Fruits Basket another

NATSUKI TAKAYA

1

FRUITS BASKET another

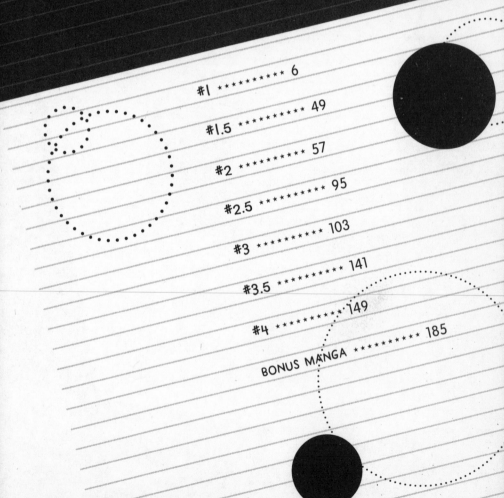

Fruits Basket another

CONTENTS

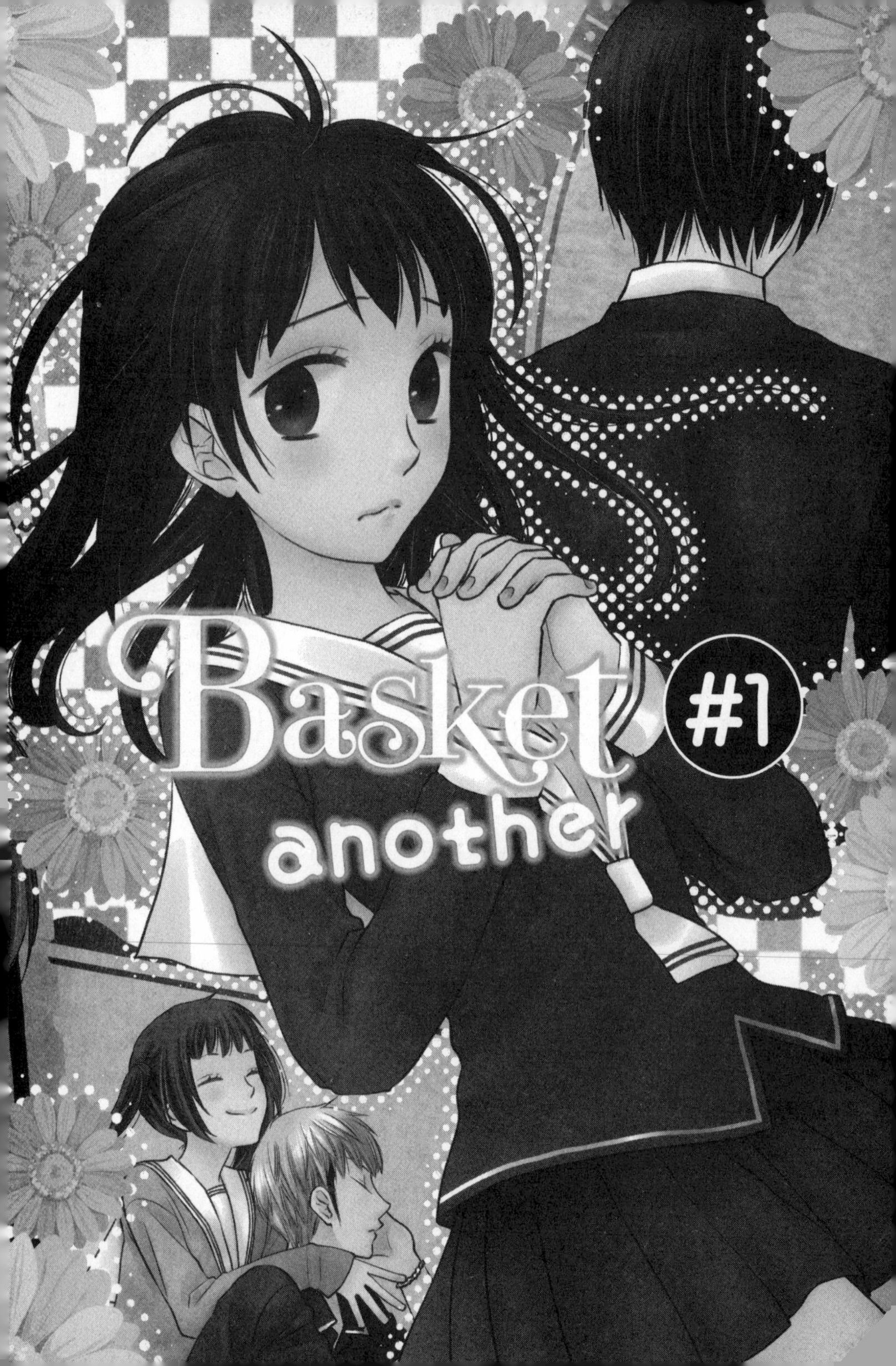
Basket another
#1

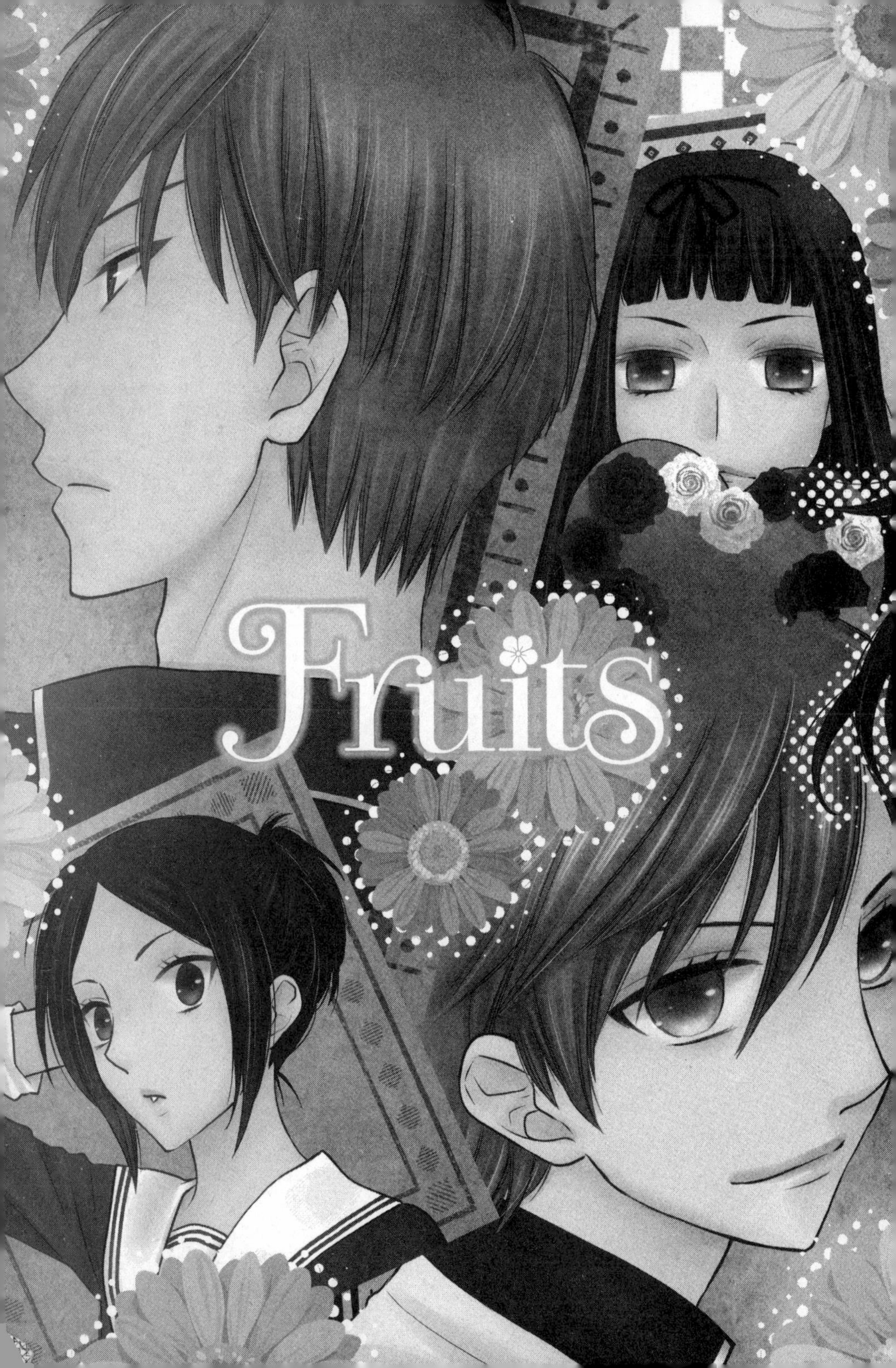
Fruits

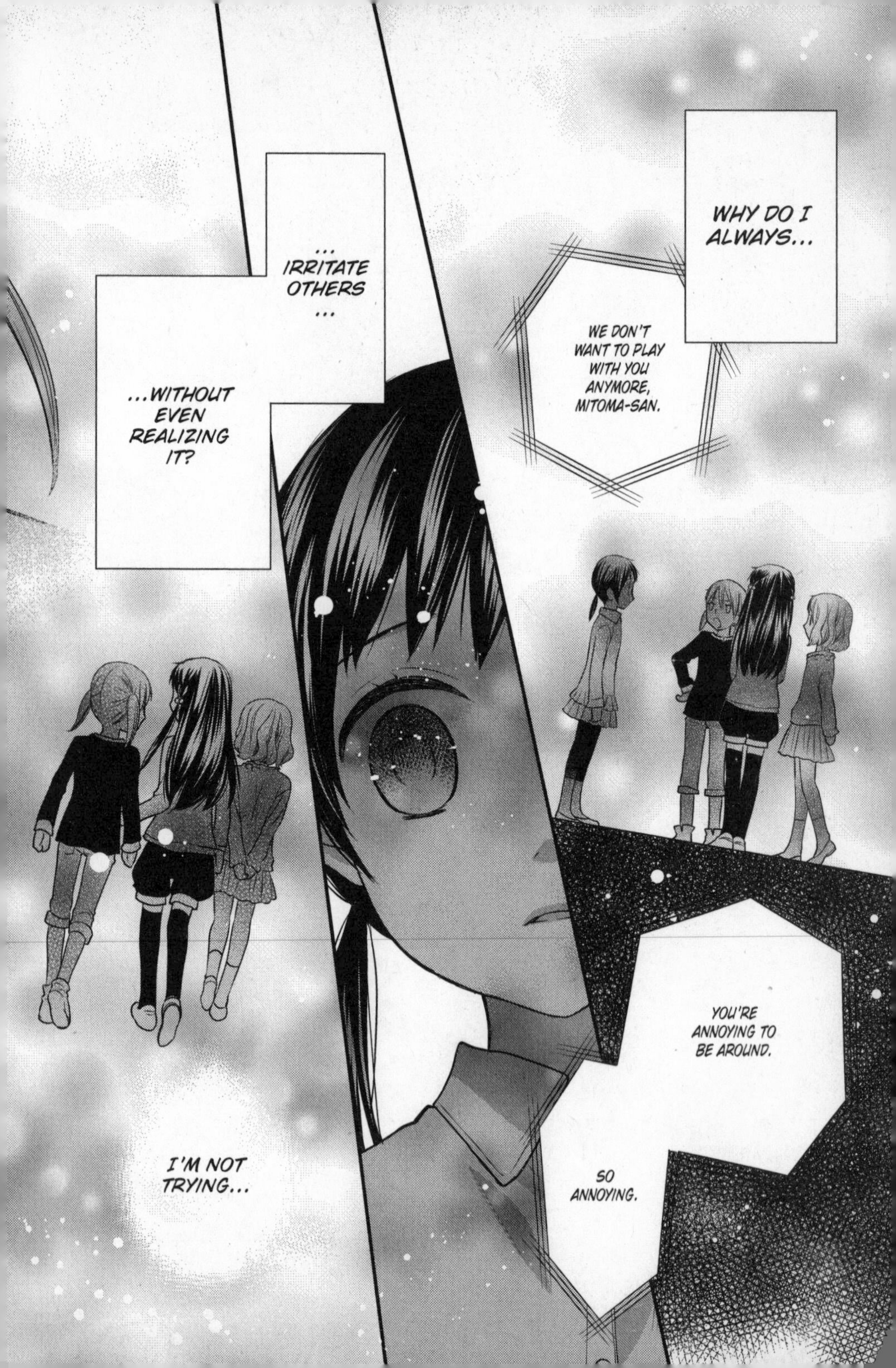
WHY DO I ALWAYS...
WE DON'T WANT TO PLAY WITH YOU ANYMORE, MITOMA-SAN.
...IRRITATE OTHERS...
...WITHOUT EVEN REALIZING IT?
YOU'RE ANNOYING TO BE AROUND.
SO ANNOYING.
I'M NOT TRYING...

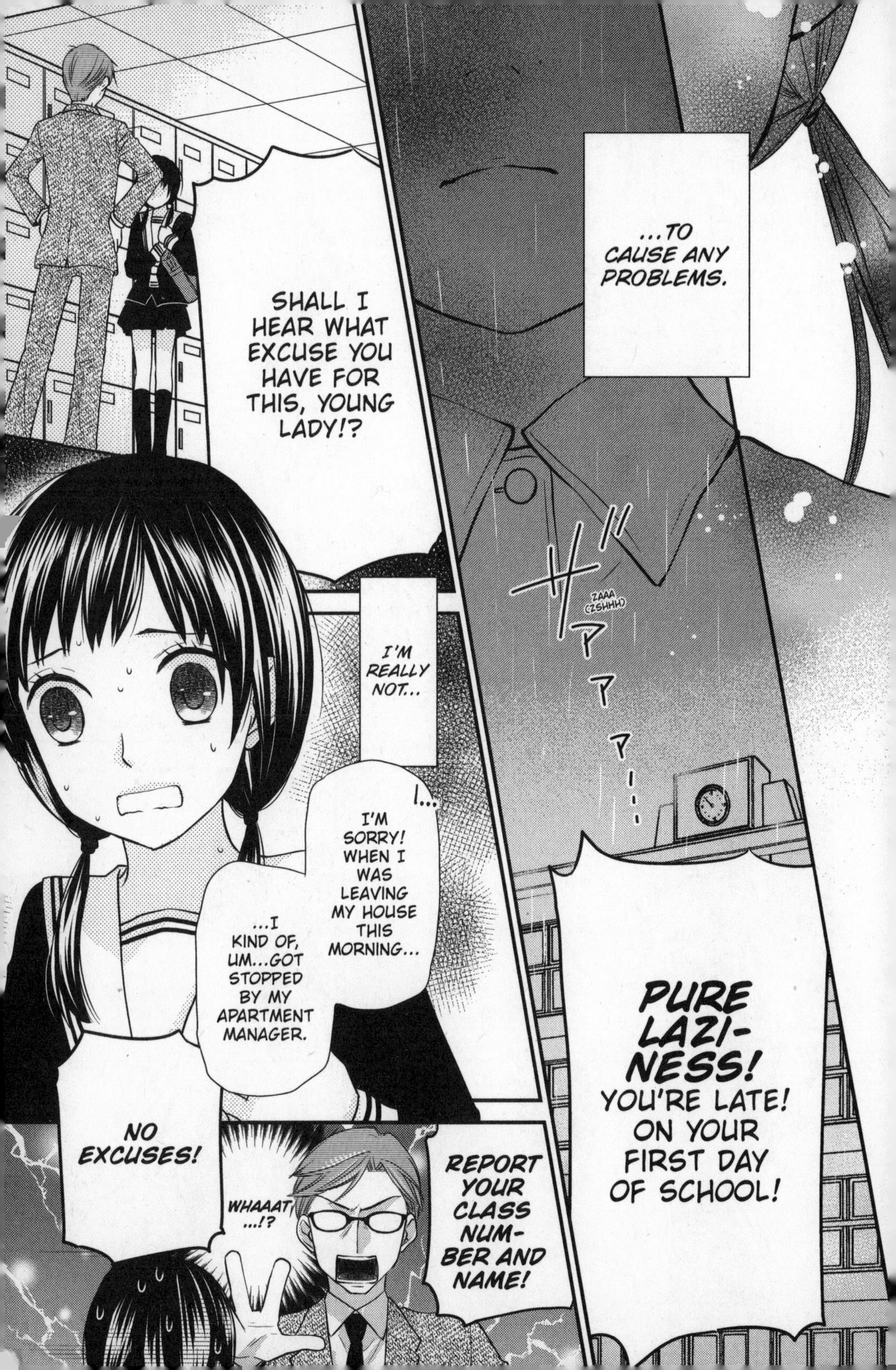
...TO CAUSE ANY PROBLEMS.
ZAAA (ZSHHH)
PURE LAZI-NESS! YOU'RE LATE! ON YOUR FIRST DAY OF SCHOOL!
SHALL I HEAR WHAT EXCUSE YOU HAVE FOR THIS, YOUNG LADY!?
I'M REALLY NOT...
I...
I'M SORRY! WHEN I WAS LEAVING MY HOUSE THIS MORNING...
...I KIND OF, UM...GOT STOPPED BY MY APARTMENT MANAGER.
REPORT YOUR CLASS NUM-BER AND NAME!
NO EXCUSES!
WHAAAT ...!?

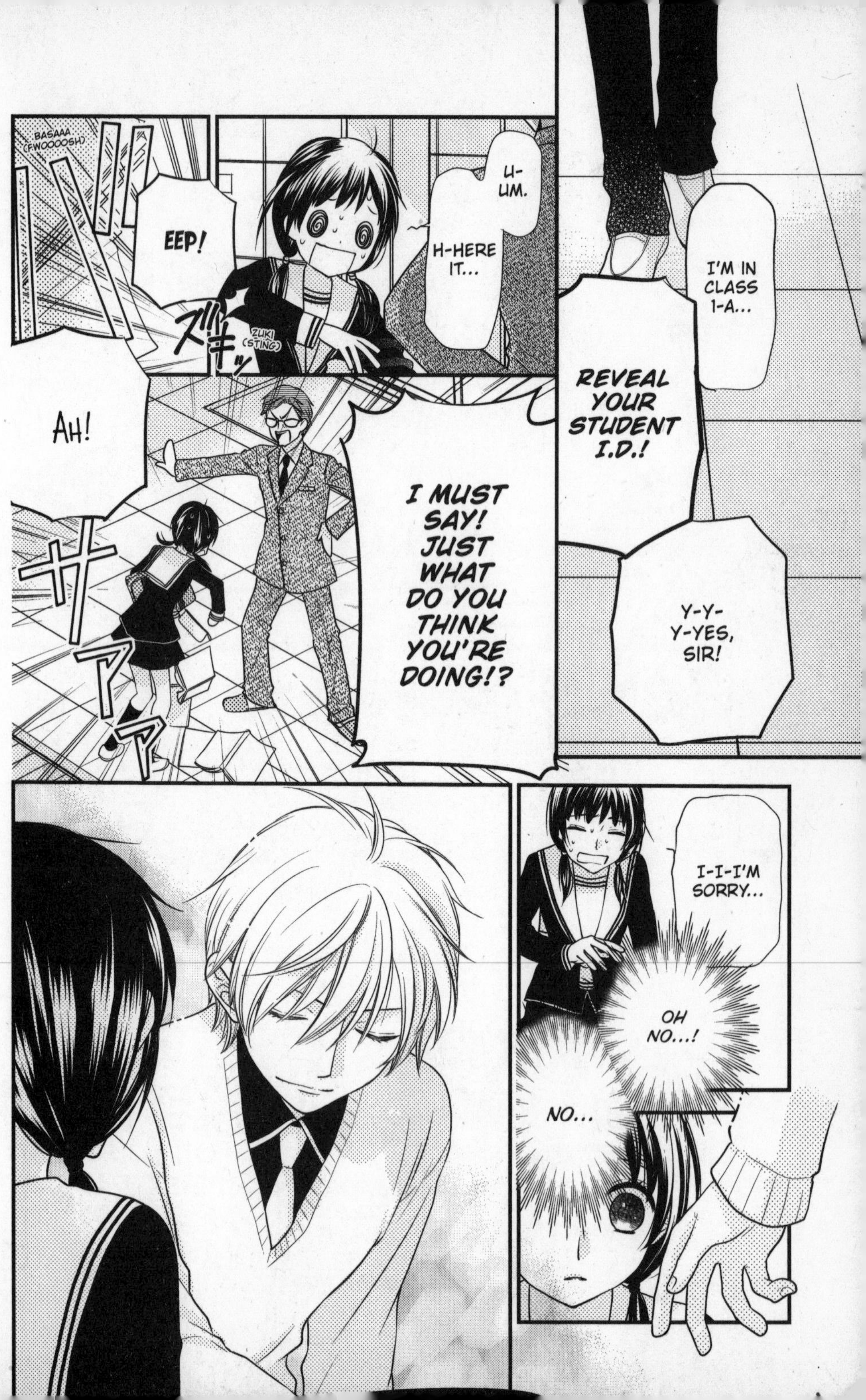
I'M IN CLASS 1-A...
REVEAL YOUR STUDENT I.D.!
Y-Y-Y-YES, SIR!
U-UM.
H-HERE IT...
ズキッ
ZUKI (STING)
BASAAA (FWOOOOSH)
EEP!
I MUST SAY! JUST WHAT DO YOU THINK YOU'RE DOING!?
AH!
サァァ
I-I-I'M SORRY...
OH NO...!
NO...

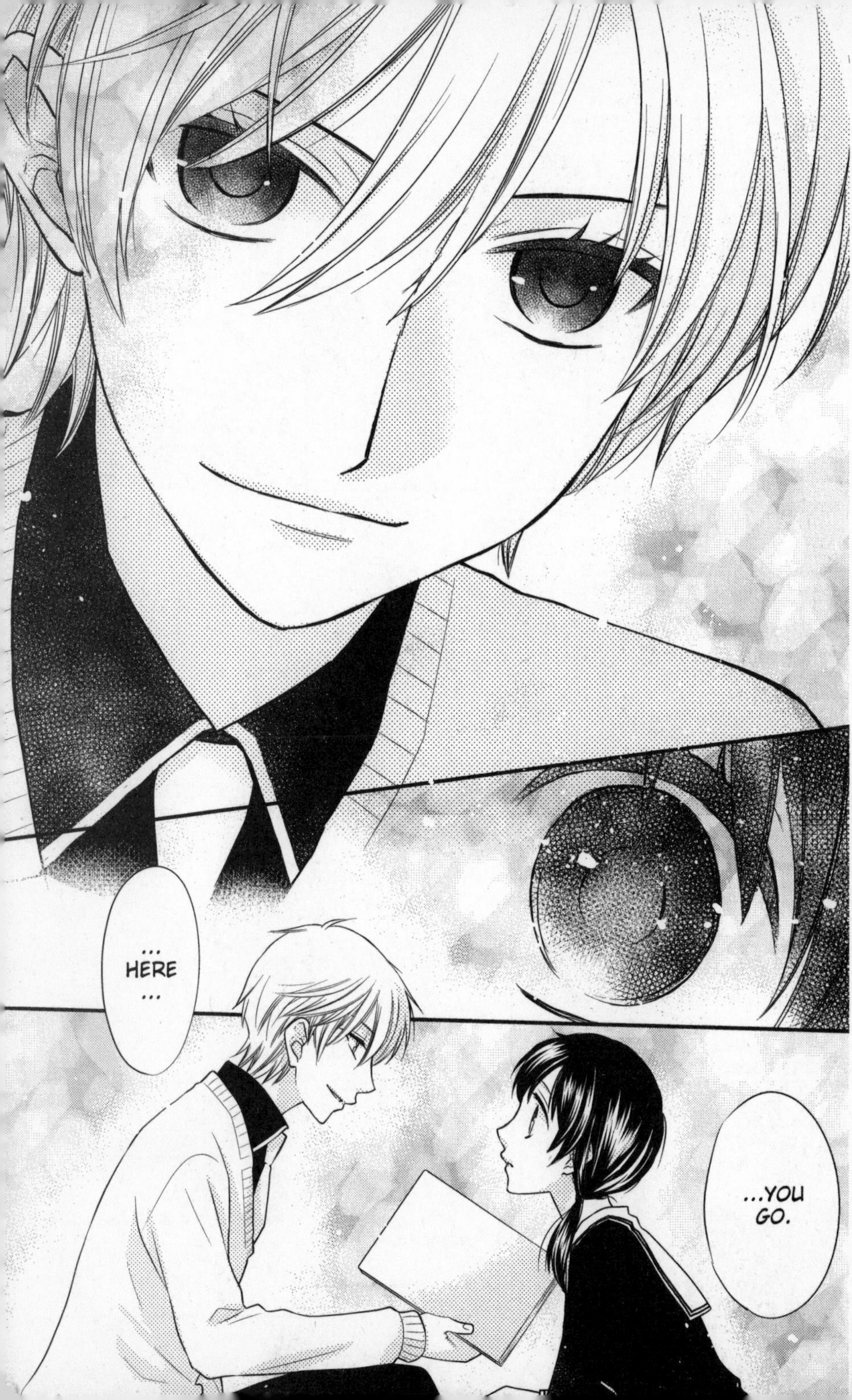
...YOU GO.
...HERE...

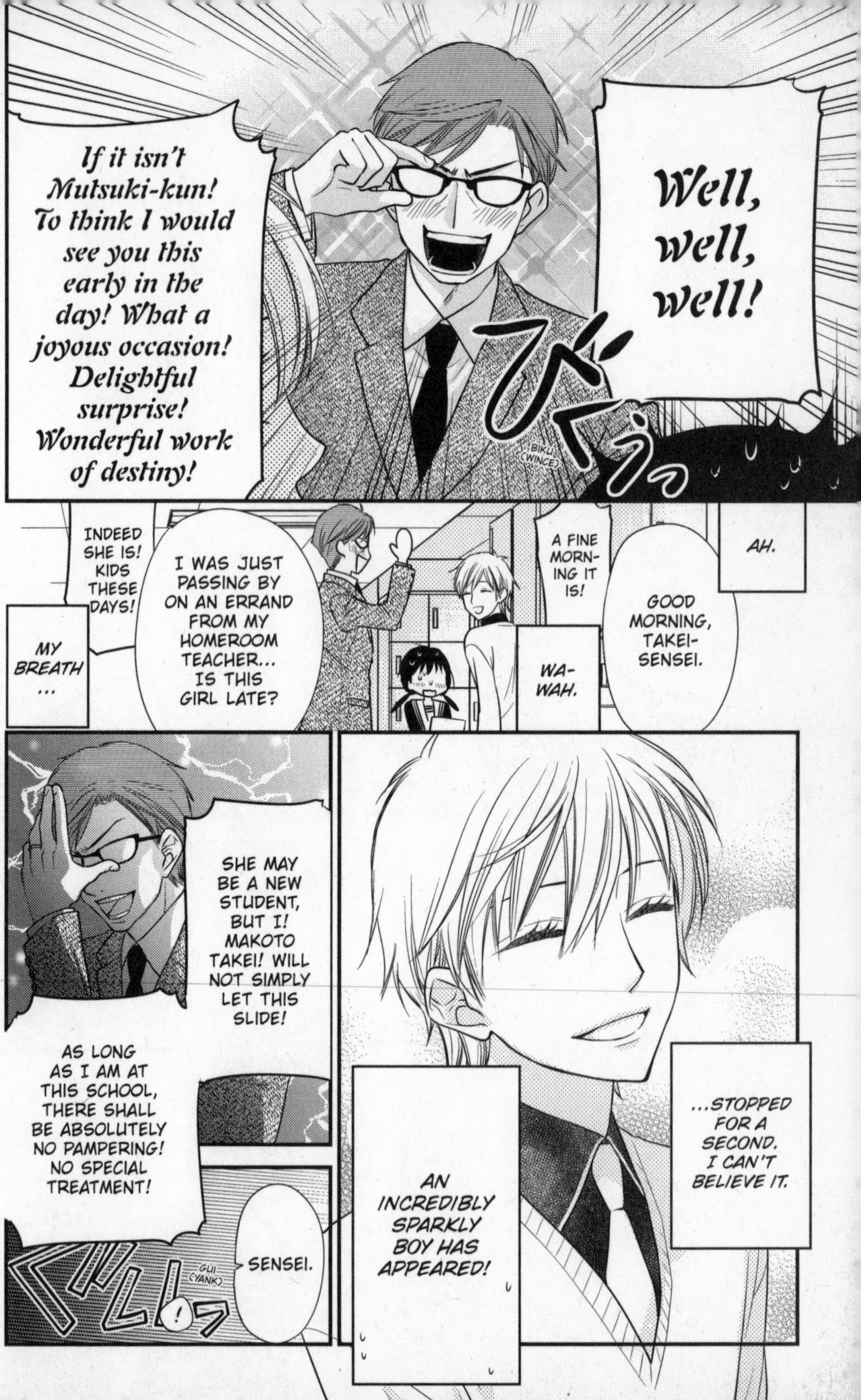
Well, well, well!
If it isn't Mutsuki-kun! To think I would see you this early in the day! What a joyous occasion! Delightful surprise! Wonderful work of destiny!
BIKU (WINCE)
AH.
GOOD MORNING, TAKEI-SENSEI.
A FINE MORNING IT IS!
WA-WAH.
I WAS JUST PASSING BY ON AN ERRAND FROM MY HOMEROOM TEACHER... IS THIS GIRL LATE?
INDEED SHE IS! KIDS THESE DAYS!
MY BREATH...
...STOPPED FOR A SECOND. I CAN'T BELIEVE IT.
AN INCREDIBLY SPARKLY BOY HAS APPEARED!
SHE MAY BE A NEW STUDENT, BUT I! MAKOTO TAKEI! WILL NOT SIMPLY LET THIS SLIDE!
AS LONG AS I AM AT THIS SCHOOL, THERE SHALL BE ABSOLUTELY NO PAMPERING! NO SPECIAL TREATMENT!
SENSEI.
GUI (YANK)

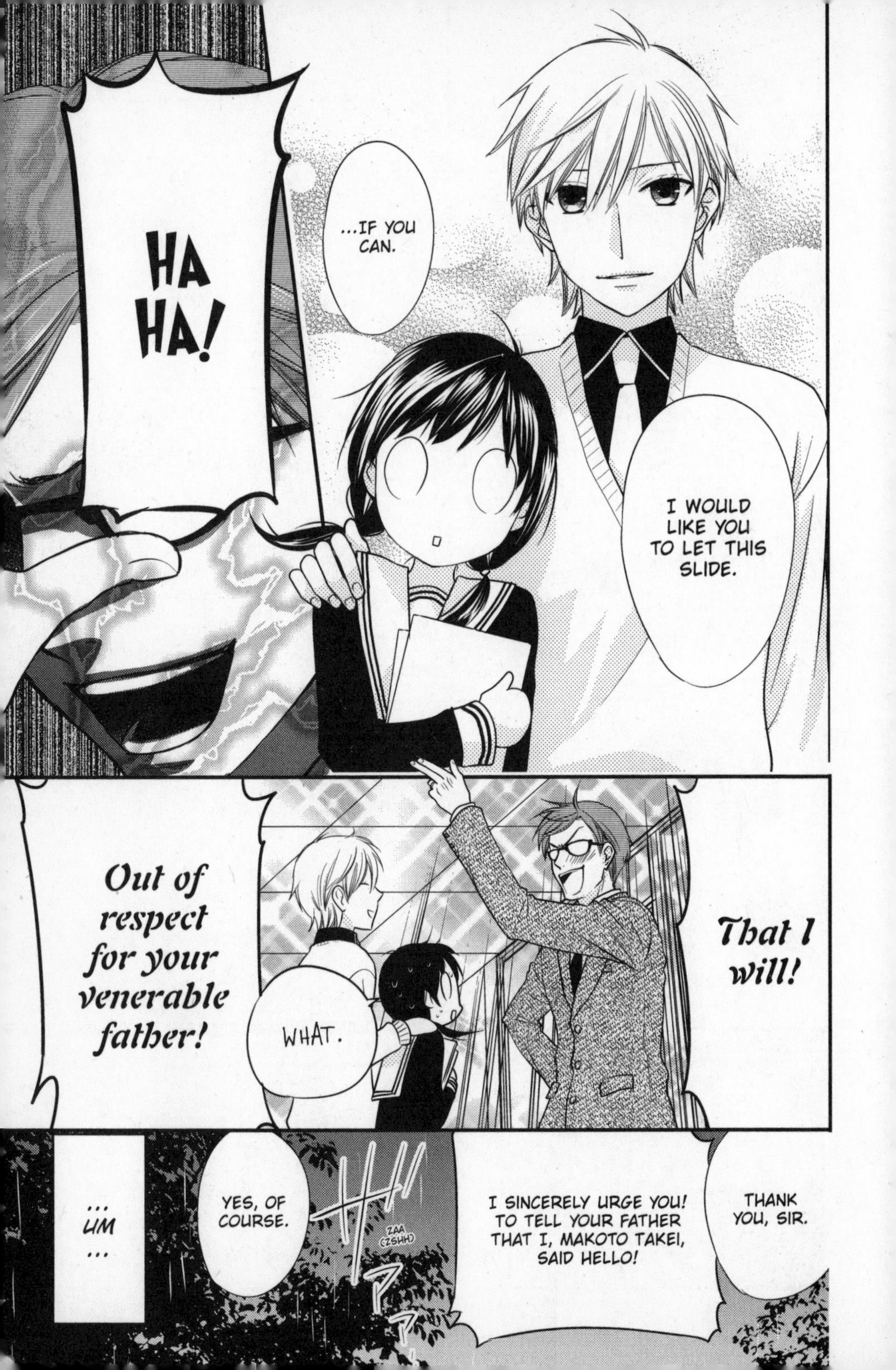
I WOULD LIKE YOU TO LET THIS SLIDE.
...IF YOU CAN.
HA HA!
That I will!
Out of respect for your venerable father!
WHAT.
THANK YOU, SIR.
I SINCERELY URGE YOU! TO TELL YOUR FATHER THAT I, MAKOTO TAKEI, SAID HELLO!
ZAA (ZSHH)
YES, OF COURSE.
... UM ...

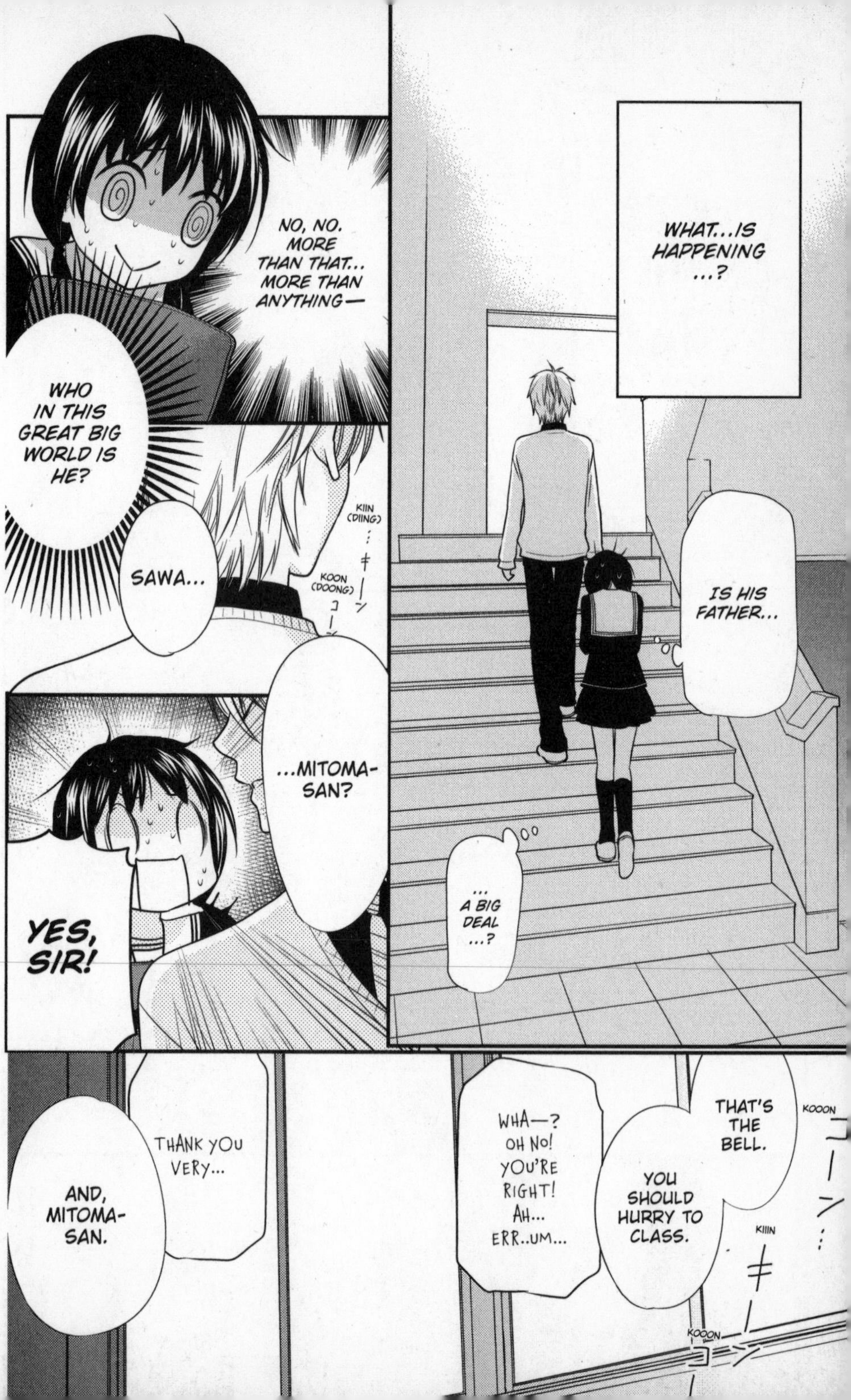
WHAT...IS HAPPENING ...?
IS HIS FATHER...
... A BIG DEAL ...?
NO, NO. MORE THAN THAT... MORE THAN ANYTHING—
WHO IN THIS GREAT BIG WORLD IS HE?
KIIN (DIING)
KOON (DOONG)
SAWA...
...MITOMA-SAN?
YES, SIR!
KOOON
KIIN
THAT'S THE BELL.
YOU SHOULD HURRY TO CLASS.
WHA—? OH NO! YOU'RE RIGHT! AH... ERR..UM...
KOOON
THANK YOU VERY...
AND, MITOMA-SAN.

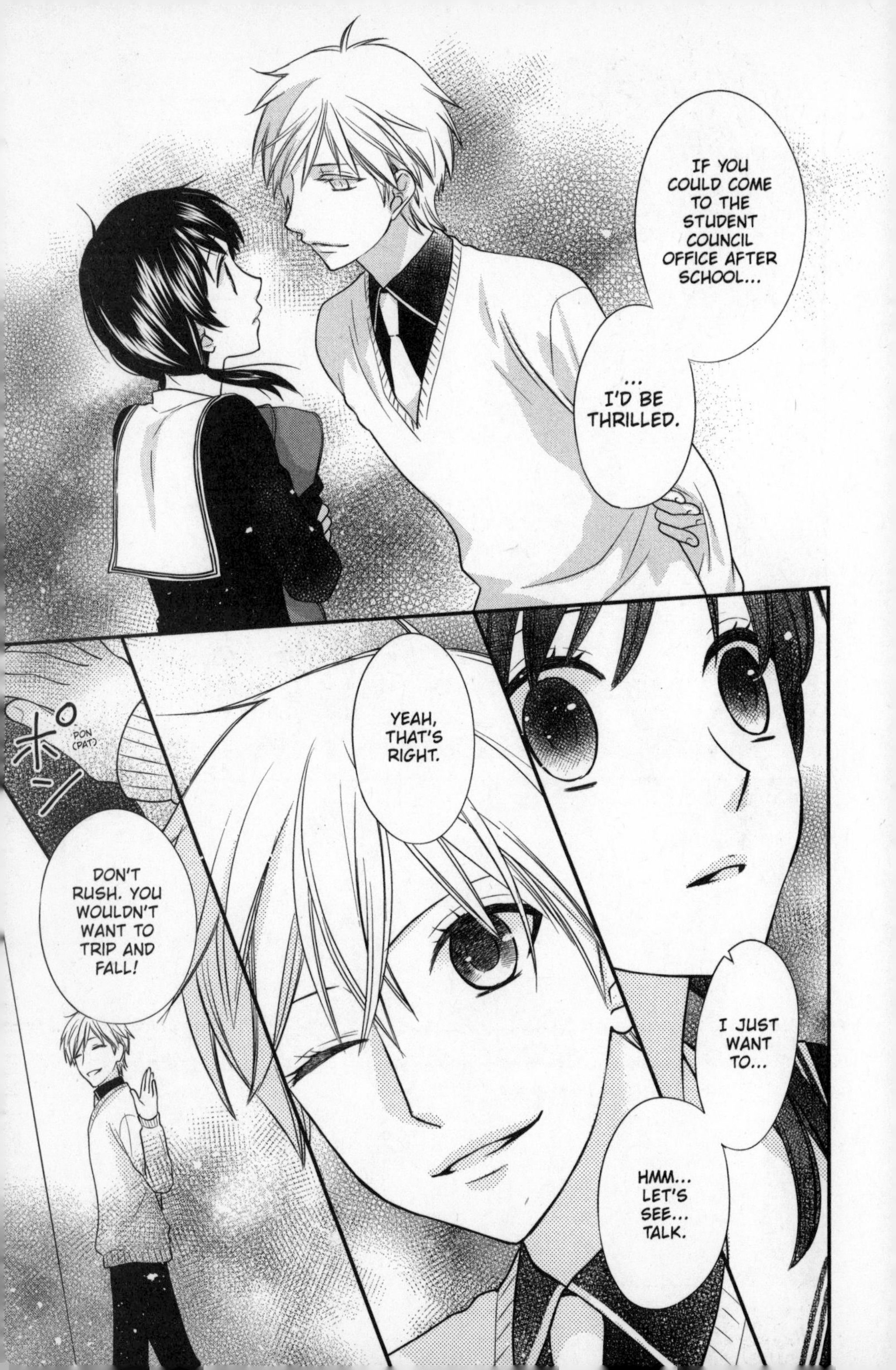
IF YOU COULD COME TO THE STUDENT COUNCIL OFFICE AFTER SCHOOL...
... I'D BE THRILLED.
I JUST WANT TO...
HMM... LET'S SEE... TALK.
YEAH, THAT'S RIGHT.
PON (PAT)
DON'T RUSH. YOU WOULDN'T WANT TO TRIP AND FALL!

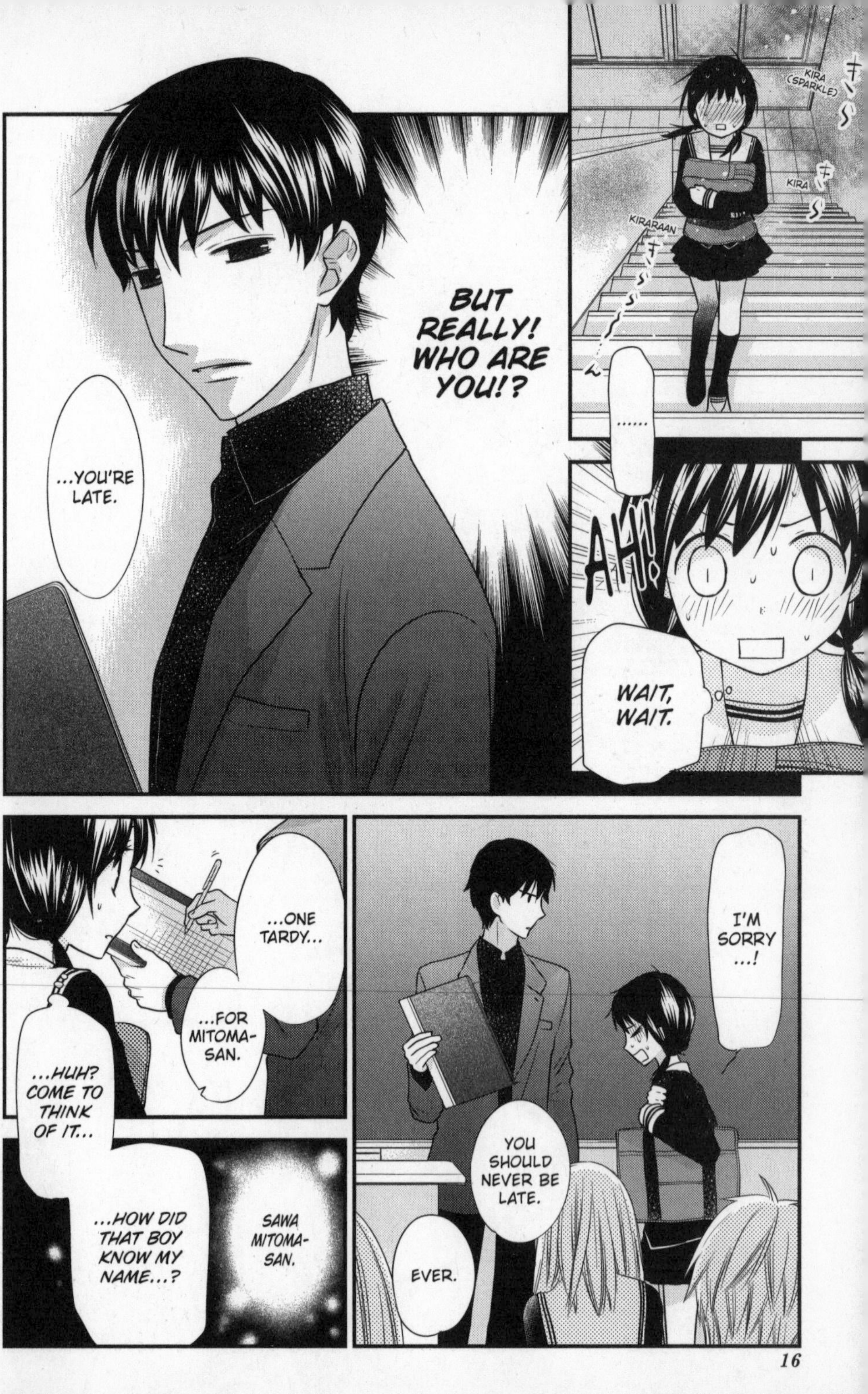
KIRA (SPARKLE)
KIRA
KIRARAAN
......
AH!
WAIT, WAIT.
BUT REALLY! WHO ARE YOU!?
...YOU'RE LATE.
I'M SORRY...!
YOU SHOULD NEVER BE LATE.
EVER.
...ONE TARDY...
...FOR MITOMA-SAN.
...HUH? COME TO THINK OF IT...
SAWA MITOMA-SAN.
...HOW DID THAT BOY KNOW MY NAME...?

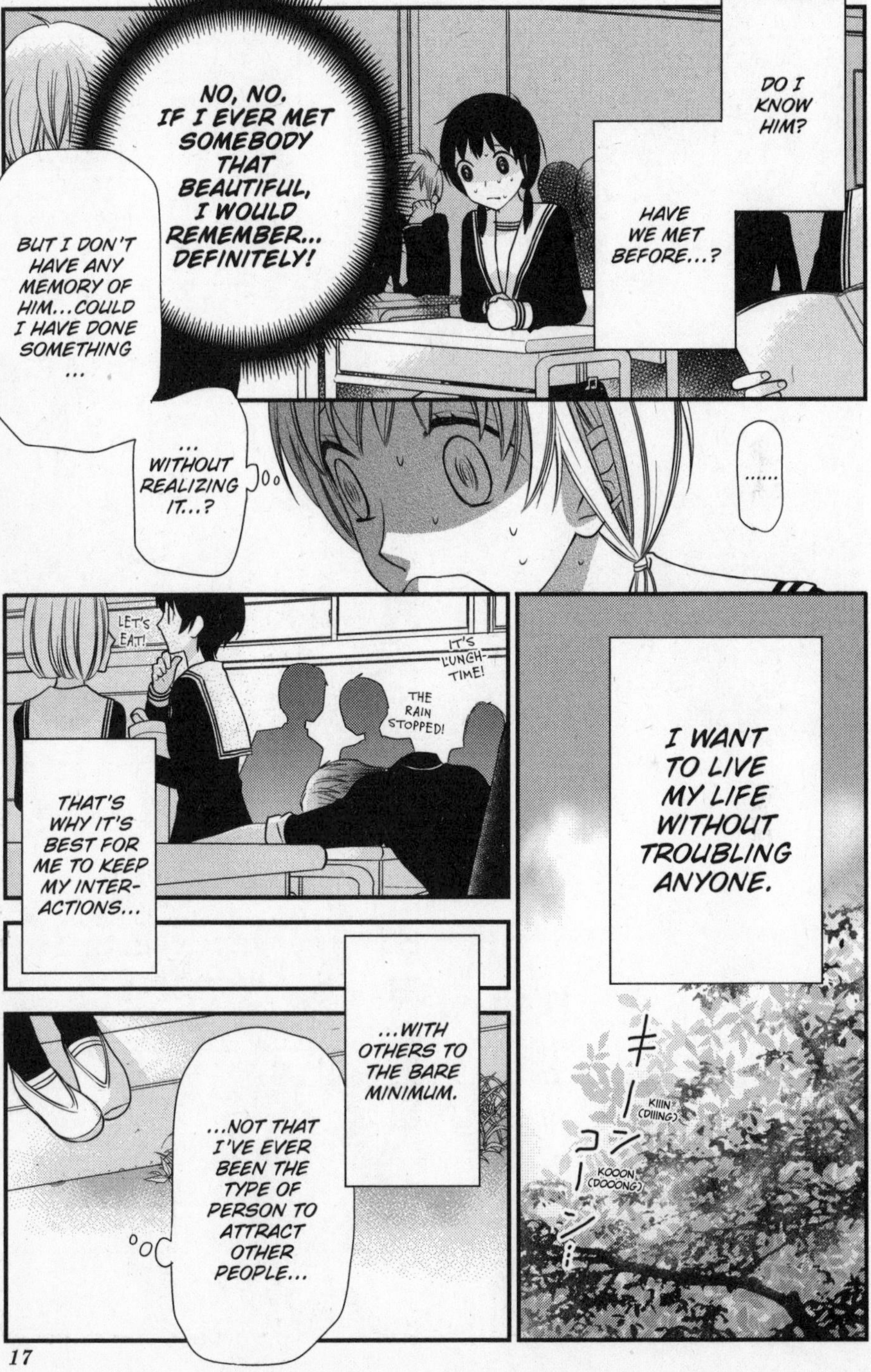
DO I KNOW HIM?
HAVE WE MET BEFORE...?
NO, NO. IF I EVER MET SOMEBODY THAT BEAUTIFUL, I WOULD REMEMBER... DEFINITELY!
BUT I DON'T HAVE ANY MEMORY OF HIM...COULD I HAVE DONE SOMETHING ...
......
... WITHOUT REALIZING IT...?
I WANT TO LIVE MY LIFE WITHOUT TROUBLING ANYONE.
キーンコーン…
KIIIN (DIIING)
KOOON (DOOONG)
IT'S LUNCH-TIME!
THE RAIN STOPPED!
LET'S EAT!
THAT'S WHY IT'S BEST FOR ME TO KEEP MY INTER-ACTIONS...
...WITH OTHERS TO THE BARE MINIMUM.
...NOT THAT I'VE EVER BEEN THE TYPE OF PERSON TO ATTRACT OTHER PEOPLE...

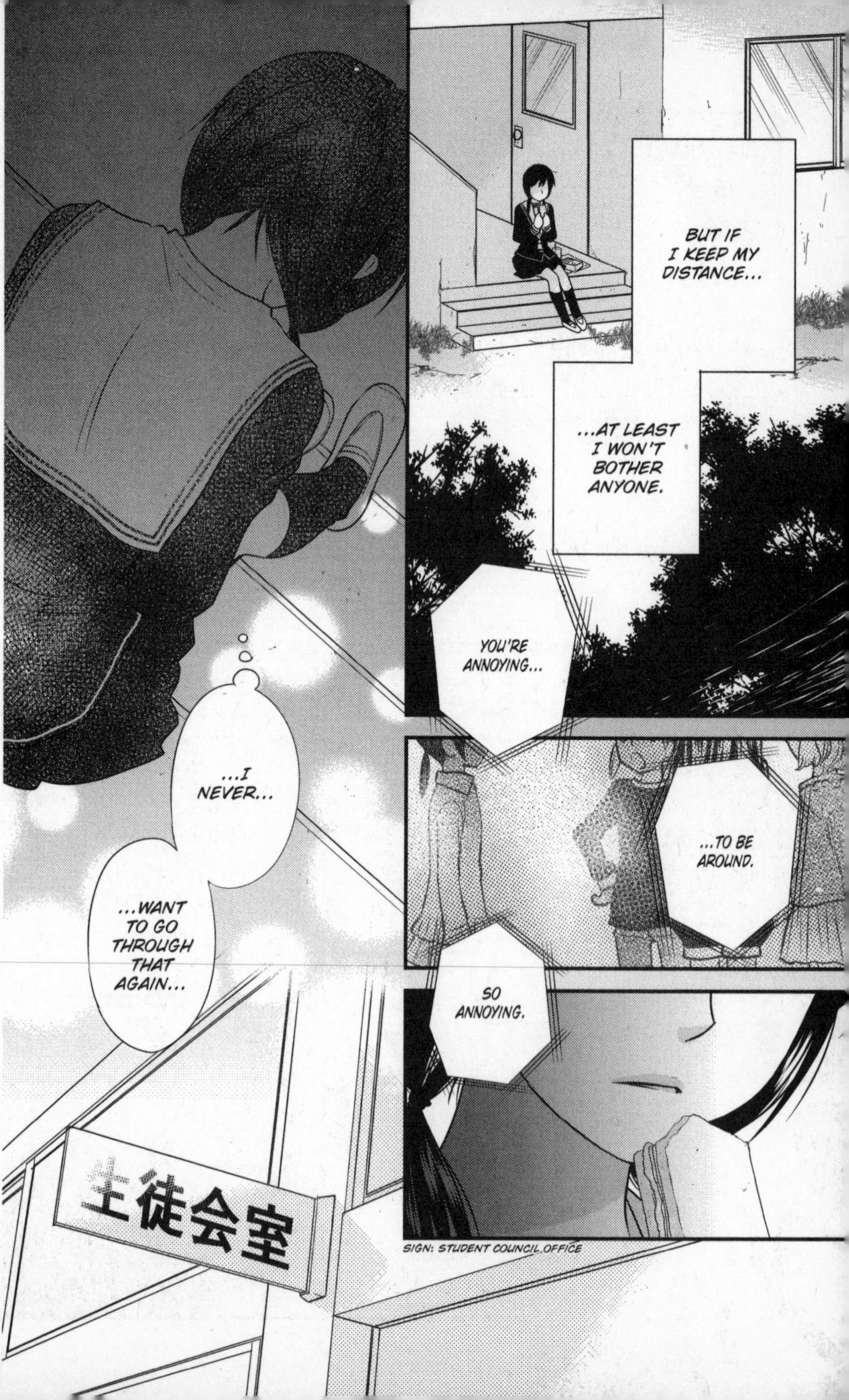
BUT IF I KEEP MY DISTANCE...
...AT LEAST I WON'T BOTHER ANYONE.
YOU'RE ANNOYING...
...TO BE AROUND.
SO ANNOYING.
...I NEVER...
...WANT TO GO THROUGH THAT AGAIN...
生徒会室
SIGN: STUDENT COUNCIL OFFICE

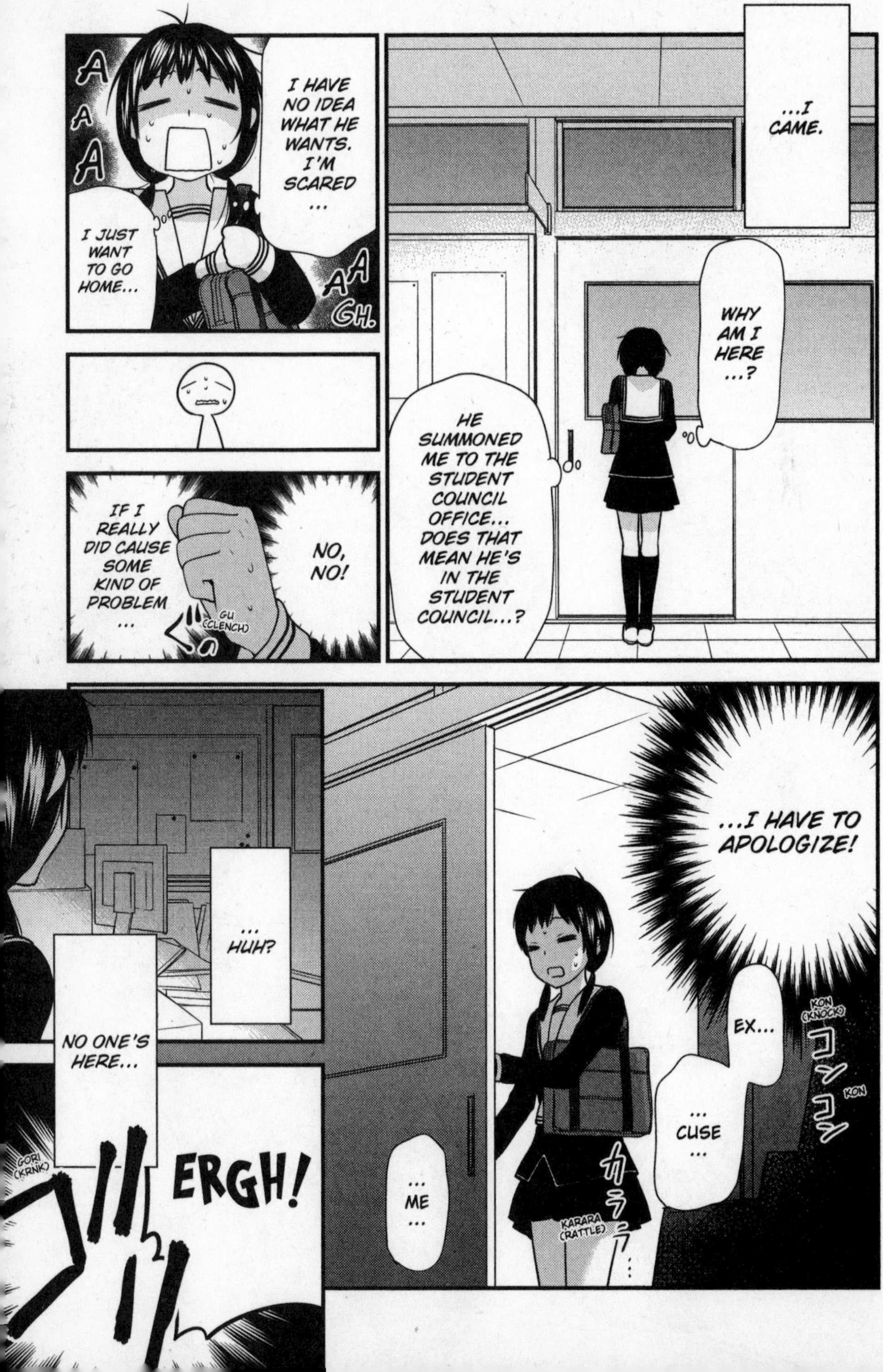
...I CAME.
WHY AM I HERE...?
HE SUMMONED ME TO THE STUDENT COUNCIL OFFICE... DOES THAT MEAN HE'S IN THE STUDENT COUNCIL...?
I HAVE NO IDEA WHAT HE WANTS. I'M SCARED...
I JUST WANT TO GO HOME...
AAAAAGH.
NO, NO!
IF I REALLY DID CAUSE SOME KIND OF PROBLEM...
GU (CLENCH)
...I HAVE TO APOLOGIZE!
KON (KNOCK)
KON
EX...
...CUSE...
...ME...
KARARA (RATTLE)
...HUH?
NO ONE'S HERE...
GORI (KRNK)
ERGH!

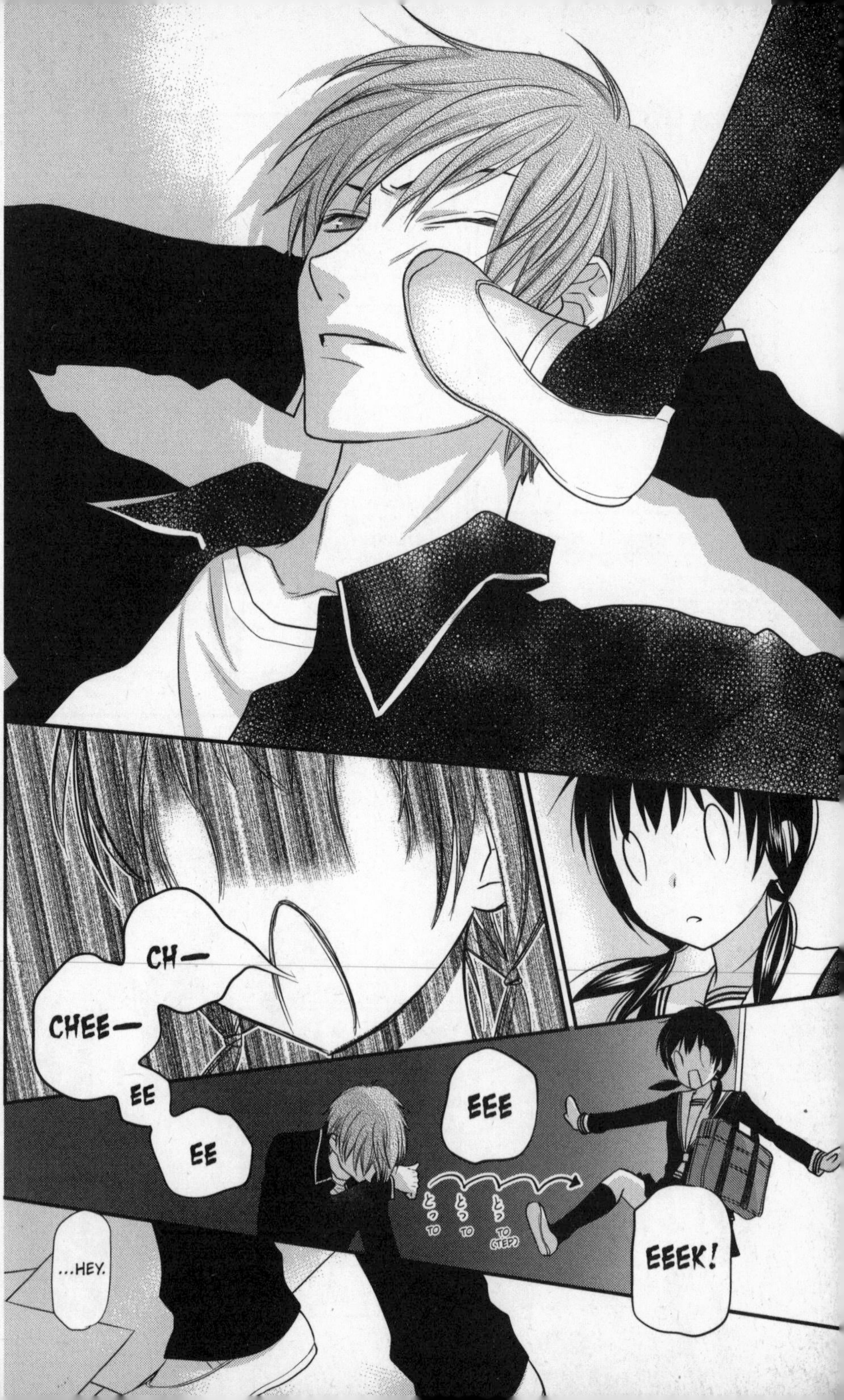
CH—
CHEE—
EE
EE
EEE
EEEK!
とっ とっ とっ
TO TO TO (STEP)
...HEY.

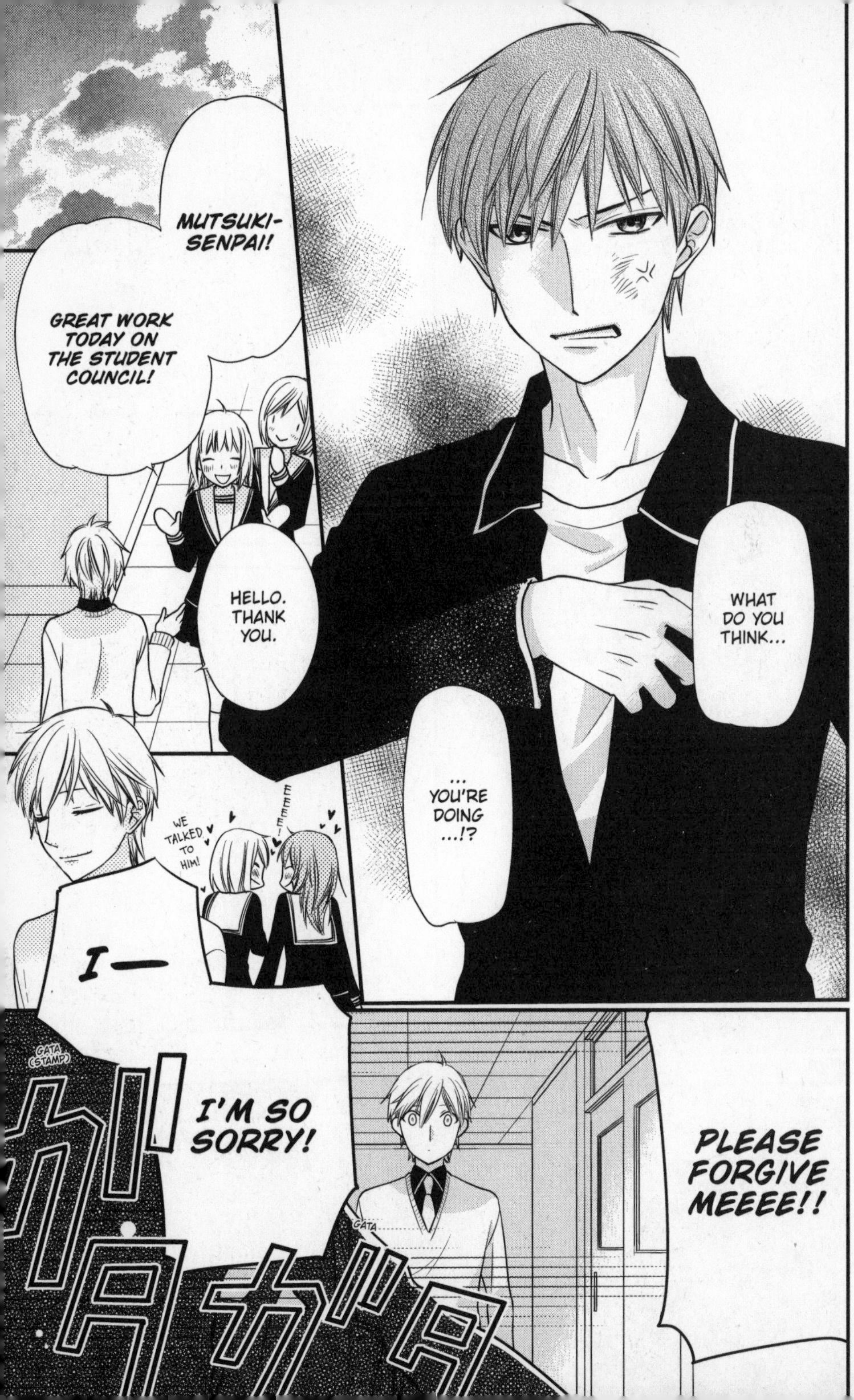
WHAT DO YOU THINK...
...YOU'RE DOING ...!?
MUTSUKI-SENPAI!
GREAT WORK TODAY ON THE STUDENT COUNCIL!
HELLO. THANK YOU.
EEEE!
WE TALKED TO HIM!
I—
PLEASE FORGIVE MEEEE!!
I'M SO SORRY!
GATA (STAMP)
GATA

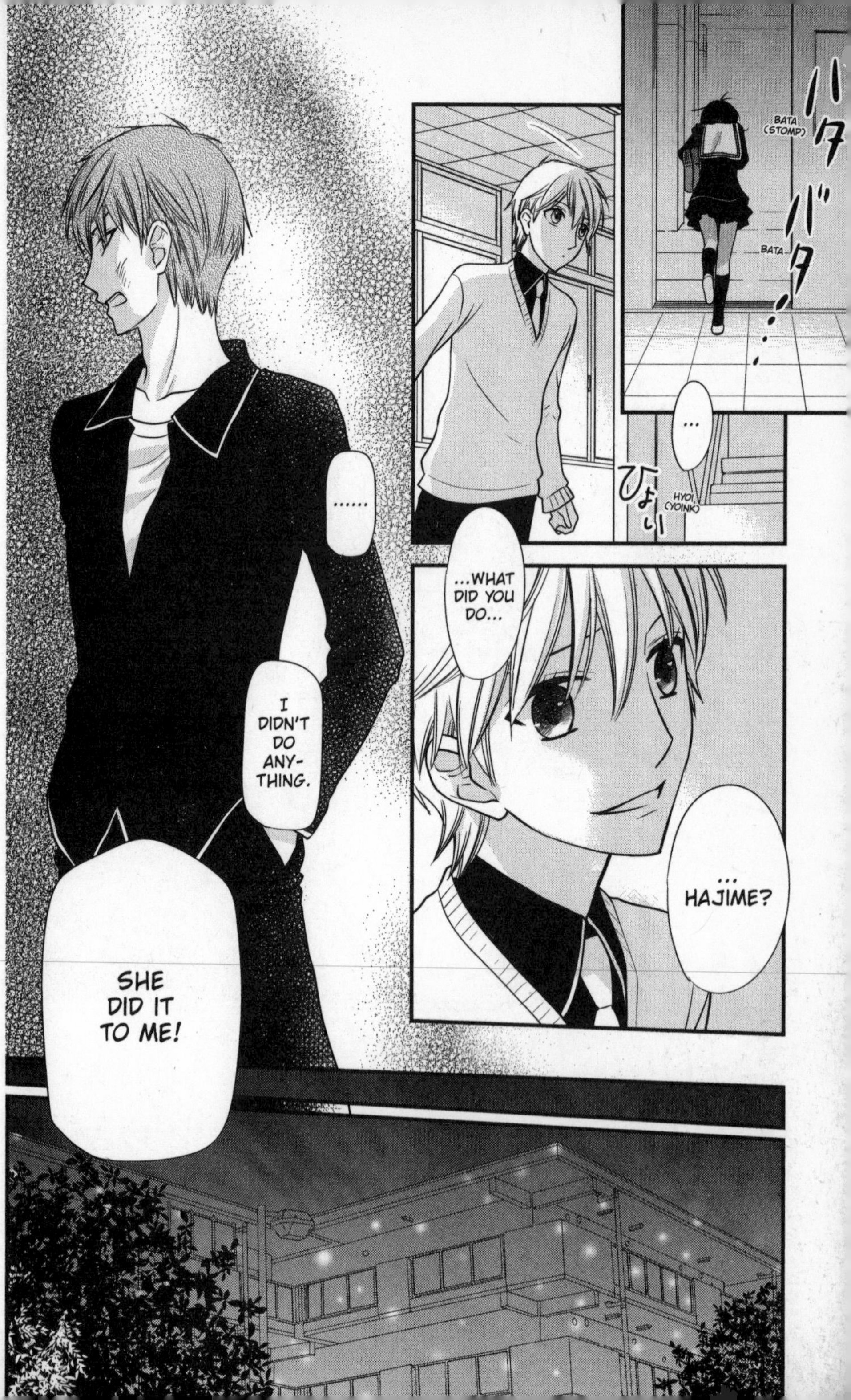

ハタバタ
BATA (STOMP)
BATA
...
ひょい
HYOI (YOINK)
...WHAT DID YOU DO...
...HAJIME?
......
I DIDN'T DO ANYTHING.
SHE DID IT TO ME!

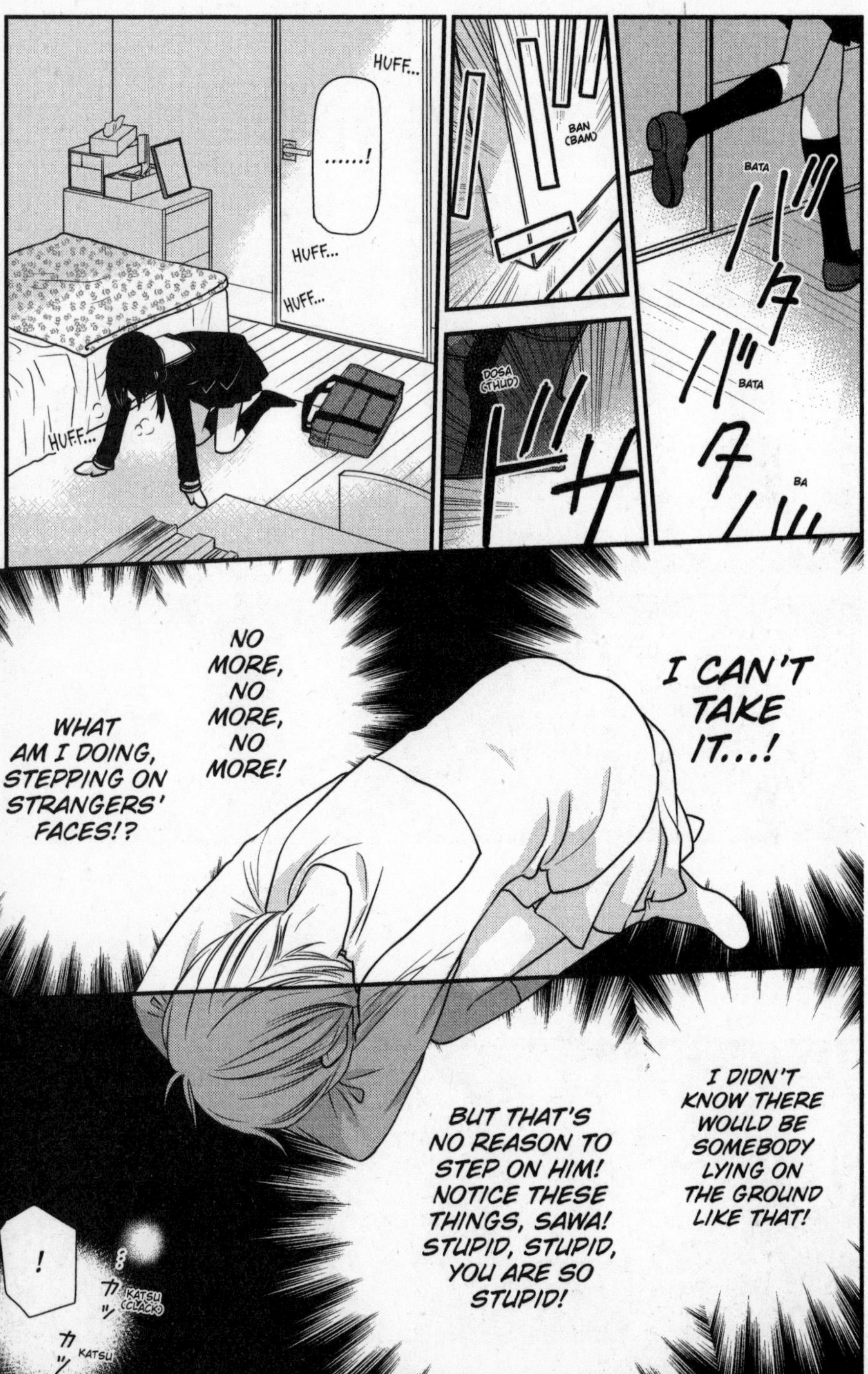

BATA
BATA
BA
BAN (BAM)
DOSA (THUD)
HUFF...
......!
HUFF...
HUFF...
HUFF...
I CAN'T TAKE IT...!
NO MORE, NO MORE, NO MORE!
WHAT AM I DOING, STEPPING ON STRANGERS' FACES!?
I DIDN'T KNOW THERE WOULD BE SOMEBODY LYING ON THE GROUND LIKE THAT!
BUT THAT'S NO REASON TO STEP ON HIM! NOTICE THESE THINGS, SAWA! STUPID, STUPID, YOU ARE SO STUPID!
KATSU (CLACK)
KATSU
!

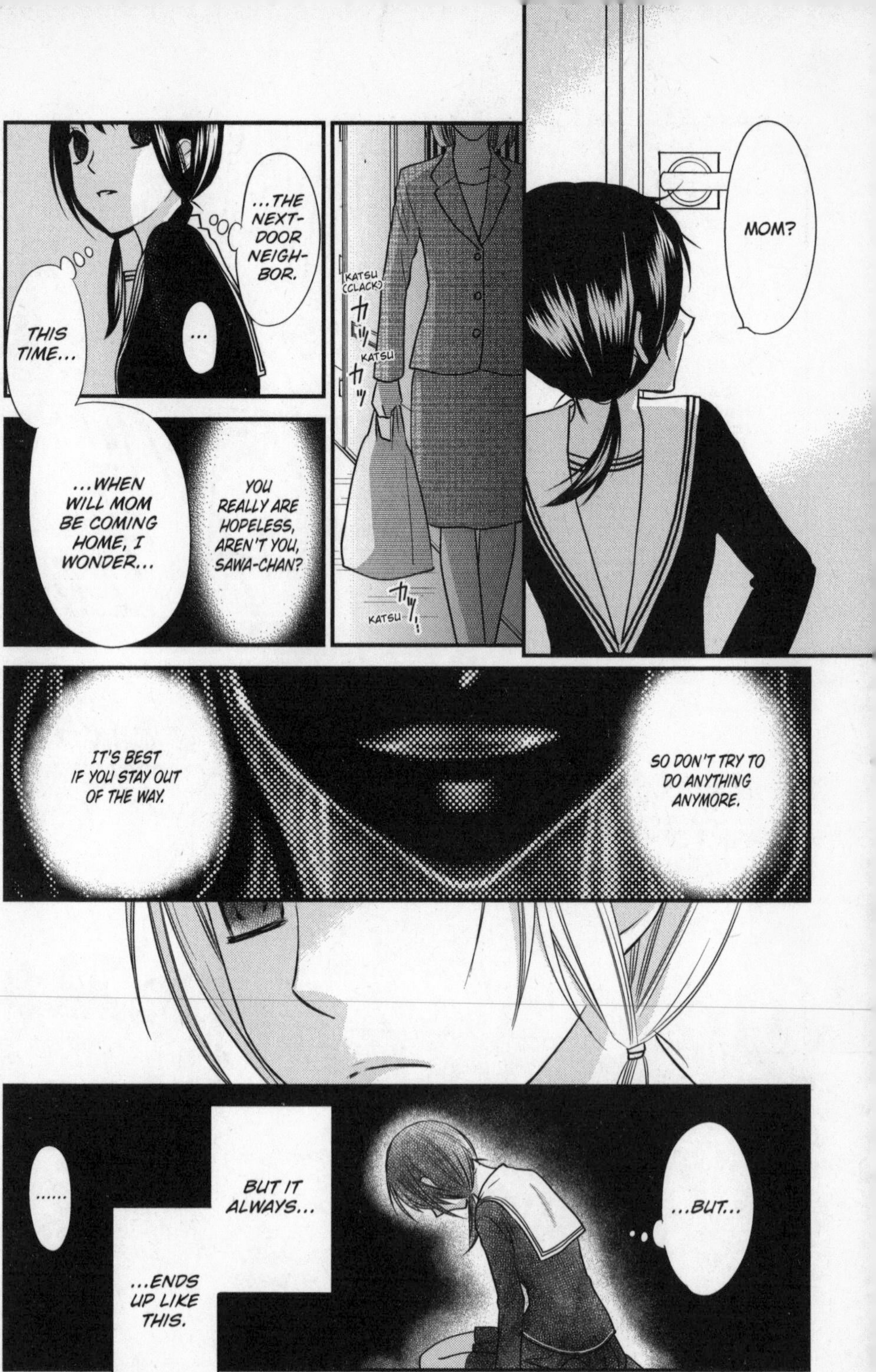
MOM?
KATSU (CLACK)
カッ
KATSU
カッ
KATSU
カッ!
...THE NEXT-DOOR NEIGHBOR.
...
THIS TIME...
...WHEN WILL MOM BE COMING HOME, I WONDER...
YOU REALLY ARE HOPELESS, AREN'T YOU, SAWA-CHAN?
SO DON'T TRY TO DO ANYTHING ANYMORE.
IT'S BEST IF YOU STAY OUT OF THE WAY.
...BUT...
BUT IT ALWAYS...
...ENDS UP LIKE THIS.
......

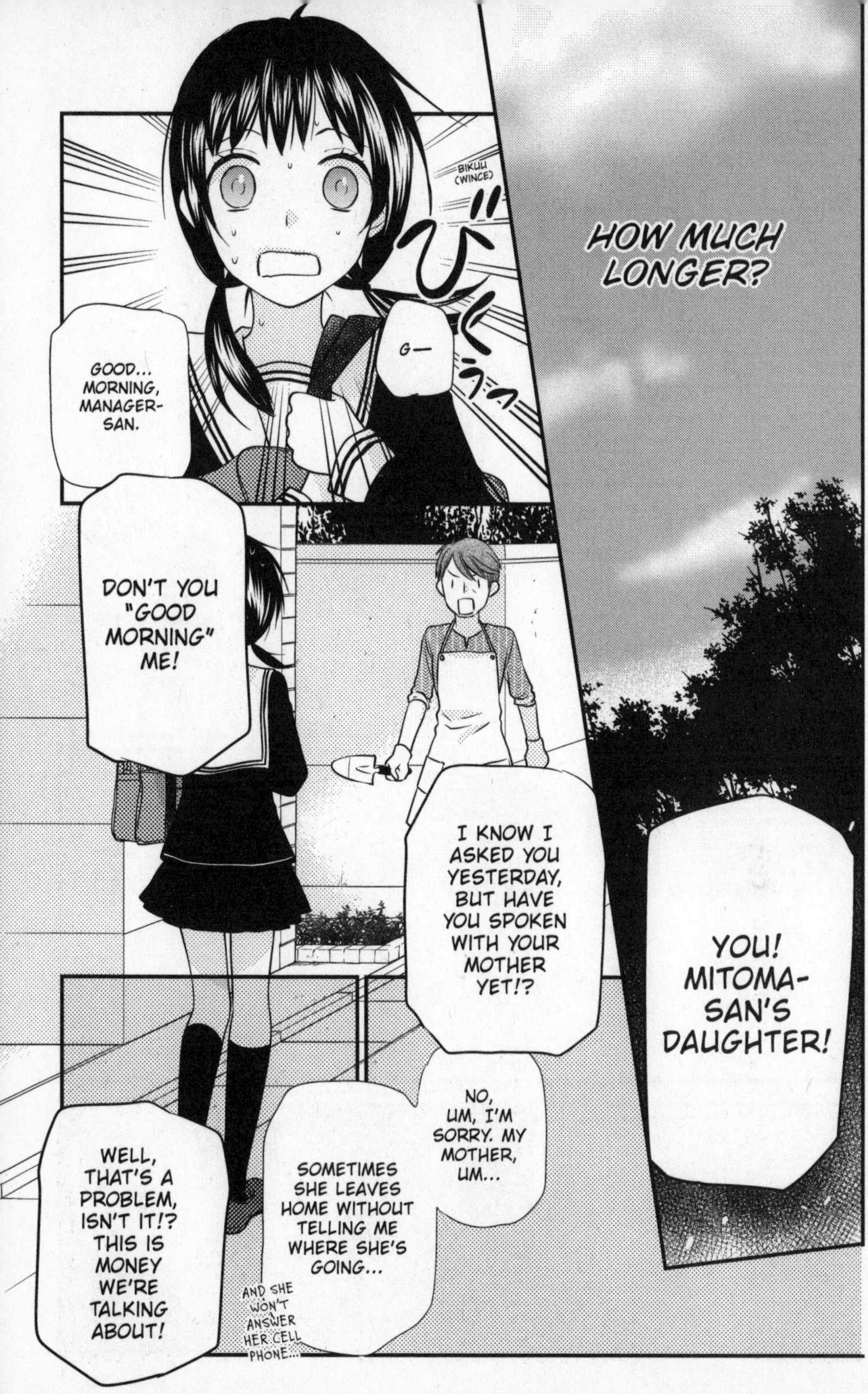
HOW MUCH LONGER?
YOU! MITOMA-SAN'S DAUGHTER!
BIKUU (WINCE)
G—
GOOD... MORNING, MANAGER-SAN.
I KNOW I ASKED YOU YESTERDAY, BUT HAVE YOU SPOKEN WITH YOUR MOTHER YET!?
DON'T YOU "GOOD MORNING" ME!
NO, UM, I'M SORRY. MY MOTHER, UM...
SOMETIMES SHE LEAVES HOME WITHOUT TELLING ME WHERE SHE'S GOING...
AND SHE WON'T ANSWER HER CELL PHONE...
WELL, THAT'S A PROBLEM, ISN'T IT!? THIS IS MONEY WE'RE TALKING ABOUT!

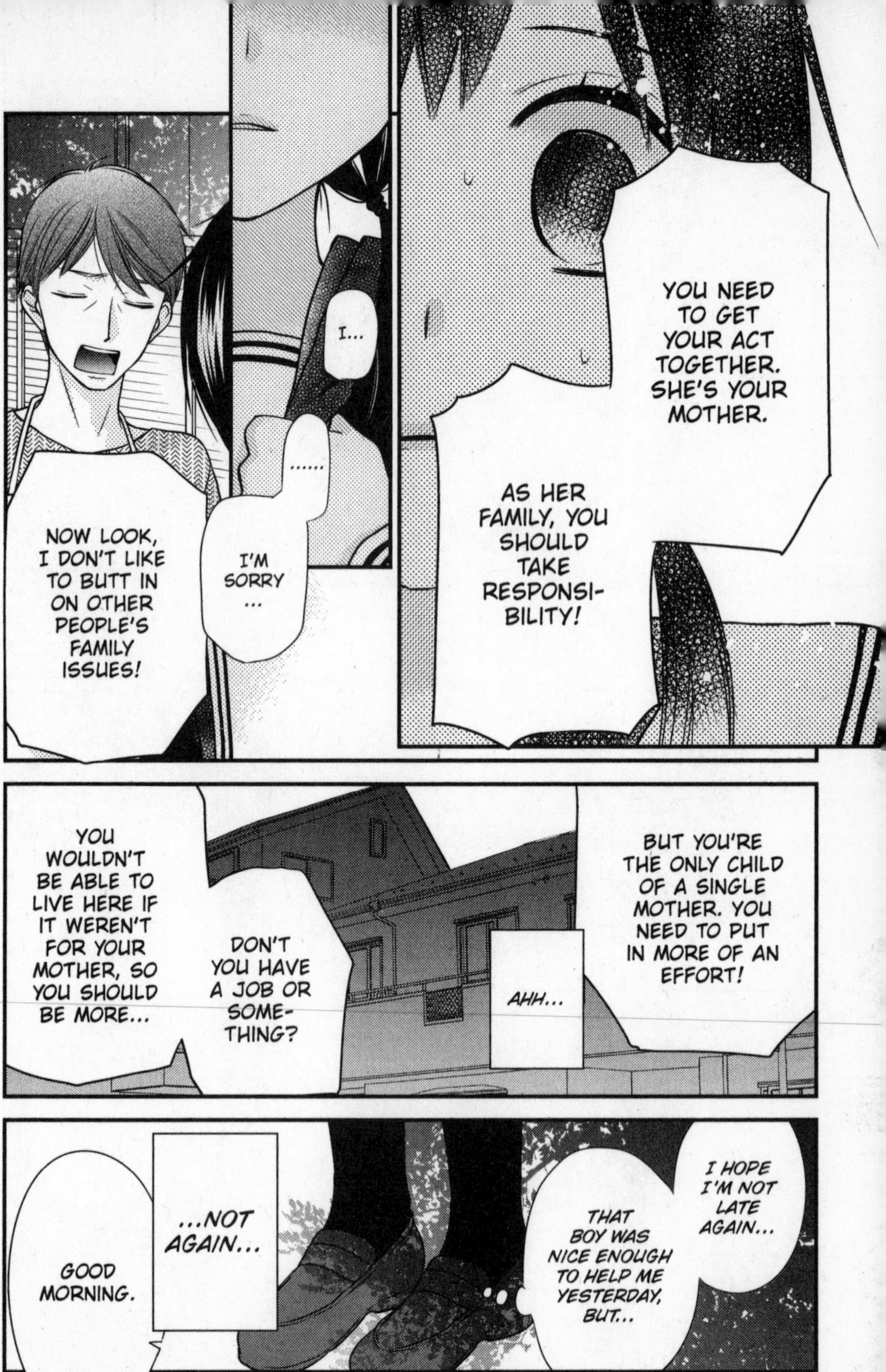
YOU NEED TO GET YOUR ACT TOGETHER. SHE'S YOUR MOTHER.
AS HER FAMILY, YOU SHOULD TAKE RESPONSI-BILITY!
I...
......
I'M SORRY ...
NOW LOOK, I DON'T LIKE TO BUTT IN ON OTHER PEOPLE'S FAMILY ISSUES!
BUT YOU'RE THE ONLY CHILD OF A SINGLE MOTHER. YOU NEED TO PUT IN MORE OF AN EFFORT!
AHH...
DON'T YOU HAVE A JOB OR SOME-THING?
YOU WOULDN'T BE ABLE TO LIVE HERE IF IT WEREN'T FOR YOUR MOTHER, SO YOU SHOULD BE MORE...
I HOPE I'M NOT LATE AGAIN...
THAT BOY WAS NICE ENOUGH TO HELP ME YESTERDAY, BUT...
...NOT AGAIN...
GOOD MORNING.

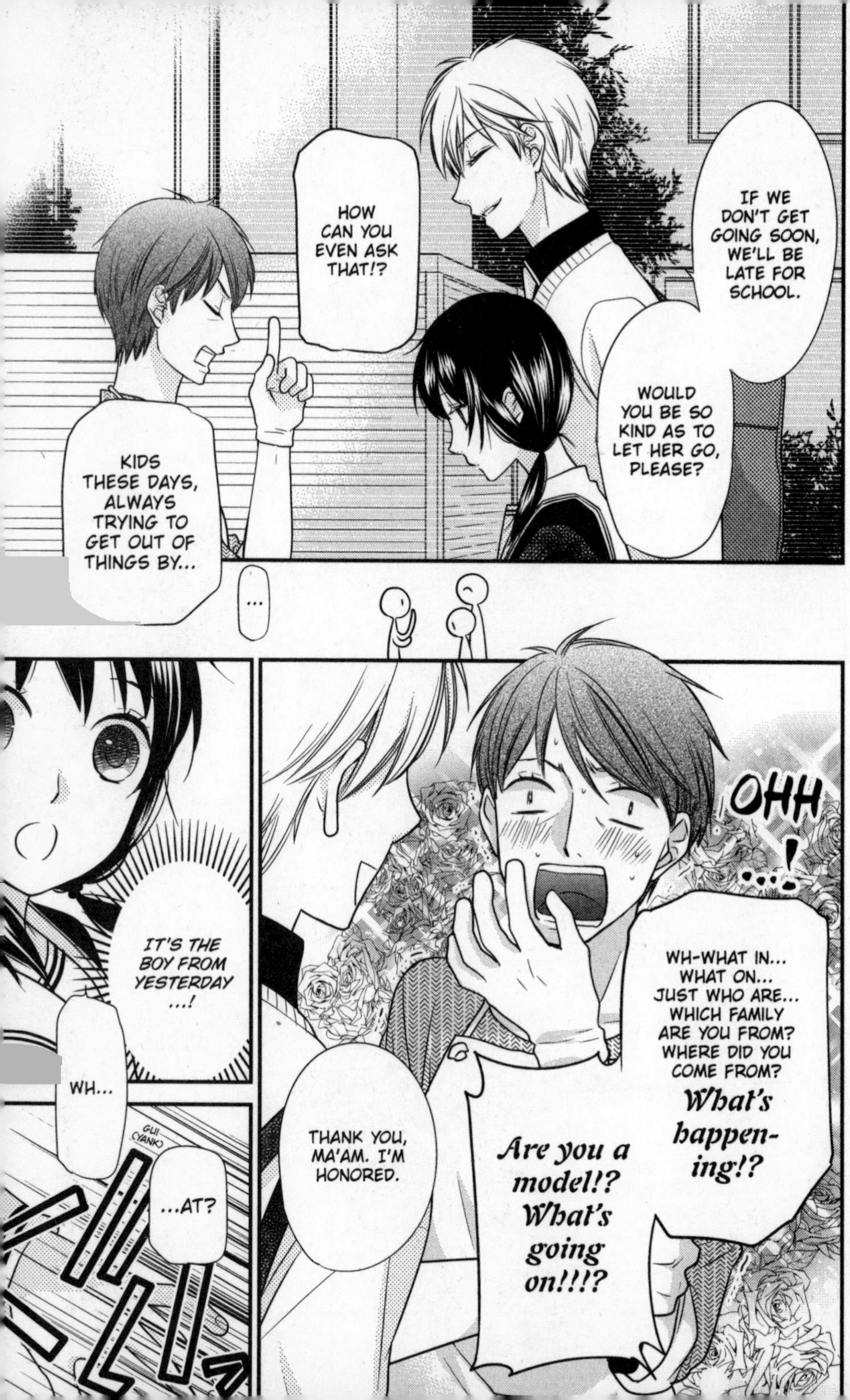
IF WE DON'T GET GOING SOON, WE'LL BE LATE FOR SCHOOL.
WOULD YOU BE SO KIND AS TO LET HER GO, PLEASE?
HOW CAN YOU EVEN ASK THAT!?
KIDS THESE DAYS, ALWAYS TRYING TO GET OUT OF THINGS BY...
...
OHH...!
WH-WHAT IN... WHAT ON... JUST WHO ARE... WHICH FAMILY ARE YOU FROM? WHERE DID YOU COME FROM? What's happen-ing!?
Are you a model!? What's going on!!!?
THANK YOU, MA'AM. I'M HONORED.
IT'S THE BOY FROM YESTERDAY...!
WH...
GUI (YANK)
...AT?

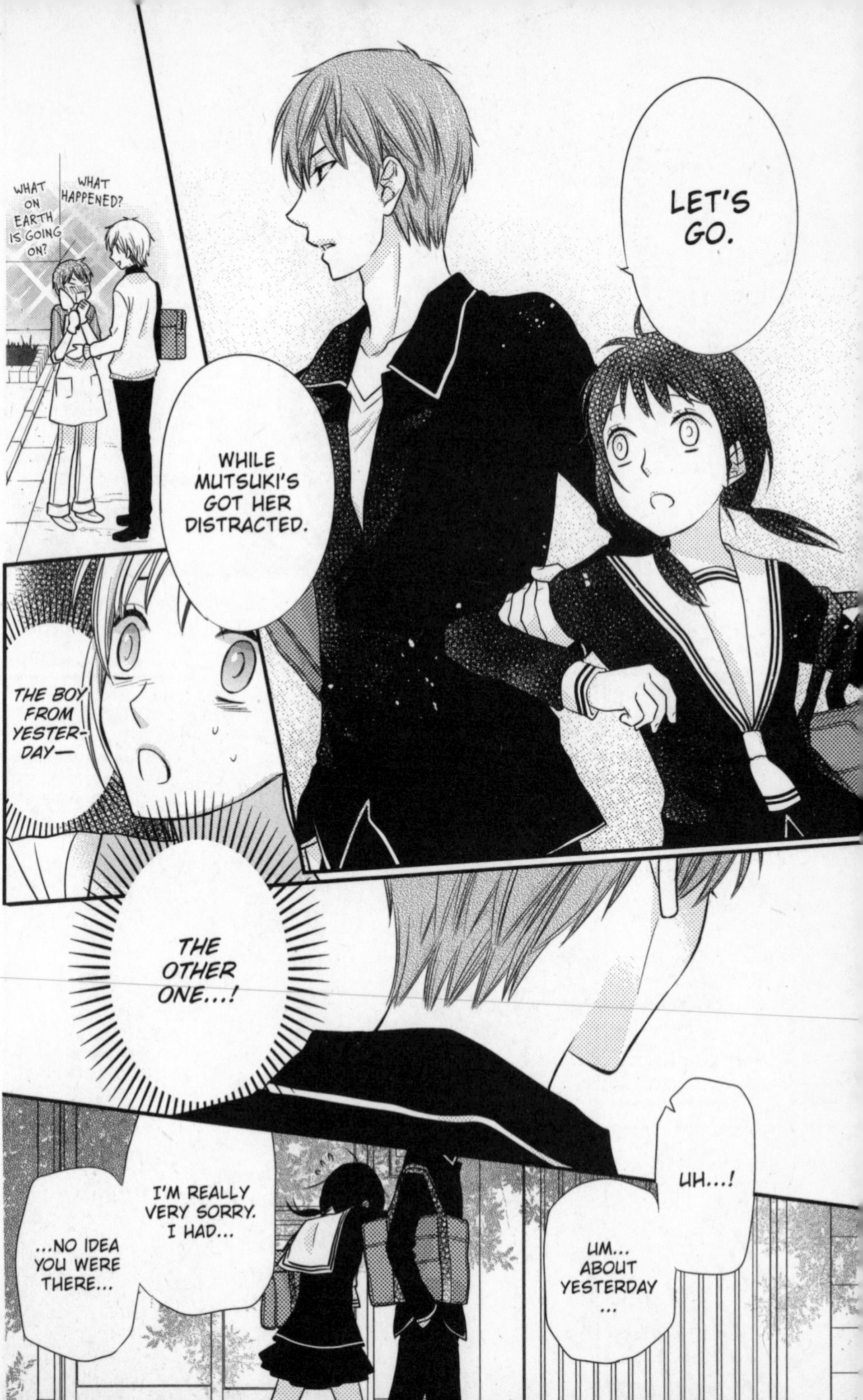
LET'S GO.
WHILE MUTSUKI'S GOT HER DISTRACTED.
WHAT HAPPENED?
WHAT ON EARTH IS GOING ON?
THE BOY FROM YESTER-DAY—
THE OTHER ONE...!
UH...!
UM... ABOUT YESTERDAY ...
I'M REALLY VERY SORRY. I HAD...
...NO IDEA YOU WERE THERE...

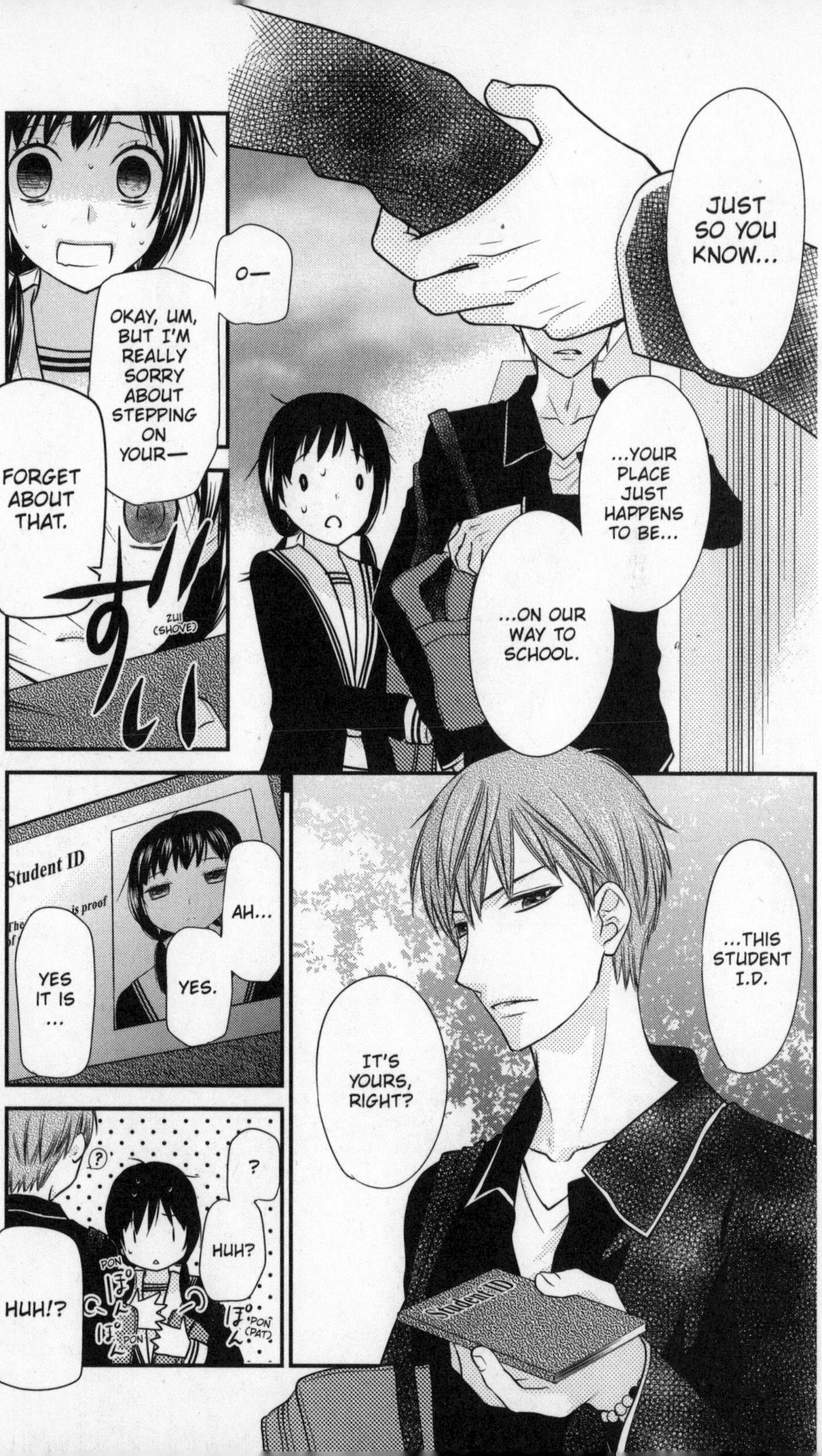
JUST SO YOU KNOW...
...YOUR PLACE JUST HAPPENS TO BE...
...ON OUR WAY TO SCHOOL.
O—
OKAY, UM, BUT I'M REALLY SORRY ABOUT STEPPING ON YOUR—
FORGET ABOUT THAT.
ZUI (SHOVE)
...THIS STUDENT I.D.
IT'S YOURS, RIGHT?
Student ID
Student ID
AH...
YES.
YES IT IS ...
?
?
HUH?
HUH!?
PON
PON
PON (PAT)

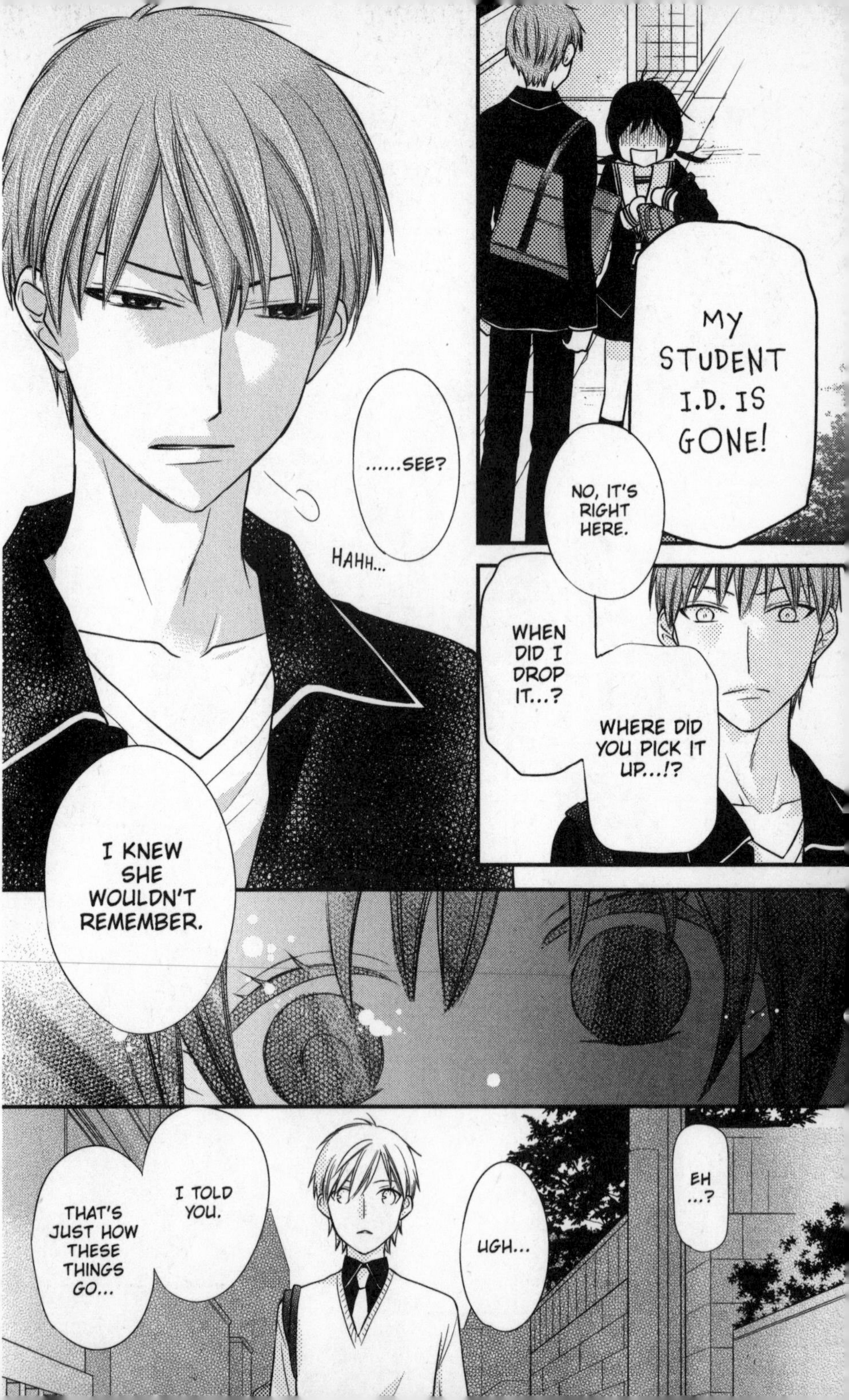
MY STUDENT I.D. IS GONE!
NO, IT'S RIGHT HERE.
WHEN DID I DROP IT...?
WHERE DID YOU PICK IT UP...!?
......SEE?
HAHH...
I KNEW SHE WOULDN'T REMEMBER.
EH ...?
UGH...
I TOLD YOU.
THAT'S JUST HOW THESE THINGS GO...

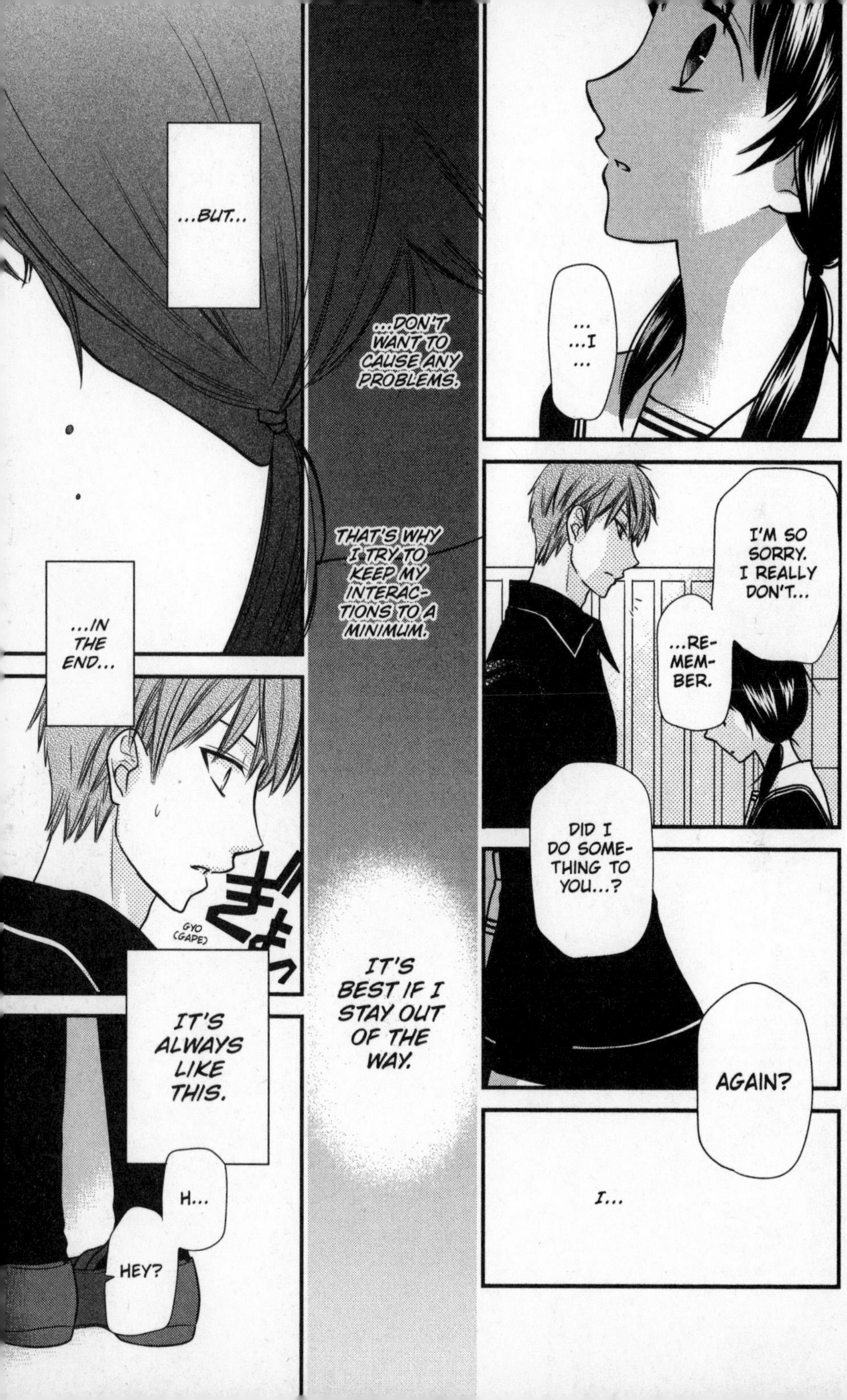
... ...I ...
I'M SO SORRY. I REALLY DON'T...
...RE-MEM-BER.
DID I DO SOME-THING TO YOU...?
AGAIN?
I...
...DON'T WANT TO CAUSE ANY PROBLEMS.
THAT'S WHY I TRY TO KEEP MY INTERAC-TIONS TO A MINIMUM.
IT'S BEST IF I STAY OUT OF THE WAY.
...BUT...
...IN THE END...
GYO (GAPE)
IT'S ALWAYS LIKE THIS.
H...
HEY?

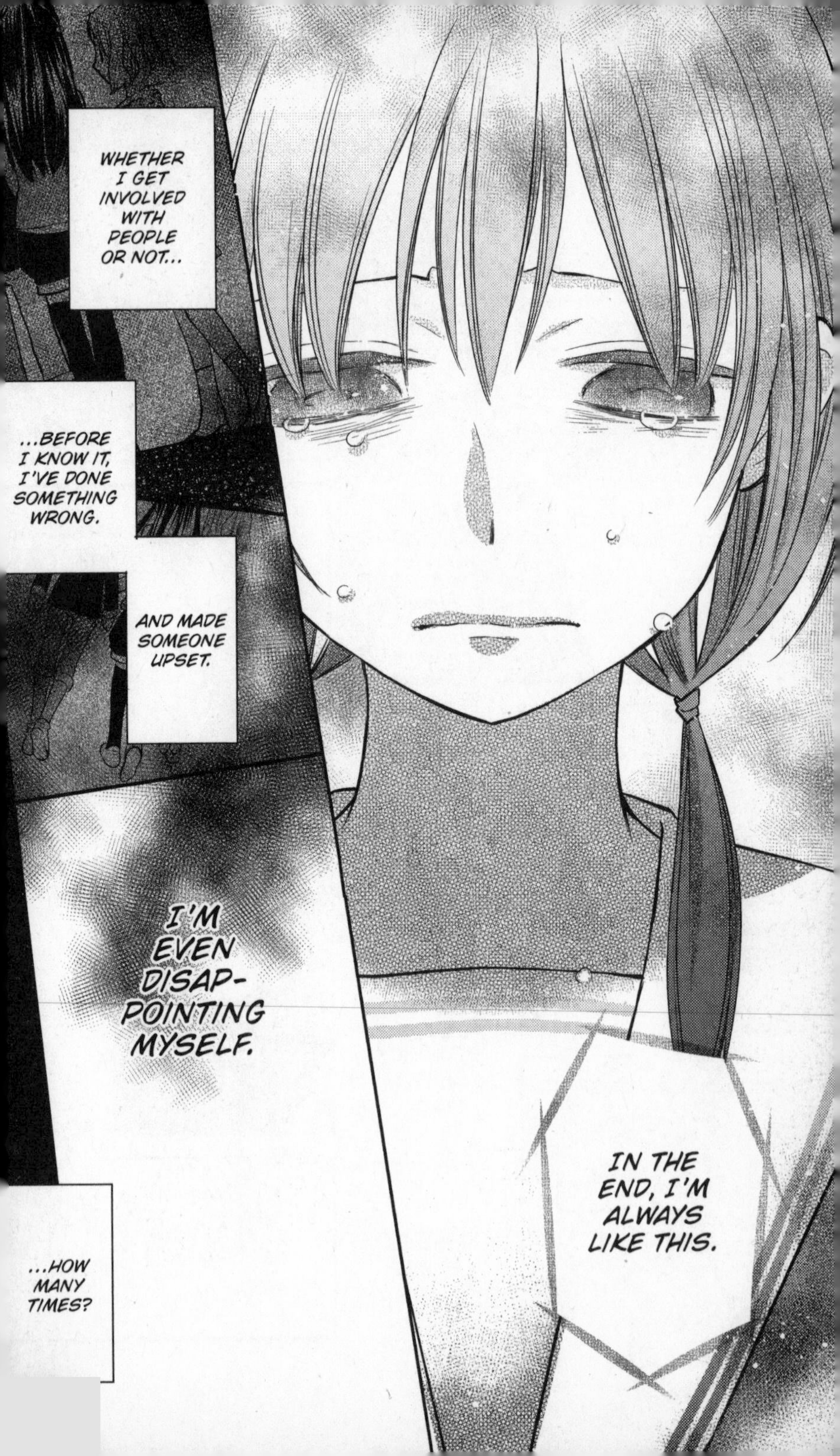
WHETHER I GET INVOLVED WITH PEOPLE OR NOT...
...BEFORE I KNOW IT, I'VE DONE SOMETHING WRONG.
AND MADE SOMEONE UPSET.
I'M EVEN DISAP-POINTING MYSELF.
IN THE END, I'M ALWAYS LIKE THIS.
...HOW MANY TIMES?

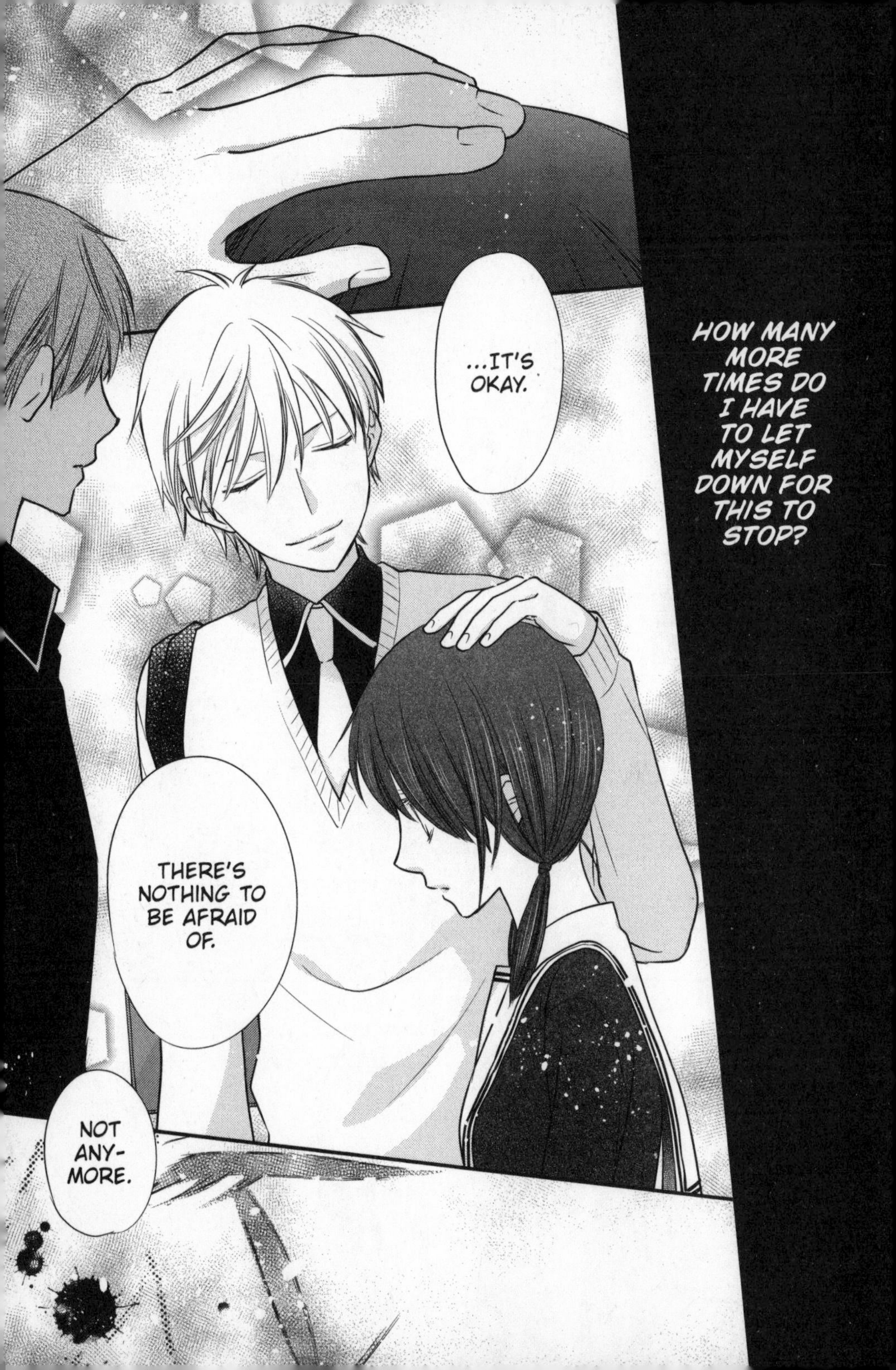
HOW MANY MORE TIMES DO I HAVE TO LET MYSELF DOWN FOR THIS TO STOP?
...IT'S OKAY.
THERE'S NOTHING TO BE AFRAID OF.
NOT ANY-MORE.

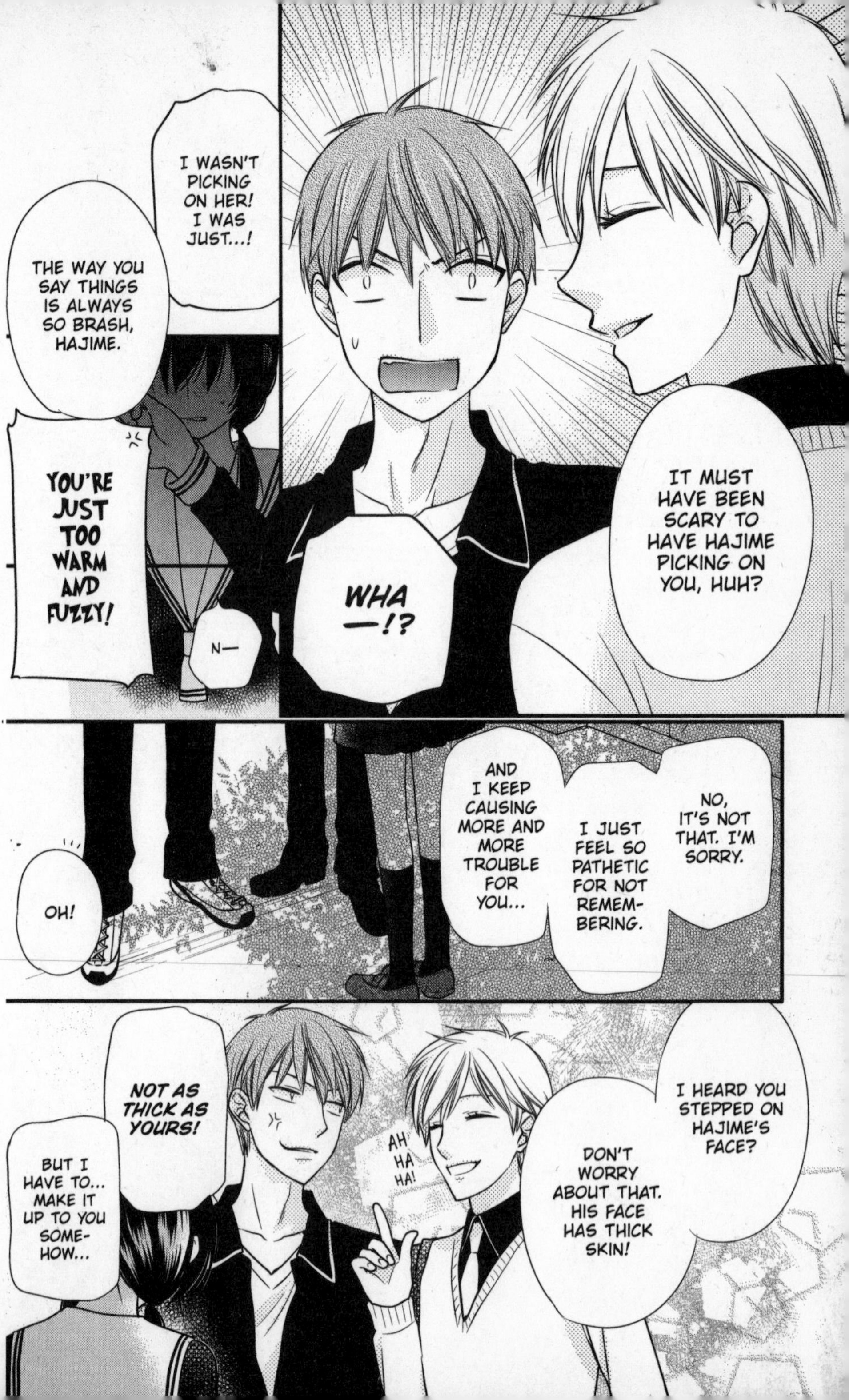
IT MUST HAVE BEEN SCARY TO HAVE HAJIME PICKING ON YOU, HUH?
WHA—!?
I WASN'T PICKING ON HER! I WAS JUST...!
THE WAY YOU SAY THINGS IS ALWAYS SO BRASH, HAJIME.
YOU'RE JUST TOO WARM AND FUZZY!
N—
NO, IT'S NOT THAT. I'M SORRY.
I JUST FEEL SO PATHETIC FOR NOT REMEMBERING.
AND I KEEP CAUSING MORE AND MORE TROUBLE FOR YOU...
OH!
I HEARD YOU STEPPED ON HAJIME'S FACE?
DON'T WORRY ABOUT THAT. HIS FACE HAS THICK SKIN!
AH HA HA!
NOT AS THICK AS YOURS!
BUT I HAVE TO... MAKE IT UP TO YOU SOMEHOW...

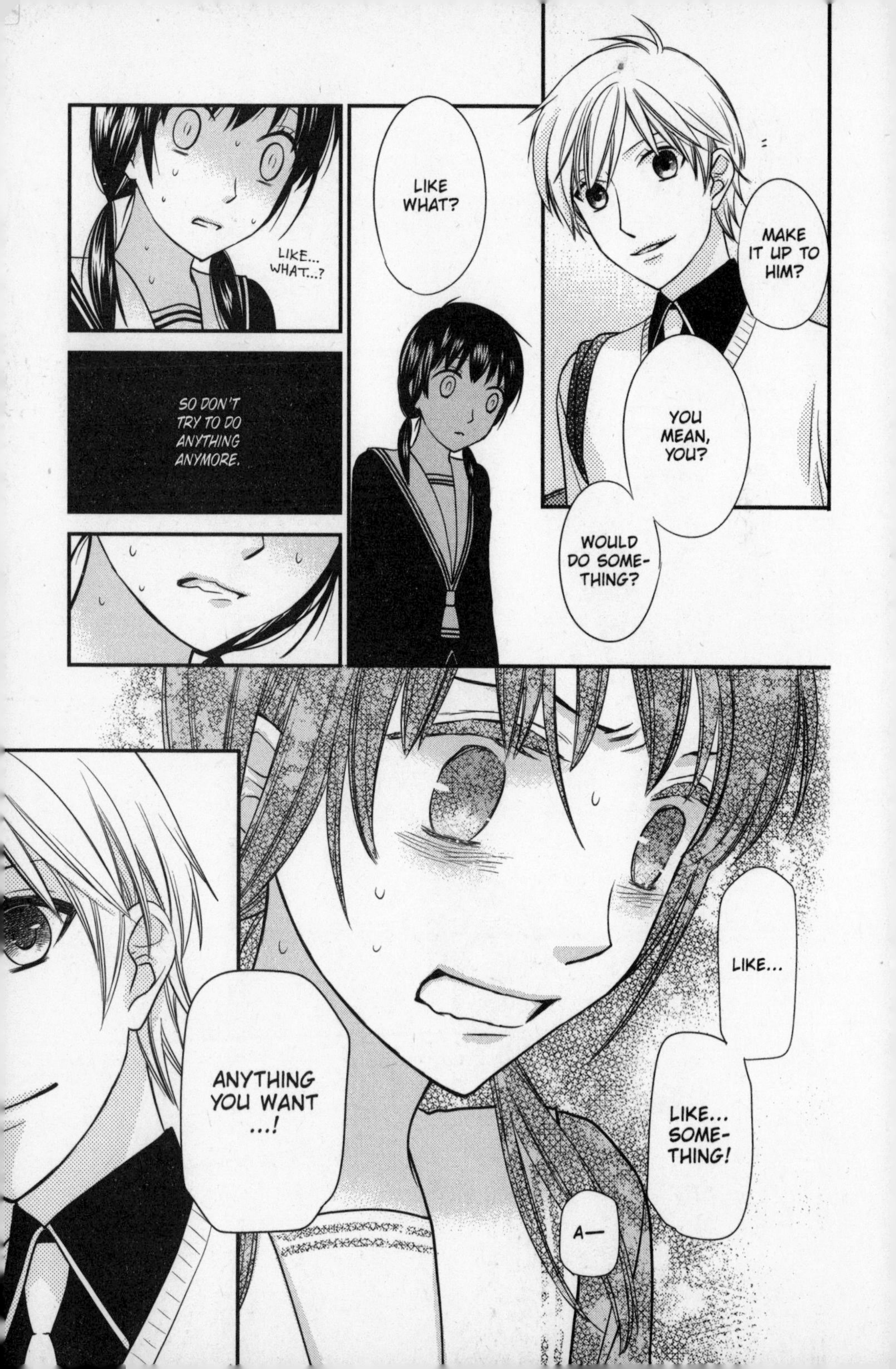
MAKE IT UP TO HIM?
YOU MEAN, YOU?
WOULD DO SOME-THING?
LIKE WHAT?
LIKE... WHAT...?
SO DON'T TRY TO DO ANYTHING ANYMORE.
LIKE...
LIKE... SOME-THING!
A—
ANYTHING YOU WANT ...!

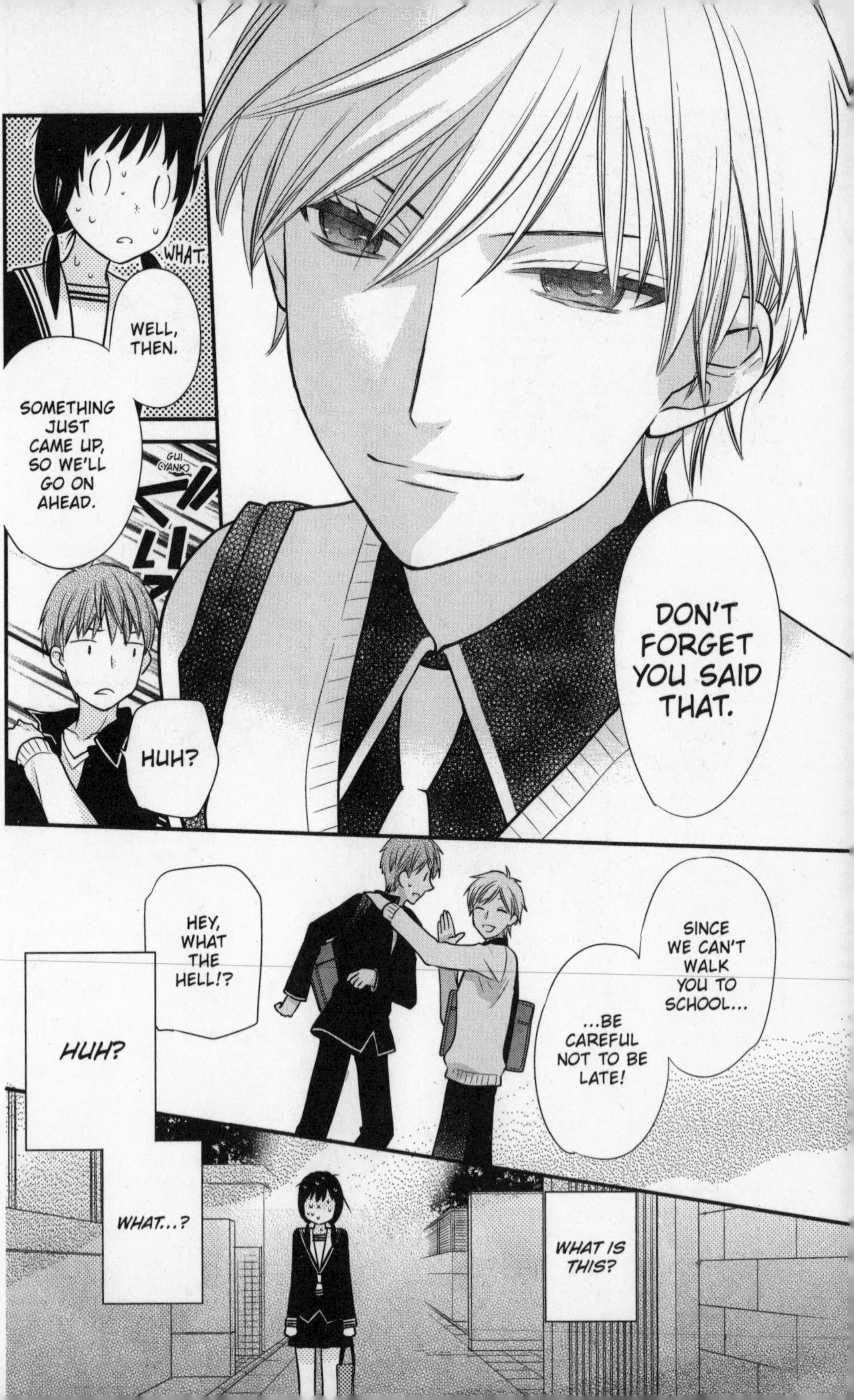
DON'T FORGET YOU SAID THAT.
WHAT.
WELL, THEN.
SOMETHING JUST CAME UP, SO WE'LL GO ON AHEAD.
GUI (YANK)
HUH?
SINCE WE CAN'T WALK YOU TO SCHOOL...
...BE CAREFUL NOT TO BE LATE!
HEY, WHAT THE HELL!?
HUH?
WHAT...?
WHAT IS THIS?

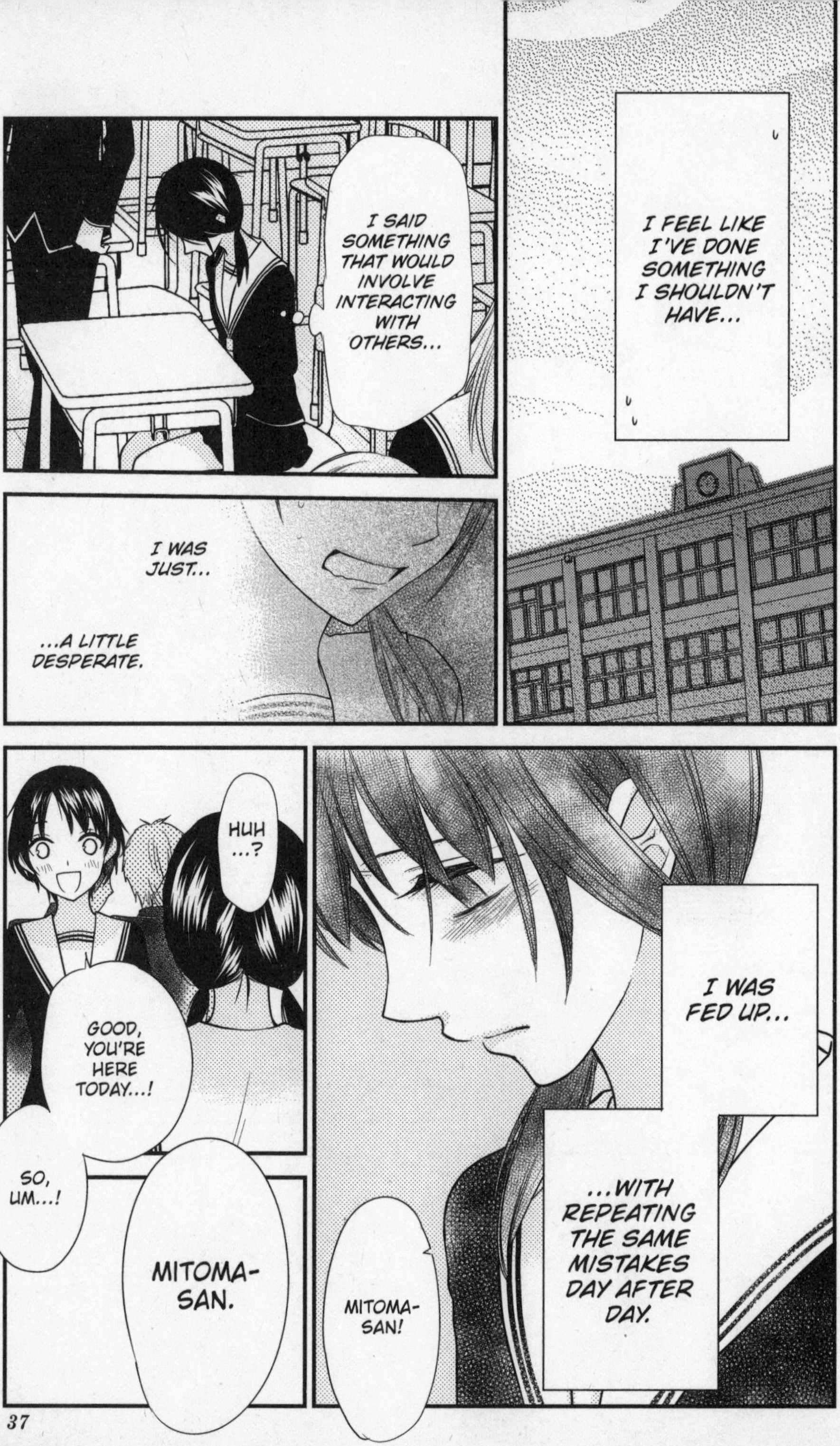
I FEEL LIKE I'VE DONE SOMETHING I SHOULDN'T HAVE...
I SAID SOMETHING THAT WOULD INVOLVE INTERACTING WITH OTHERS...
I WAS JUST...
...A LITTLE DESPERATE.
I WAS FED UP...
...WITH REPEATING THE SAME MISTAKES DAY AFTER DAY.
HUH ...?
GOOD, YOU'RE HERE TODAY...!
SO, UM...!
MITOMA-SAN!
MITOMA-SAN.

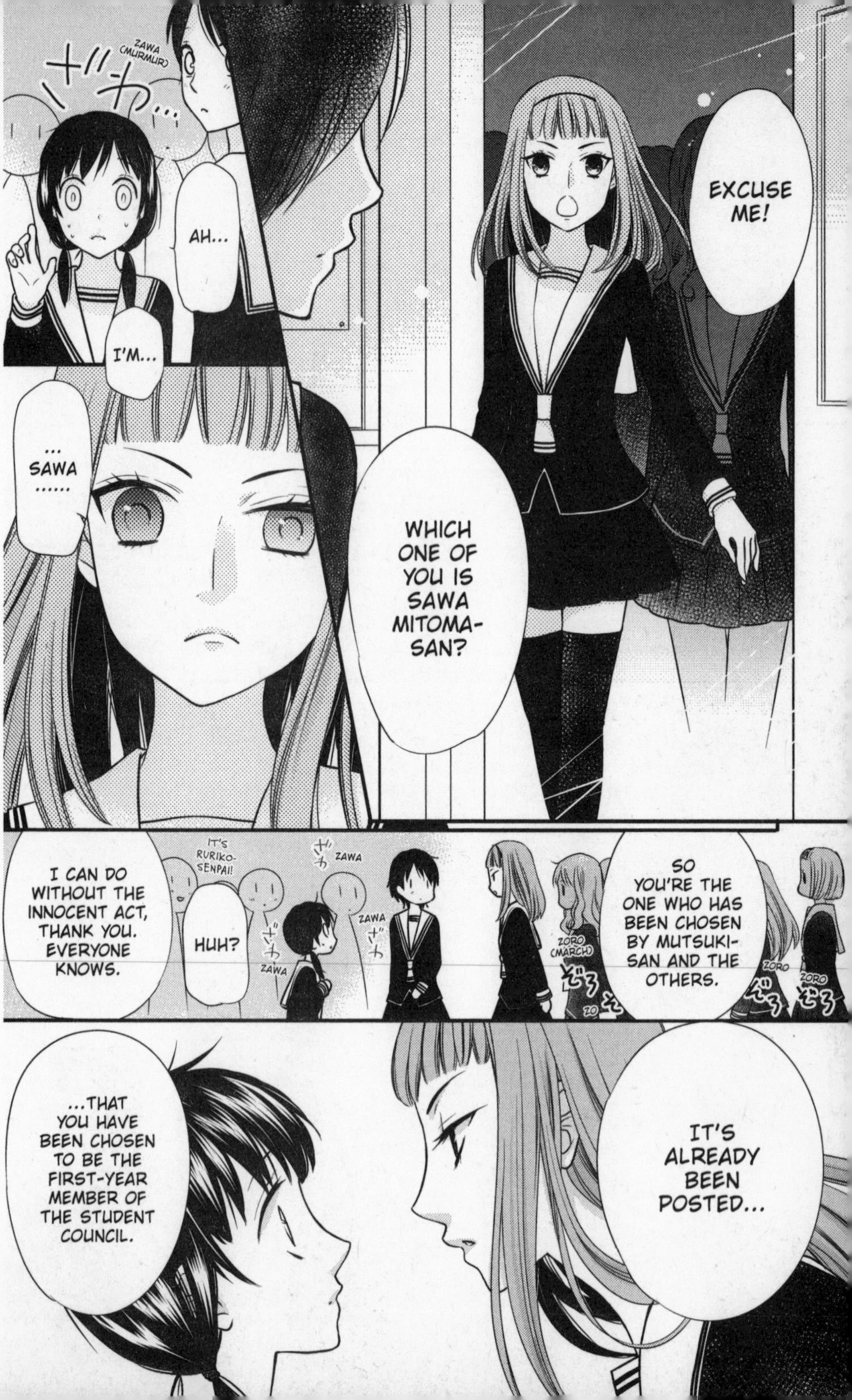
EXCUSE ME!
WHICH ONE OF YOU IS SAWA MITOMA-SAN?
ZAWA (MURMUR)
AH...
I'M...
... SAWA ......
SO YOU'RE THE ONE WHO HAS BEEN CHOSEN BY MUTSUKI-SAN AND THE OTHERS.
ZORO (MARCH)
ZORO
ZORO
ZO
ZAWA
ZAWA
IT'S RURIKO-SENPAI!
ZAWA
HUH?
I CAN DO WITHOUT THE INNOCENT ACT, THANK YOU. EVERYONE KNOWS.
IT'S ALREADY BEEN POSTED...
...THAT YOU HAVE BEEN CHOSEN TO BE THE FIRST-YEAR MEMBER OF THE STUDENT COUNCIL.

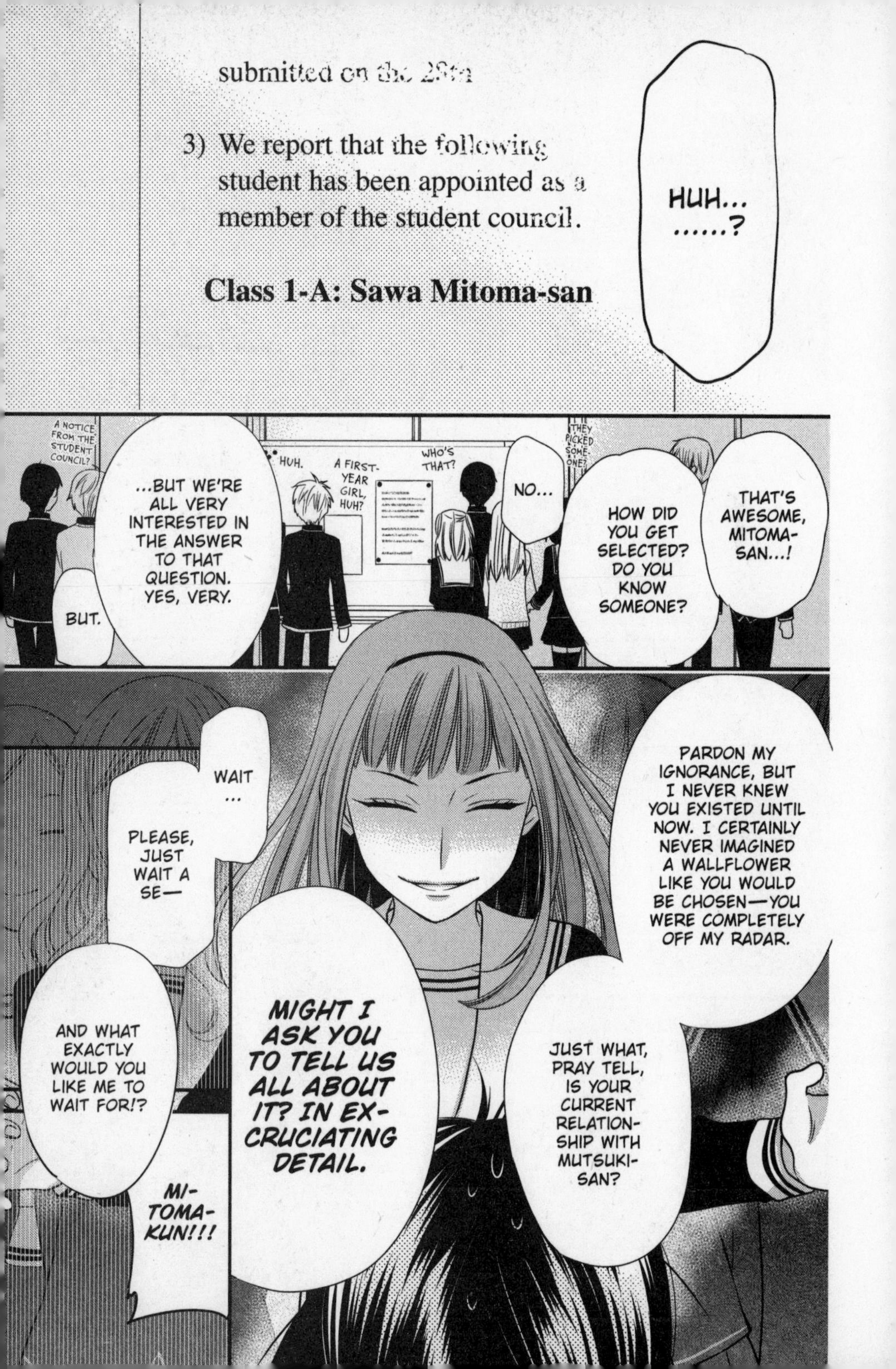
submitted on the 28th
3) We report that the following student has been appointed as a member of the student council.
Class 1-A: Sawa Mitoma-san
HUH... ......?
THEY PICKED SOME-ONE?
THAT'S AWESOME, MITOMA-SAN...!
HOW DID YOU GET SELECTED? DO YOU KNOW SOMEONE?
NO...
WHO'S THAT?
A FIRST-YEAR GIRL, HUH?
HUH.
A NOTICE FROM THE STUDENT COUNCIL?
BUT.
...BUT WE'RE ALL VERY INTERESTED IN THE ANSWER TO THAT QUESTION. YES, VERY.
PARDON MY IGNORANCE, BUT I NEVER KNEW YOU EXISTED UNTIL NOW. I CERTAINLY NEVER IMAGINED A WALLFLOWER LIKE YOU WOULD BE CHOSEN—YOU WERE COMPLETELY OFF MY RADAR.
JUST WHAT, PRAY TELL, IS YOUR CURRENT RELATION-SHIP WITH MUTSUKI-SAN?
MIGHT I ASK YOU TO TELL US ALL ABOUT IT? IN EX-CRUCIATING DETAIL.
WAIT ...
PLEASE, JUST WAIT A SE—
AND WHAT EXACTLY WOULD YOU LIKE ME TO WAIT FOR!?
MI-TOMA-KUN!!!

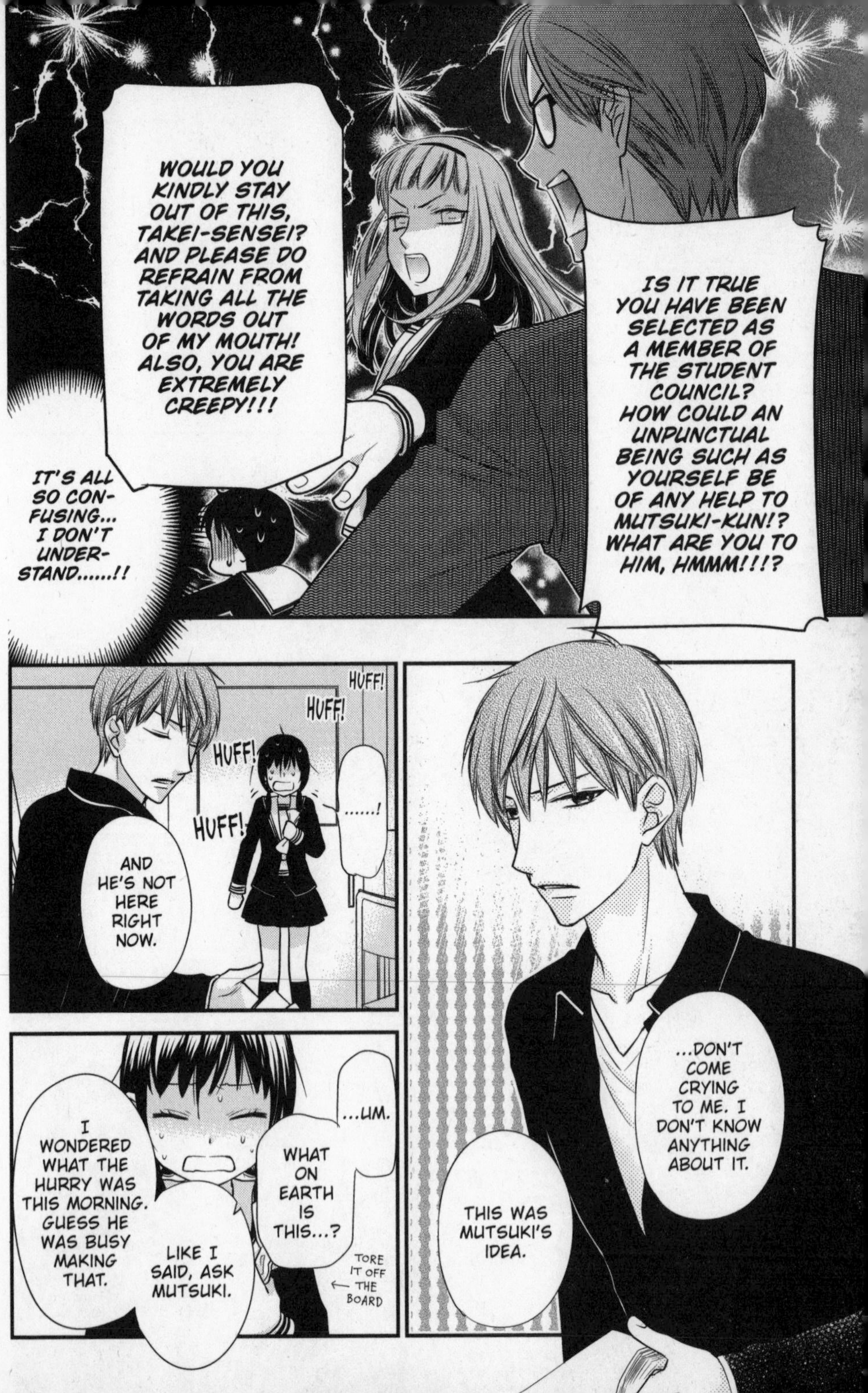
IS IT TRUE YOU HAVE BEEN SELECTED AS A MEMBER OF THE STUDENT COUNCIL? HOW COULD AN UNPUNCTUAL BEING SUCH AS YOURSELF BE OF ANY HELP TO MUTSUKI-KUN!? WHAT ARE YOU TO HIM, HMMM!!!?
WOULD YOU KINDLY STAY OUT OF THIS, TAKEI-SENSEI? AND PLEASE DO REFRAIN FROM TAKING ALL THE WORDS OUT OF MY MOUTH! ALSO, YOU ARE EXTREMELY CREEPY!!!
IT'S ALL SO CON-FUSING... I DON'T UNDER-STAND......!!
...DON'T COME CRYING TO ME. I DON'T KNOW ANYTHING ABOUT IT.
THIS WAS MUTSUKI'S IDEA.
HUFF!
HUFF!
HUFF!
HUFF!
......!
AND HE'S NOT HERE RIGHT NOW.
...UM.
WHAT ON EARTH IS THIS...?
I WONDERED WHAT THE HURRY WAS THIS MORNING. GUESS HE WAS BUSY MAKING THAT.
LIKE I SAID, ASK MUTSUKI.
TORE IT OFF THE BOARD

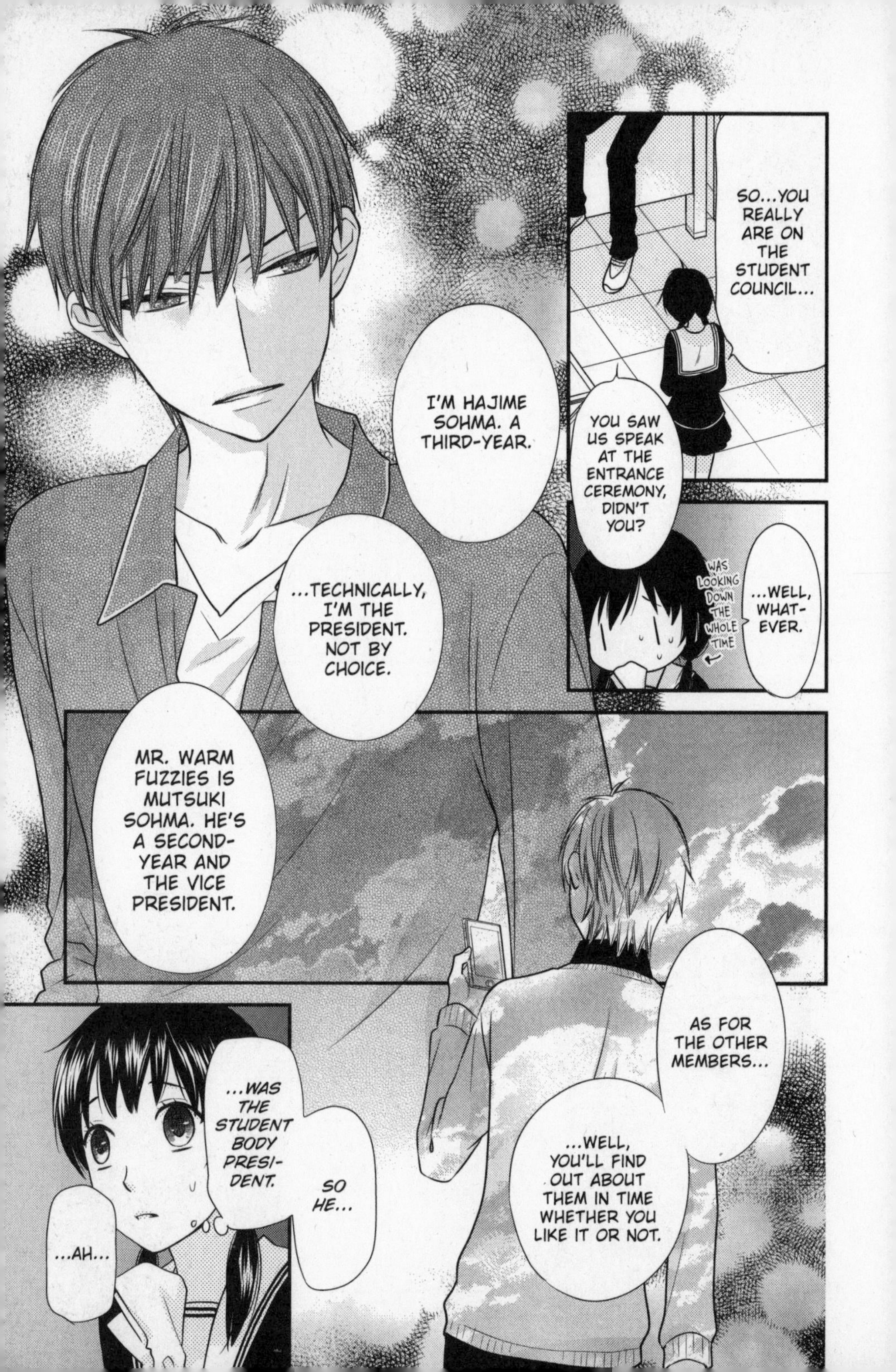
SO...YOU REALLY ARE ON THE STUDENT COUNCIL...
YOU SAW US SPEAK AT THE ENTRANCE CEREMONY, DIDN'T YOU?
WAS LOOKING DOWN THE WHOLE TIME
...WELL, WHATEVER.
I'M HAJIME SOHMA. A THIRD-YEAR.
...TECHNICALLY, I'M THE PRESIDENT. NOT BY CHOICE.
MR. WARM FUZZIES IS MUTSUKI SOHMA. HE'S A SECOND-YEAR AND THE VICE PRESIDENT.
AS FOR THE OTHER MEMBERS...
...WELL, YOU'LL FIND OUT ABOUT THEM IN TIME WHETHER YOU LIKE IT OR NOT.
SO HE...
...WAS THE STUDENT BODY PRESIDENT.
...AH...

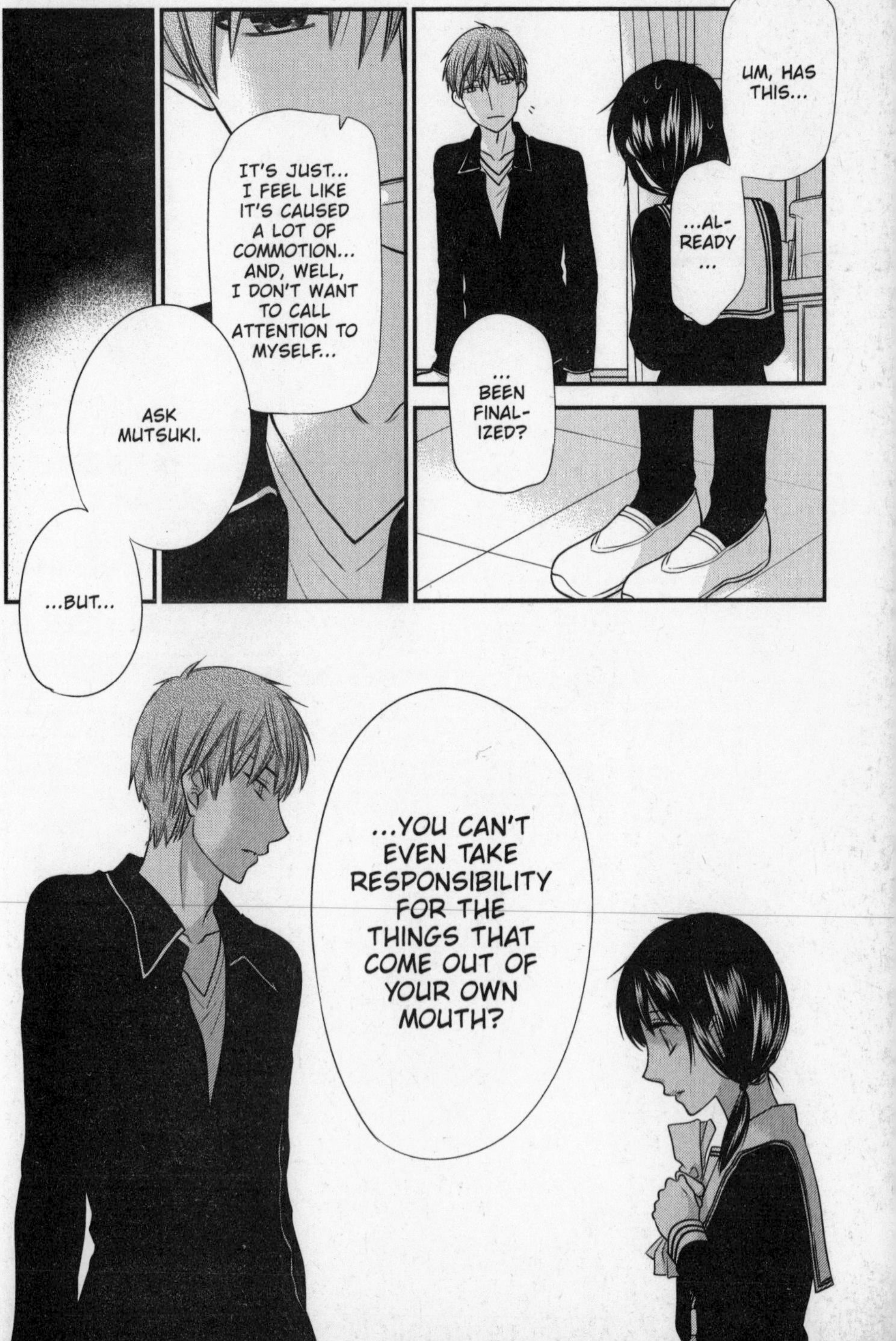
UM, HAS THIS...
...AL-READY...
...BEEN FINAL-IZED?
IT'S JUST... I FEEL LIKE IT'S CAUSED A LOT OF COMMOTION... AND, WELL, I DON'T WANT TO CALL ATTENTION TO MYSELF...
ASK MUTSUKI.
...BUT...
...YOU CAN'T EVEN TAKE RESPONSIBILITY FOR THE THINGS THAT COME OUT OF YOUR OWN MOUTH?

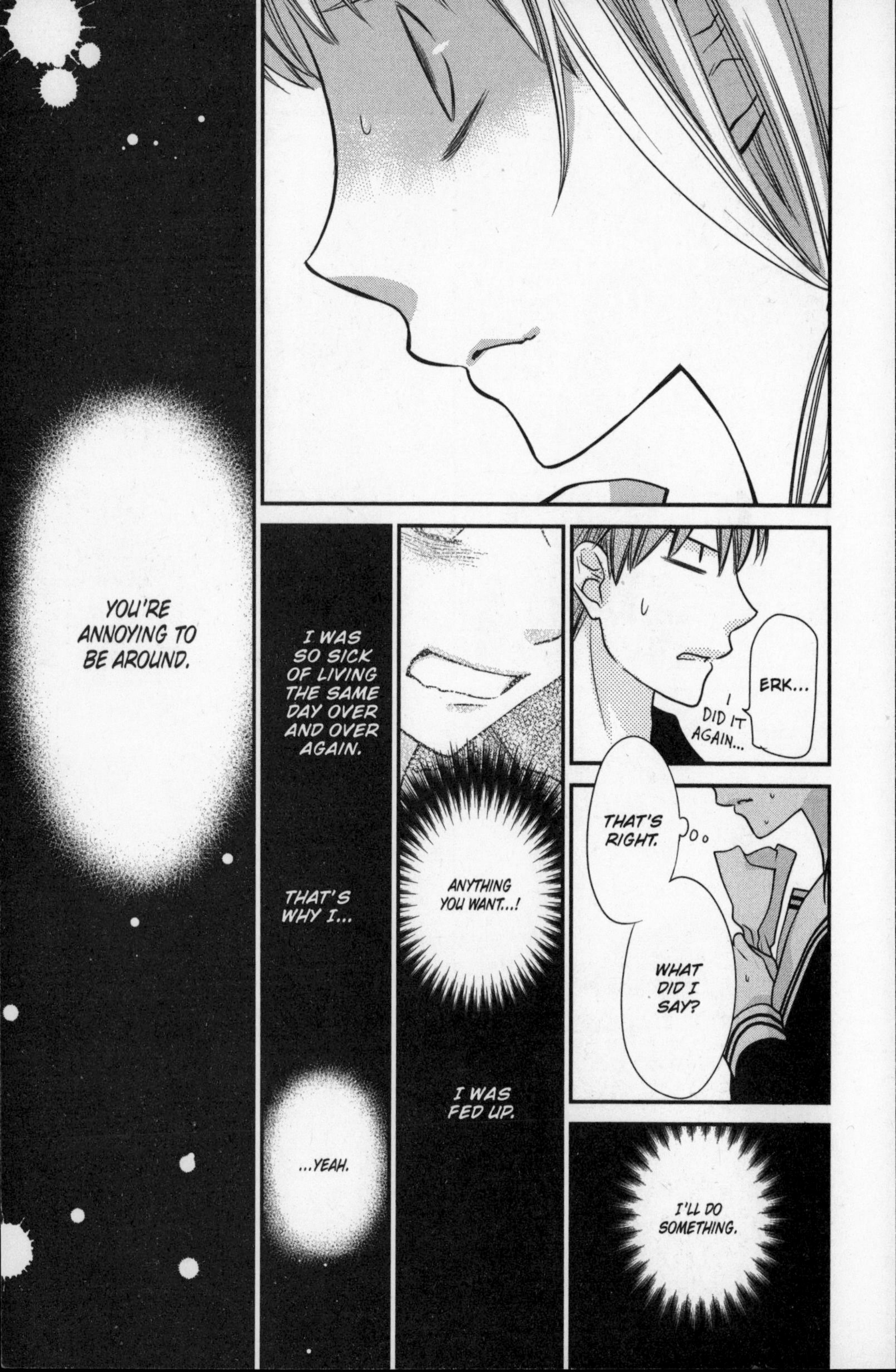
ERK...
I DID IT AGAIN...
THAT'S RIGHT.
WHAT DID I SAY?
I WAS SO SICK OF LIVING THE SAME DAY OVER AND OVER AGAIN.
THAT'S WHY I...
ANYTHING YOU WANT...!
I WAS FED UP.
I'LL DO SOMETHING.
YOU'RE ANNOYING TO BE AROUND.
...YEAH.

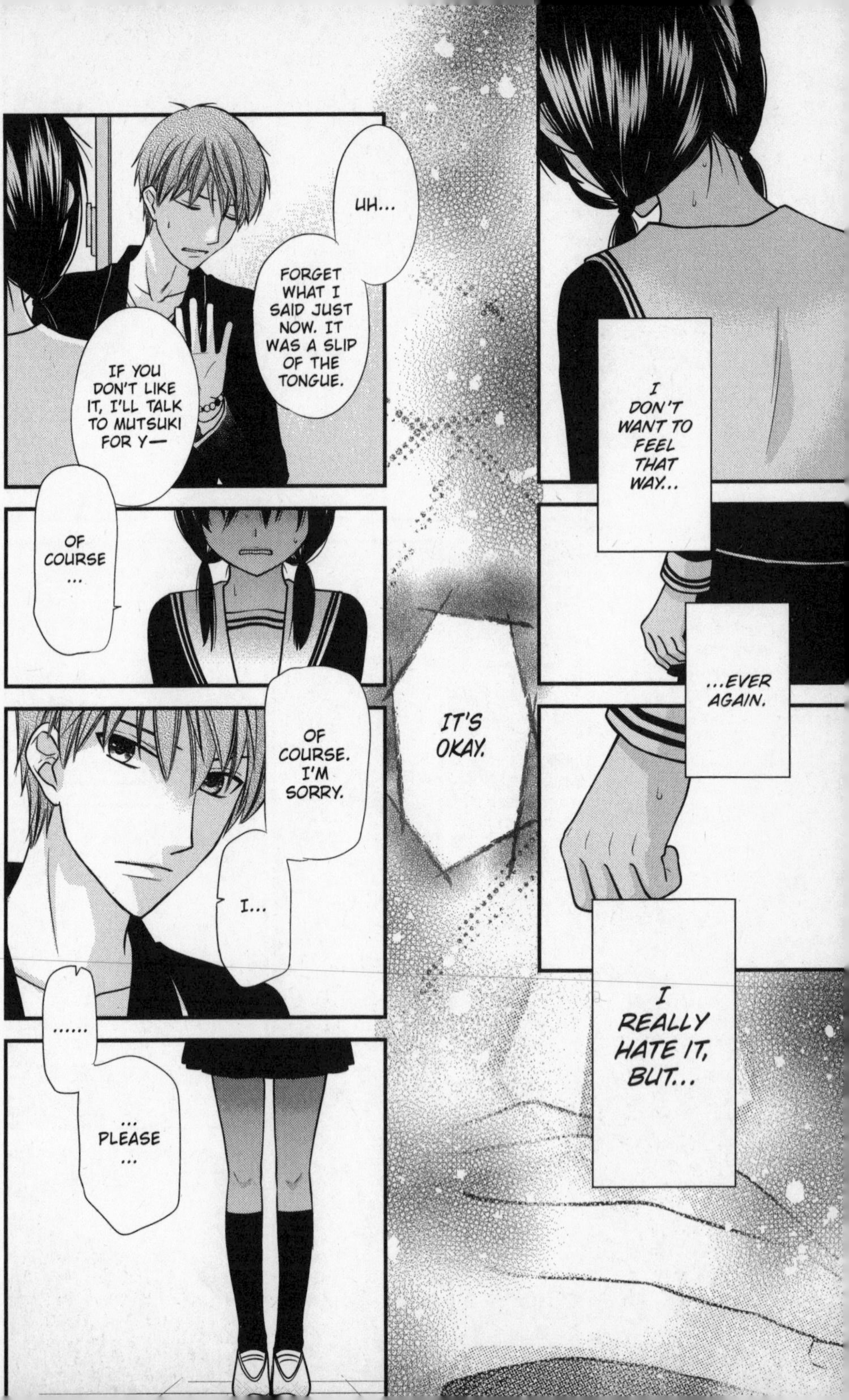
I DON'T WANT TO FEEL THAT WAY...
...EVER AGAIN.
I REALLY HATE IT, BUT...
UH...
FORGET WHAT I SAID JUST NOW. IT WAS A SLIP OF THE TONGUE.
IF YOU DON'T LIKE IT, I'LL TALK TO MUTSUKI FOR Y—
OF COURSE...
IT'S OKAY.
OF COURSE. I'M SORRY.
I...
......
...PLEASE...

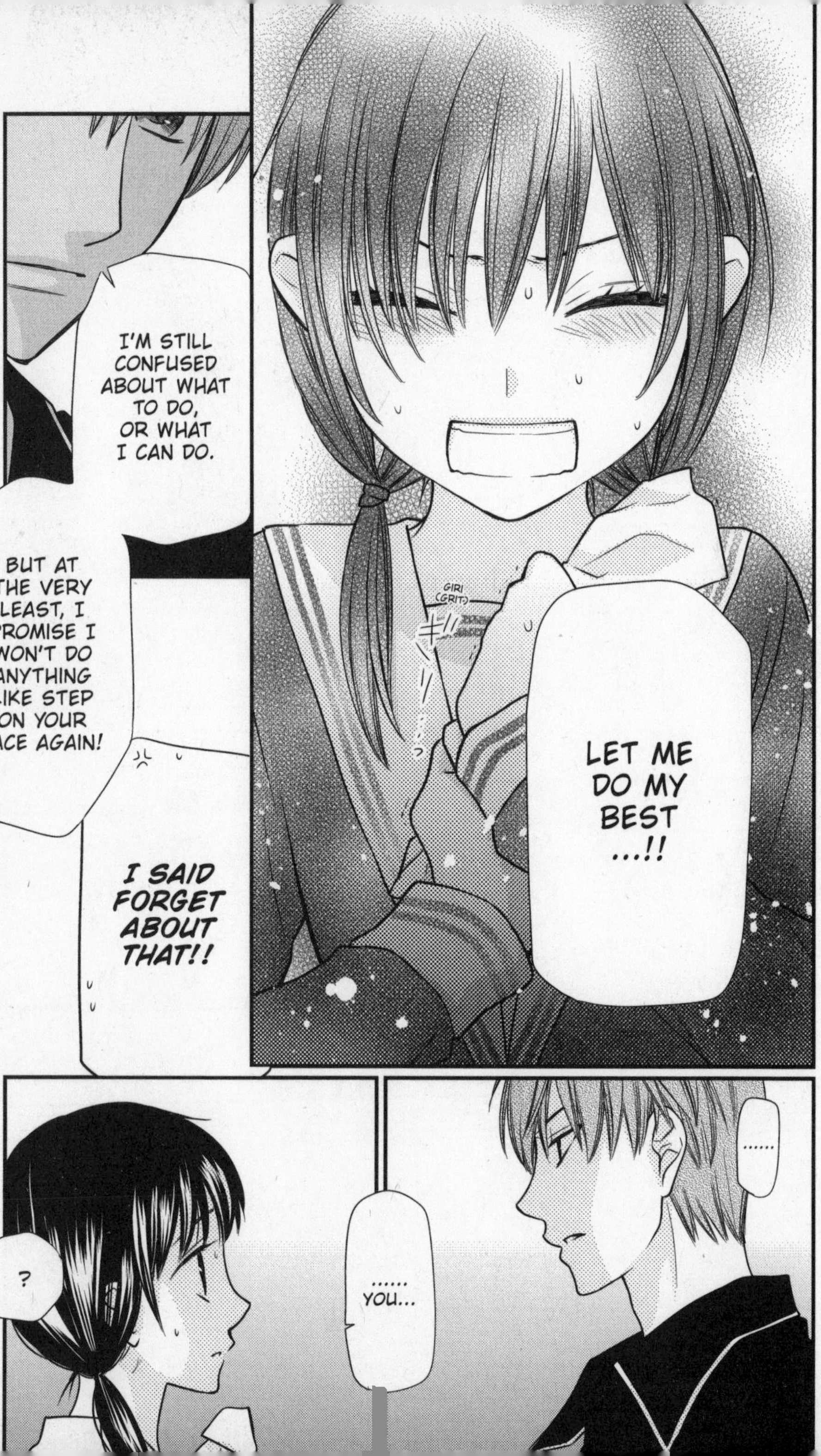
I'M STILL CONFUSED ABOUT WHAT TO DO, OR WHAT I CAN DO.
BUT AT THE VERY LEAST, I PROMISE I WON'T DO ANYTHING LIKE STEP ON YOUR FACE AGAIN!
GIRI (GRIT)
LET ME DO MY BEST ...!!
I SAID FORGET ABOUT THAT!!
......
...... YOU...
?

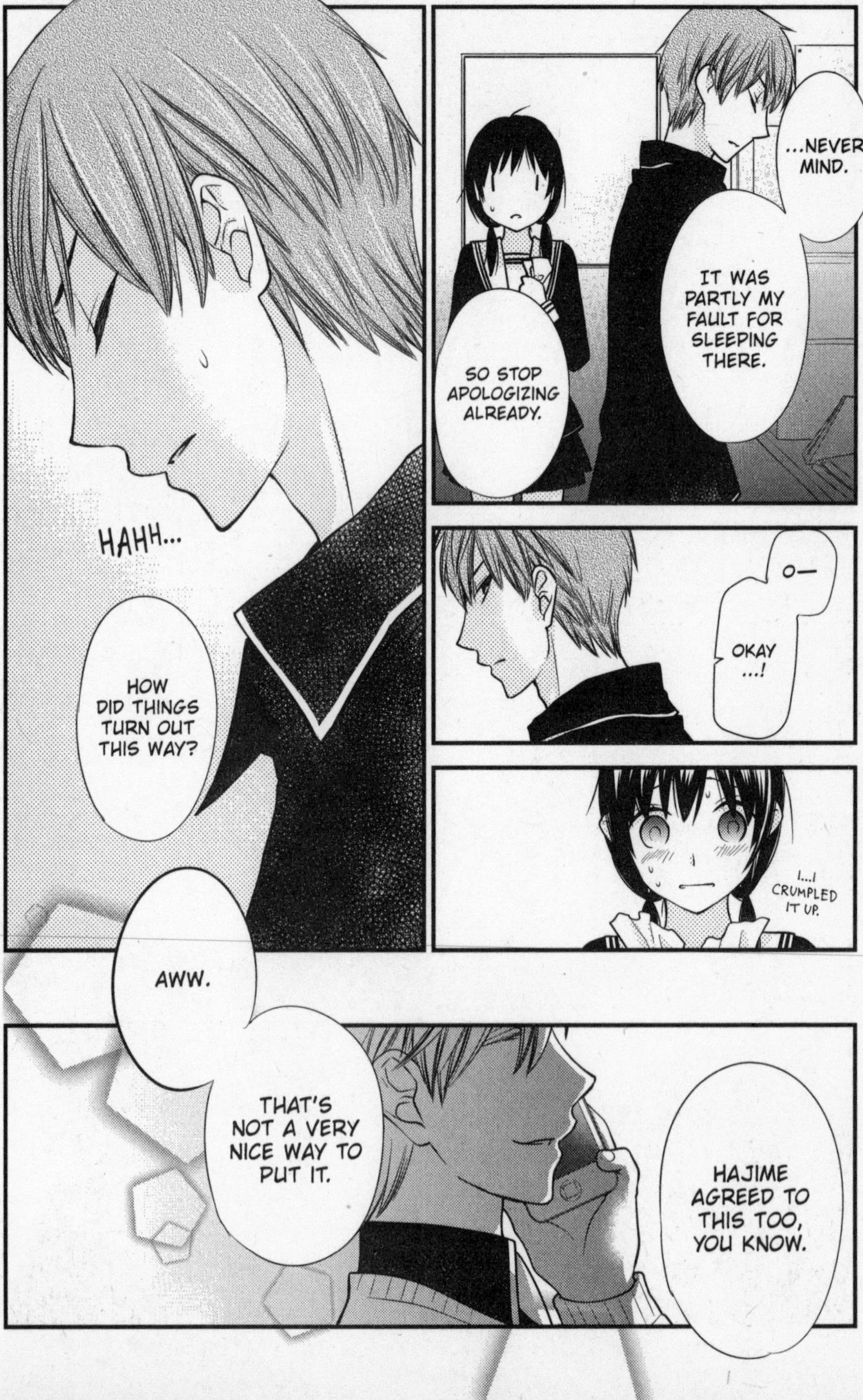
...NEVER MIND.
IT WAS PARTLY MY FAULT FOR SLEEPING THERE.
SO STOP APOLOGIZING ALREADY.
O—
OKAY ...!
I...I CRUMPLED IT UP.
HAHH...
HOW DID THINGS TURN OUT THIS WAY?
AWW.
THAT'S NOT A VERY NICE WAY TO PUT IT.
HAJIME AGREED TO THIS TOO, YOU KNOW.

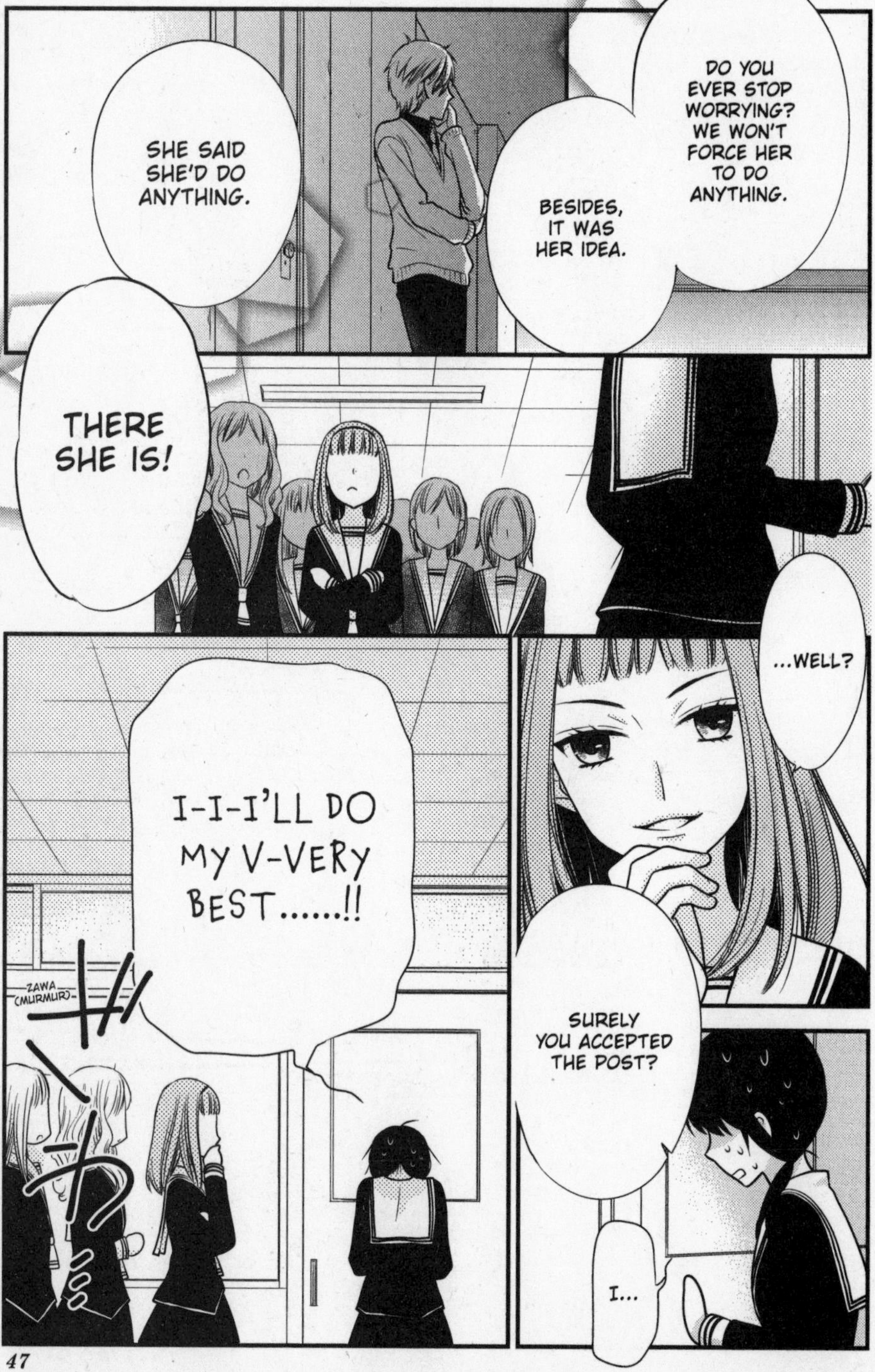
DO YOU EVER STOP WORRYING? WE WON'T FORCE HER TO DO ANYTHING.
BESIDES, IT WAS HER IDEA.
SHE SAID SHE'D DO ANYTHING.
THERE SHE IS!
...WELL?
SURELY YOU ACCEPTED THE POST?
I...
I-I-I'LL DO MY V-VERY BEST......!!
ZAWA (MURMUR)

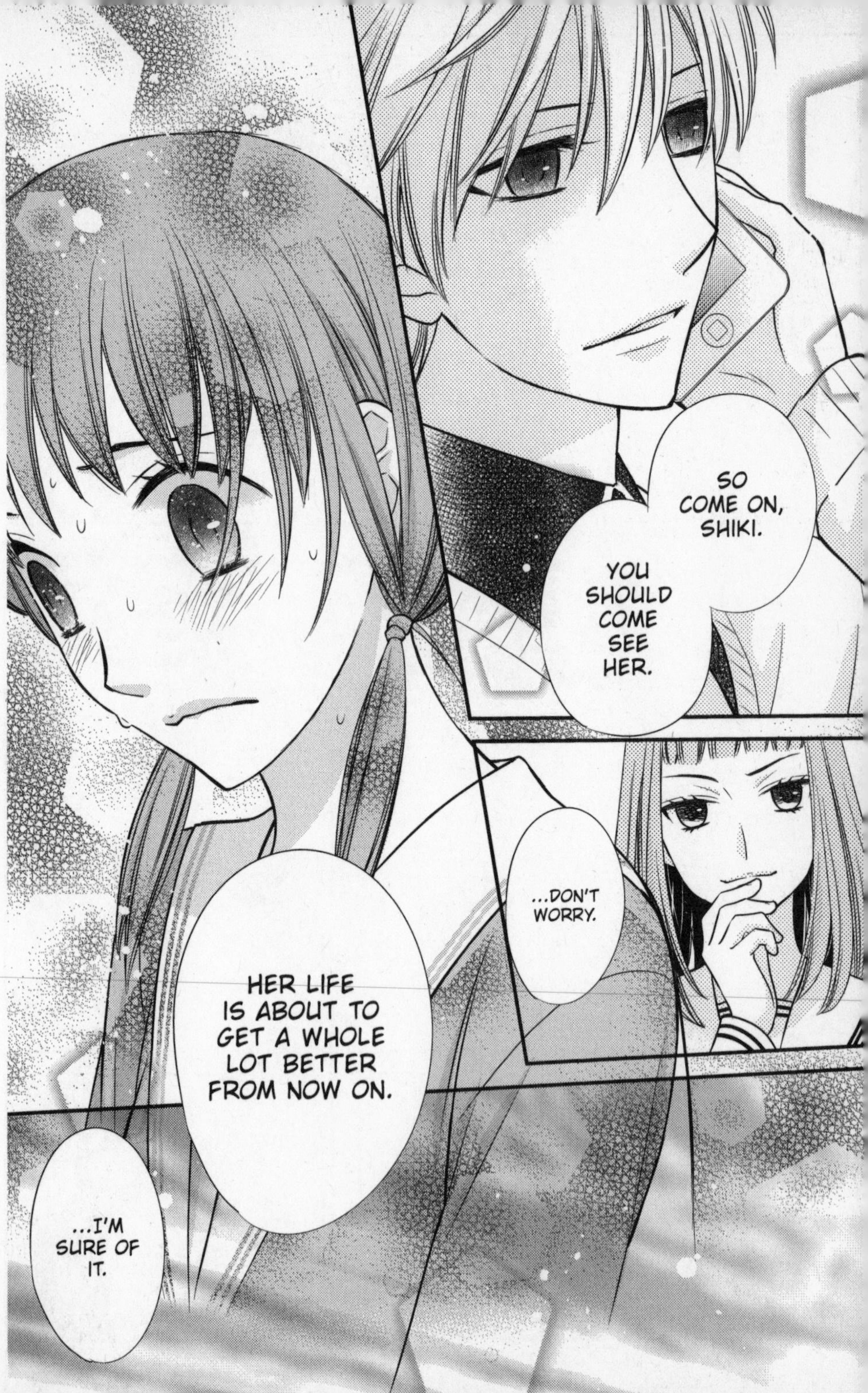
SO COME ON, SHIKI.
YOU SHOULD COME SEE HER.
...DON'T WORRY.
HER LIFE IS ABOUT TO GET A WHOLE LOT BETTER FROM NOW ON.
...I'M SURE OF IT.

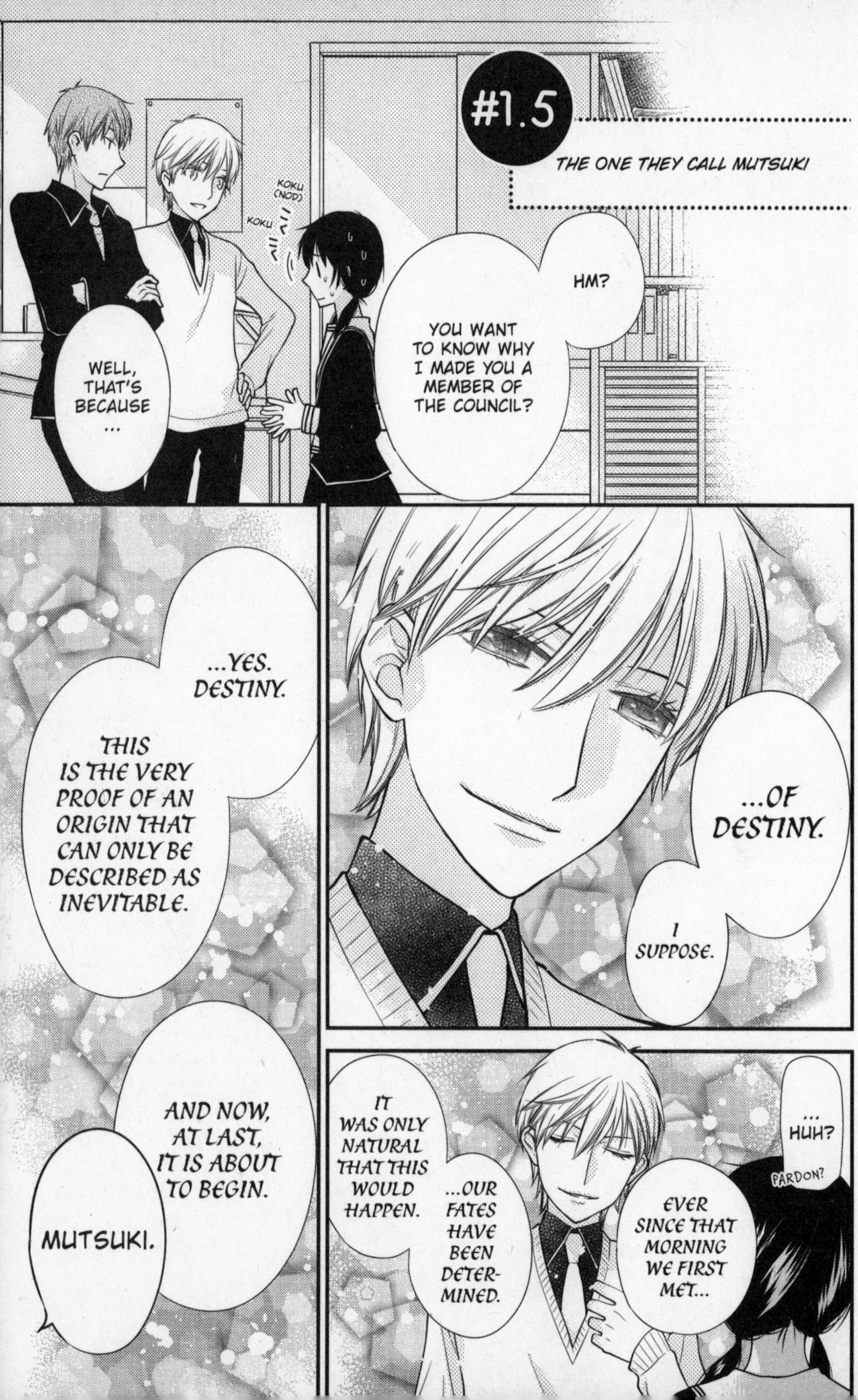
#1.5
THE ONE THEY CALL MUTSUKI
HM?
YOU WANT TO KNOW WHY I MADE YOU A MEMBER OF THE COUNCIL?
KOKU (NOD)
KOKU
WELL, THAT'S BECAUSE ...
...OF DESTINY.
I SUPPOSE.
... HUH?
PARDON?
EVER SINCE THAT MORNING WE FIRST MET...
...OUR FATES HAVE BEEN DETER-MINED.
IT WAS ONLY NATURAL THAT THIS WOULD HAPPEN.
...YES. DESTINY.
THIS IS THE VERY PROOF OF AN ORIGIN THAT CAN ONLY BE DESCRIBED AS INEVITABLE.
AND NOW, AT LAST, IT IS ABOUT TO BEGIN.
MUTSUKI.

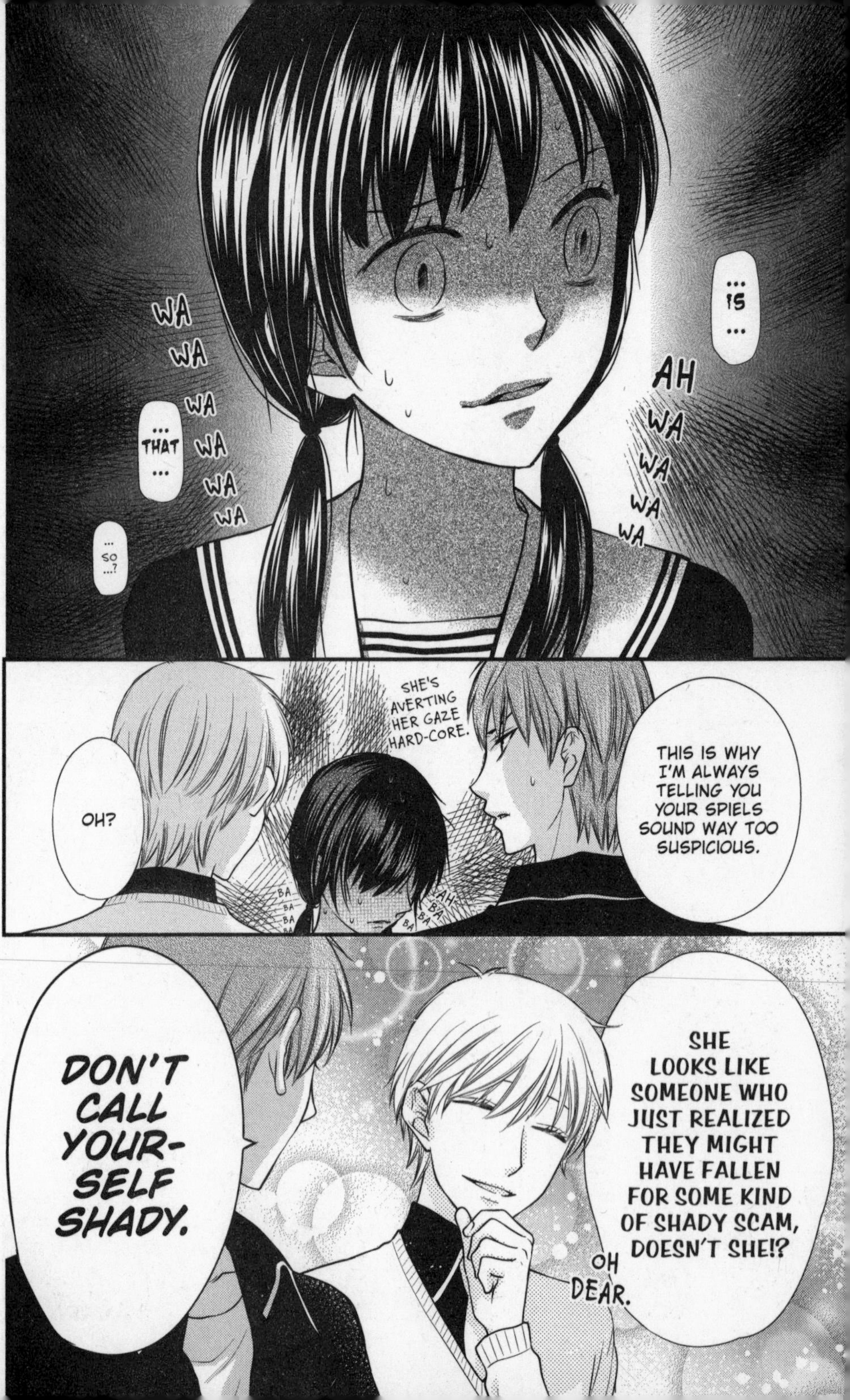

...IS...
AH WA WA WA WA
WA WA WA WA WA WA
...THAT...
...SO...?
THIS IS WHY I'M ALWAYS TELLING YOU YOUR SPIELS SOUND WAY TOO SUSPICIOUS.
SHE'S AVERTING HER GAZE HARD-CORE.
OH?
SHE LOOKS LIKE SOMEONE WHO JUST REALIZED THEY MIGHT HAVE FALLEN FOR SOME KIND OF SHADY SCAM, DOESN'T SHE!?
OH DEAR.
DON'T CALL YOUR-SELF SHADY.

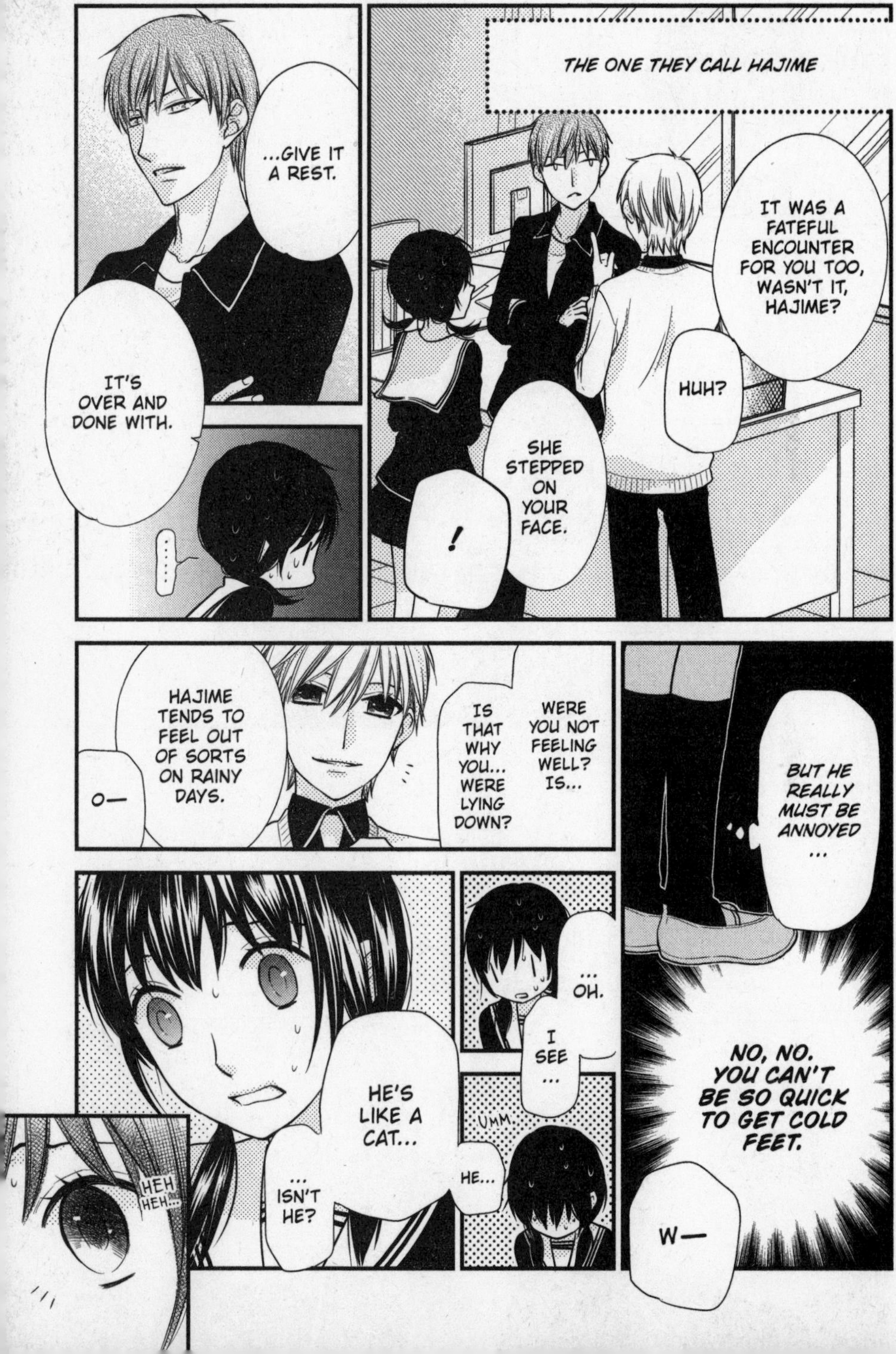
THE ONE THEY CALL HAJIME
IT WAS A FATEFUL ENCOUNTER FOR YOU TOO, WASN'T IT, HAJIME?
HUH?
SHE STEPPED ON YOUR FACE.
!
...GIVE IT A REST.
IT'S OVER AND DONE WITH.
......
BUT HE REALLY MUST BE ANNOYED ...
NO, NO. YOU CAN'T BE SO QUICK TO GET COLD FEET.
W—
WERE YOU NOT FEELING WELL? IS...
IS THAT WHY YOU... WERE LYING DOWN?
HAJIME TENDS TO FEEL OUT OF SORTS ON RAINY DAYS.
O—
...OH.
I SEE...
UMM.
HE...
HE'S LIKE A CAT...
...ISN'T HE?
HEH HEH...

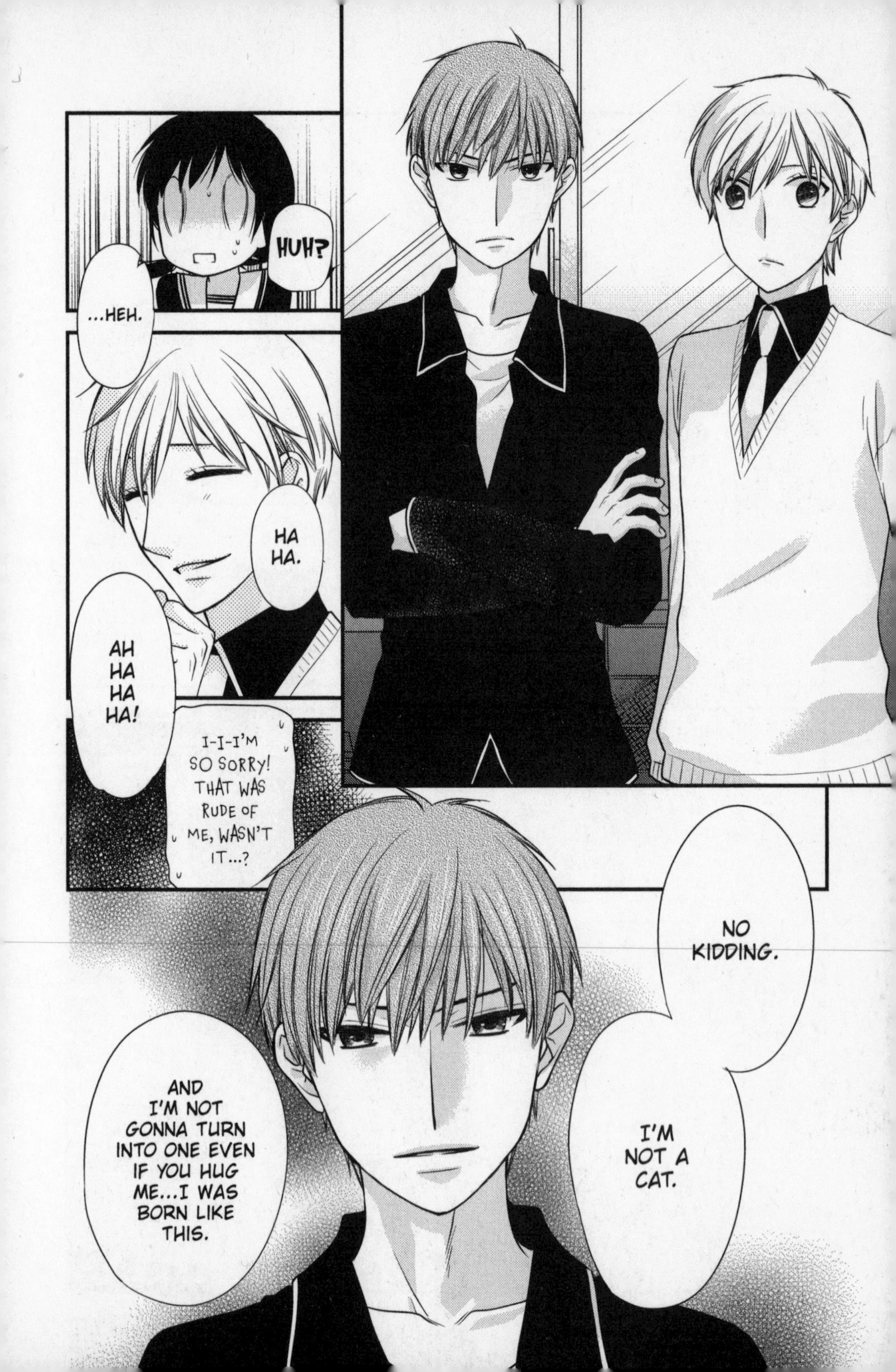
HUH?
...HEH.
HA HA.
AH HA HA HA!
I-I-I'M SO SORRY! THAT WAS RUDE OF ME, WASN'T IT...?
NO KIDDING.
I'M NOT A CAT.
AND I'M NOT GONNA TURN INTO ONE EVEN IF YOU HUG ME...I WAS BORN LIKE THIS.

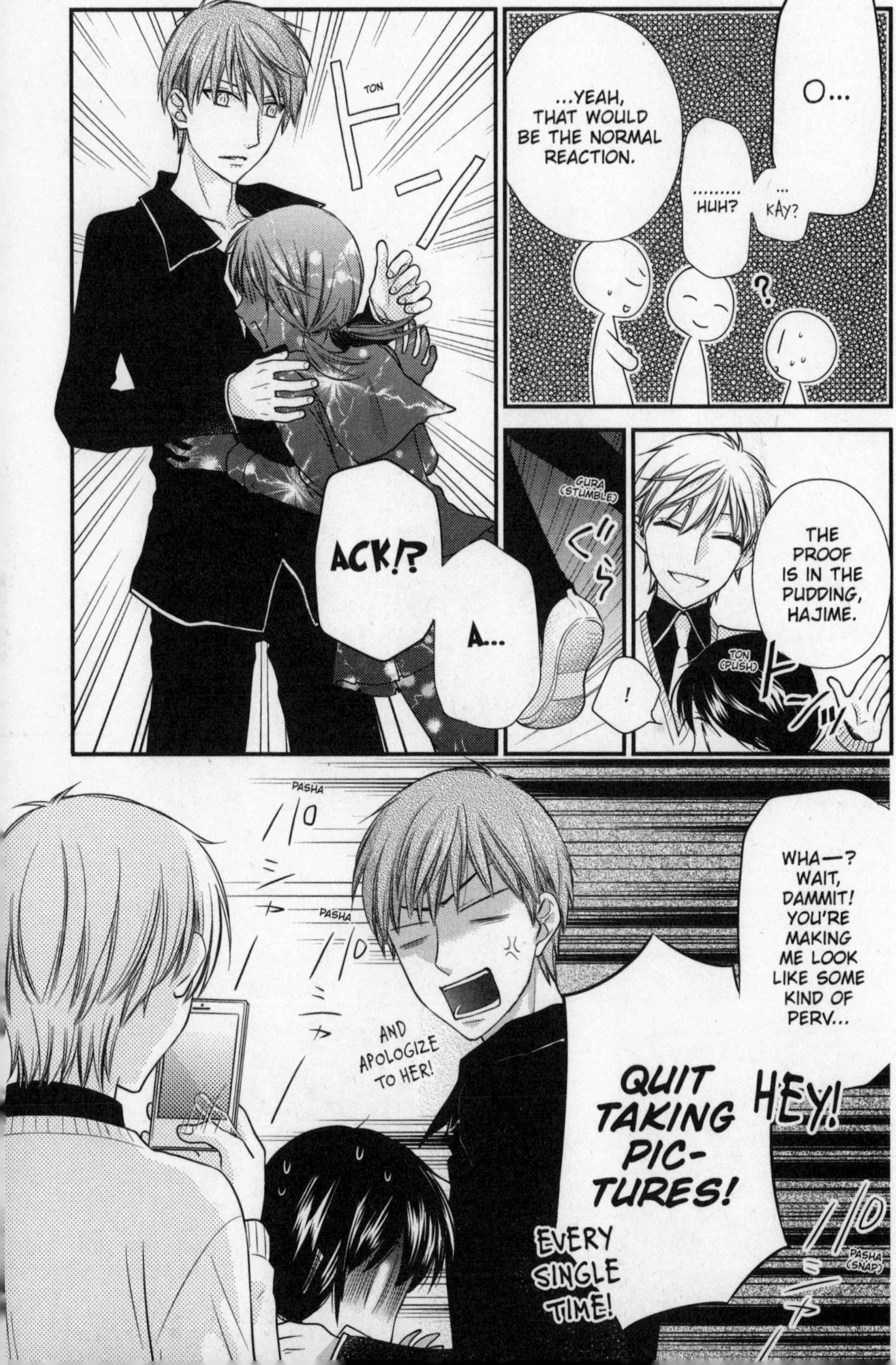
O...
...KAY?
.........HUH?
...YEAH, THAT WOULD BE THE NORMAL REACTION.
THE PROOF IS IN THE PUDDING, HAJIME.
TON (PUSH)
GURA (STUMBLE)
!
TON
ACK!?
A...
WHA—? WAIT, DAMMIT! YOU'RE MAKING ME LOOK LIKE SOME KIND OF PERV...
HEY!
QUIT TAKING PIC-TURES!
PASHA (SNAP)
EVERY SINGLE TIME!
AND APOLOGIZE TO HER!
PASHA
PASHA

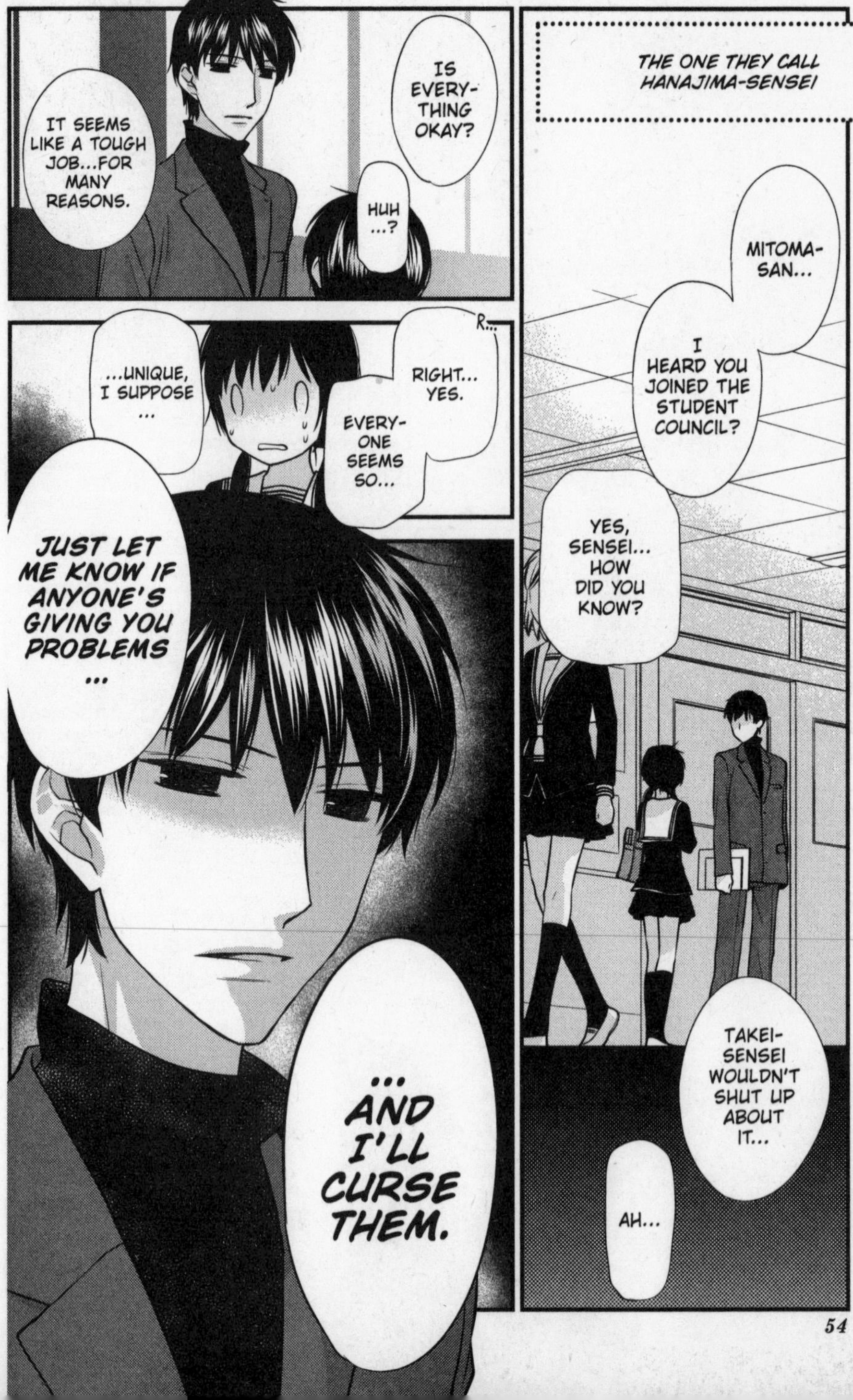
THE ONE THEY CALL HANAJIMA-SENSEI
MITOMA-SAN...
I HEARD YOU JOINED THE STUDENT COUNCIL?
YES, SENSEI... HOW DID YOU KNOW?
TAKEI-SENSEI WOULDN'T SHUT UP ABOUT IT...
AH...
IS EVERYTHING OKAY?
HUH...?
IT SEEMS LIKE A TOUGH JOB...FOR MANY REASONS.
R...
RIGHT... YES.
EVERYONE SEEMS SO...
...UNIQUE, I SUPPOSE...
JUST LET ME KNOW IF ANYONE'S GIVING YOU PROBLEMS...
...AND I'LL CURSE THEM.

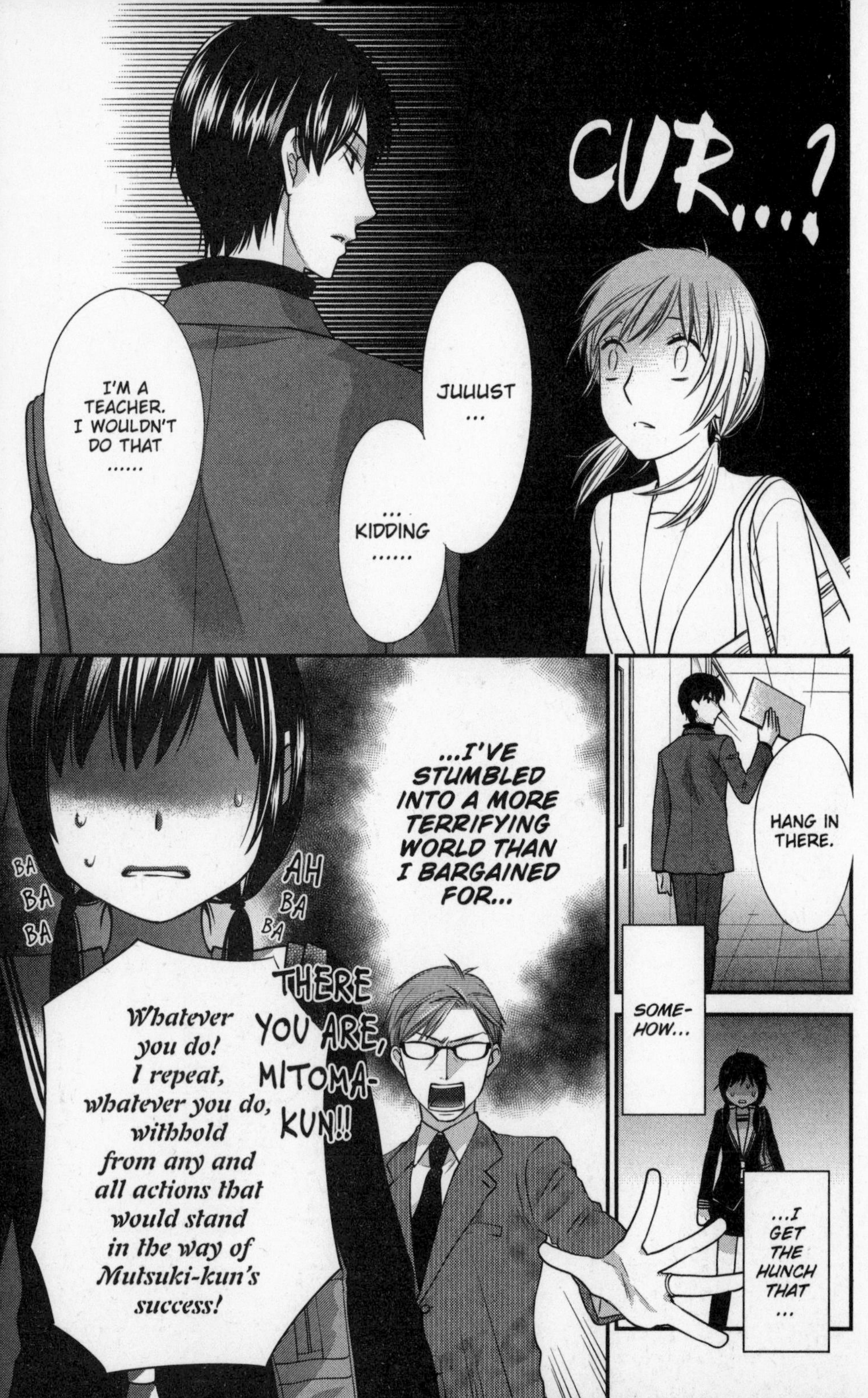
CUR...?
JUUUST ...
... KIDDING ......
I'M A TEACHER. I WOULDN'T DO THAT ......
HANG IN THERE.
SOME-HOW...
...I GET THE HUNCH THAT ...
...I'VE STUMBLED INTO A MORE TERRIFYING WORLD THAN I BARGAINED FOR...
AH BA BA
BA BA BA
THERE YOU ARE, MITOMA-KUN!!
Whatever you do! I repeat, whatever you do, withhold from any and all actions that would stand in the way of Mutsuki-kun's success!

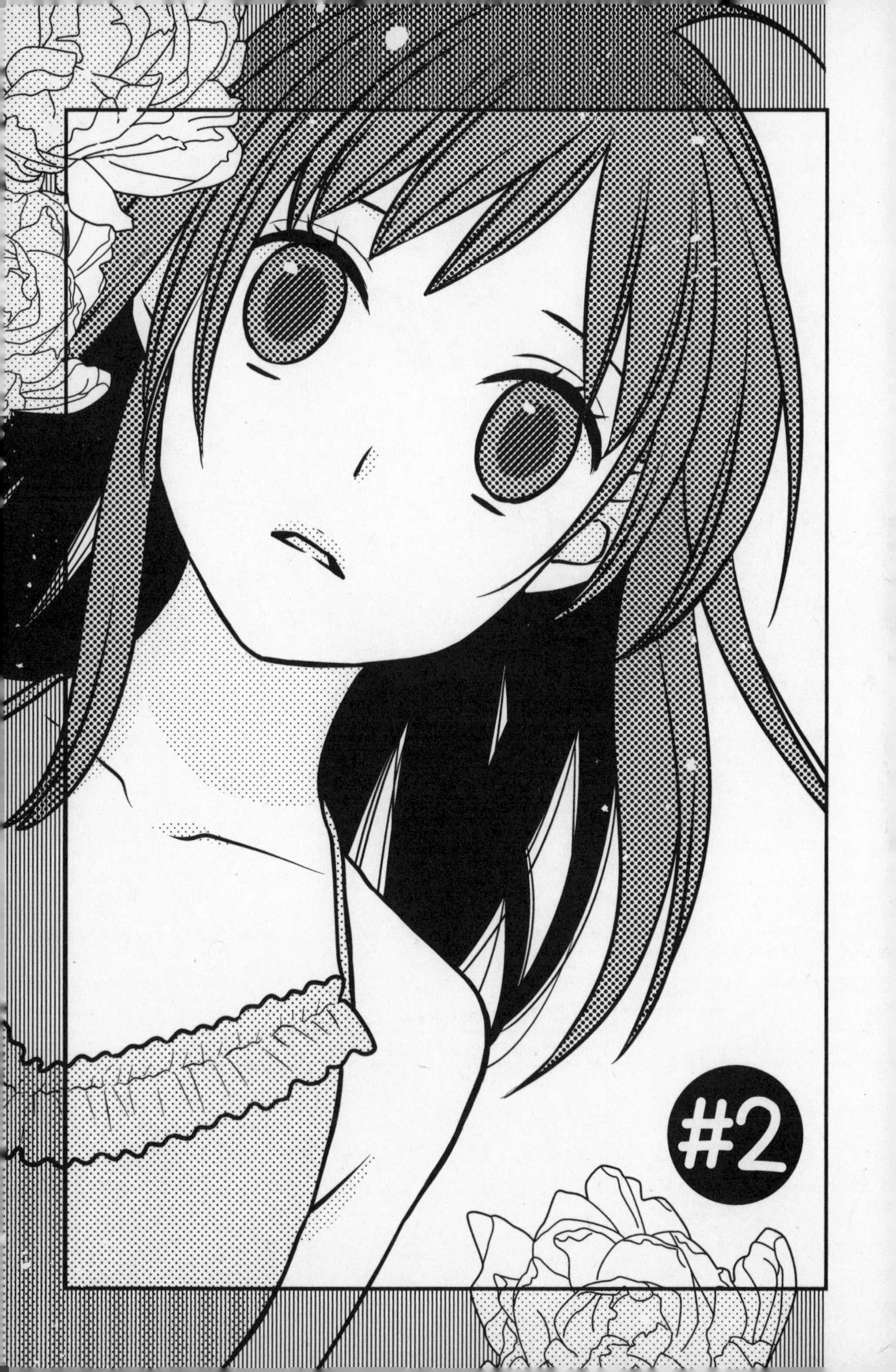
#2

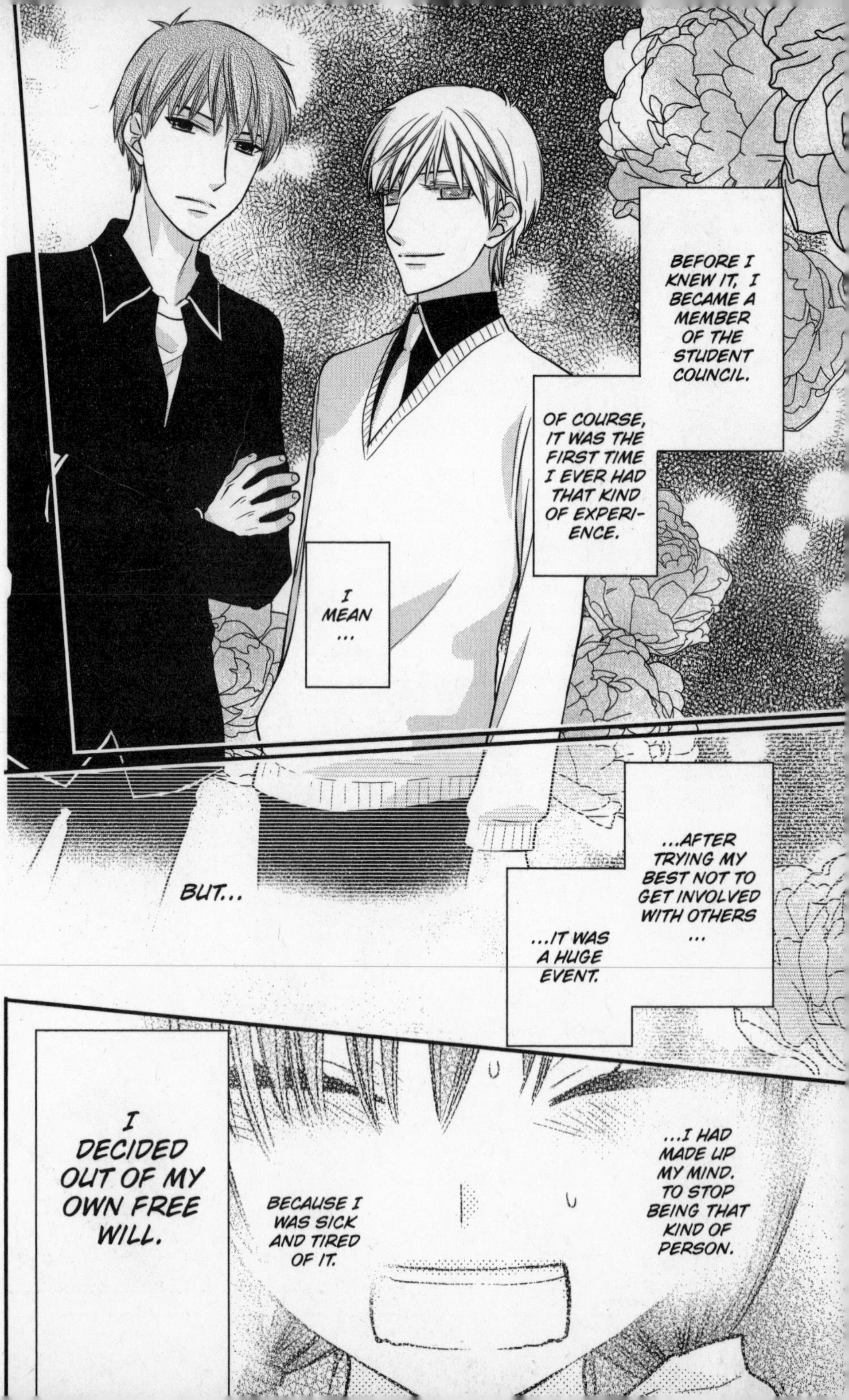
BEFORE I KNEW IT, I BECAME A MEMBER OF THE STUDENT COUNCIL.
OF COURSE, IT WAS THE FIRST TIME I EVER HAD THAT KIND OF EXPERI-ENCE.
I MEAN ...
...AFTER TRYING MY BEST NOT TO GET INVOLVED WITH OTHERS ...
...IT WAS A HUGE EVENT.
BUT...
...I HAD MADE UP MY MIND.
TO STOP BEING THAT KIND OF PERSON.
BECAUSE I WAS SICK AND TIRED OF IT.
I DECIDED OUT OF MY OWN FREE WILL.

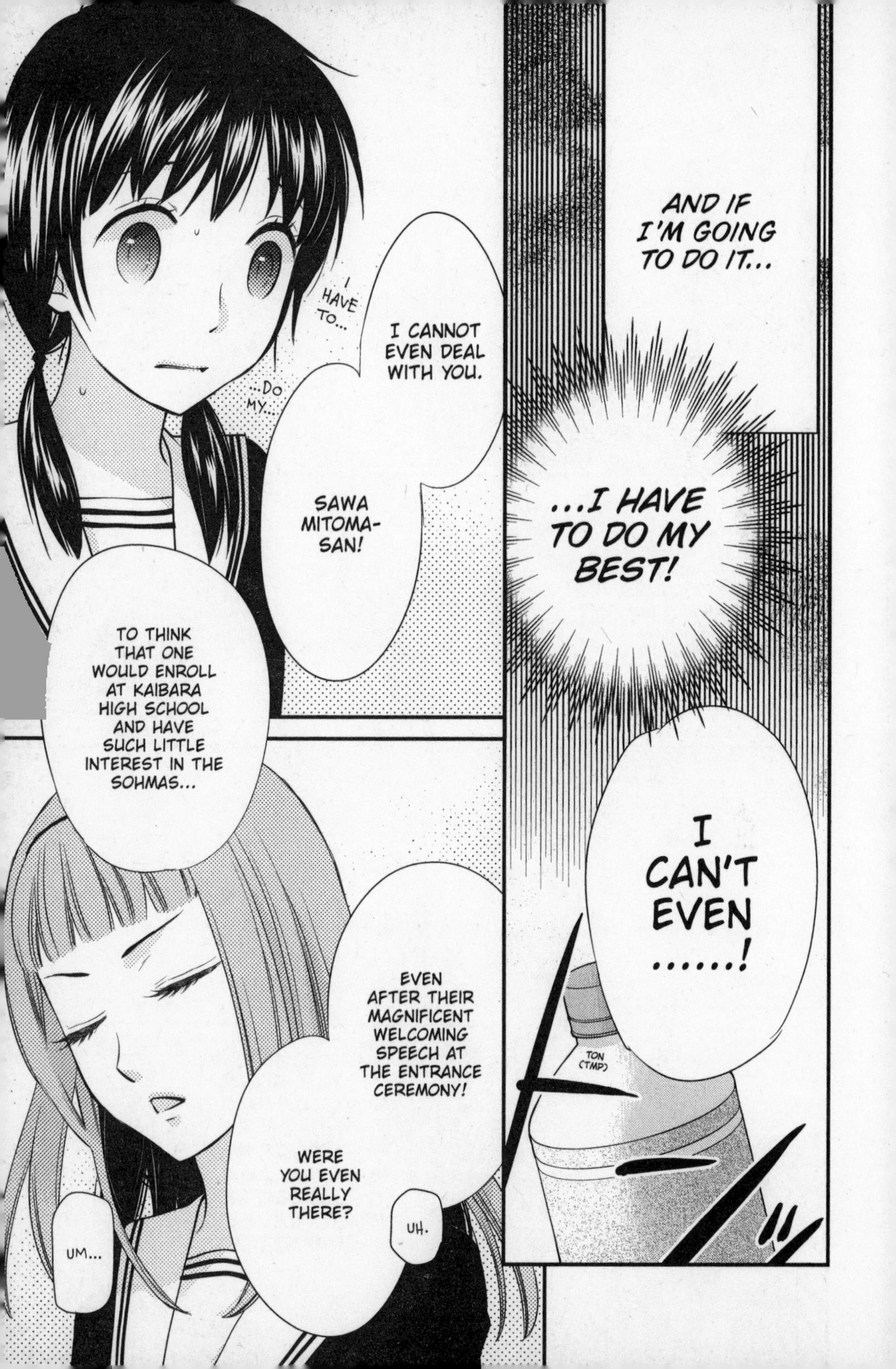
AND IF I'M GOING TO DO IT...
...I HAVE TO DO MY BEST!
I CAN'T EVEN ......!
TON (TMP)
I CANNOT EVEN DEAL WITH YOU.
SAWA MITOMA-SAN!
I HAVE TO...
...DO MY...
TO THINK THAT ONE WOULD ENROLL AT KAIBARA HIGH SCHOOL AND HAVE SUCH LITTLE INTEREST IN THE SOHMAS...
EVEN AFTER THEIR MAGNIFICENT WELCOMING SPEECH AT THE ENTRANCE CEREMONY!
WERE YOU EVEN REALLY THERE?
UH.
UM...

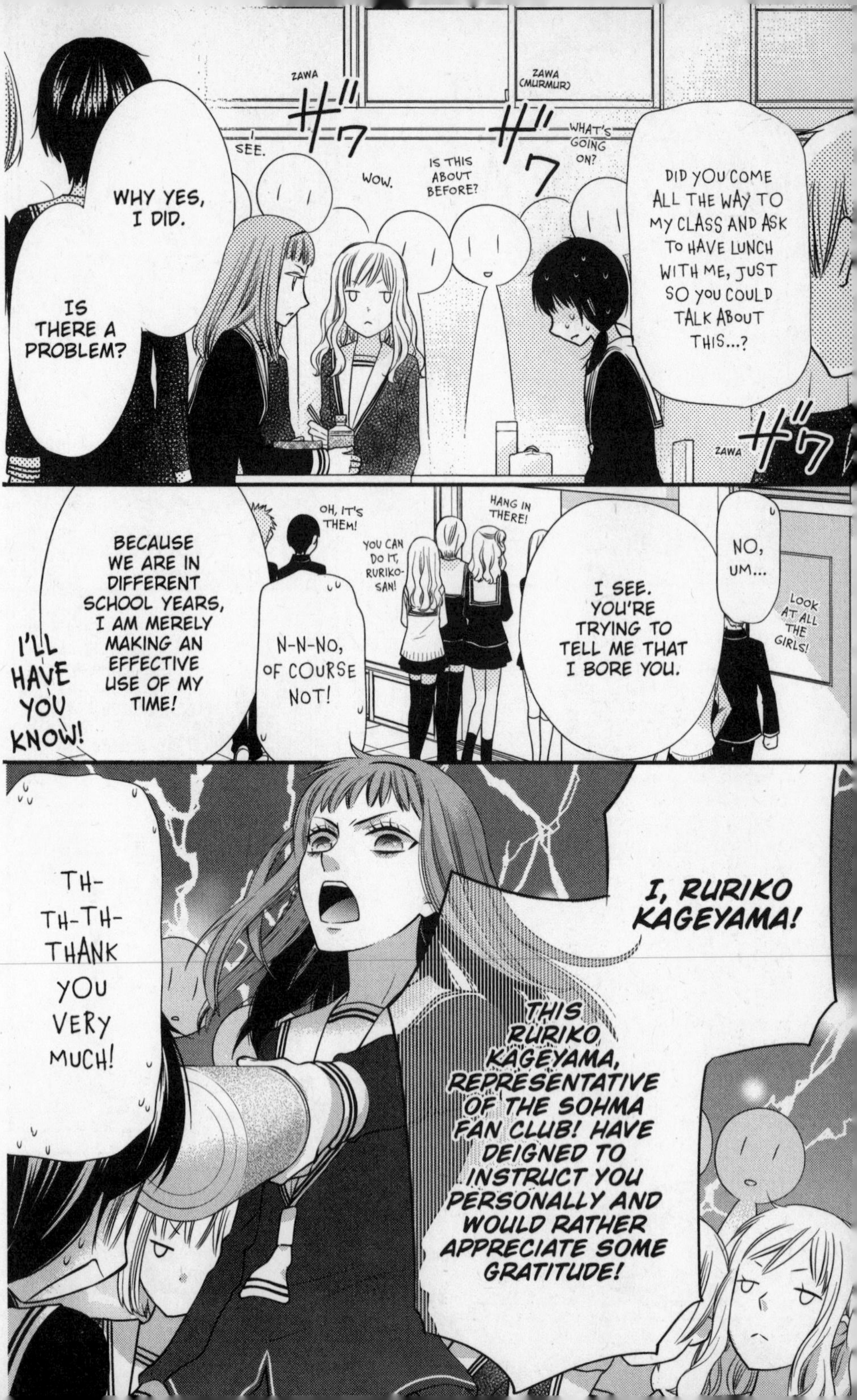
DID YOU COME ALL THE WAY TO MY CLASS AND ASK TO HAVE LUNCH WITH ME, JUST SO YOU COULD TALK ABOUT THIS...?
ZAWA
WHAT'S GOING ON?
ZAWA (MURMUR)
IS THIS ABOUT BEFORE?
WOW.
I SEE.
ZAWA
WHY YES, I DID.
IS THERE A PROBLEM?
NO, UM...
LOOK AT ALL THE GIRLS!
I SEE. YOU'RE TRYING TO TELL ME THAT I BORE YOU.
HANG IN THERE!
OH, IT'S THEM!
YOU CAN DO IT, RURIKO-SAN!
N-N-NO, OF COURSE NOT!
BECAUSE WE ARE IN DIFFERENT SCHOOL YEARS, I AM MERELY MAKING AN EFFECTIVE USE OF MY TIME!
I'LL HAVE YOU KNOW!
I, RURIKO KAGEYAMA!
THIS RURIKO KAGEYAMA, REPRESENTATIVE OF THE SOHMA FAN CLUB! HAVE DEIGNED TO INSTRUCT YOU PERSONALLY AND WOULD RATHER APPRECIATE SOME GRATITUDE!
TH-TH-TH-THANK YOU VERY MUCH!

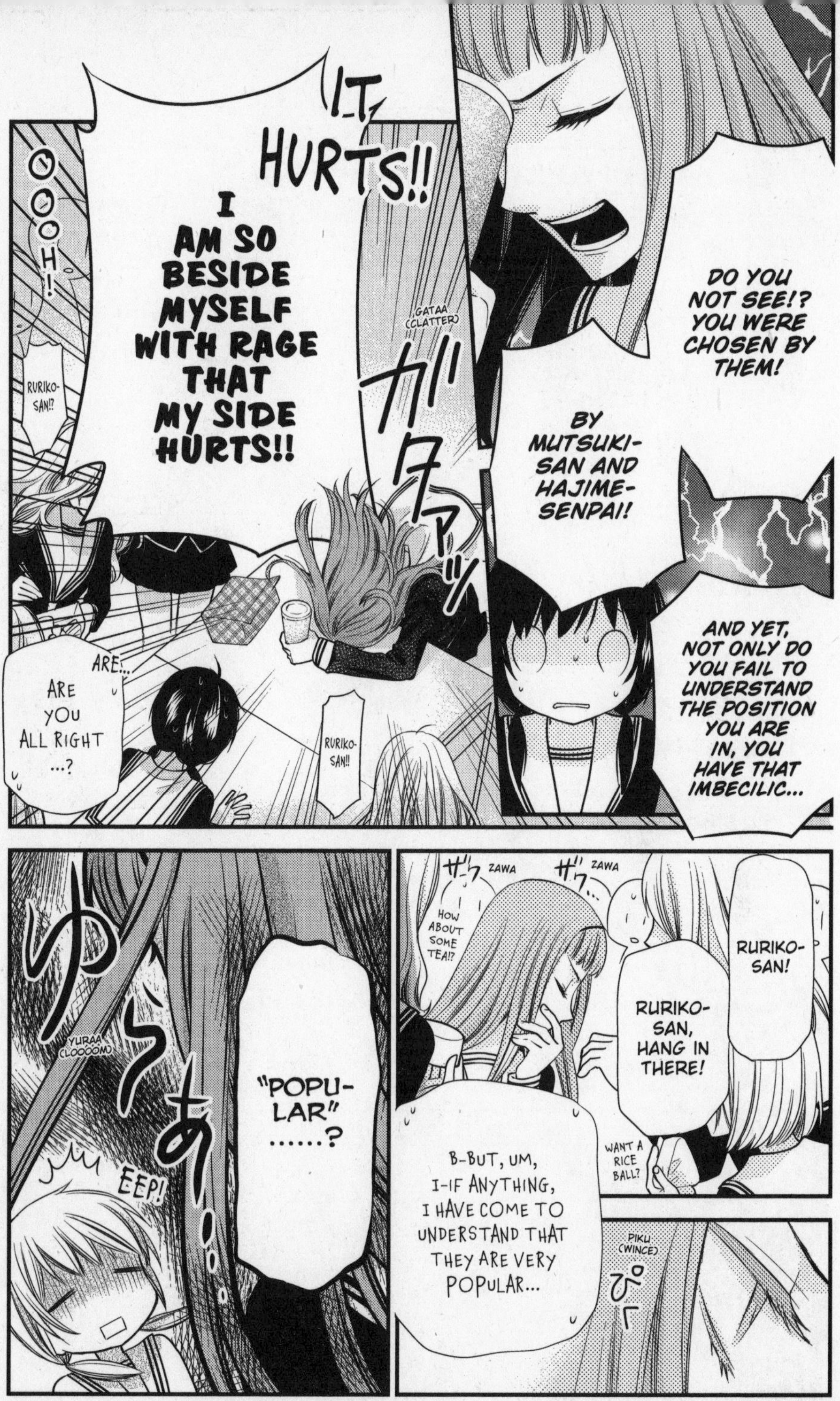

DO YOU NOT SEE!? YOU WERE CHOSEN BY THEM!
BY MUTSUKI-SAN AND HAJIME-SENPAI!
AND YET, NOT ONLY DO YOU FAIL TO UNDERSTAND THE POSITION YOU ARE IN, YOU HAVE THAT IMBECILIC...
IT, HURTS!!
I AM SO BESIDE MYSELF WITH RAGE THAT MY SIDE HURTS!!
GATAA (CLATTER)
OOOH!
RURIKO-SAN!?
ARE...
ARE YOU ALL RIGHT ...?
RURIKO-SAN!!
ZAWA
ZAWA
HOW ABOUT SOME TEA!?
RURIKO-SAN!
RURIKO-SAN, HANG IN THERE!
WANT A RICE BALL?
B-BUT, UM, I-IF ANYTHING, I HAVE COME TO UNDERSTAND THAT THEY ARE VERY POPULAR...
PIKU (WINCE)
YURAA (LOOOOM)
"POPULAR" ......?
EEP!

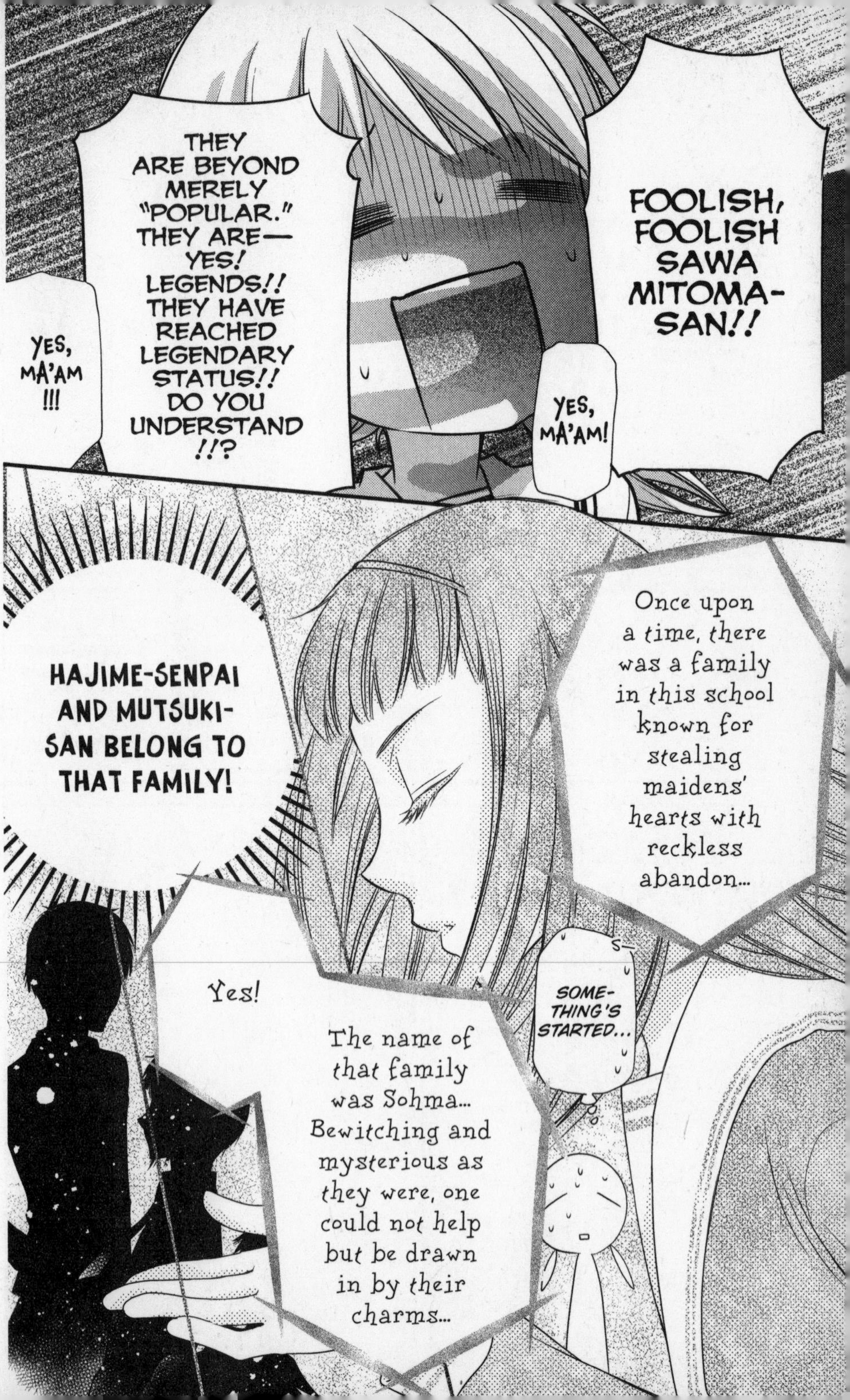
FOOLISH, FOOLISH SAWA MITOMA-SAN!!
YES, MA'AM!
THEY ARE BEYOND MERELY "POPULAR." THEY ARE—YES! LEGENDS!! THEY HAVE REACHED LEGENDARY STATUS!! DO YOU UNDERSTAND!!?
YES, MA'AM!!!
Once upon a time, there was a family in this school known for stealing maidens' hearts with reckless abandon...
HAJIME-SENPAI AND MUTSUKI-SAN BELONG TO THAT FAMILY!
SOMETHING'S STARTED...
The name of that family was Sohma... Bewitching and mysterious as they were, one could not help but be drawn in by their charms...
Yes!

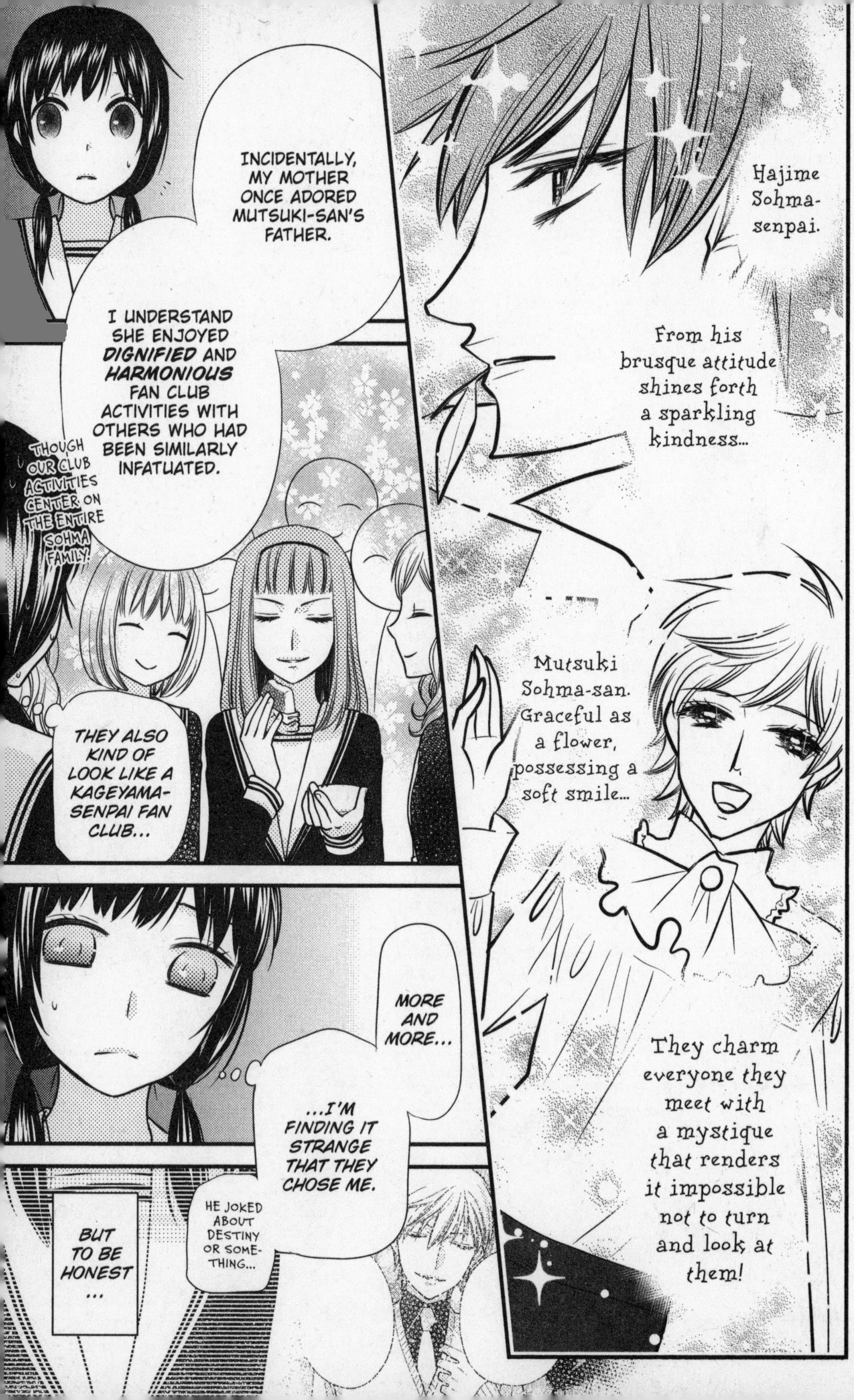
Hajime Sohma-senpai.
From his brusque attitude shines forth a sparkling kindness...
Mutsuki Sohma-san. Graceful as a flower, possessing a soft smile...
They charm everyone they meet with a mystique that renders it impossible not to turn and look at them!
INCIDENTALLY, MY MOTHER ONCE ADORED MUTSUKI-SAN'S FATHER.
I UNDERSTAND SHE ENJOYED ***DIGNIFIED*** AND ***HARMONIOUS*** FAN CLUB ACTIVITIES WITH OTHERS WHO HAD BEEN SIMILARLY INFATUATED.
THOUGH OUR CLUB ACTIVITIES CENTER ON THE ENTIRE SOHMA FAMILY.
THEY ALSO KIND OF LOOK LIKE A KAGEYAMA-SENPAI FAN CLUB...
MORE AND MORE...
...I'M FINDING IT STRANGE THAT THEY CHOSE ME.
HE JOKED ABOUT DESTINY OR SOMETHING...
BUT TO BE HONEST ...

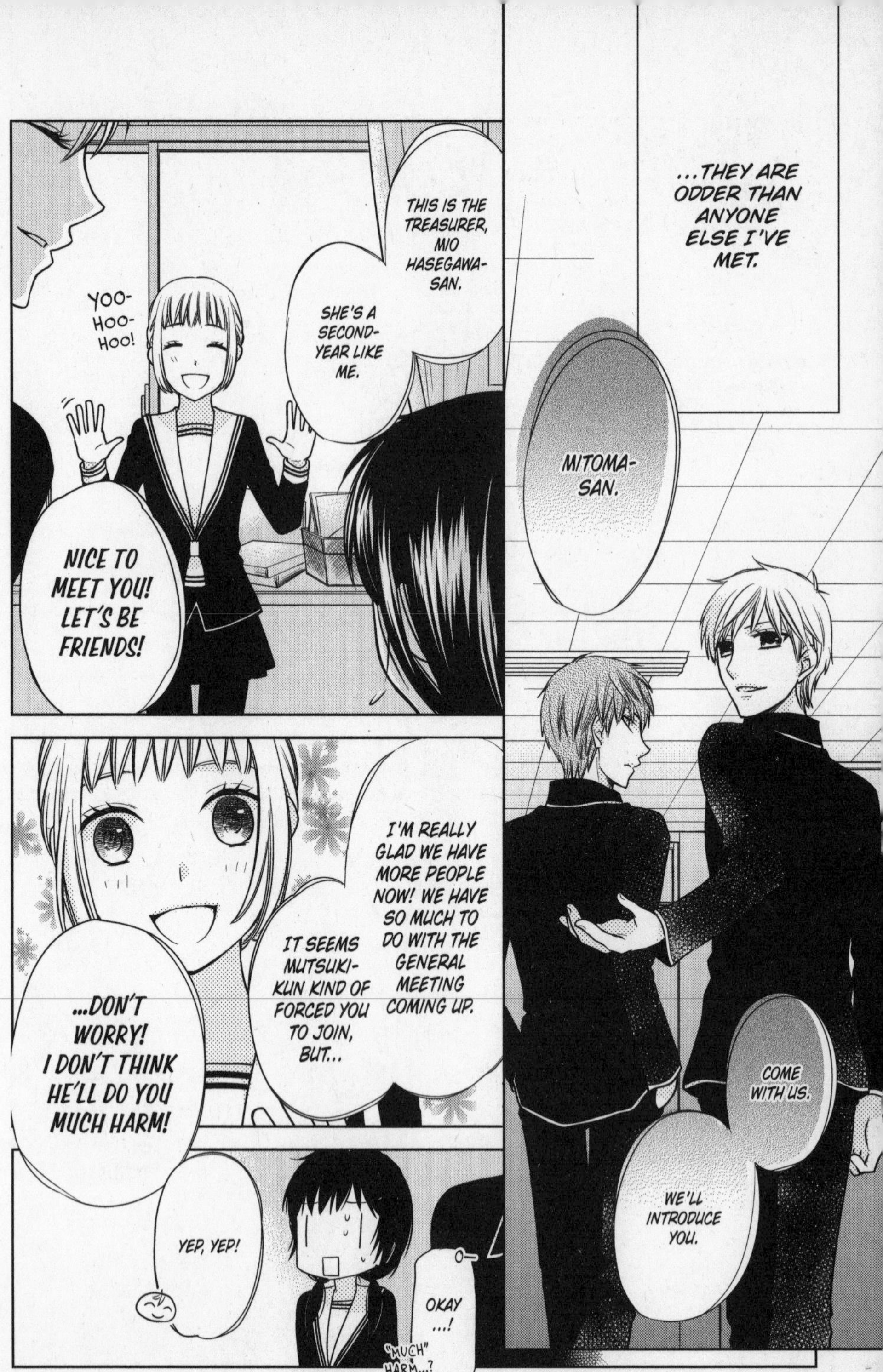
...THEY ARE ODDER THAN ANYONE ELSE I'VE MET.
MITOMA-SAN.
COME WITH US.
WE'LL INTRODUCE YOU.
THIS IS THE TREASURER, MIO HASEGAWA-SAN.
SHE'S A SECOND-YEAR LIKE ME.
YOO-HOO-HOO!
NICE TO MEET YOU! LET'S BE FRIENDS!
I'M REALLY GLAD WE HAVE MORE PEOPLE NOW! WE HAVE SO MUCH TO DO WITH THE GENERAL MEETING COMING UP.
IT SEEMS MUTSUKI-KUN KIND OF FORCED YOU TO JOIN, BUT...
...DON'T WORRY! I DON'T THINK HE'LL DO YOU MUCH HARM!
OKAY ...!
YEP, YEP!
"MUCH" HARM...?

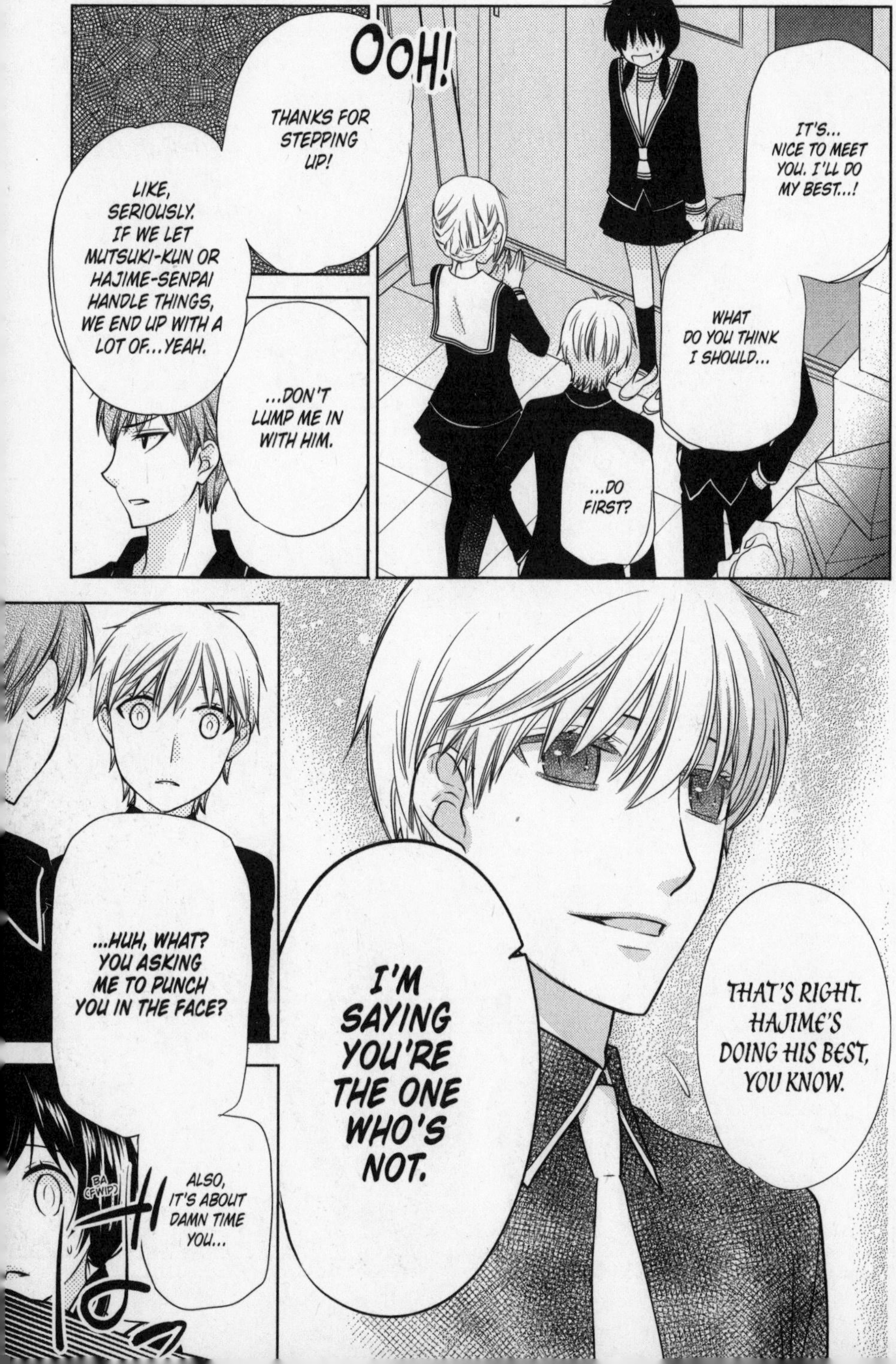
IT'S... NICE TO MEET YOU. I'LL DO MY BEST...!
WHAT DO YOU THINK I SHOULD...
...DO FIRST?
OOH!
THANKS FOR STEPPING UP!
LIKE, SERIOUSLY. IF WE LET MUTSUKI-KUN OR HAJIME-SENPAI HANDLE THINGS, WE END UP WITH A LOT OF...YEAH.
...DON'T LUMP ME IN WITH HIM.
THAT'S RIGHT. HAJIME'S DOING HIS BEST, YOU KNOW.
I'M SAYING YOU'RE THE ONE WHO'S NOT.
...HUH, WHAT? YOU ASKING ME TO PUNCH YOU IN THE FACE?
BA (FWIP)
ALSO, IT'S ABOUT DAMN TIME YOU...

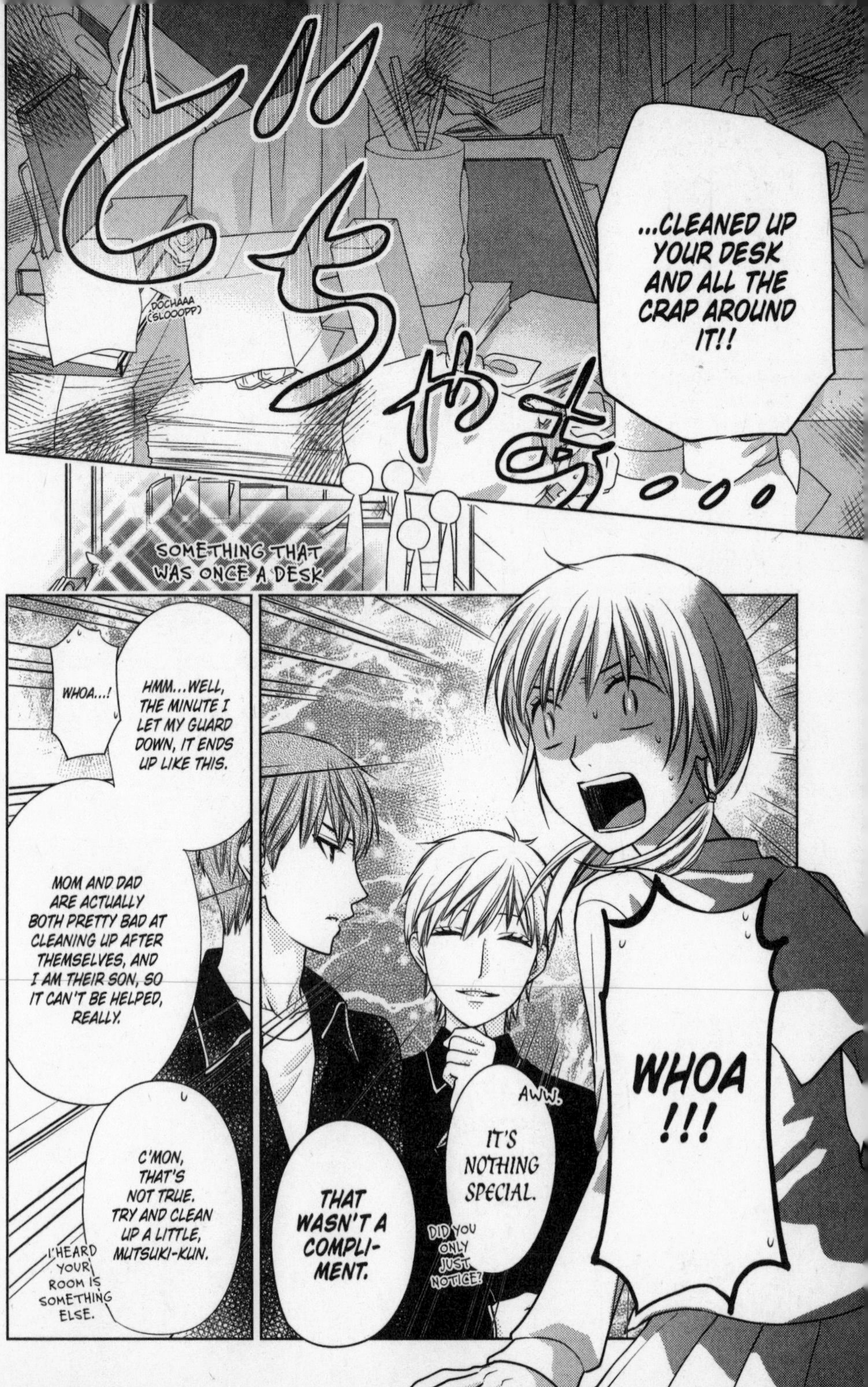
...CLEANED UP YOUR DESK AND ALL THE CRAP AROUND IT!!
DOCHAAA (SLOOOPP)
SOMETHING THAT WAS ONCE A DESK
WHOA !!!
AWW.
IT'S NOTHING SPECIAL.
THAT WASN'T A COMPLIMENT.
DID YOU ONLY JUST NOTICE?
WHOA...!
HMM...WELL, THE MINUTE I LET MY GUARD DOWN, IT ENDS UP LIKE THIS.
MOM AND DAD ARE ACTUALLY BOTH PRETTY BAD AT CLEANING UP AFTER THEMSELVES, AND I AM THEIR SON, SO IT CAN'T BE HELPED, REALLY.
C'MON, THAT'S NOT TRUE. TRY AND CLEAN UP A LITTLE, MUTSUKI-KUN.
I HEARD YOUR ROOM IS SOMETHING ELSE.

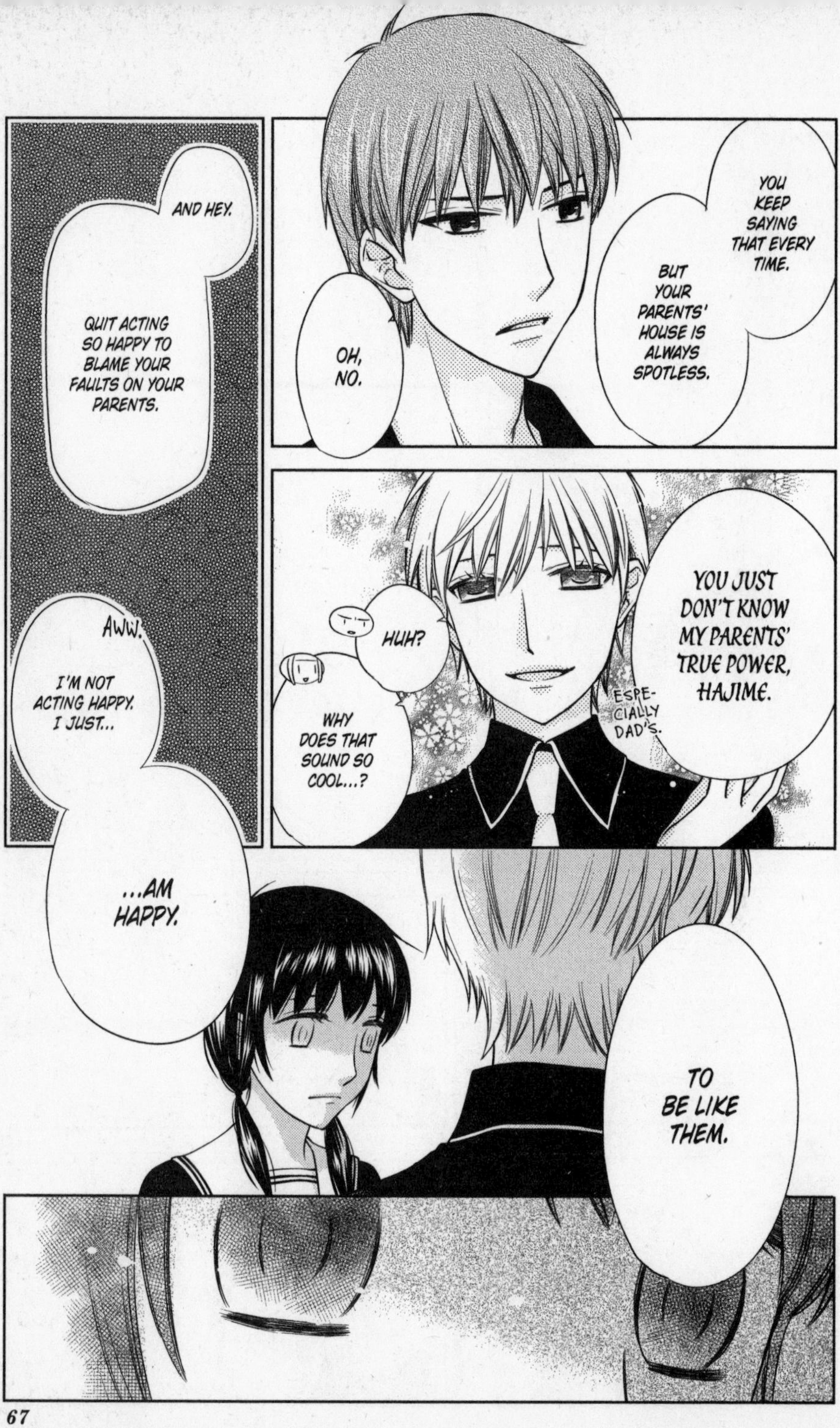
YOU KEEP SAYING THAT EVERY TIME.
BUT YOUR PARENTS' HOUSE IS ALWAYS SPOTLESS.
OH, NO.
YOU JUST DON'T KNOW MY PARENTS' TRUE POWER, HAJIME.
ESPE-CIALLY DAD'S.
HUH?
WHY DOES THAT SOUND SO COOL...?
AND HEY.
QUIT ACTING SO HAPPY TO BLAME YOUR FAULTS ON YOUR PARENTS.
AWW.
I'M NOT ACTING HAPPY. I JUST...
...AM HAPPY.
TO BE LIKE THEM.

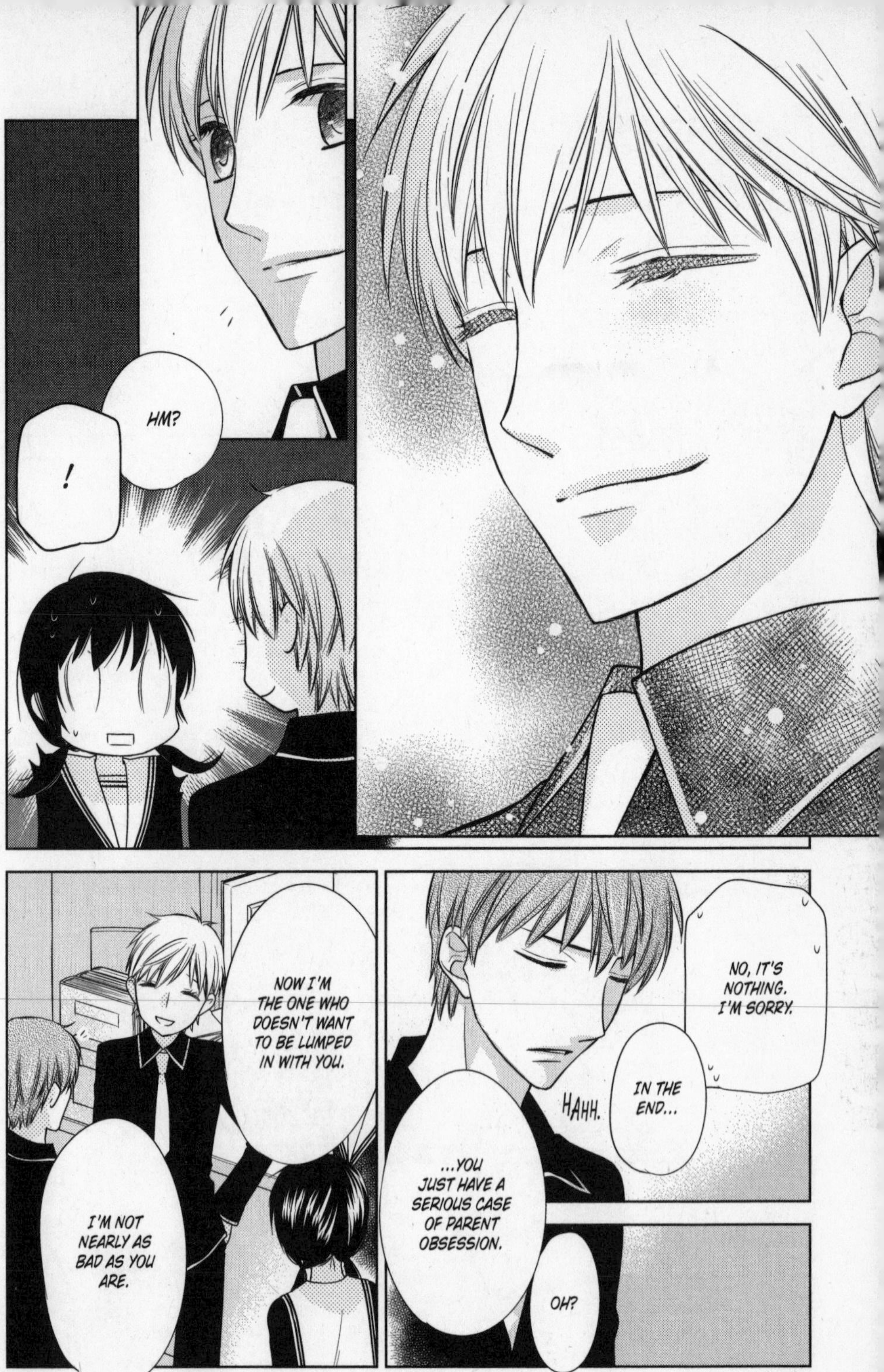
HM?
!
NO, IT'S NOTHING. I'M SORRY.
HAHH.
IN THE END...
...YOU JUST HAVE A SERIOUS CASE OF PARENT OBSESSION.
OH?
NOW I'M THE ONE WHO DOESN'T WANT TO BE LUMPED IN WITH YOU.
I'M NOT NEARLY AS BAD AS YOU ARE.

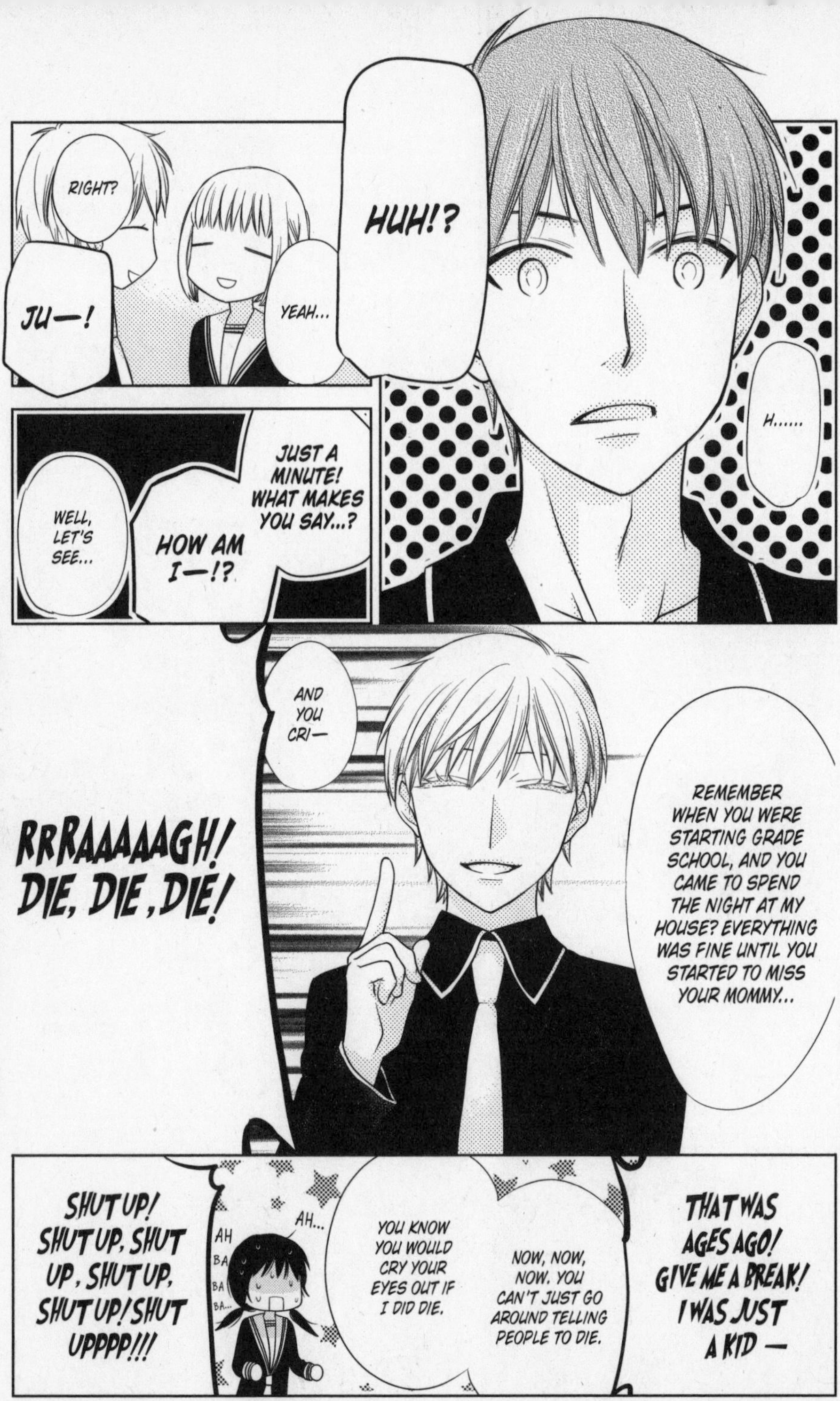
RIGHT?
JU—!
YEAH...
HUH!?
H......
JUST A MINUTE! WHAT MAKES YOU SAY...?
HOW AM I—!?
WELL, LET'S SEE...
REMEMBER WHEN YOU WERE STARTING GRADE SCHOOL, AND YOU CAME TO SPEND THE NIGHT AT MY HOUSE? EVERYTHING WAS FINE UNTIL YOU STARTED TO MISS YOUR MOMMY...
AND YOU CRI—
RRRAAAAAGH! DIE, DIE, DIE!
THAT WAS AGES AGO! GIVE ME A BREAK! I WAS JUST A KID—
NOW, NOW, NOW. YOU CAN'T JUST GO AROUND TELLING PEOPLE TO DIE.
YOU KNOW YOU WOULD CRY YOUR EYES OUT IF I DID DIE.
AH...
AH BA BA BA...
SHUT UP! SHUT UP, SHUT UP, SHUT UP, SHUT UP! SHUT UPPPP!!!

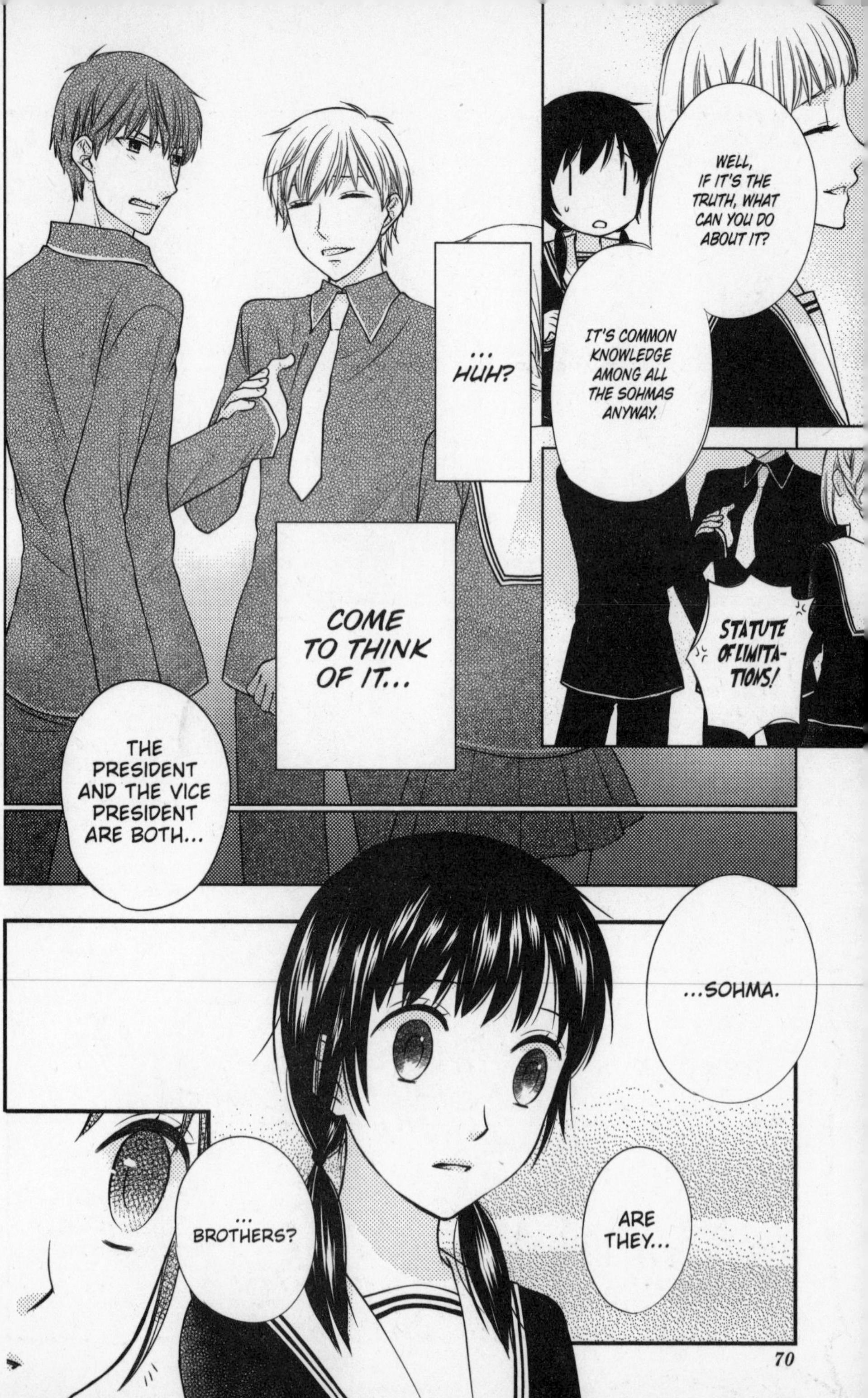
WELL, IF IT'S THE TRUTH, WHAT CAN YOU DO ABOUT IT?
IT'S COMMON KNOWLEDGE AMONG ALL THE SOHMAS ANYWAY.
STATUTE OF LIMITA-TIONS!
...HUH?
COME TO THINK OF IT...
THE PRESIDENT AND THE VICE PRESIDENT ARE BOTH...
...SOHMA.
ARE THEY...
...BROTHERS?

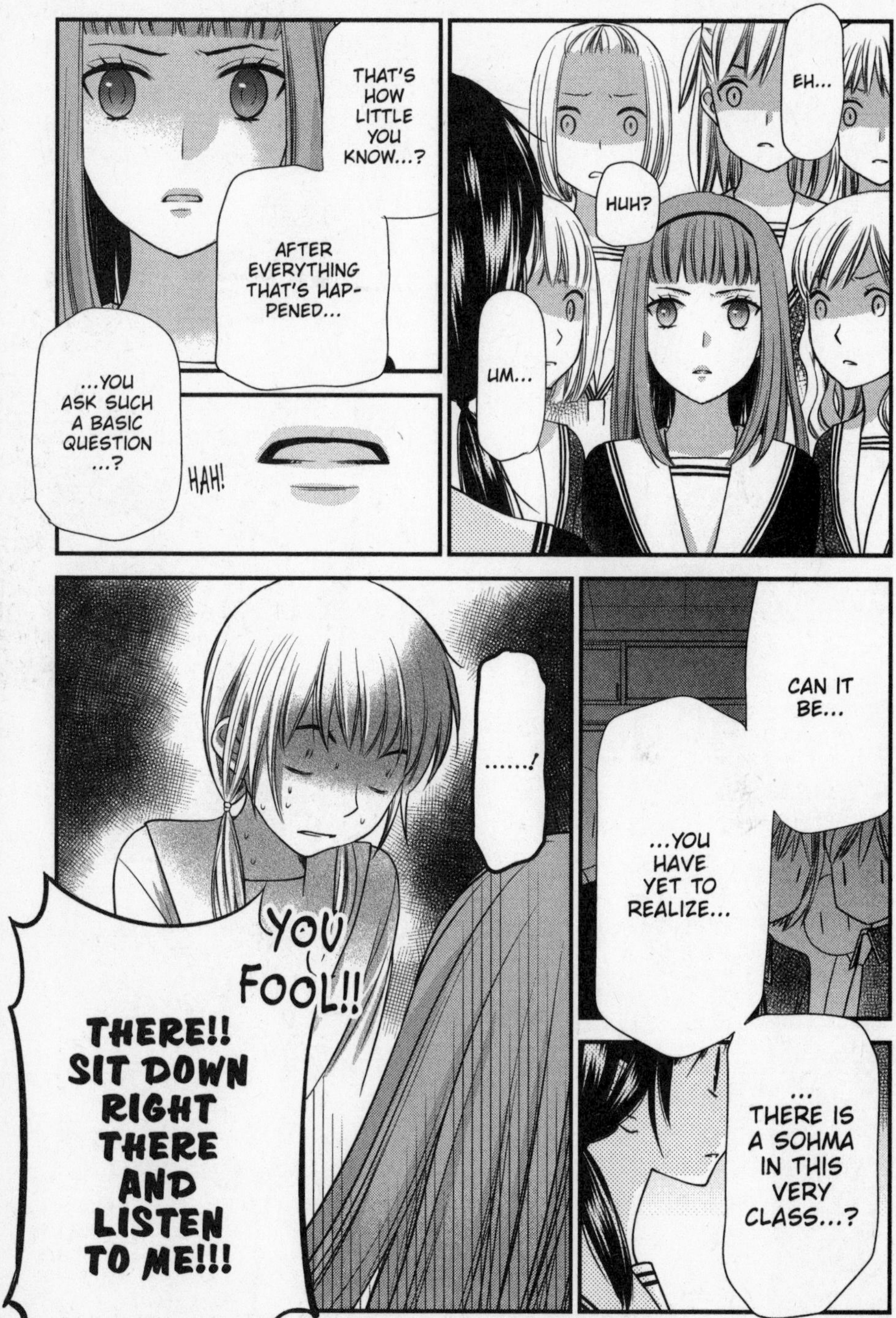
EH...
HUH?
UM...
THAT'S HOW LITTLE YOU KNOW...?
AFTER EVERYTHING THAT'S HAP-PENED...
...YOU ASK SUCH A BASIC QUESTION ...?
HAH!
CAN IT BE...
...YOU HAVE YET TO REALIZE...
... THERE IS A SOHMA IN THIS VERY CLASS...?
.......!
YOU FOOL!!
THERE!! SIT DOWN RIGHT THERE AND LISTEN TO ME!!!

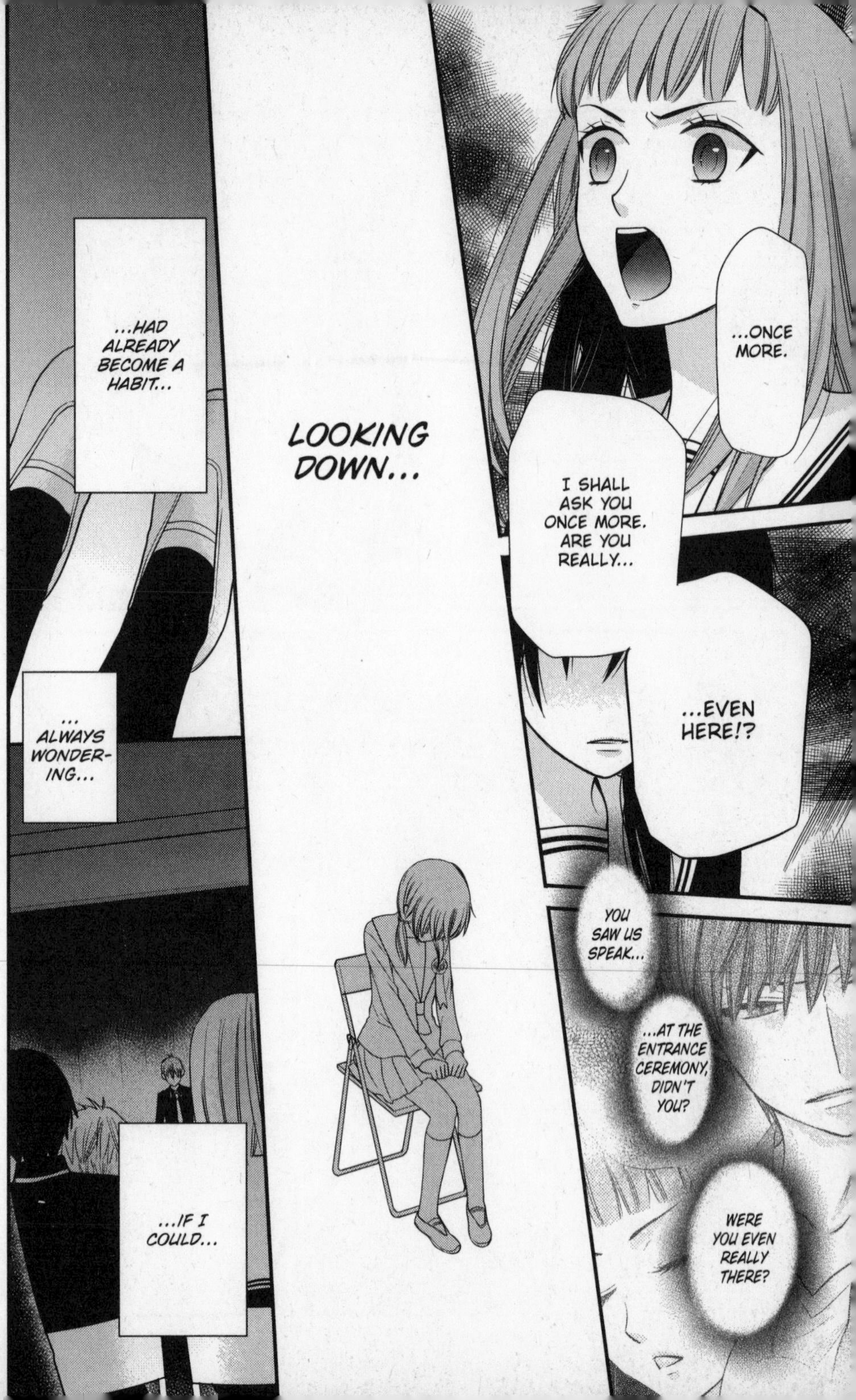
...ONCE MORE.
I SHALL ASK YOU ONCE MORE. ARE YOU REALLY...
...EVEN HERE!?
YOU SAW US SPEAK...
...AT THE ENTRANCE CEREMONY, DIDN'T YOU?
WERE YOU EVEN REALLY THERE?
LOOKING DOWN...
...HAD ALREADY BECOME A HABIT...
...ALWAYS WONDER-ING...
...IF I COULD...

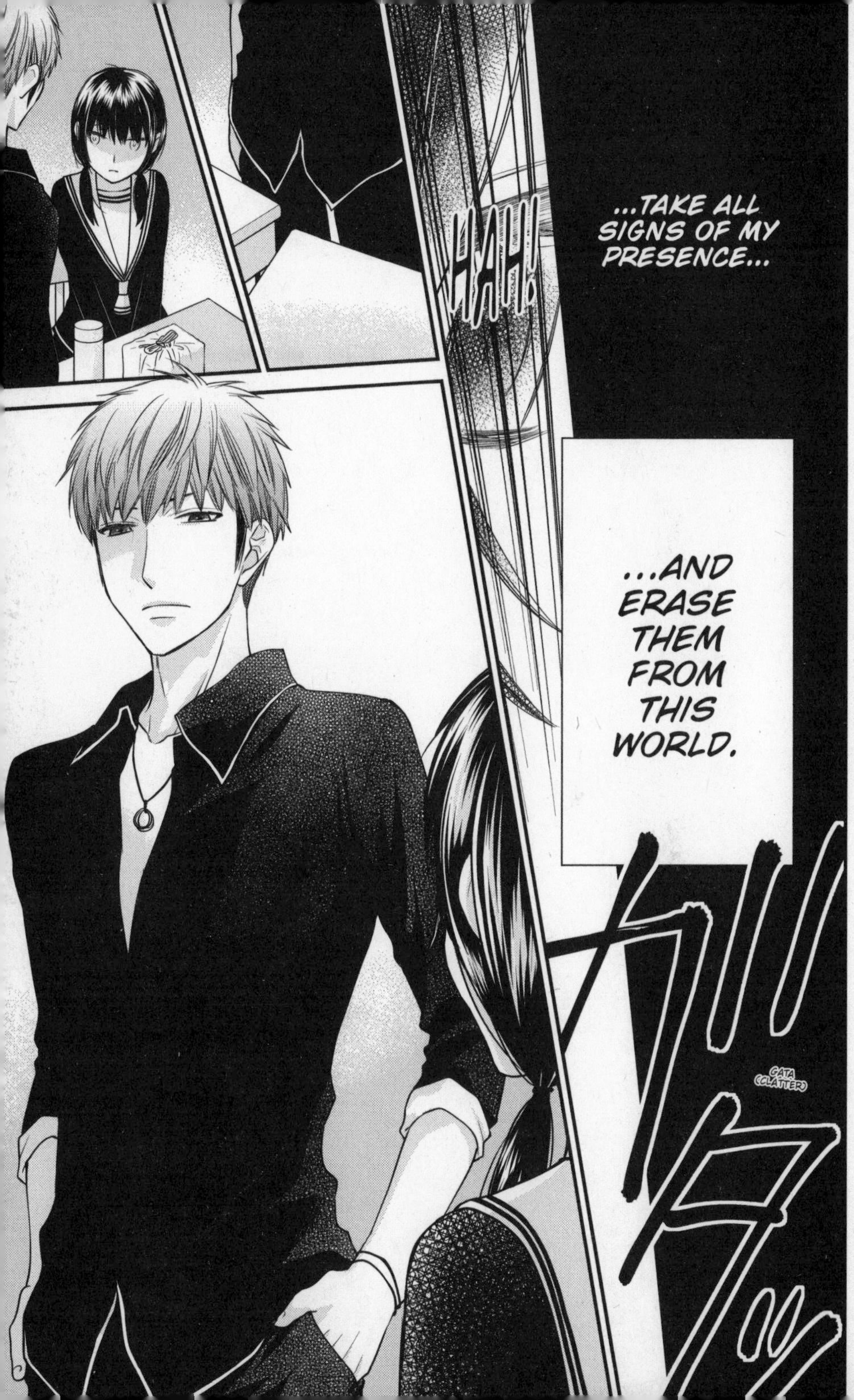
...TAKE ALL SIGNS OF MY PRESENCE...
HAH!
...AND ERASE THEM FROM THIS WORLD.
GATA (CLATTER)

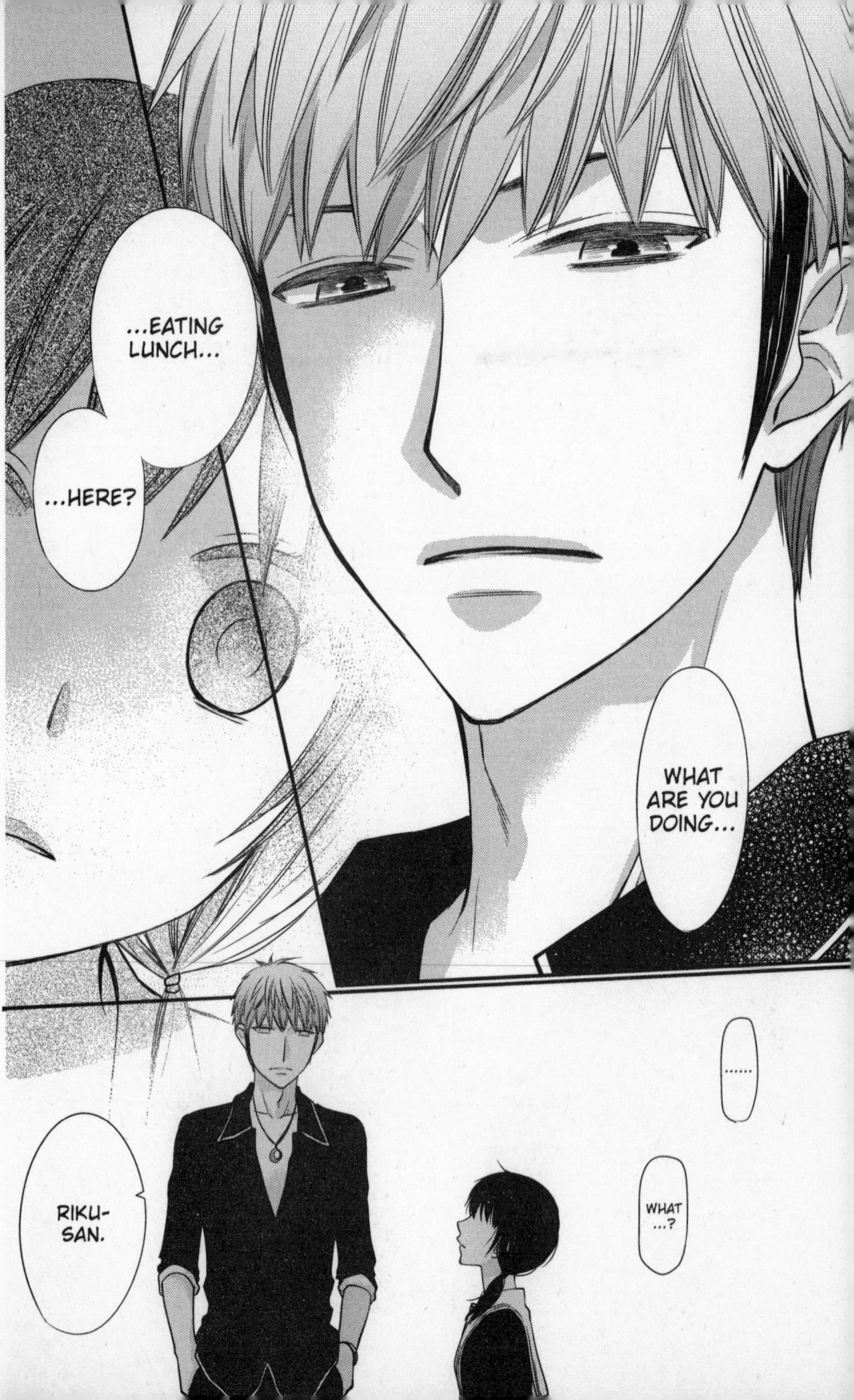
WHAT ARE YOU DOING...
...EATING LUNCH...
...HERE?
......
WHAT ...?
RIKU-SAN.

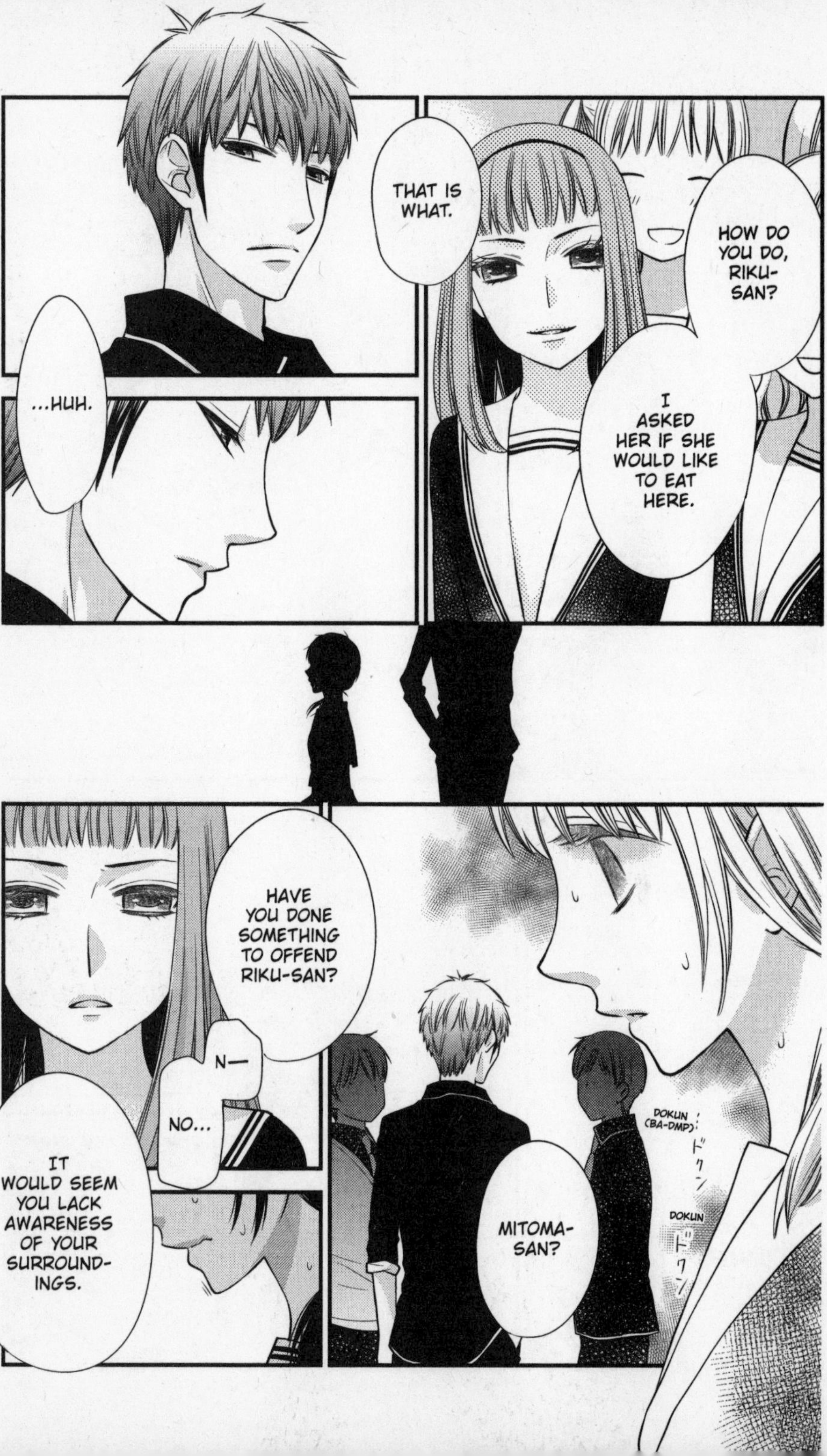
HOW DO YOU DO, RIKU-SAN?
I ASKED HER IF SHE WOULD LIKE TO EAT HERE.
THAT IS WHAT.
...HUH.
DOKUN (BA-DMP)
ドクン
DOKUN
ドクン
MITOMA-SAN?
HAVE YOU DONE SOMETHING TO OFFEND RIKU-SAN?
N—
NO...
IT WOULD SEEM YOU LACK AWARENESS OF YOUR SURROUND-INGS.

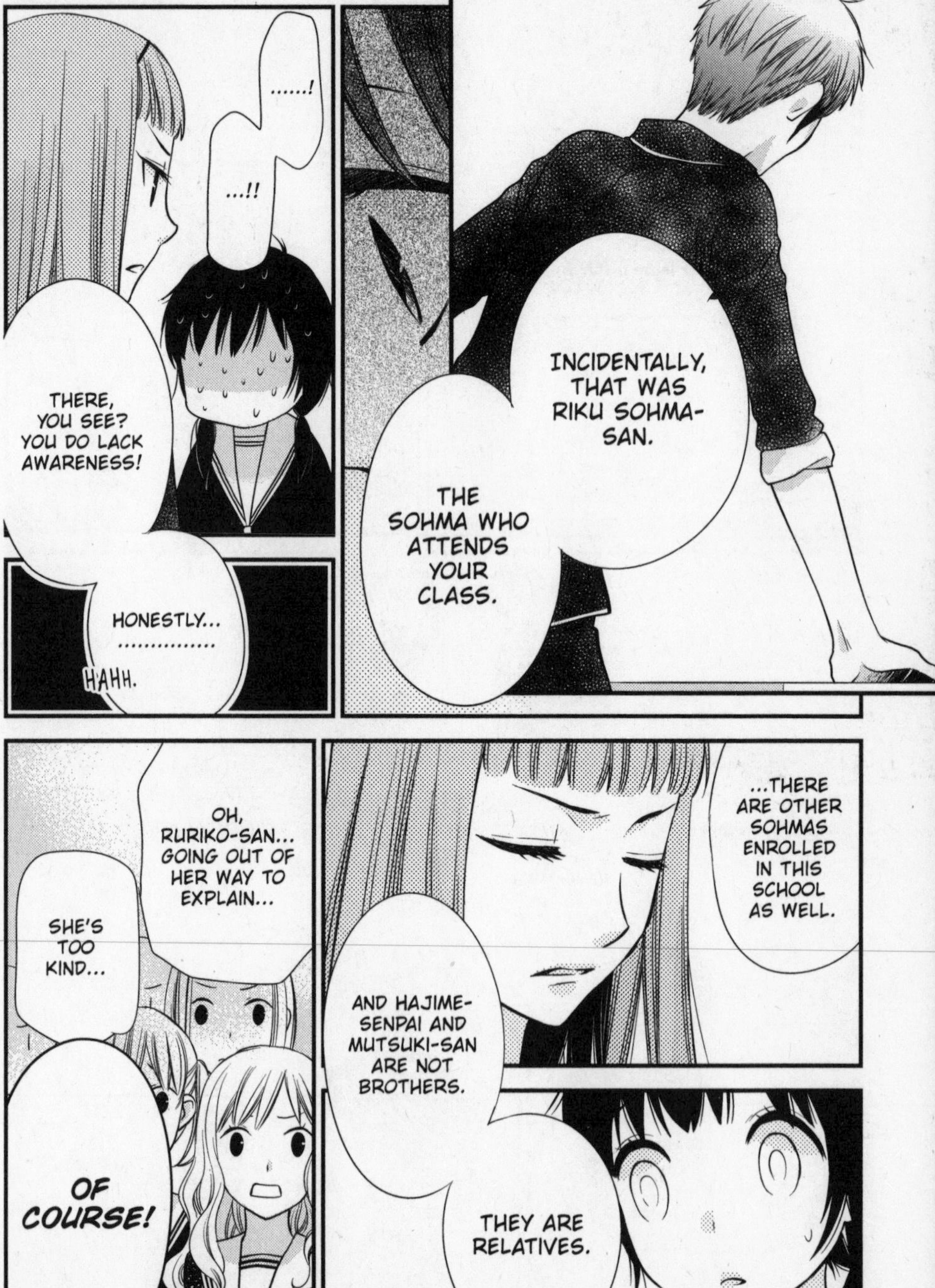
INCIDENTALLY, THAT WAS RIKU SOHMA-SAN.
THE SOHMA WHO ATTENDS YOUR CLASS.
......!
...!!
THERE, YOU SEE? YOU DO LACK AWARENESS!
HONESTLY... ....
HAHH.
...THERE ARE OTHER SOHMAS ENROLLED IN THIS SCHOOL AS WELL.
AND HAJIME-SENPAI AND MUTSUKI-SAN ARE NOT BROTHERS.
THEY ARE RELATIVES.
OH, RURIKO-SAN... GOING OUT OF HER WAY TO EXPLAIN...
SHE'S TOO KIND...
OF COURSE!

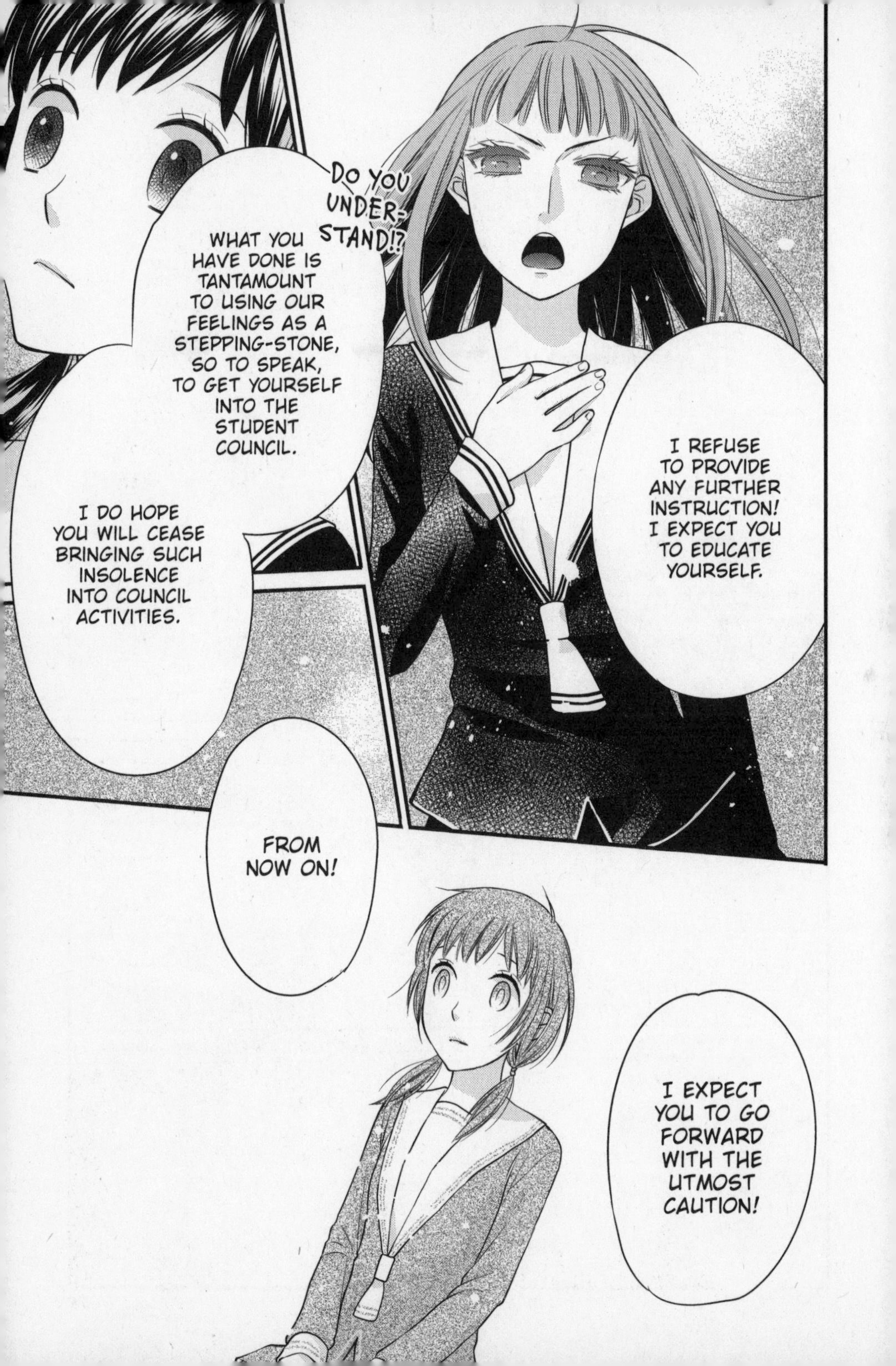
DO YOU UNDERSTAND!?
I REFUSE TO PROVIDE ANY FURTHER INSTRUCTION! I EXPECT YOU TO EDUCATE YOURSELF.
WHAT YOU HAVE DONE IS TANTAMOUNT TO USING OUR FEELINGS AS A STEPPING-STONE, SO TO SPEAK, TO GET YOURSELF INTO THE STUDENT COUNCIL.
I DO HOPE YOU WILL CEASE BRINGING SUCH INSOLENCE INTO COUNCIL ACTIVITIES.
FROM NOW ON!
I EXPECT YOU TO GO FORWARD WITH THE UTMOST CAUTION!

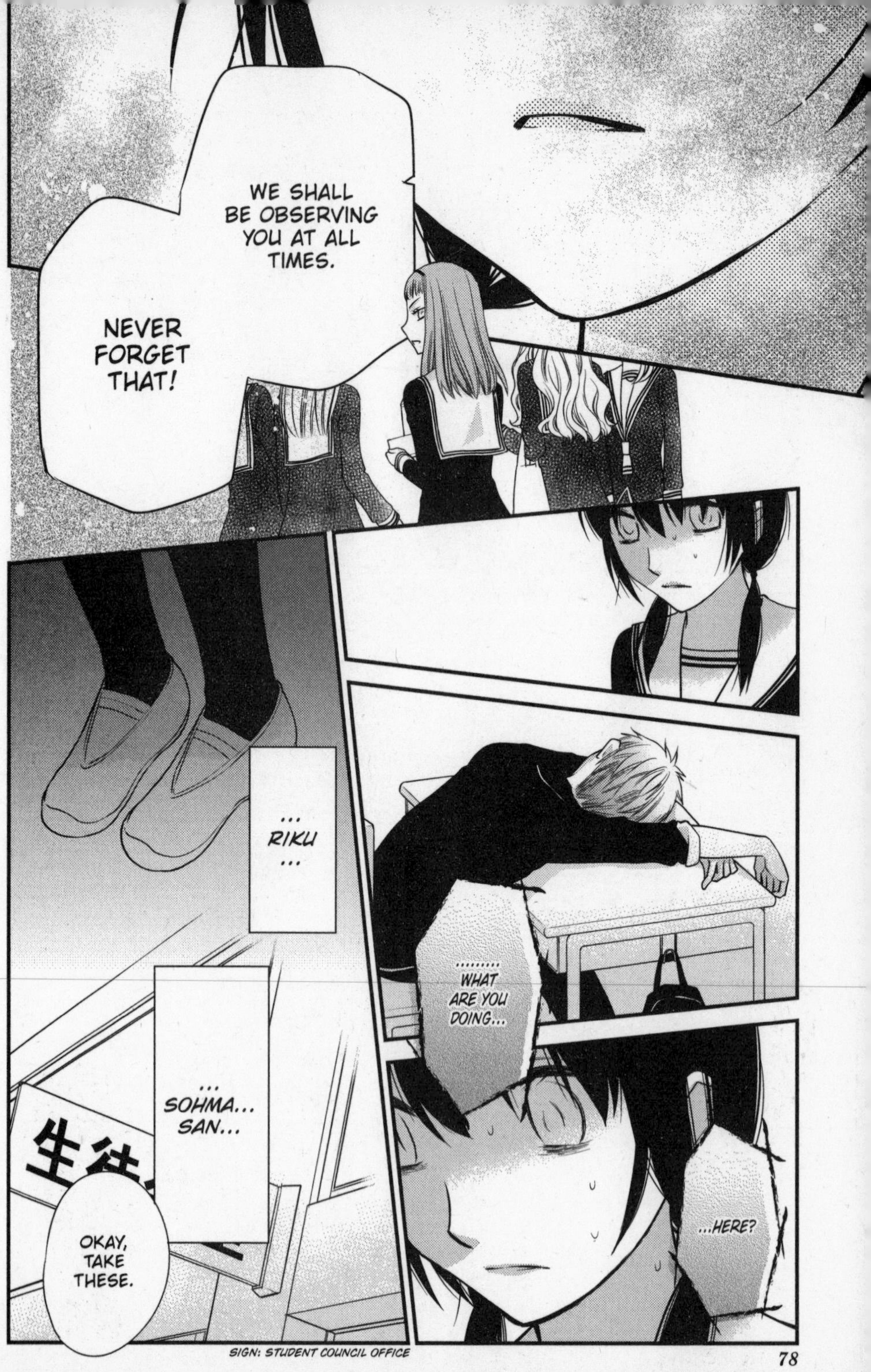
WE SHALL BE OBSERVING YOU AT ALL TIMES.
NEVER FORGET THAT!
.... WHAT ARE YOU DOING...
...HERE?
...RIKU...
...SOHMA... SAN...
生徒
OKAY, TAKE THESE.

SIGN: STUDENT COUNCIL OFFICE

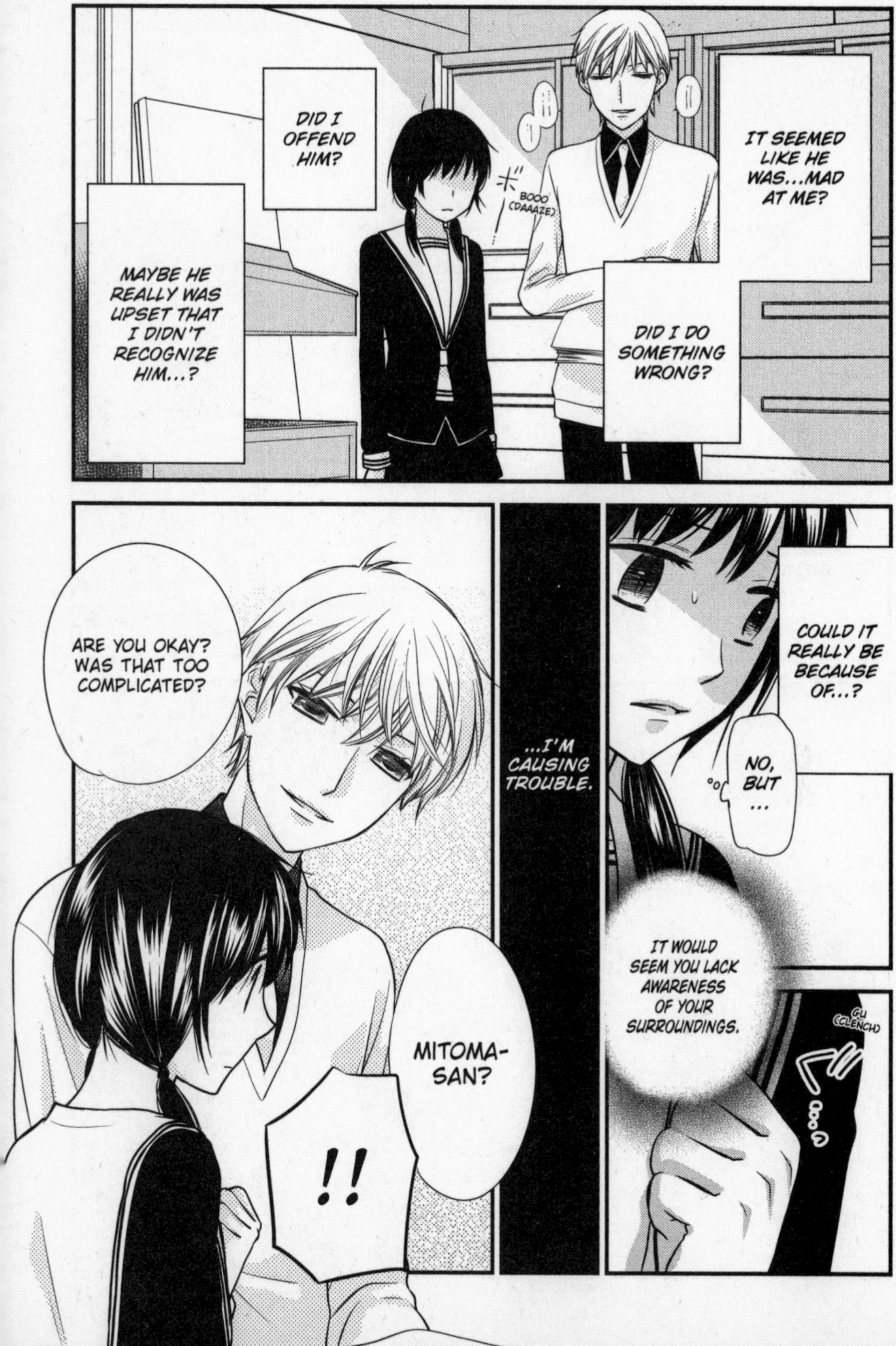
IT SEEMED LIKE HE WAS...MAD AT ME?
BOOO (DAAAZE)
DID I OFFEND HIM?
DID I DO SOMETHING WRONG?
MAYBE HE REALLY WAS UPSET THAT I DIDN'T RECOGNIZE HIM...?
COULD IT REALLY BE BECAUSE OF...?
NO, BUT ...
IT WOULD SEEM YOU LACK AWARENESS OF YOUR SURROUNDINGS.
GU (CLENCH)
...I'M CAUSING TROUBLE.
ARE YOU OKAY? WAS THAT TOO COMPLICATED?
MITOMA-SAN?
!!

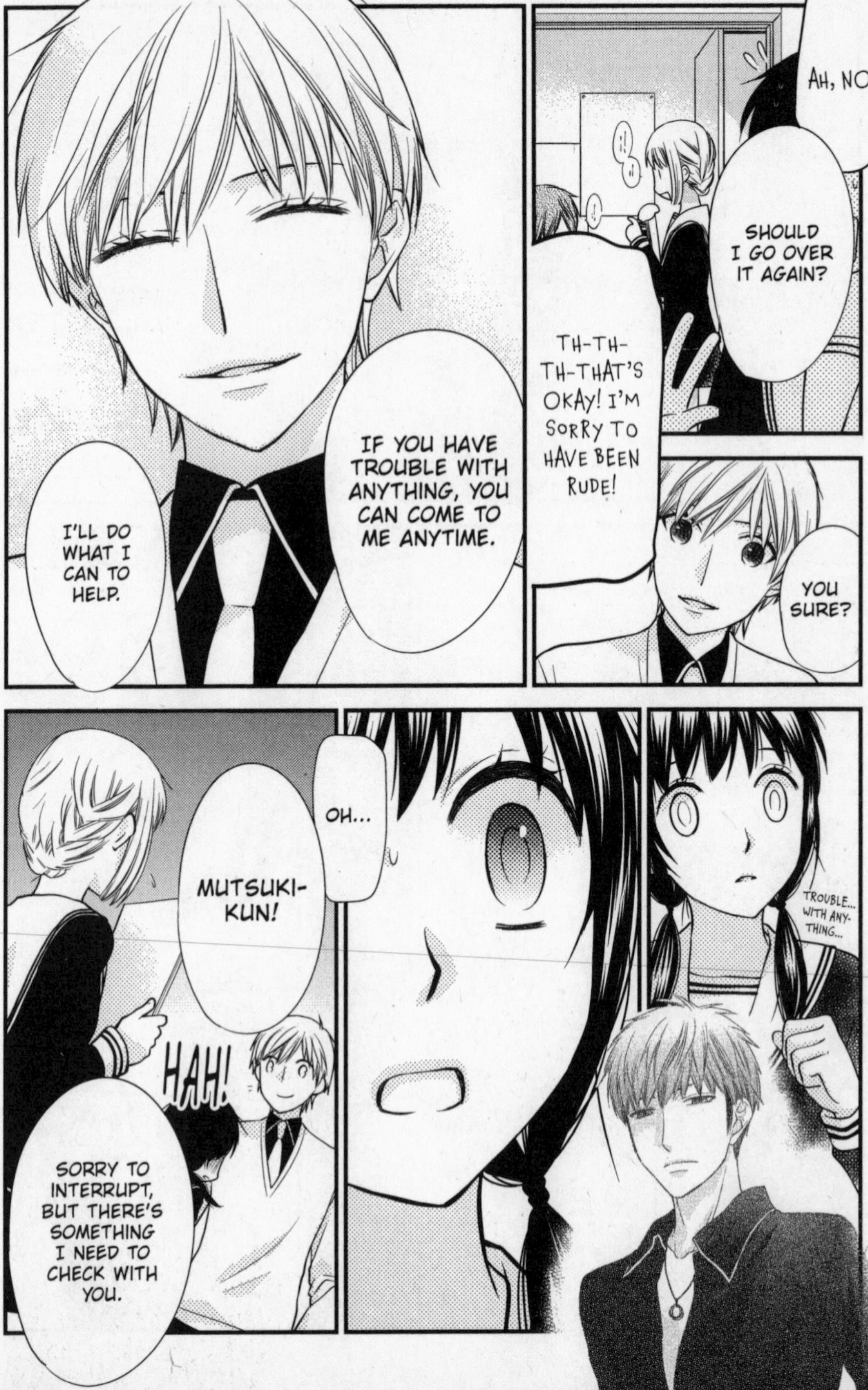
AH, NO!
SHOULD I GO OVER IT AGAIN?
TH-TH-TH-THAT'S OKAY! I'M SORRY TO HAVE BEEN RUDE!
YOU SURE?
IF YOU HAVE TROUBLE WITH ANYTHING, YOU CAN COME TO ME ANYTIME.
I'LL DO WHAT I CAN TO HELP.
TROUBLE... WITH ANYTHING...
OH...
MUTSUKI-KUN!
HAH!
SORRY TO INTERRUPT, BUT THERE'S SOMETHING I NEED TO CHECK WITH YOU.

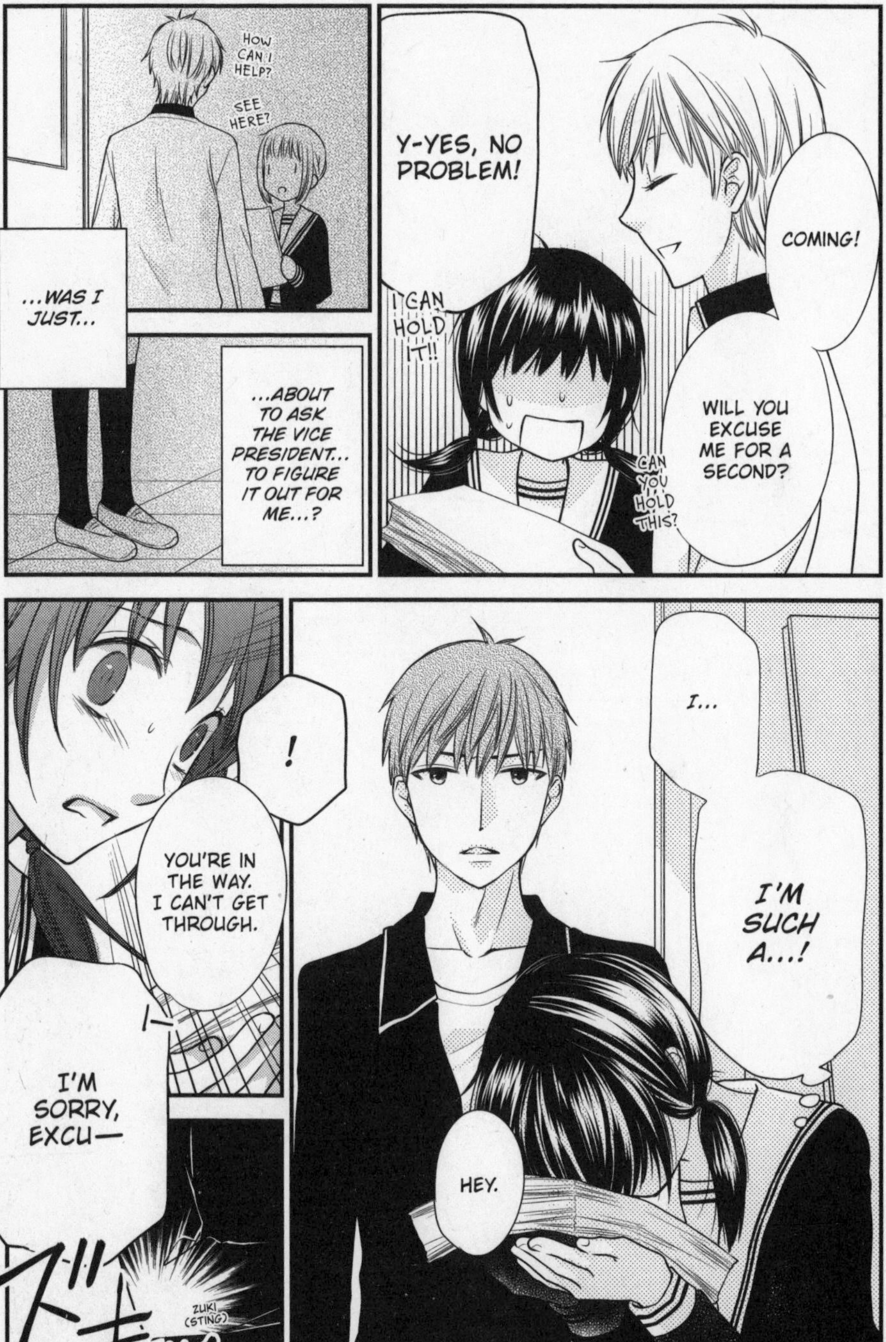
COMING!
WILL YOU EXCUSE ME FOR A SECOND?
CAN YOU HOLD THIS?
Y-YES, NO PROBLEM!
I CAN HOLD IT!!
HOW CAN I HELP?
SEE HERE?
...WAS I JUST...
...ABOUT TO ASK THE VICE PRESIDENT... TO FIGURE IT OUT FOR ME...?
I...
I'M SUCH A...!
HEY.
!
YOU'RE IN THE WAY. I CAN'T GET THROUGH.
I'M SORRY, EXCU—
ZUKI (STING)

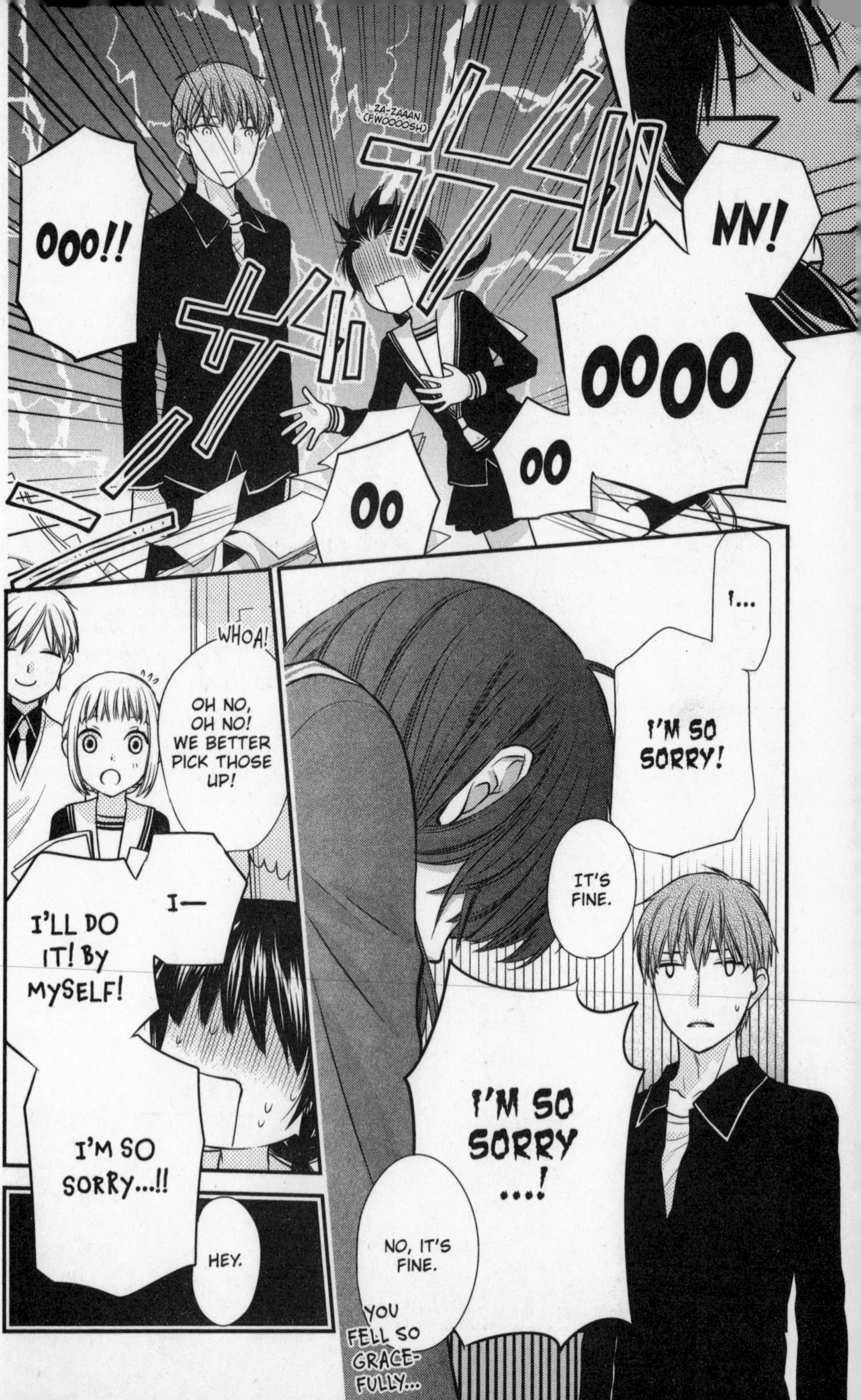
ZA-ZAAAN (FWOOOOSH)
NN!
OOOO
OO
OO
OOO!!
I...
I'M SO SORRY!
IT'S FINE.
I'M SO SORRY...!
NO, IT'S FINE.
YOU FELL SO GRACE-FULLY...
WHOA!
OH NO, OH NO! WE BETTER PICK THOSE UP!
I—
I'LL DO IT! BY MYSELF!
I'M SO SORRY...!!
HEY.

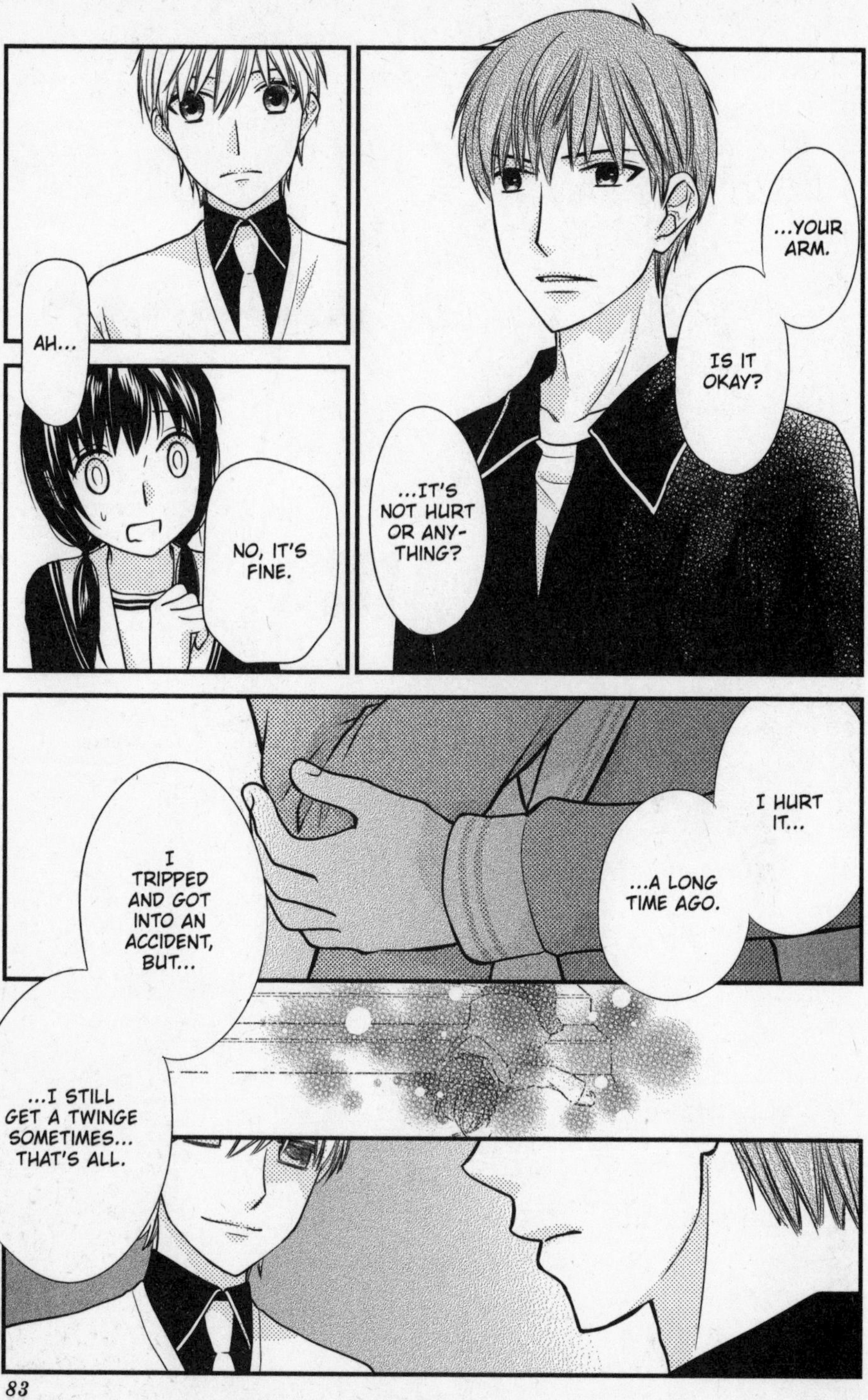
...YOUR ARM.
IS IT OKAY?
...IT'S NOT HURT OR ANYTHING?
AH...
NO, IT'S FINE.
I HURT IT...
...A LONG TIME AGO.
I TRIPPED AND GOT INTO AN ACCIDENT, BUT...
...I STILL GET A TWINGE SOMETIMES... THAT'S ALL.

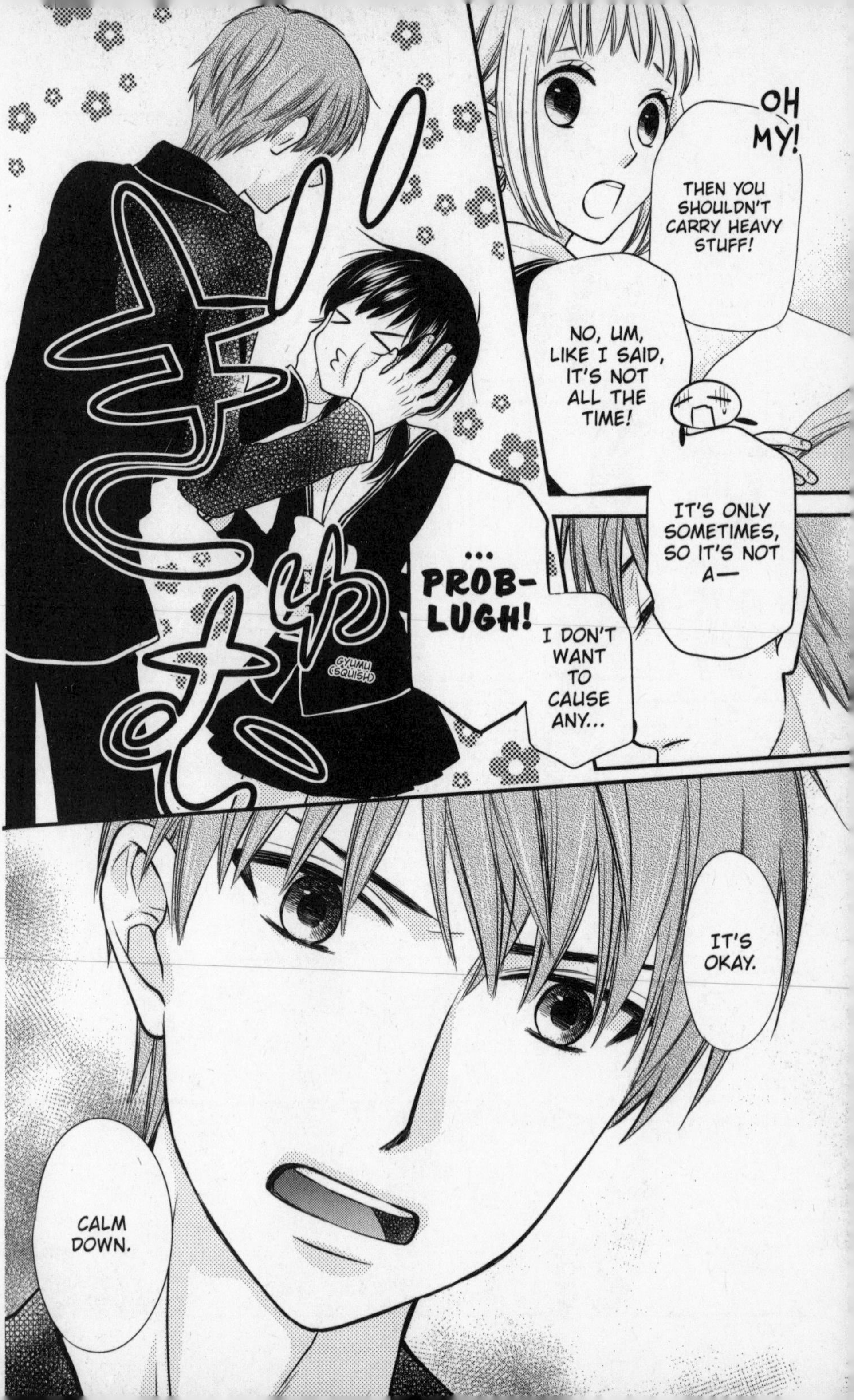
OH MY!
THEN YOU SHOULDN'T CARRY HEAVY STUFF!
NO, UM, LIKE I SAID, IT'S NOT ALL THE TIME!
IT'S ONLY SOMETIMES, SO IT'S NOT A—
I DON'T WANT TO CAUSE ANY...
... PROB-LUGH!
GYUMU (SQUISH)
IT'S OKAY.
CALM DOWN.

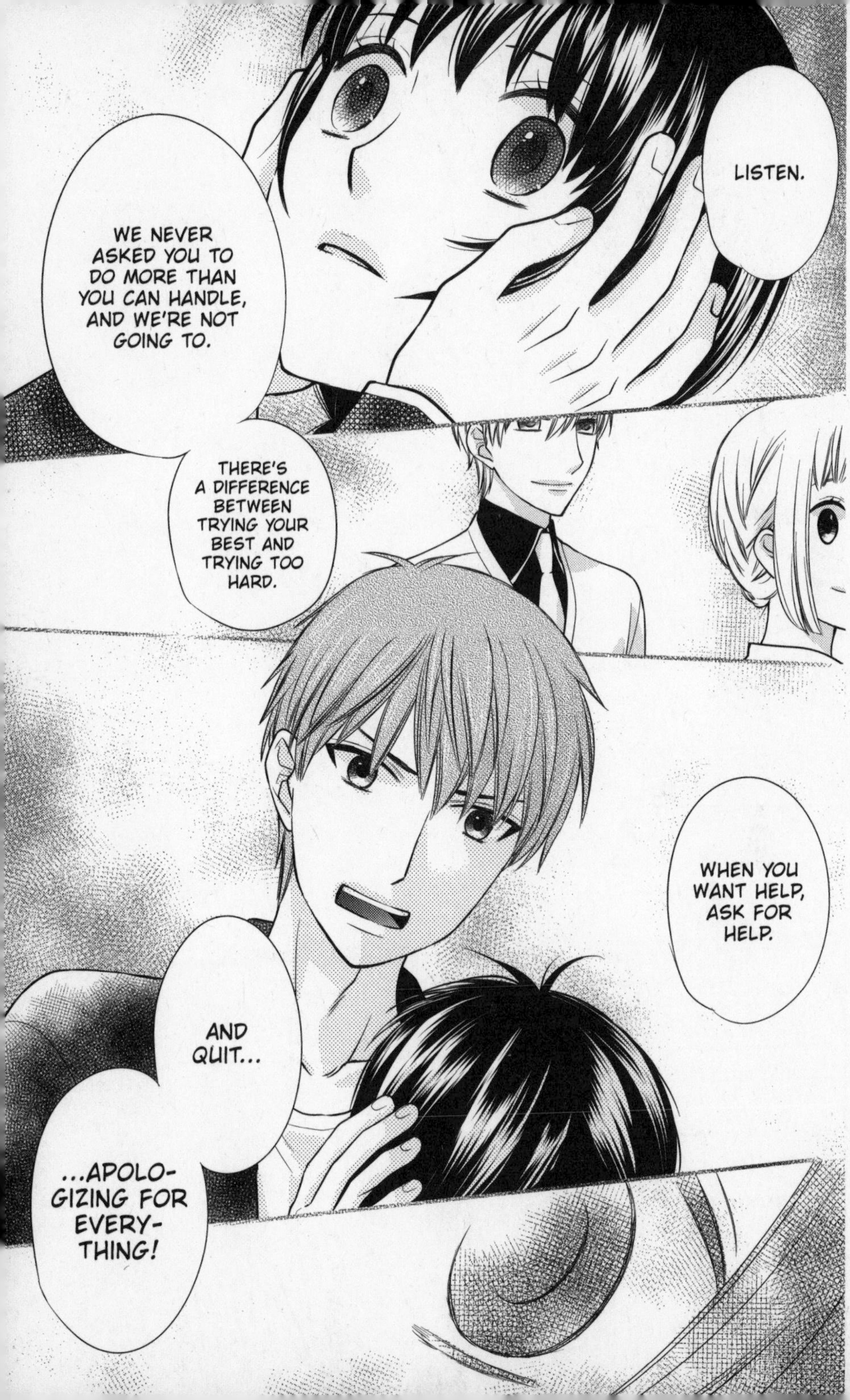
LISTEN.
WE NEVER ASKED YOU TO DO MORE THAN YOU CAN HANDLE, AND WE'RE NOT GOING TO.
THERE'S A DIFFERENCE BETWEEN TRYING YOUR BEST AND TRYING TOO HARD.
WHEN YOU WANT HELP, ASK FOR HELP.
AND QUIT...
...APOLO-GIZING FOR EVERY-THING!

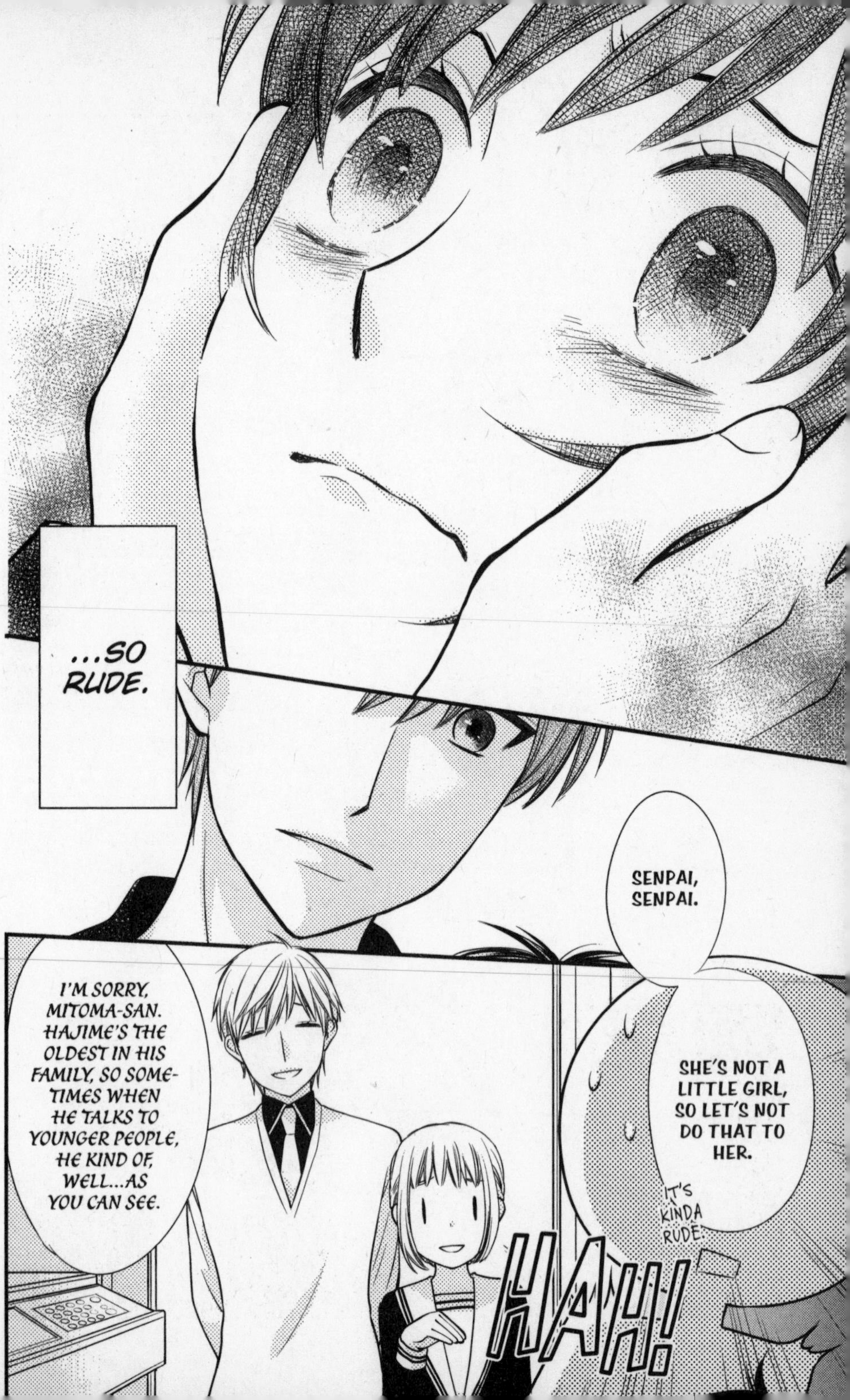
...SO RUDE.
SENPAI, SENPAI.
SHE'S NOT A LITTLE GIRL, SO LET'S NOT DO THAT TO HER.
IT'S KINDA RUDE.
HAH!
I'M SORRY, MITOMA-SAN. HAJIME'S THE OLDEST IN HIS FAMILY, SO SOME-TIMES WHEN HE TALKS TO YOUNGER PEOPLE, HE KIND OF, WELL...AS YOU CAN SEE.

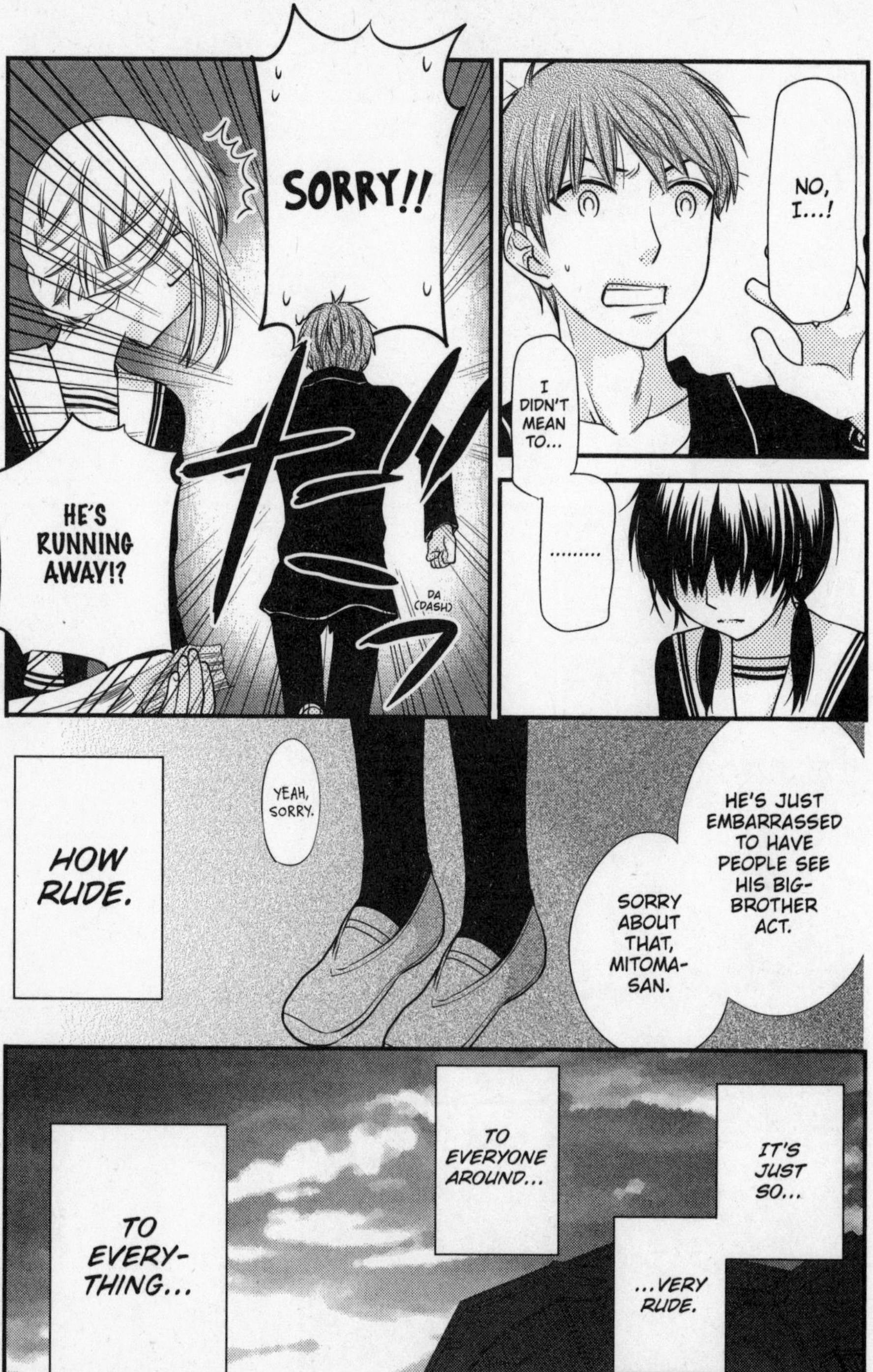
NO, I...!
I DIDN'T MEAN TO...
....
SORRY!!
HE'S RUNNING AWAY!?
DA (DASH)
HE'S JUST EMBARRASSED TO HAVE PEOPLE SEE HIS BIG-BROTHER ACT.
SORRY ABOUT THAT, MITOMA-SAN.
YEAH, SORRY.
HOW RUDE.
IT'S JUST SO...
...VERY RUDE.
TO EVERYONE AROUND...
TO EVERY-THING...

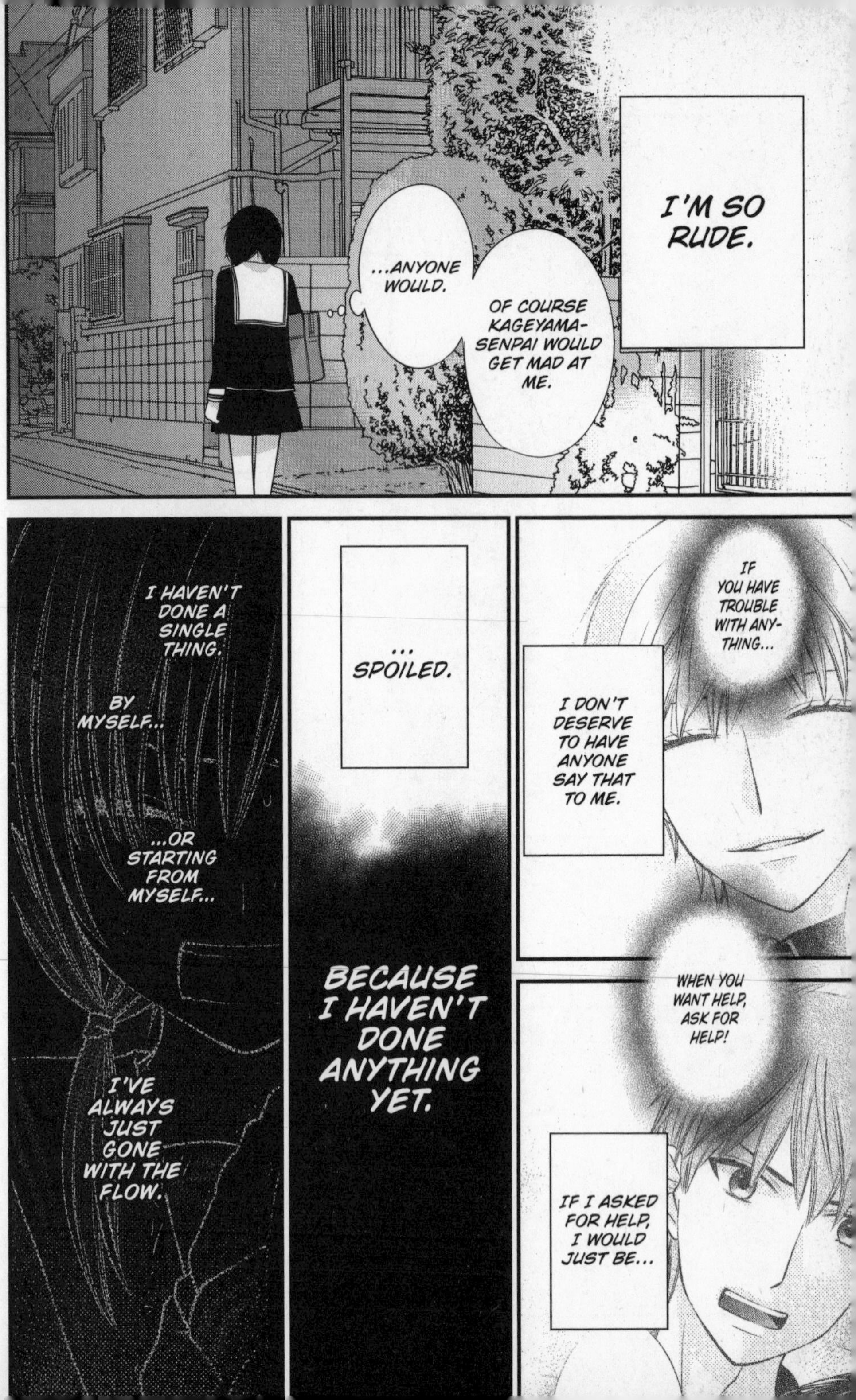
I'M SO RUDE.
OF COURSE KAGEYAMA-SENPAI WOULD GET MAD AT ME.
...ANYONE WOULD.
IF YOU HAVE TROUBLE WITH ANY-THING...
I DON'T DESERVE TO HAVE ANYONE SAY THAT TO ME.
WHEN YOU WANT HELP, ASK FOR HELP!
IF I ASKED FOR HELP, I WOULD JUST BE...
...SPOILED.
BECAUSE I HAVEN'T DONE ANYTHING YET.
I HAVEN'T DONE A SINGLE THING.
BY MYSELF...
...OR STARTING FROM MYSELF...
I'VE ALWAYS JUST GONE WITH THE FLOW.

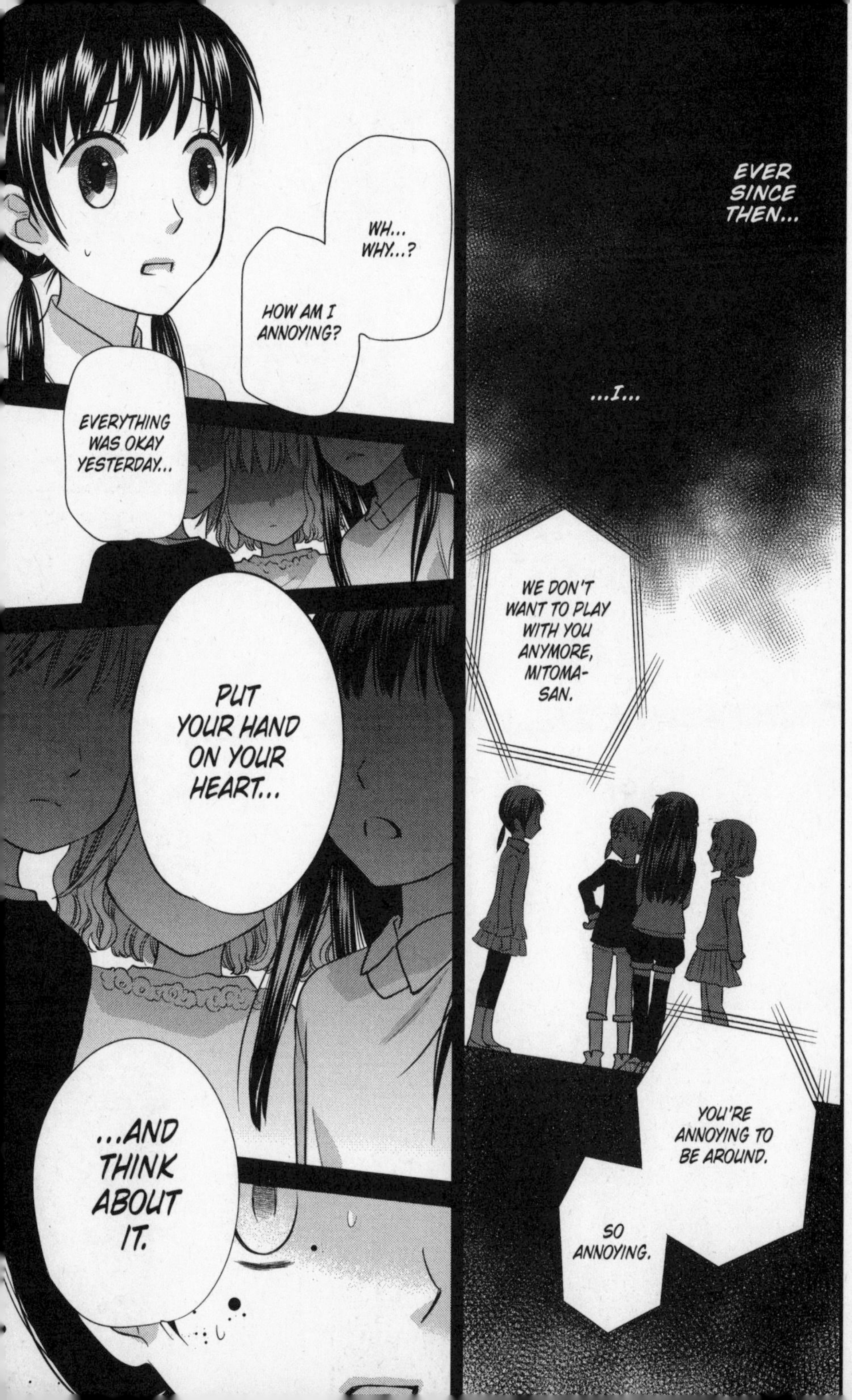

EVER SINCE THEN...
...I...
WE DON'T WANT TO PLAY WITH YOU ANYMORE, MITOMA-SAN.
YOU'RE ANNOYING TO BE AROUND.
SO ANNOYING.
WH... WHY...?
HOW AM I ANNOYING?
EVERYTHING WAS OKAY YESTERDAY...
PUT YOUR HAND ON YOUR HEART...
...AND THINK ABOUT IT.

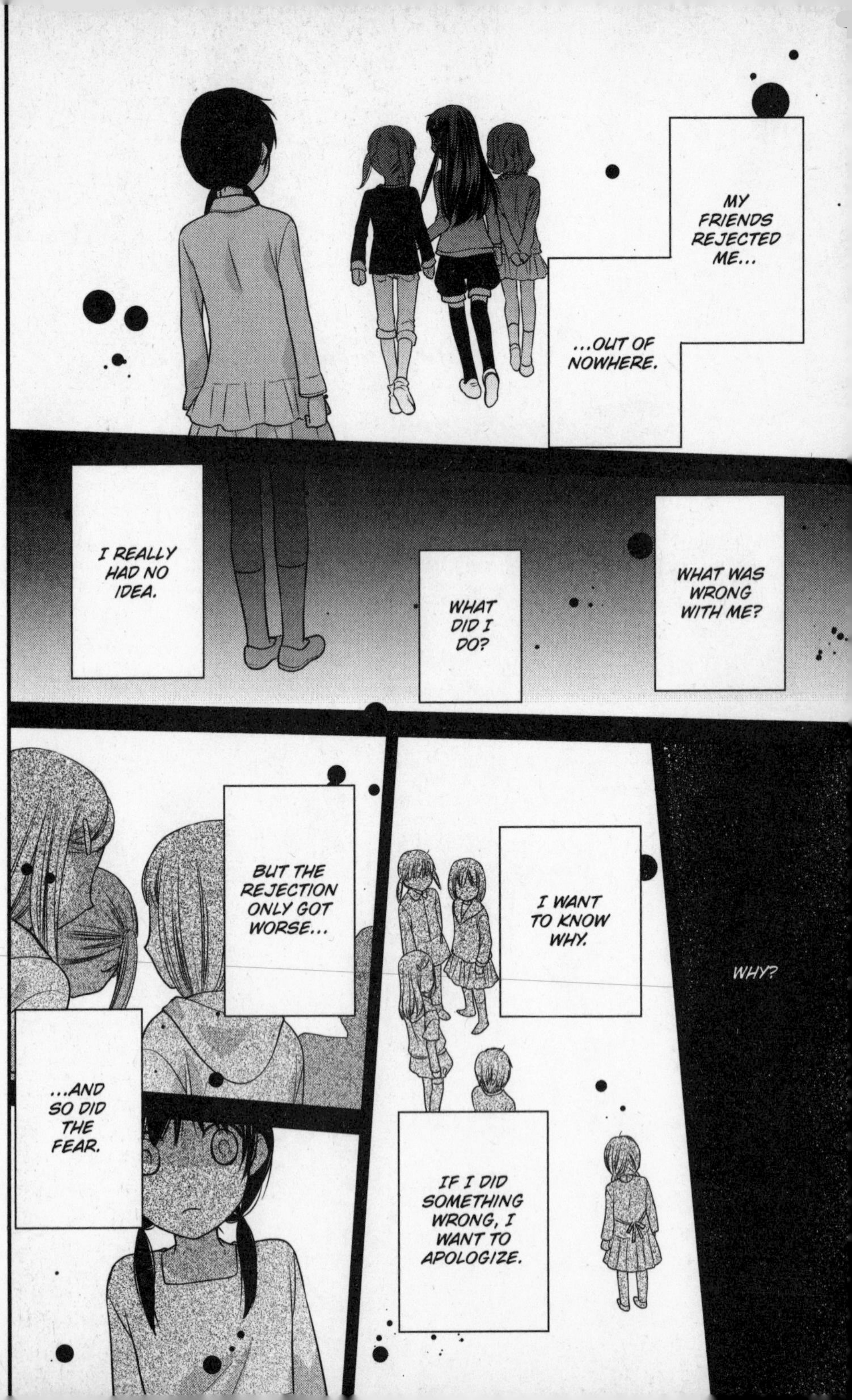
MY FRIENDS REJECTED ME...
...OUT OF NOWHERE.
WHAT WAS WRONG WITH ME?
WHAT DID I DO?
I REALLY HAD NO IDEA.
I WANT TO KNOW WHY.
WHY?
IF I DID SOMETHING WRONG, I WANT TO APOLOGIZE.
BUT THE REJECTION ONLY GOT WORSE...
...AND SO DID THE FEAR.

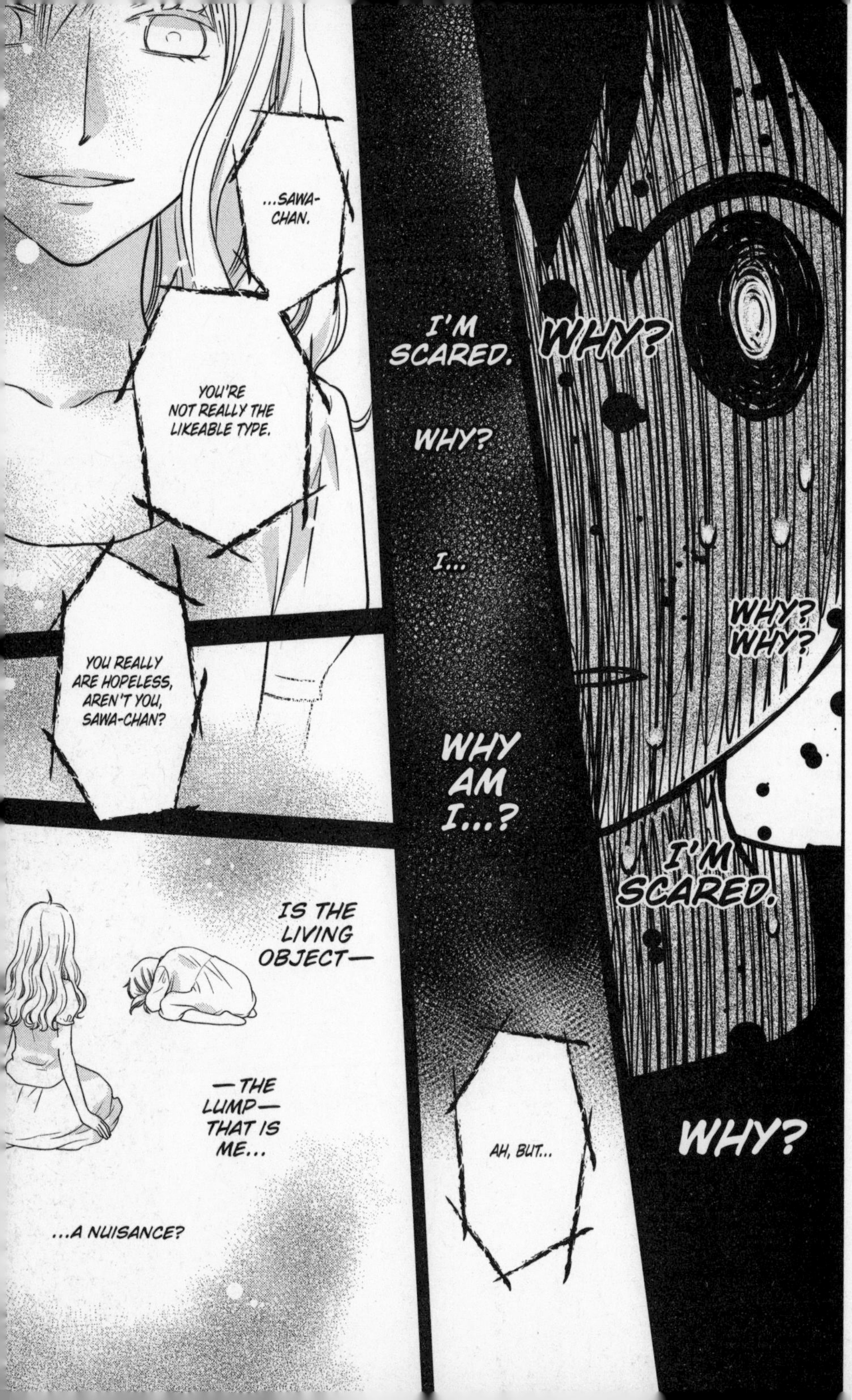
WHY?
I'M SCARED.
WHY?
I...
WHY? WHY?
WHY AM I...?
I'M SCARED.
WHY?
AH, BUT...
...SAWA-CHAN.
YOU'RE NOT REALLY THE LIKEABLE TYPE.
YOU REALLY ARE HOPELESS, AREN'T YOU, SAWA-CHAN?
IS THE LIVING OBJECT—
—THE LUMP— THAT IS ME...
...A NUISANCE?

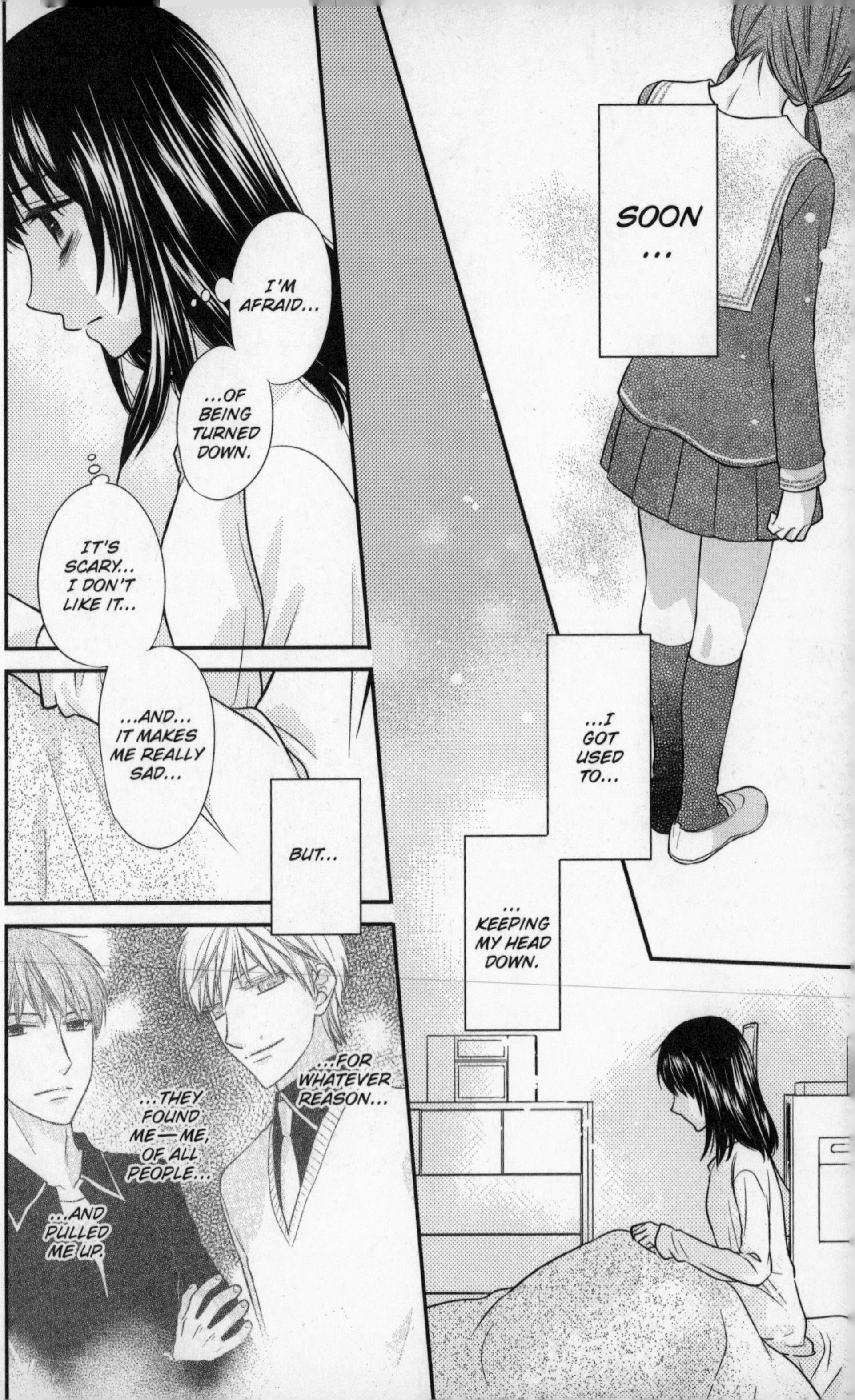
SOON ...
...I GOT USED TO...
...KEEPING MY HEAD DOWN.
I'M AFRAID...
...OF BEING TURNED DOWN.
IT'S SCARY... I DON'T LIKE IT...
...AND... IT MAKES ME REALLY SAD...
BUT...
...FOR WHATEVER REASON...
...THEY FOUND ME—ME, OF ALL PEOPLE...
...AND PULLED ME UP.

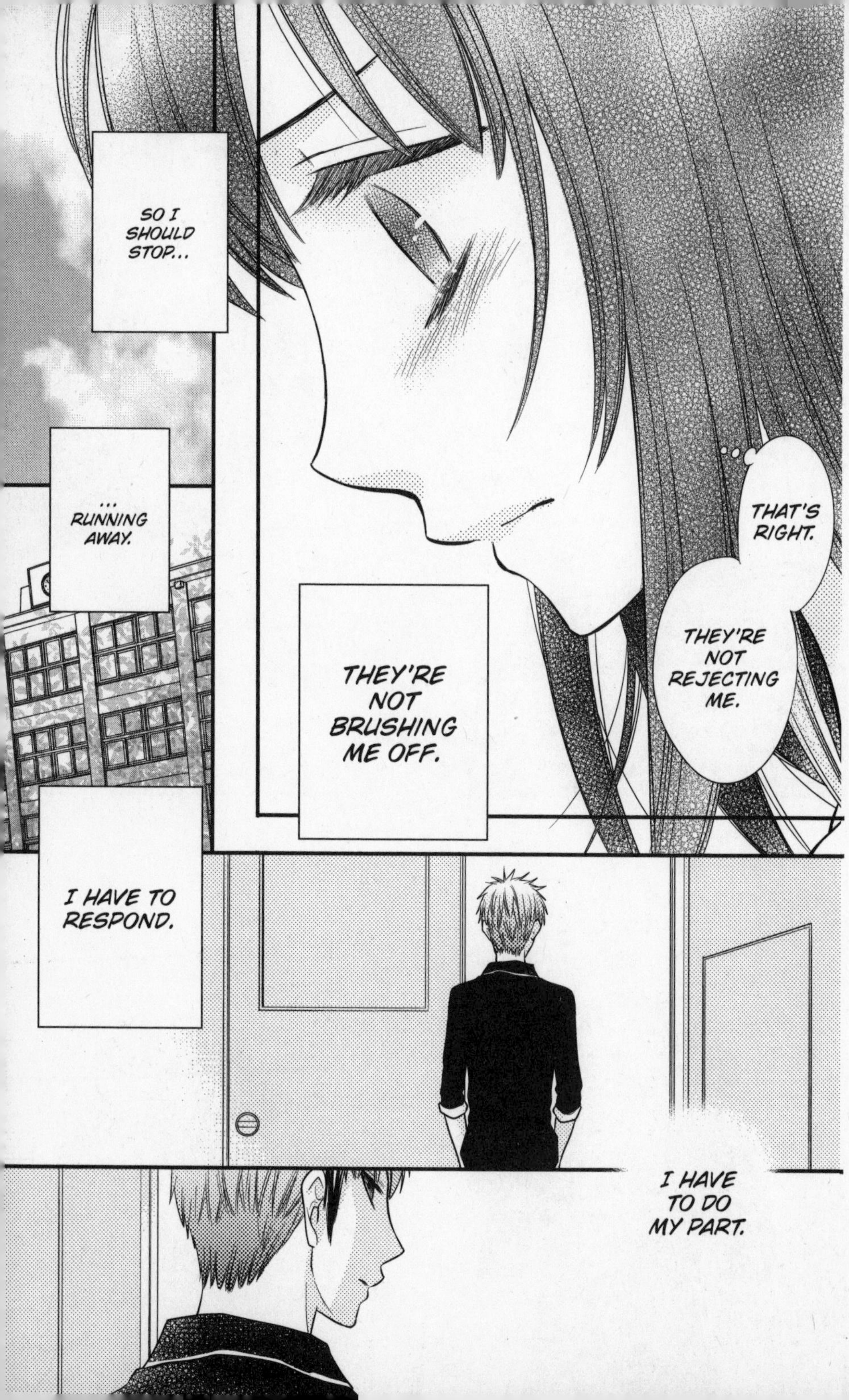
THAT'S RIGHT.
THEY'RE NOT REJECTING ME.
THEY'RE NOT BRUSHING ME OFF.
SO I SHOULD STOP...
... RUNNING AWAY.
I HAVE TO RESPOND.
I HAVE TO DO MY PART.

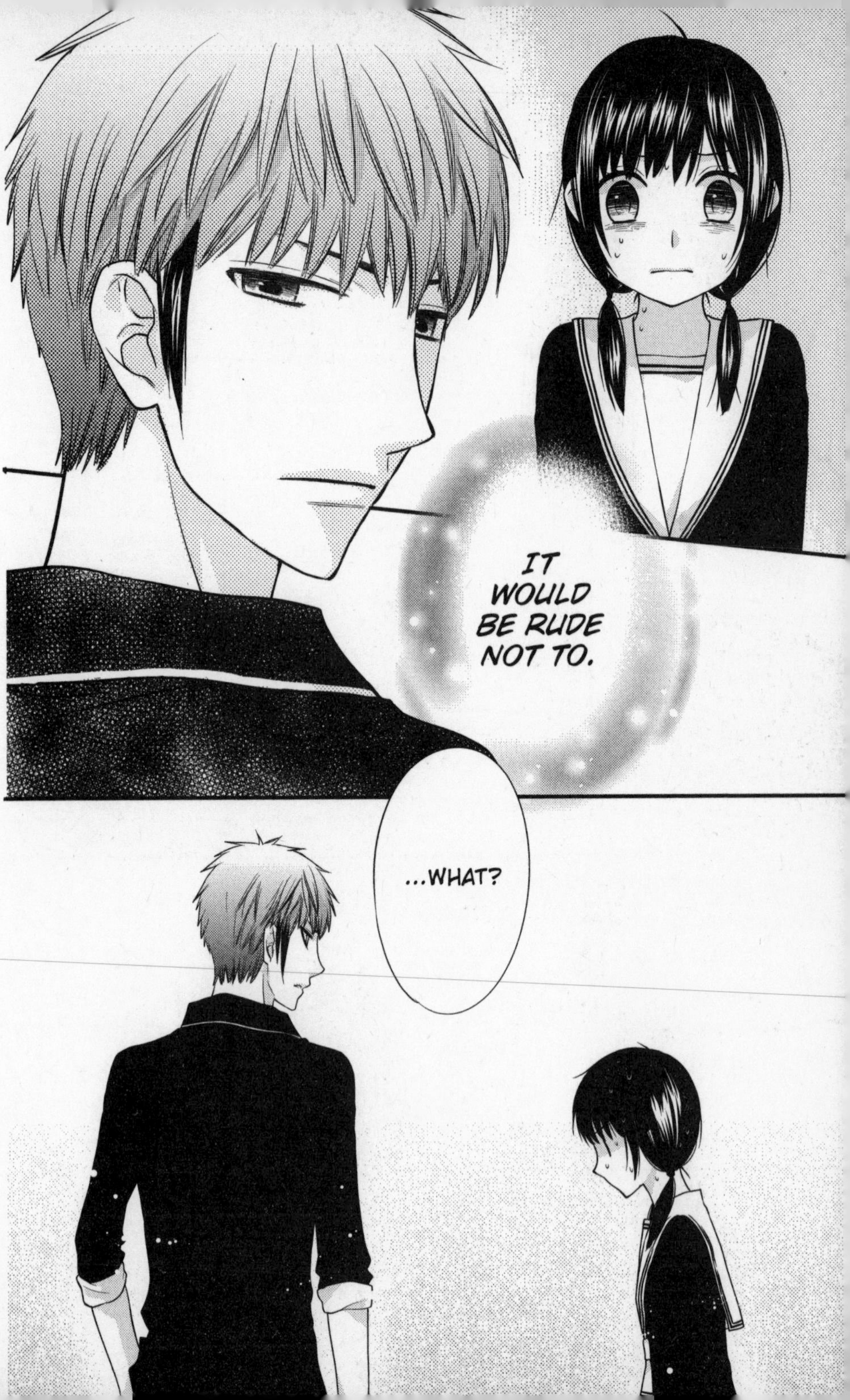
IT WOULD BE RUDE NOT TO.
...WHAT?

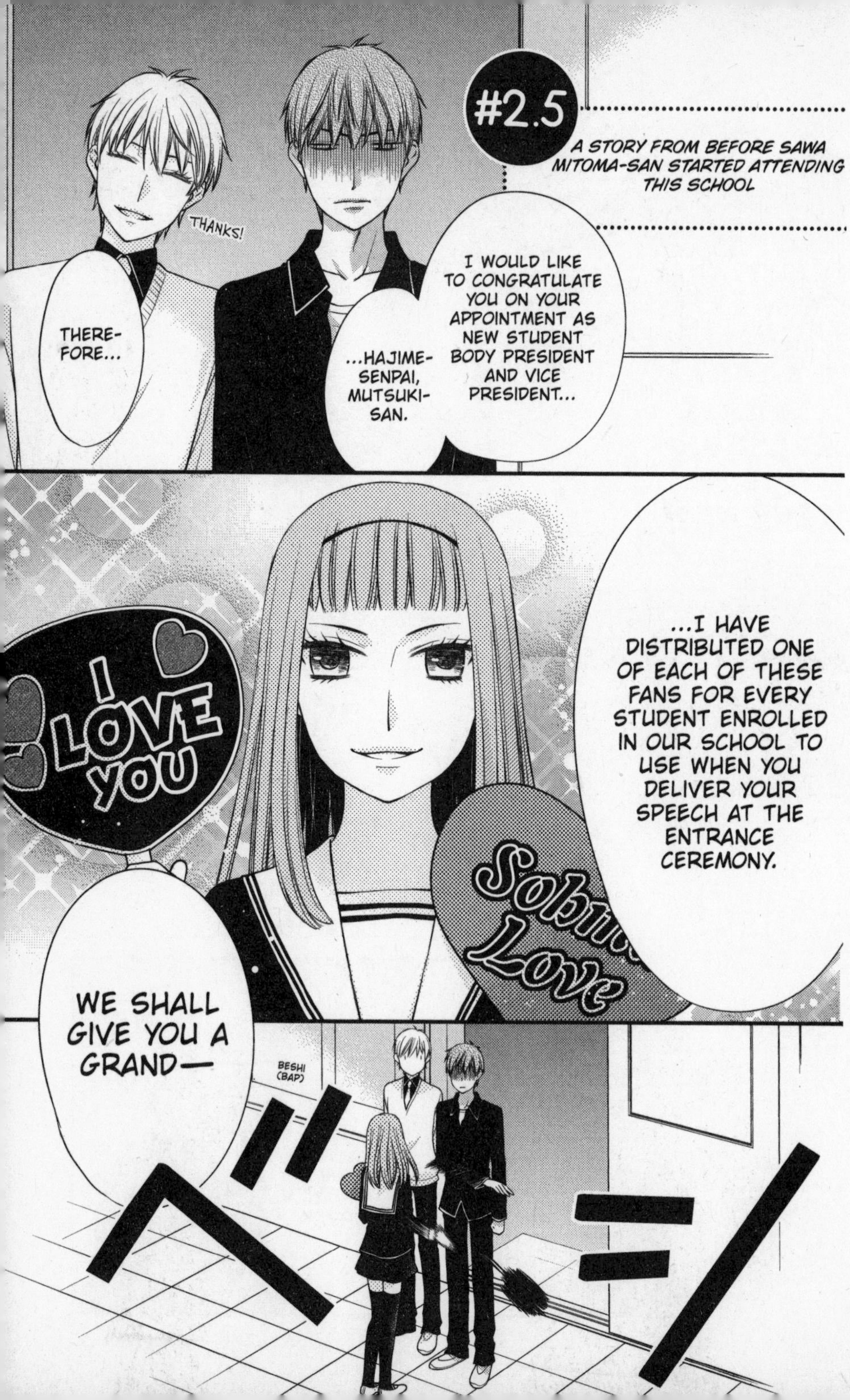
#2.5
A STORY FROM BEFORE SAWA MITOMA-SAN STARTED ATTENDING THIS SCHOOL
I WOULD LIKE TO CONGRATULATE YOU ON YOUR APPOINTMENT AS NEW STUDENT BODY PRESIDENT AND VICE PRESIDENT...
...HAJIME-SENPAI, MUTSUKI-SAN.
THANKS!
THERE-FORE...
...I HAVE DISTRIBUTED ONE OF EACH OF THESE FANS FOR EVERY STUDENT ENROLLED IN OUR SCHOOL TO USE WHEN YOU DELIVER YOUR SPEECH AT THE ENTRANCE CEREMONY.
I LOVE YOU
WE SHALL GIVE YOU A GRAND—
BESHI (BAP)

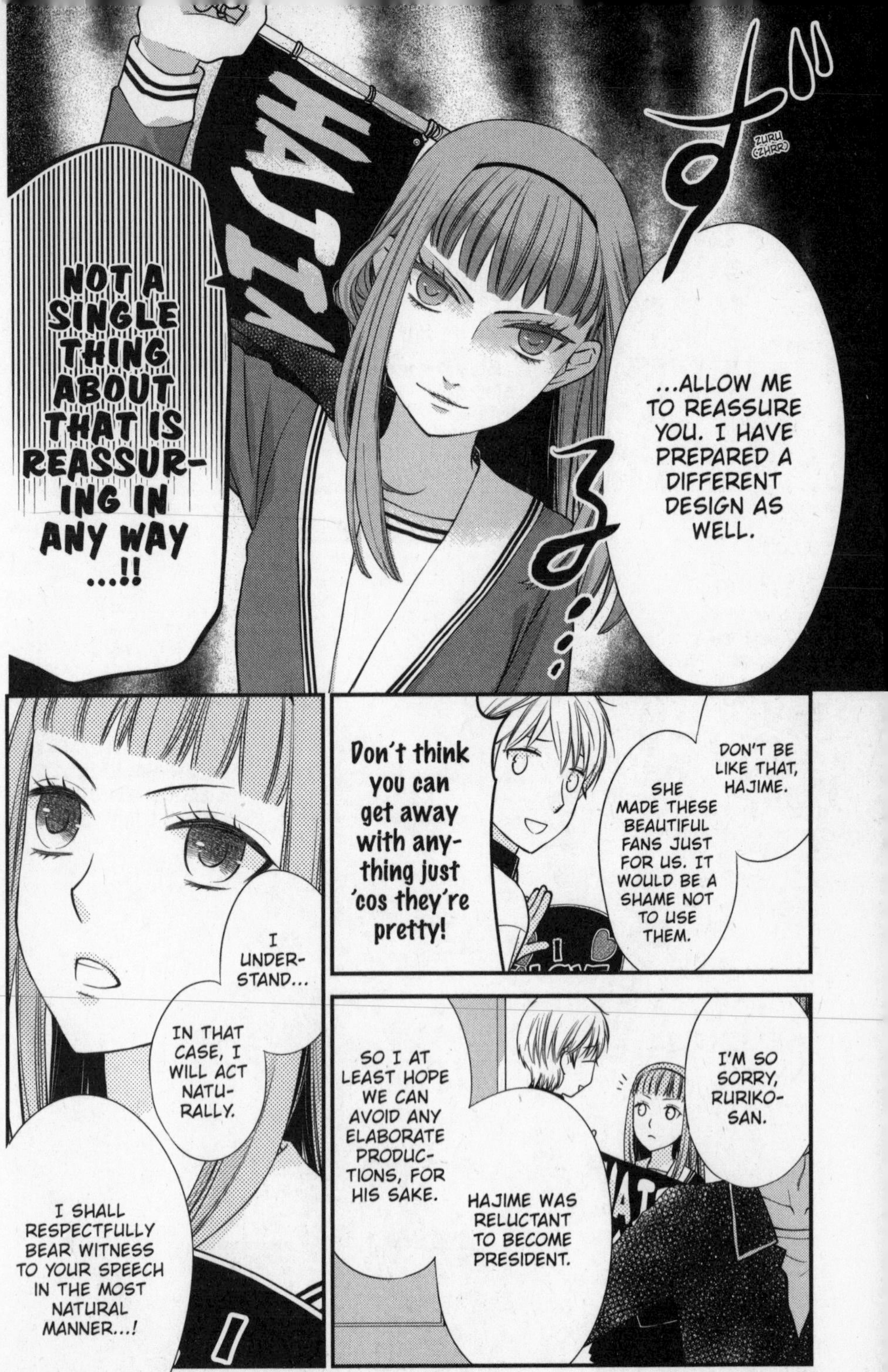
ZURU (ZHRR)
...ALLOW ME TO REASSURE YOU. I HAVE PREPARED A DIFFERENT DESIGN AS WELL.
NOT A SINGLE THING ABOUT THAT IS REASSURING IN ANY WAY...!!
DON'T BE LIKE THAT, HAJIME.
SHE MADE THESE BEAUTIFUL FANS JUST FOR US. IT WOULD BE A SHAME NOT TO USE THEM.
Don't think you can get away with anything just 'cos they're pretty!
I'M SO SORRY, RURIKO-SAN.
HAJIME WAS RELUCTANT TO BECOME PRESIDENT.
SO I AT LEAST HOPE WE CAN AVOID ANY ELABORATE PRODUCTIONS, FOR HIS SAKE.
I UNDERSTAND...
IN THAT CASE, I WILL ACT NATURALLY.
I SHALL RESPECTFULLY BEAR WITNESS TO YOUR SPEECH IN THE MOST NATURAL MANNER...!

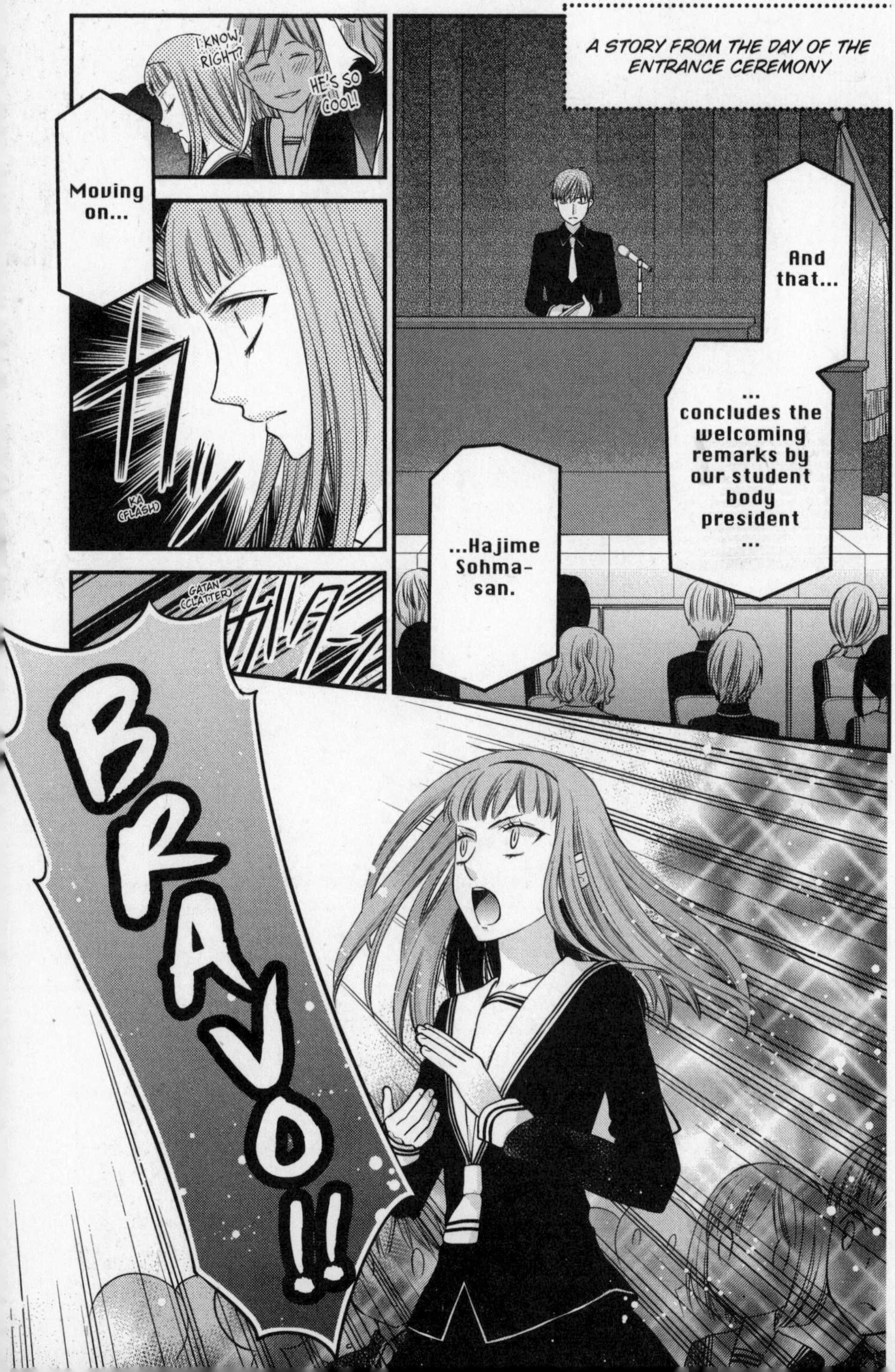
A STORY FROM THE DAY OF THE ENTRANCE CEREMONY
And that...
...
concludes the welcoming remarks by our student body president
...
...Hajime Sohma-san.
I KNOW, RIGHT?
HE'S SO COOL!!
Moving on...
KA (FLASH)
GATAN (CLATTER)
BRAVO!!

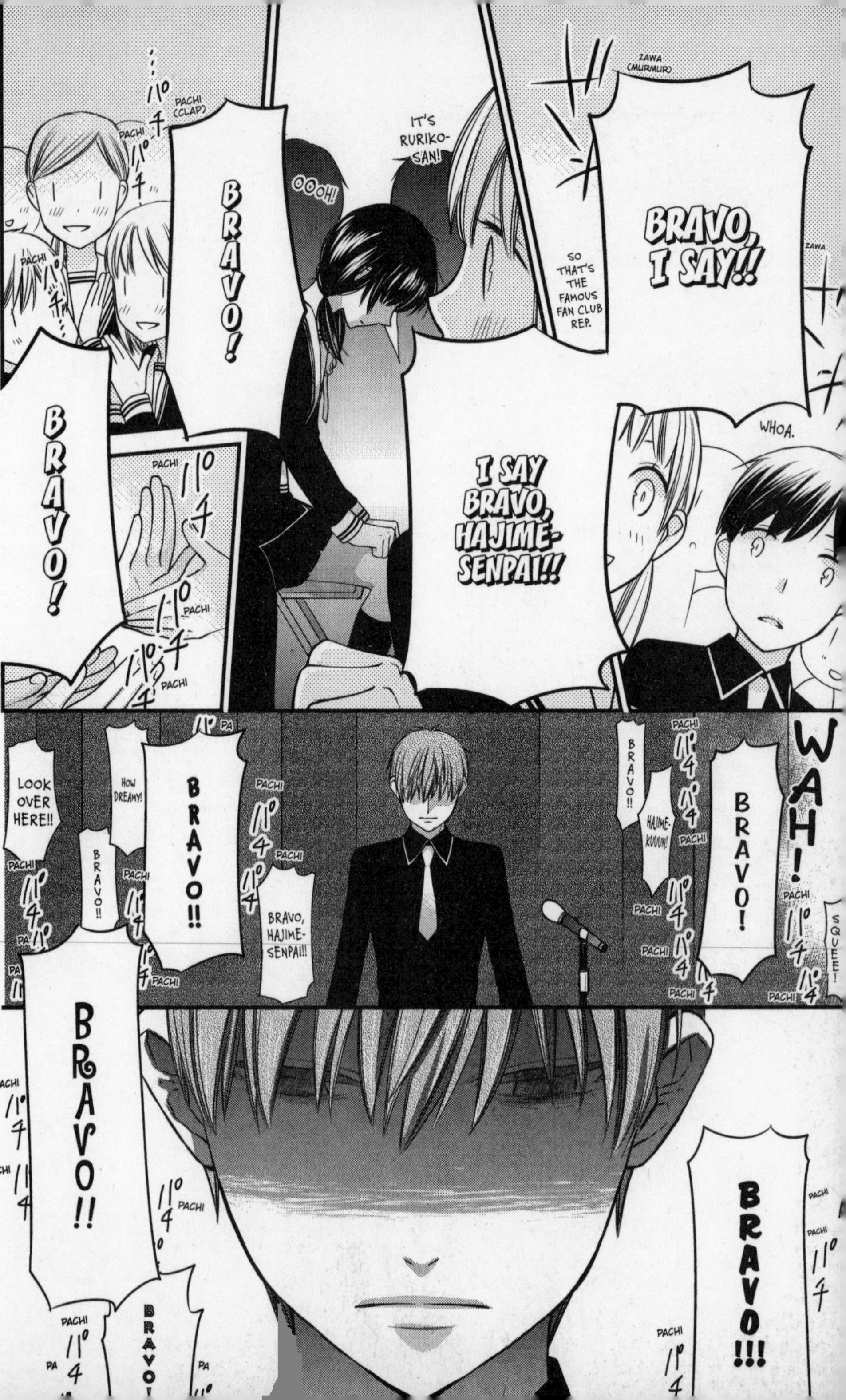
ZAWA (MURMUR)
BRAVO, I SAY!!
ZAWA
SO THAT'S THE FAMOUS FAN CLUB REP.
IT'S RURIKO-SAN!
OOOH!
WHOA.
I SAY BRAVO, HAJIME-SENPAI!!
BRAVO!
PACHI (CLAP)
PACHI
BRAVO!
PACHI
PACHI
PACHI
WAH!
SQUEE!
PACHI
BRAVO!
PACHI
HAJIME-KUUUN!
BRAVO!!
PACHI
BRAVO, HAJIME-SENPAI!!!
PACHI
BRAVO!!
PA
HOW DREAMY!
BRAVO!!
LOOK OVER HERE!!
PACHI
BRAVO!!!
PACHI
BRAVO!!
PACHI
BRAVO
PA

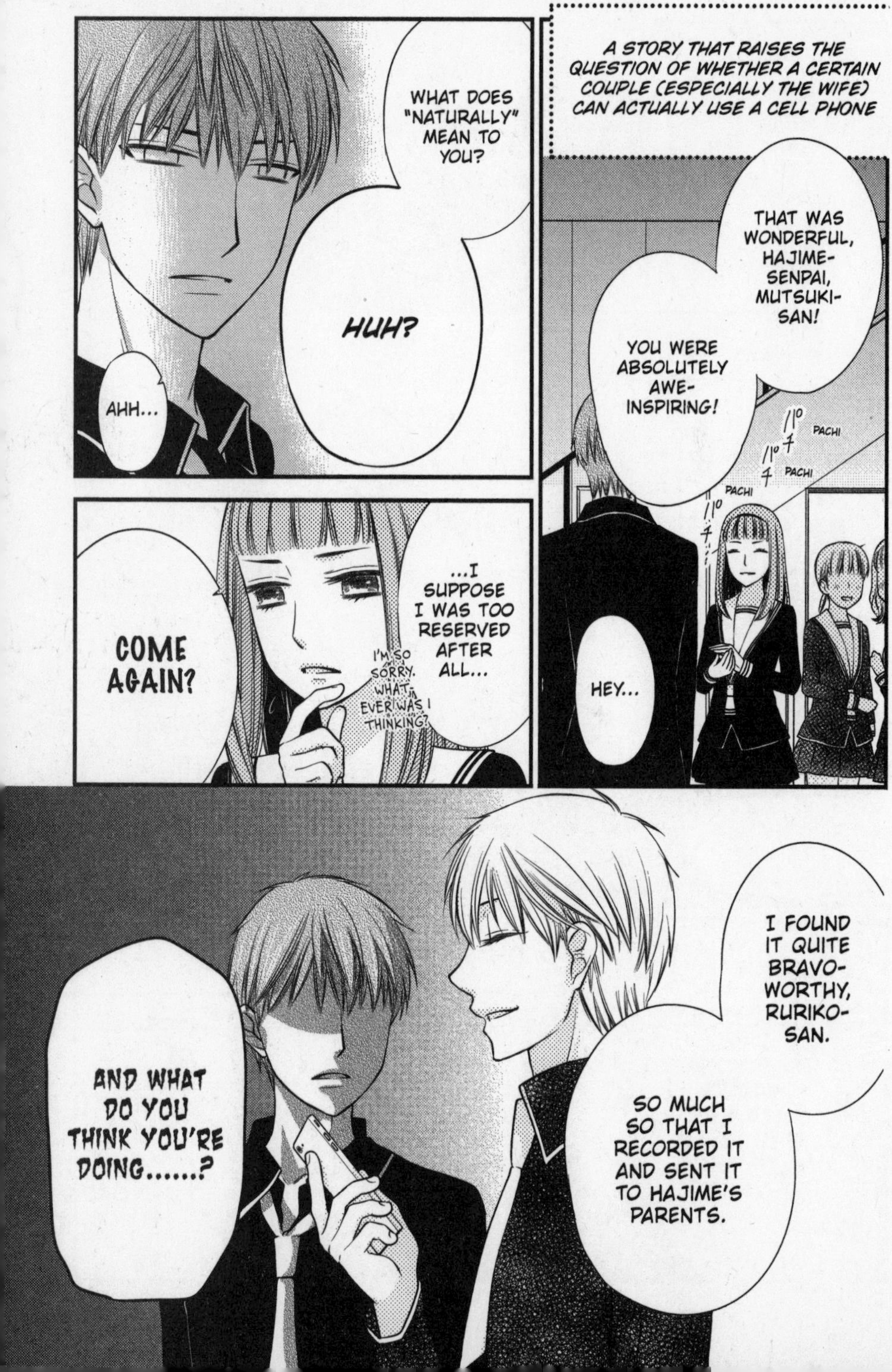
A STORY THAT RAISES THE QUESTION OF WHETHER A CERTAIN COUPLE (ESPECIALLY THE WIFE) CAN ACTUALLY USE A CELL PHONE
THAT WAS WONDERFUL, HAJIME-SENPAI, MUTSUKI-SAN!
YOU WERE ABSOLUTELY AWE-INSPIRING!
PACHI
PACHI
PACHI
HEY...
WHAT DOES "NATURALLY" MEAN TO YOU?
HUH?
AHH...
...I SUPPOSE I WAS TOO RESERVED AFTER ALL...
I'M SO SORRY. WHATEVER WAS I THINKING?
COME AGAIN?
I FOUND IT QUITE BRAVO-WORTHY, RURIKO-SAN.
SO MUCH SO THAT I RECORDED IT AND SENT IT TO HAJIME'S PARENTS.
AND WHAT DO YOU THINK YOU'RE DOING......?

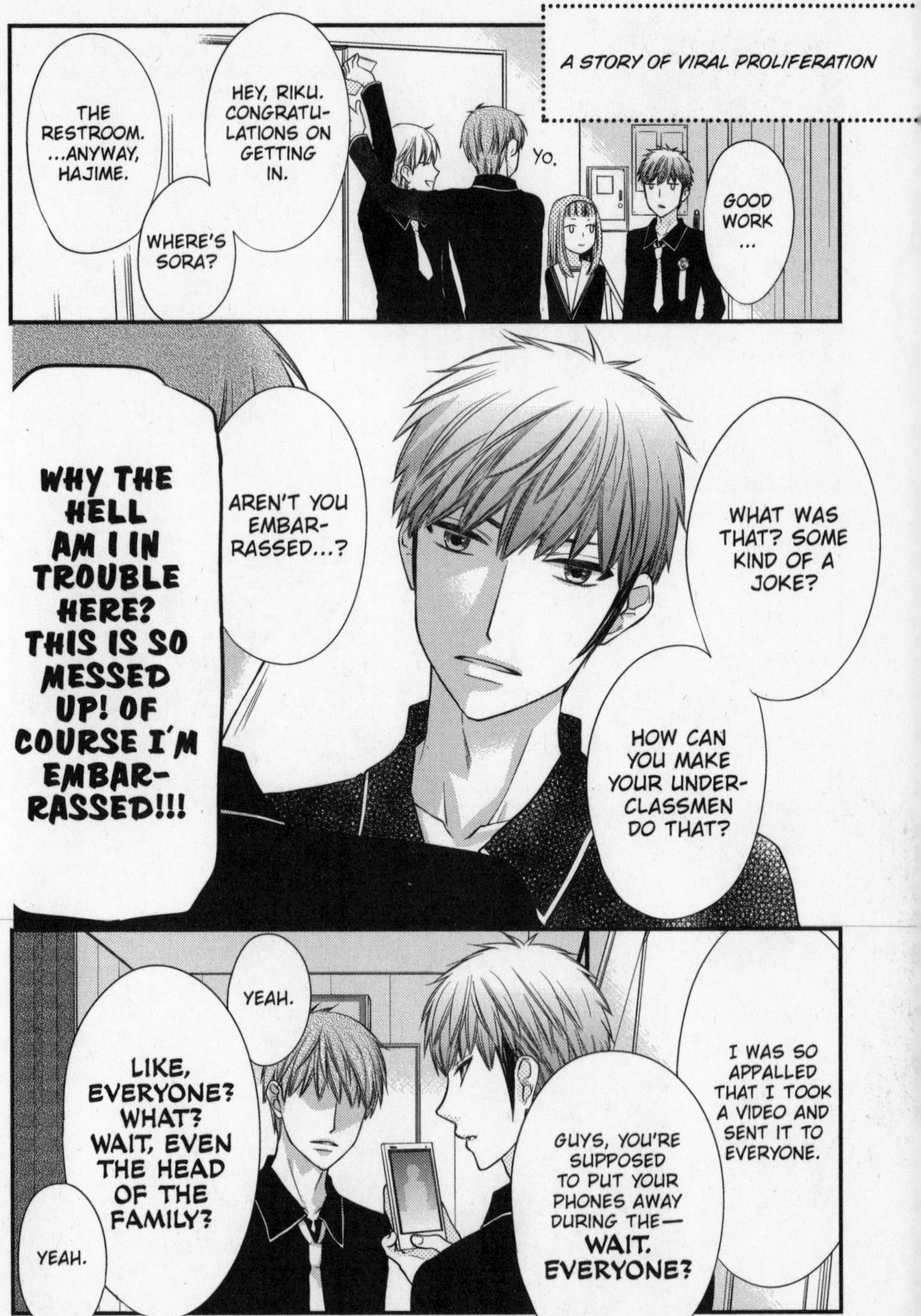
A STORY OF VIRAL PROLIFERATION
GOOD WORK ...
YO.
HEY, RIKU. CONGRATULATIONS ON GETTING IN.
WHERE'S SORA?
THE RESTROOM. ...ANYWAY, HAJIME.
WHAT WAS THAT? SOME KIND OF A JOKE?
HOW CAN YOU MAKE YOUR UNDERCLASSMEN DO THAT?
AREN'T YOU EMBARRASSED...?
WHY THE HELL AM I IN TROUBLE HERE? THIS IS SO MESSED UP! OF COURSE I'M EMBARRASSED!!!
I WAS SO APPALLED THAT I TOOK A VIDEO AND SENT IT TO EVERYONE.
GUYS, YOU'RE SUPPOSED TO PUT YOUR PHONES AWAY DURING THE— WAIT. EVERYONE?
YEAH.
LIKE, EVERYONE? WHAT? WAIT, EVEN THE HEAD OF THE FAMILY?
YEAH.

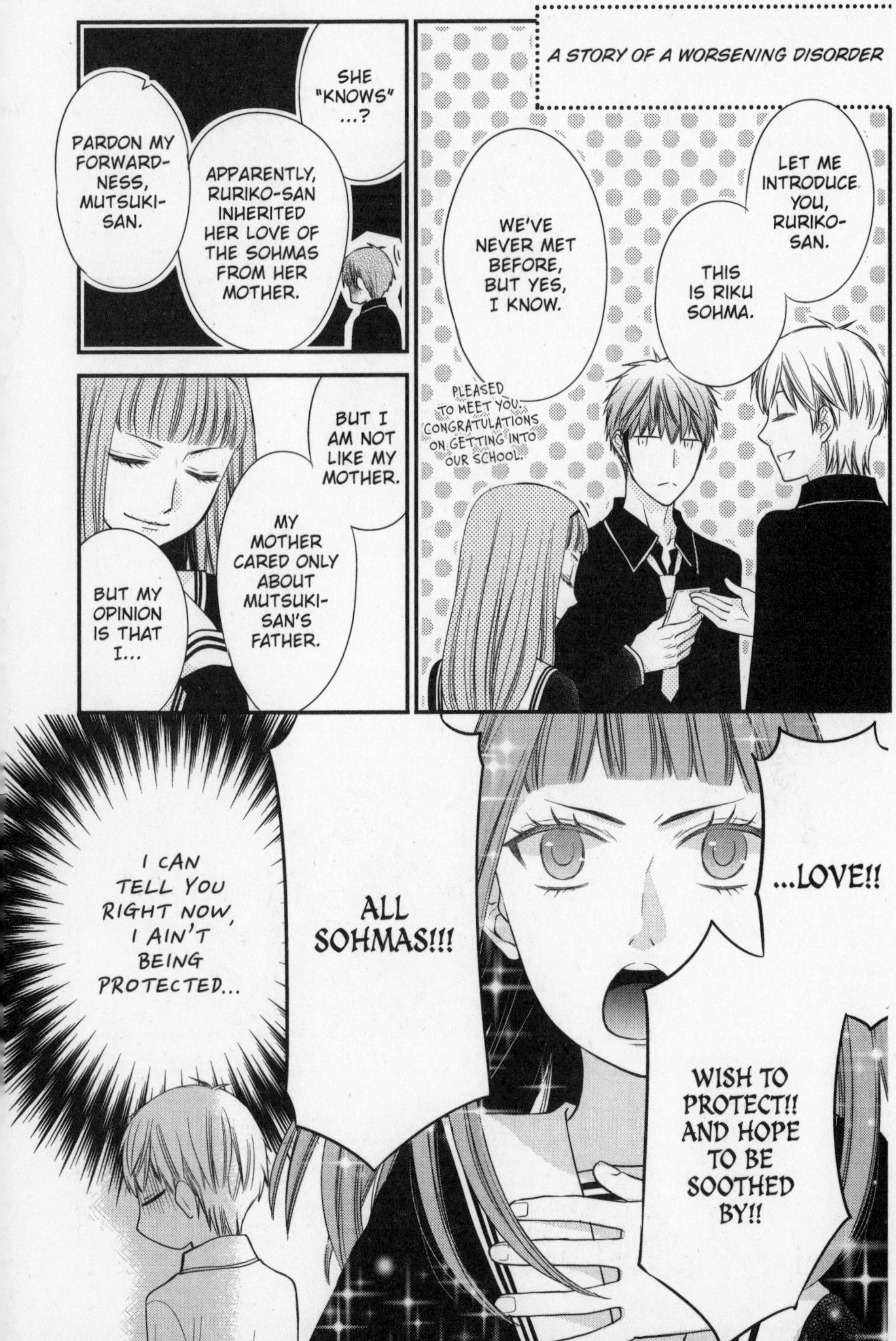
A STORY OF A WORSENING DISORDER
LET ME INTRODUCE YOU, RURIKO-SAN.
THIS IS RIKU SOHMA.
WE'VE NEVER MET BEFORE, BUT YES, I KNOW.
PLEASED TO MEET YOU. CONGRATULATIONS ON GETTING INTO OUR SCHOOL.
SHE "KNOWS" ...?
APPARENTLY, RURIKO-SAN INHERITED HER LOVE OF THE SOHMAS FROM HER MOTHER.
PARDON MY FORWARD-NESS, MUTSUKI-SAN.
BUT I AM NOT LIKE MY MOTHER.
MY MOTHER CARED ONLY ABOUT MUTSUKI-SAN'S FATHER.
BUT MY OPINION IS THAT I...
...LOVE!!
ALL SOHMAS!!!
WISH TO PROTECT!! AND HOPE TO BE SOOTHED BY!!
I CAN TELL YOU RIGHT NOW, I AIN'T BEING PROTECTED...

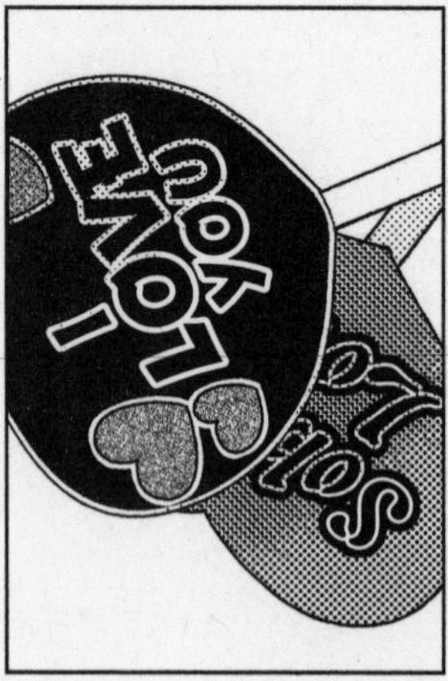
I LOVE YOU

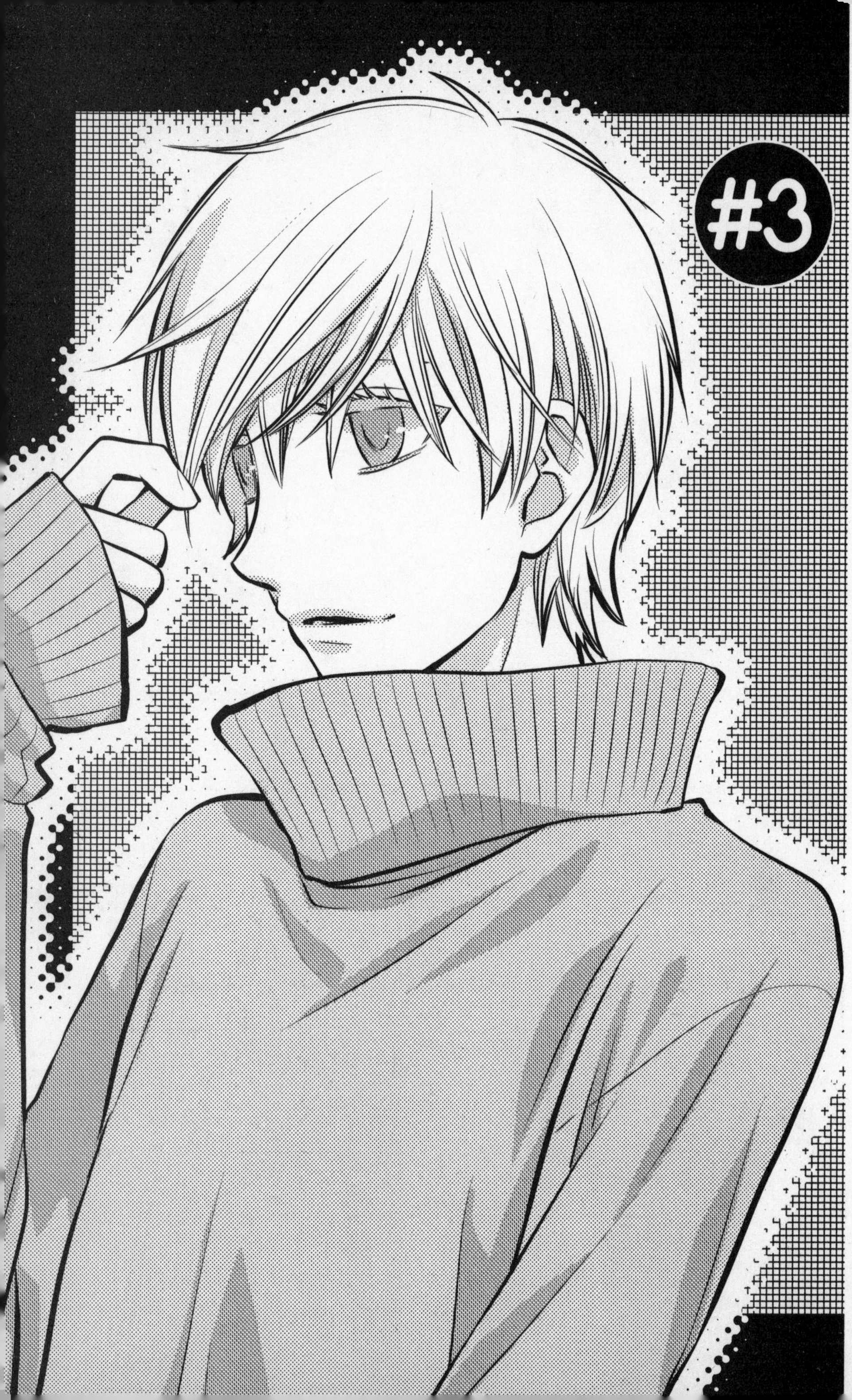
#3

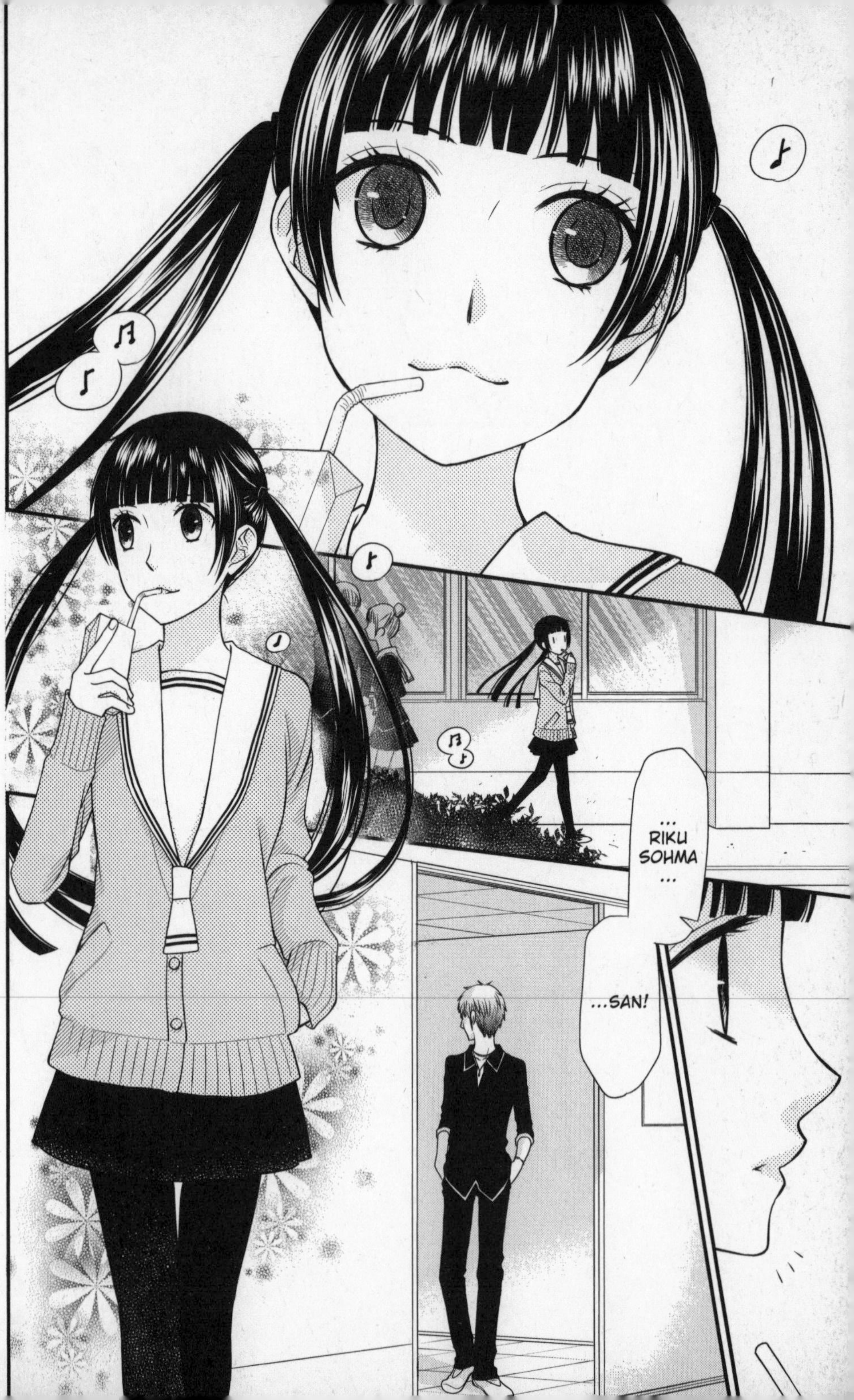
...RIKU SOHMA ...
...SAN!

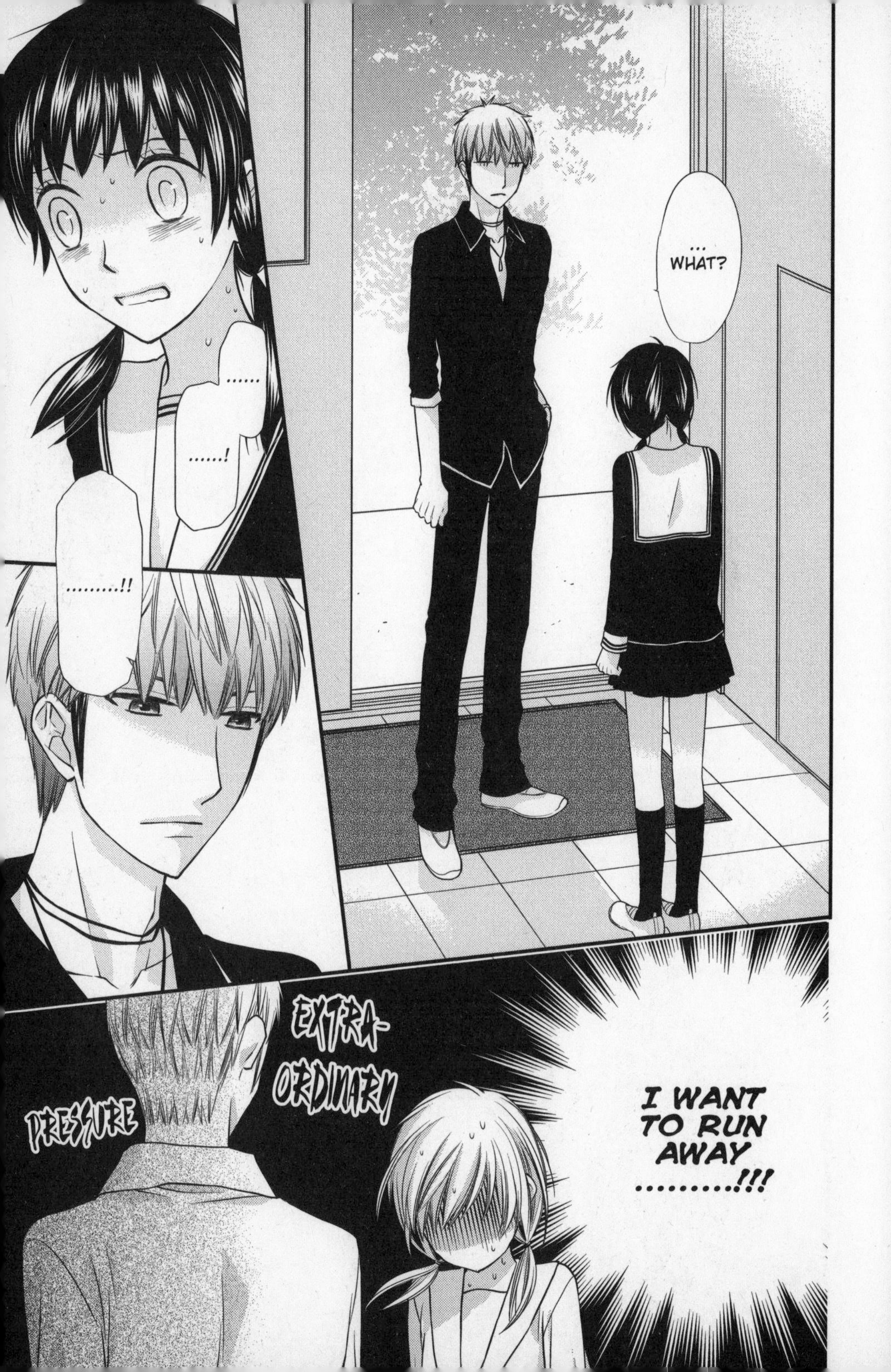
... WHAT?
......
......!
..........!!
I WANT TO RUN AWAY ....!!!
EXTRA-ORDINARY
PRESSURE

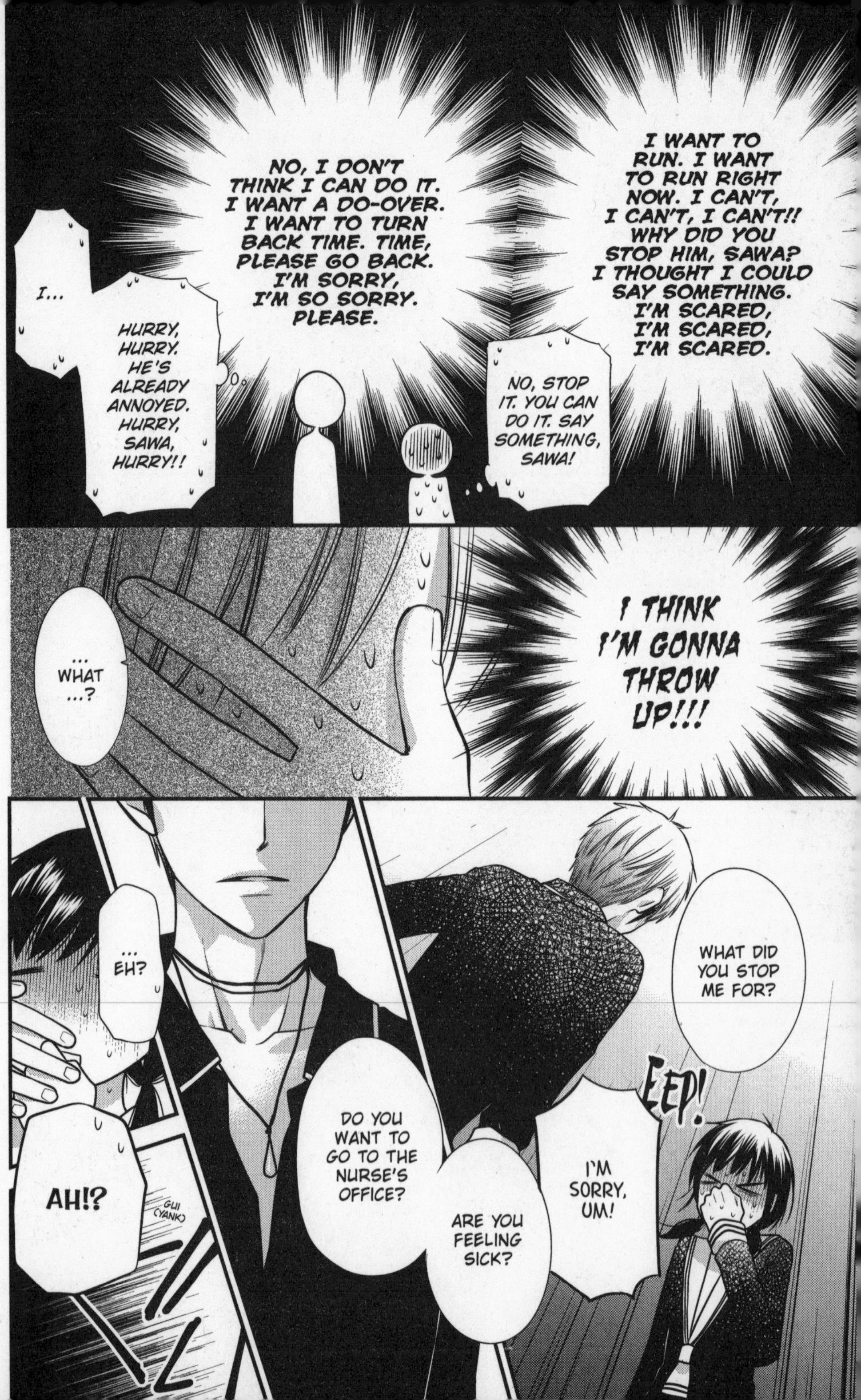
I WANT TO RUN. I WANT TO RUN RIGHT NOW. I CAN'T, I CAN'T, I CAN'T!! WHY DID YOU STOP HIM, SAWA? I THOUGHT I COULD SAY SOMETHING. I'M SCARED, I'M SCARED, I'M SCARED.
NO, I DON'T THINK I CAN DO IT. I WANT A DO-OVER. I WANT TO TURN BACK TIME. TIME, PLEASE GO BACK. I'M SORRY, I'M SO SORRY. PLEASE.
NO, STOP IT. YOU CAN DO IT. SAY SOMETHING, SAWA!
HURRY, HURRY. HE'S ALREADY ANNOYED. HURRY, SAWA, HURRY!!
I...
I THINK I'M GONNA THROW UP!!!
...WHAT...?
WHAT DID YOU STOP ME FOR?
EEP!
I'M SORRY, UM!
...EH?
DO YOU WANT TO GO TO THE NURSE'S OFFICE?
ARE YOU FEELING SICK?
AH!?
GUI (YANK)

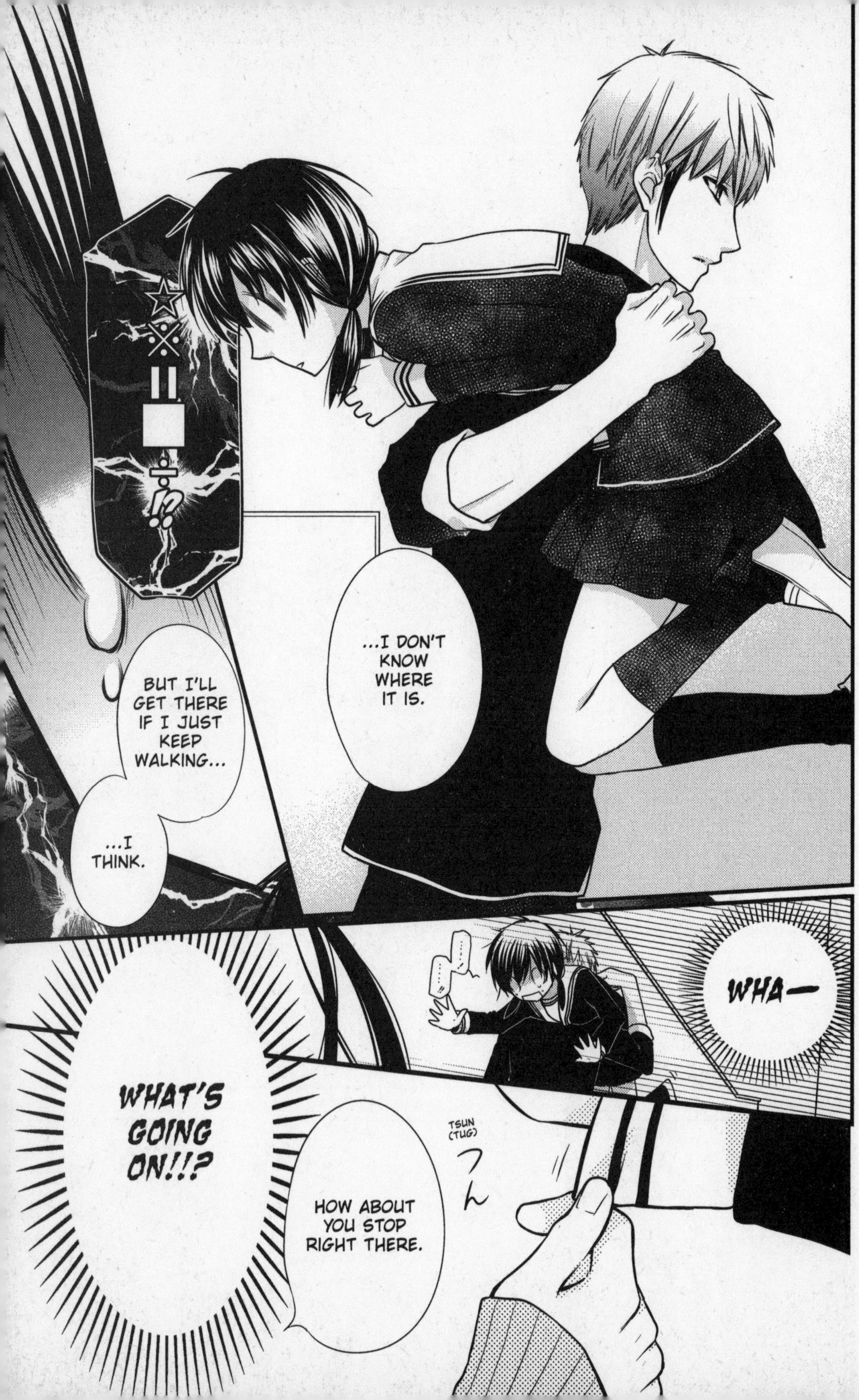
...I DON'T KNOW WHERE IT IS.
BUT I'LL GET THERE IF I JUST KEEP WALKING...
...I THINK.
WHA—
WHAT'S GOING ON!!?
TSUN (TUG)
HOW ABOUT YOU STOP RIGHT THERE.

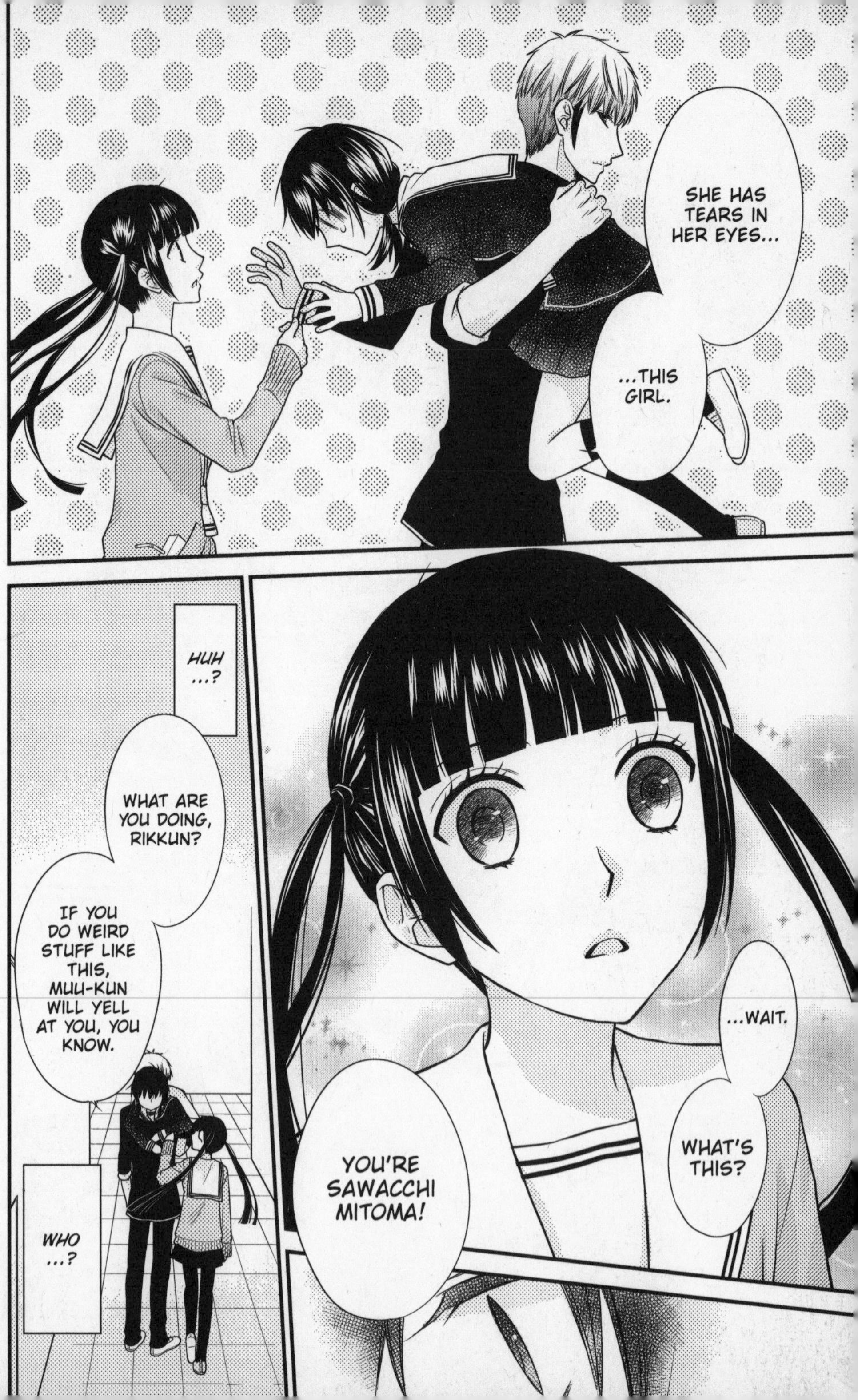
SHE HAS TEARS IN HER EYES...
...THIS GIRL.
...WAIT.
WHAT'S THIS?
YOU'RE SAWACCHI MITOMA!
HUH ...?
WHAT ARE YOU DOING, RIKKUN?
IF YOU DO WEIRD STUFF LIKE THIS, MUU-KUN WILL YELL AT YOU, YOU KNOW.
WHO ...?

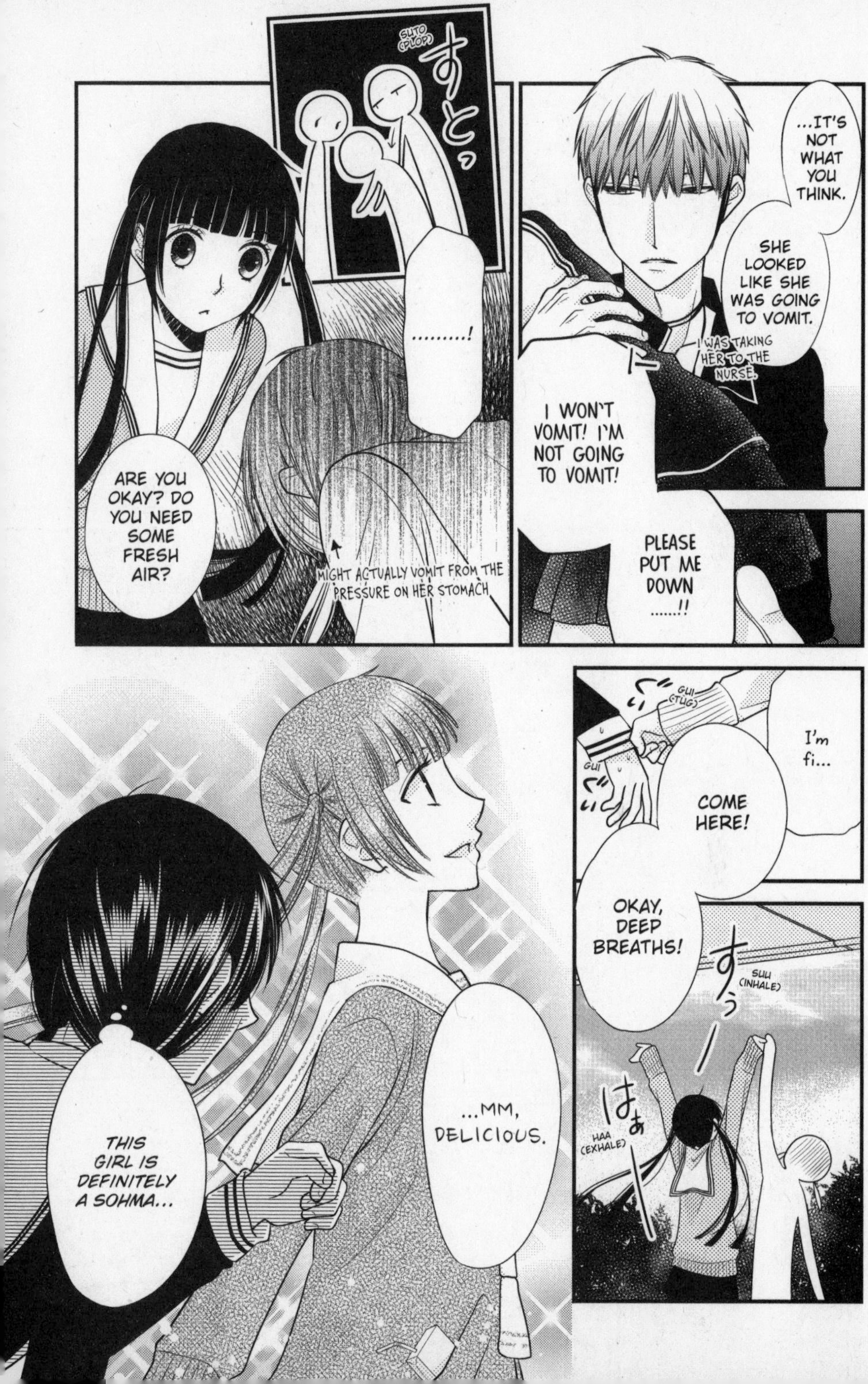
...IT'S NOT WHAT YOU THINK.
SHE LOOKED LIKE SHE WAS GOING TO VOMIT.
I WAS TAKING HER TO THE NURSE.
I WON'T VOMIT! I'M NOT GOING TO VOMIT!
PLEASE PUT ME DOWN ......!!
SUTO (PLOP)
..........!
ARE YOU OKAY? DO YOU NEED SOME FRESH AIR?
MIGHT ACTUALLY VOMIT FROM THE PRESSURE ON HER STOMACH
GUI (TUG)
GUI
I'm fi...
COME HERE!
OKAY, DEEP BREATHS!
SUU (INHALE)
HAA (EXHALE)
...MM, DELICIOUS.
THIS GIRL IS DEFINITELY A SOHMA...

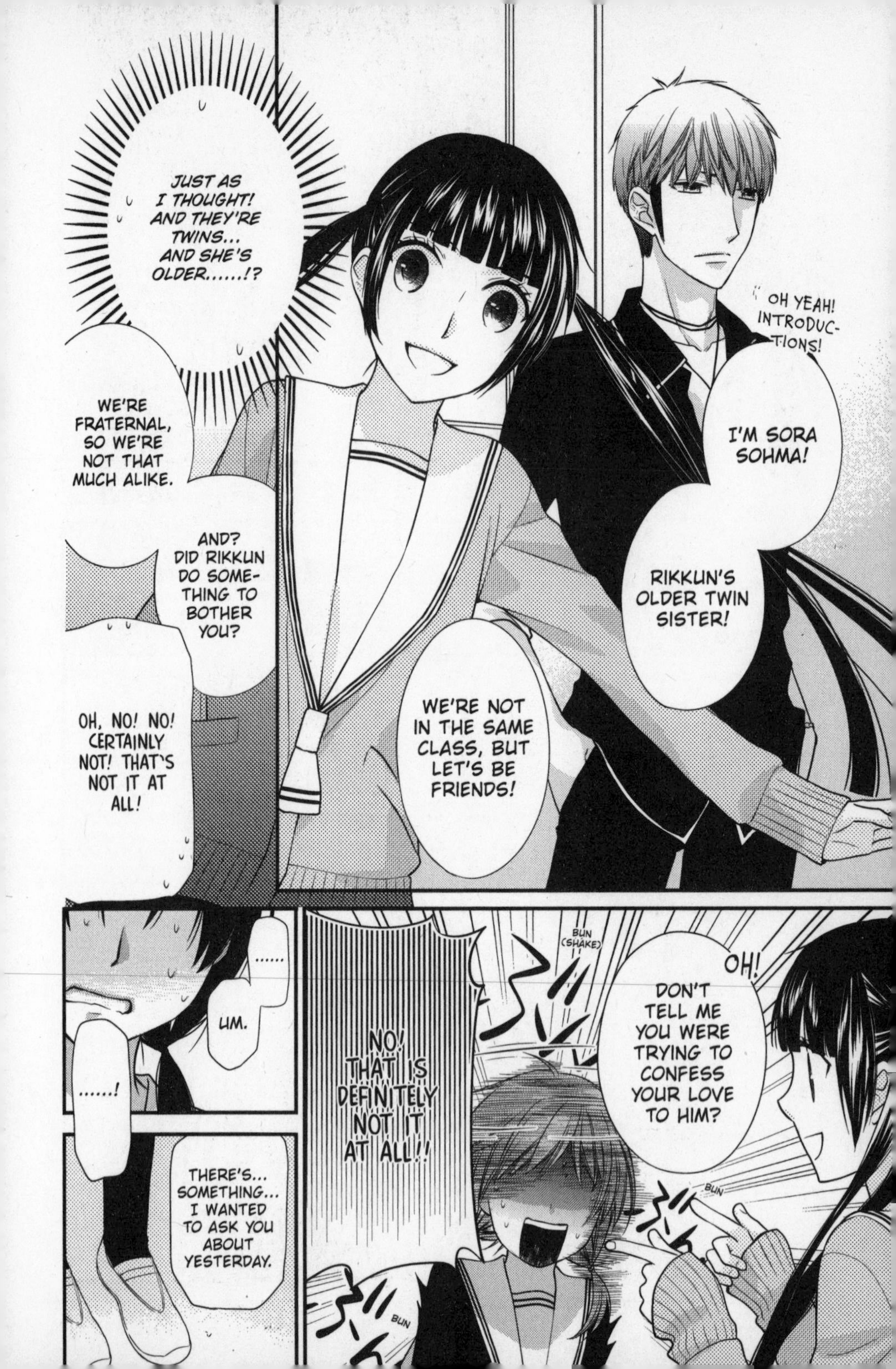
OH YEAH! INTRODUCTIONS!
I'M SORA SOHMA!
RIKKUN'S OLDER TWIN SISTER!
WE'RE NOT IN THE SAME CLASS, BUT LET'S BE FRIENDS!
JUST AS I THOUGHT! AND THEY'RE TWINS... AND SHE'S OLDER......!?
WE'RE FRATERNAL, SO WE'RE NOT THAT MUCH ALIKE.
AND? DID RIKKUN DO SOMETHING TO BOTHER YOU?
OH, NO! NO! CERTAINLY NOT! THAT'S NOT IT AT ALL!
OH!
DON'T TELL ME YOU WERE TRYING TO CONFESS YOUR LOVE TO HIM?
BUN (SHAKE)
BUN
NO! THAT IS DEFINITELY NOT IT AT ALL!!
BUN
......
UM.
......!
THERE'S... SOMETHING... I WANTED TO ASK YOU ABOUT YESTERDAY.

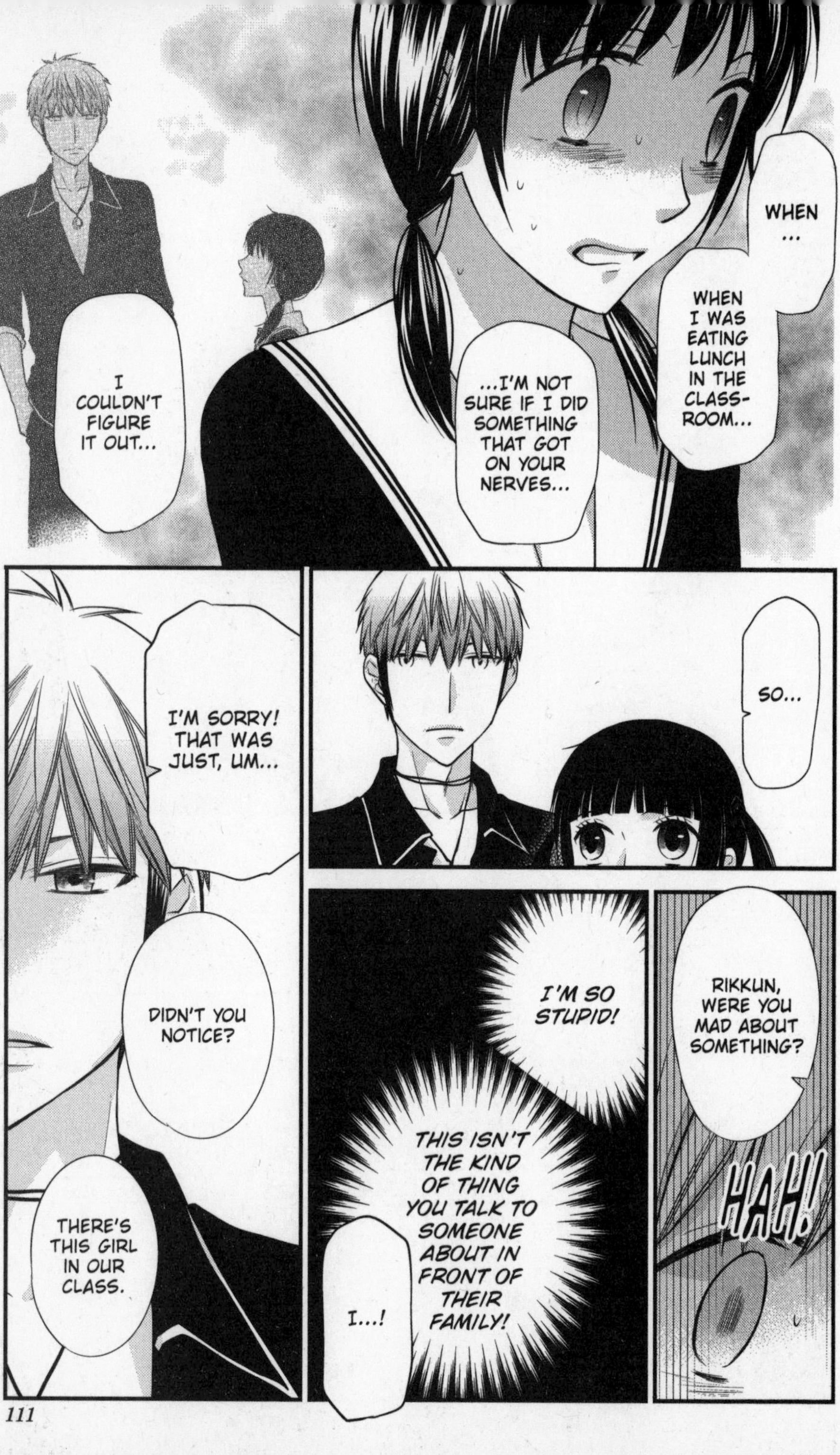
WHEN ...
WHEN I WAS EATING LUNCH IN THE CLASS-ROOM...
...I'M NOT SURE IF I DID SOMETHING THAT GOT ON YOUR NERVES...
I COULDN'T FIGURE IT OUT...
SO...
RIKKUN, WERE YOU MAD ABOUT SOMETHING?
HAH!
I'M SO STUPID!
THIS ISN'T THE KIND OF THING YOU TALK TO SOMEONE ABOUT IN FRONT OF THEIR FAMILY!
I...!
I'M SORRY! THAT WAS JUST, UM...
DIDN'T YOU NOTICE?
THERE'S THIS GIRL IN OUR CLASS.

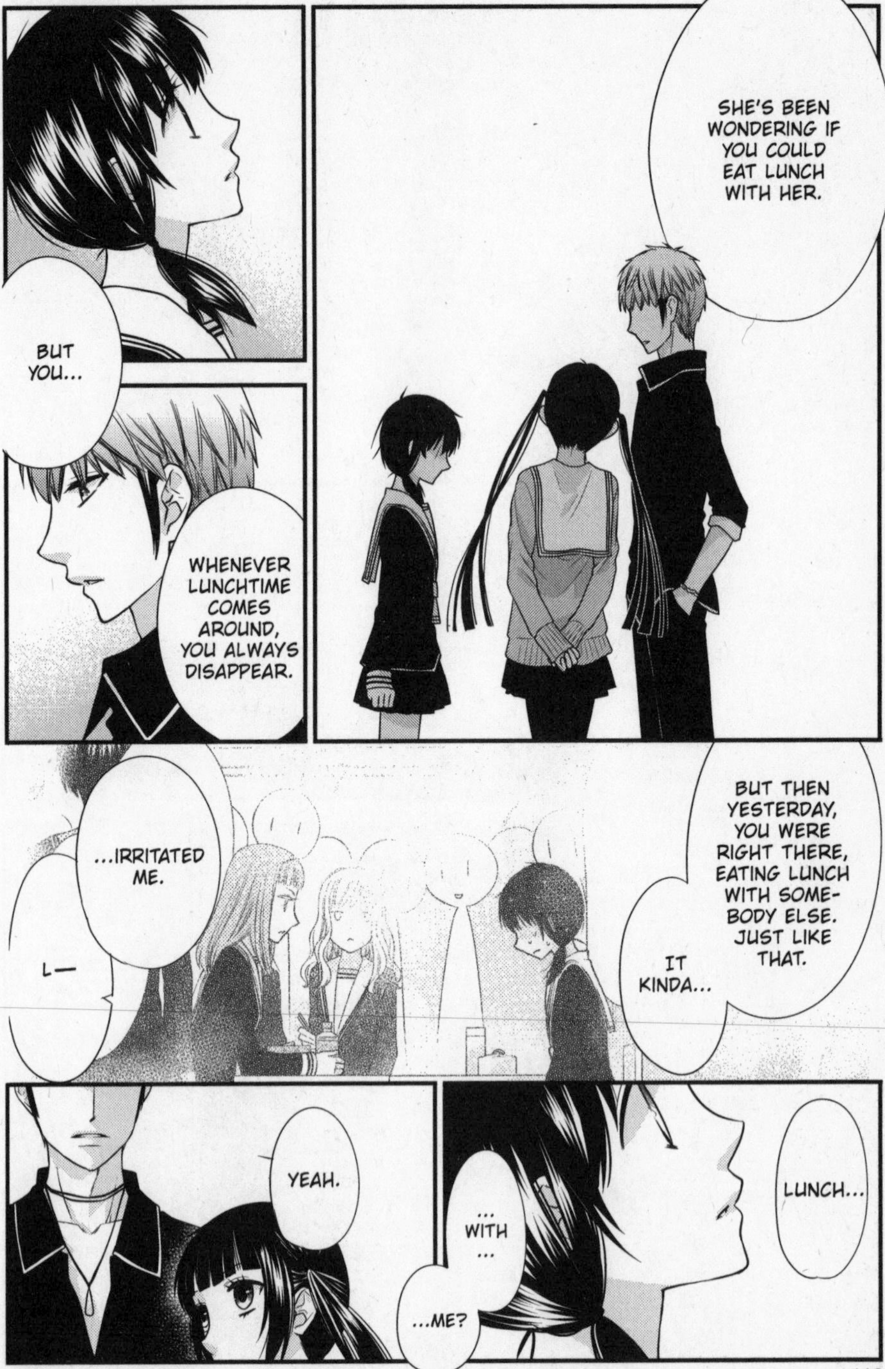
SHE'S BEEN WONDERING IF YOU COULD EAT LUNCH WITH HER.
BUT YOU...
WHENEVER LUNCHTIME COMES AROUND, YOU ALWAYS DISAPPEAR.
BUT THEN YESTERDAY, YOU WERE RIGHT THERE, EATING LUNCH WITH SOME-BODY ELSE. JUST LIKE THAT.
IT KINDA...
...IRRITATED ME.
I—
LUNCH...
...WITH...
...ME?
YEAH.

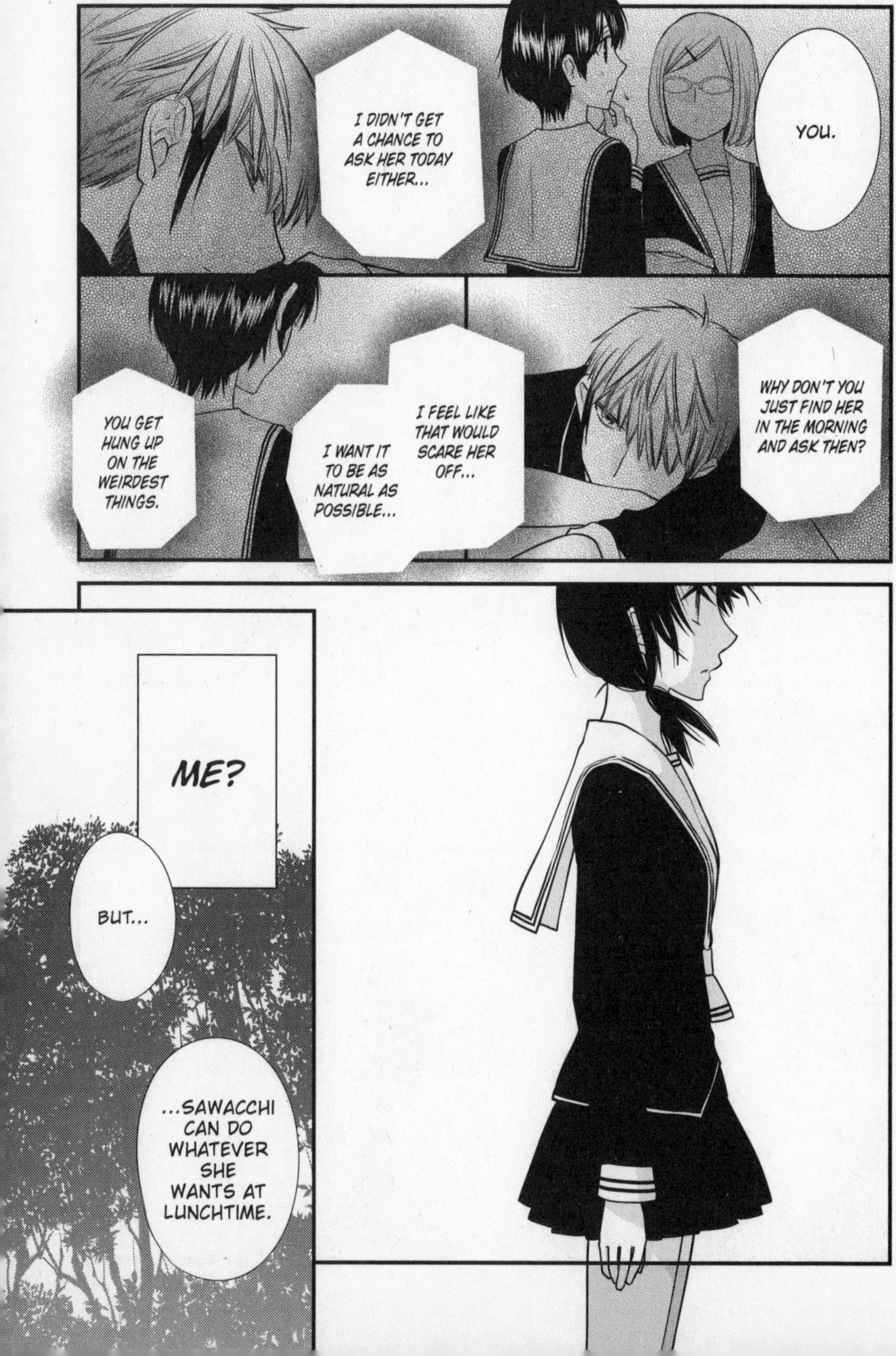
YOU.
I DIDN'T GET A CHANCE TO ASK HER TODAY EITHER...
WHY DON'T YOU JUST FIND HER IN THE MORNING AND ASK THEN?
I FEEL LIKE THAT WOULD SCARE HER OFF...
I WANT IT TO BE AS NATURAL AS POSSIBLE...
YOU GET HUNG UP ON THE WEIRDEST THINGS.
ME?
BUT...
...SAWACCHI CAN DO WHATEVER SHE WANTS AT LUNCHTIME.

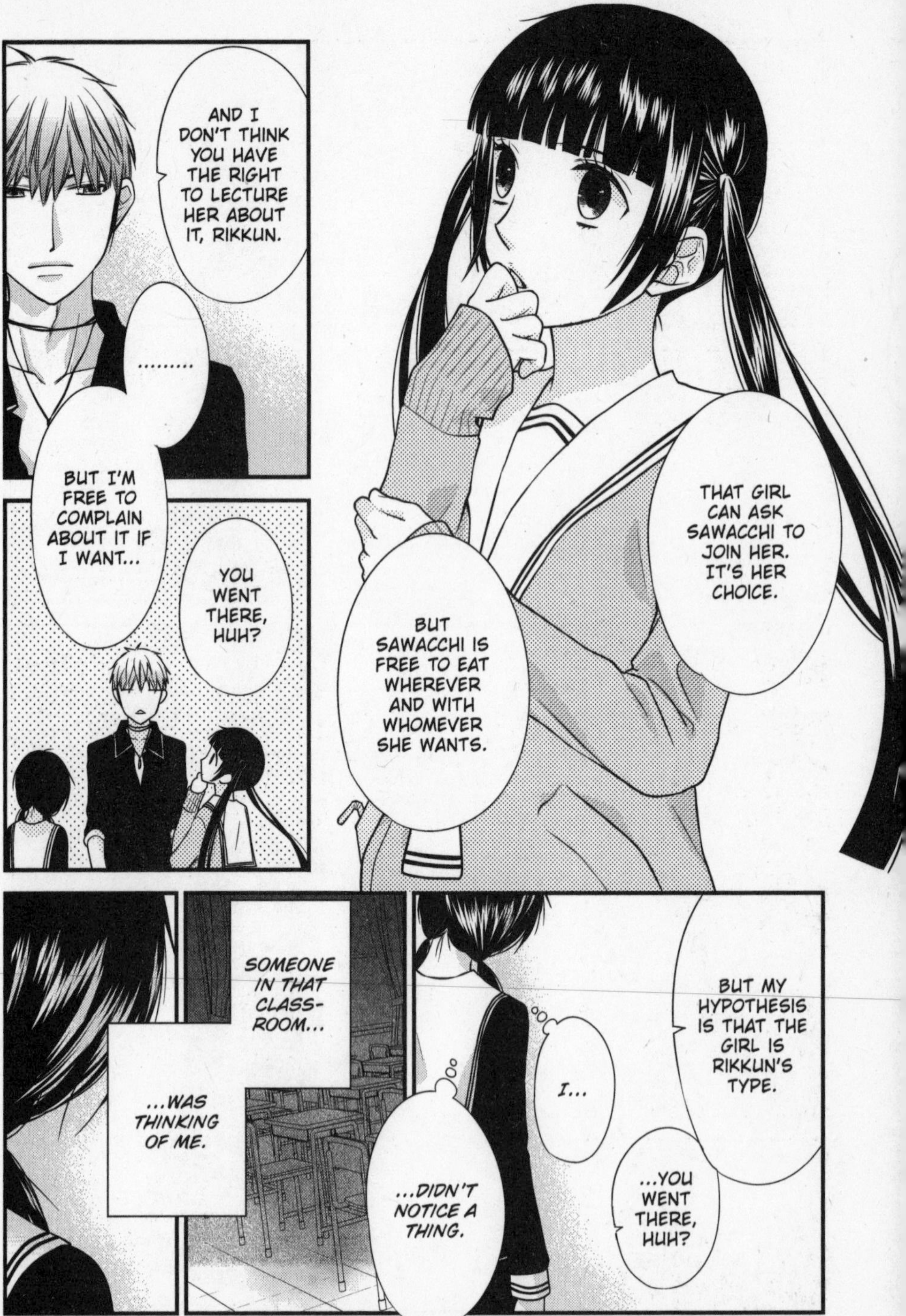
THAT GIRL CAN ASK SAWACCHI TO JOIN HER. IT'S HER CHOICE.
BUT SAWACCHI IS FREE TO EAT WHEREVER AND WITH WHOMEVER SHE WANTS.
AND I DON'T THINK YOU HAVE THE RIGHT TO LECTURE HER ABOUT IT, RIKKUN.
....
BUT I'M FREE TO COMPLAIN ABOUT IT IF I WANT...
YOU WENT THERE, HUH?
BUT MY HYPOTHESIS IS THAT THE GIRL IS RIKKUN'S TYPE.
I...
...YOU WENT THERE, HUH?
...DIDN'T NOTICE A THING.
SOMEONE IN THAT CLASS-ROOM...
...WAS THINKING OF ME.

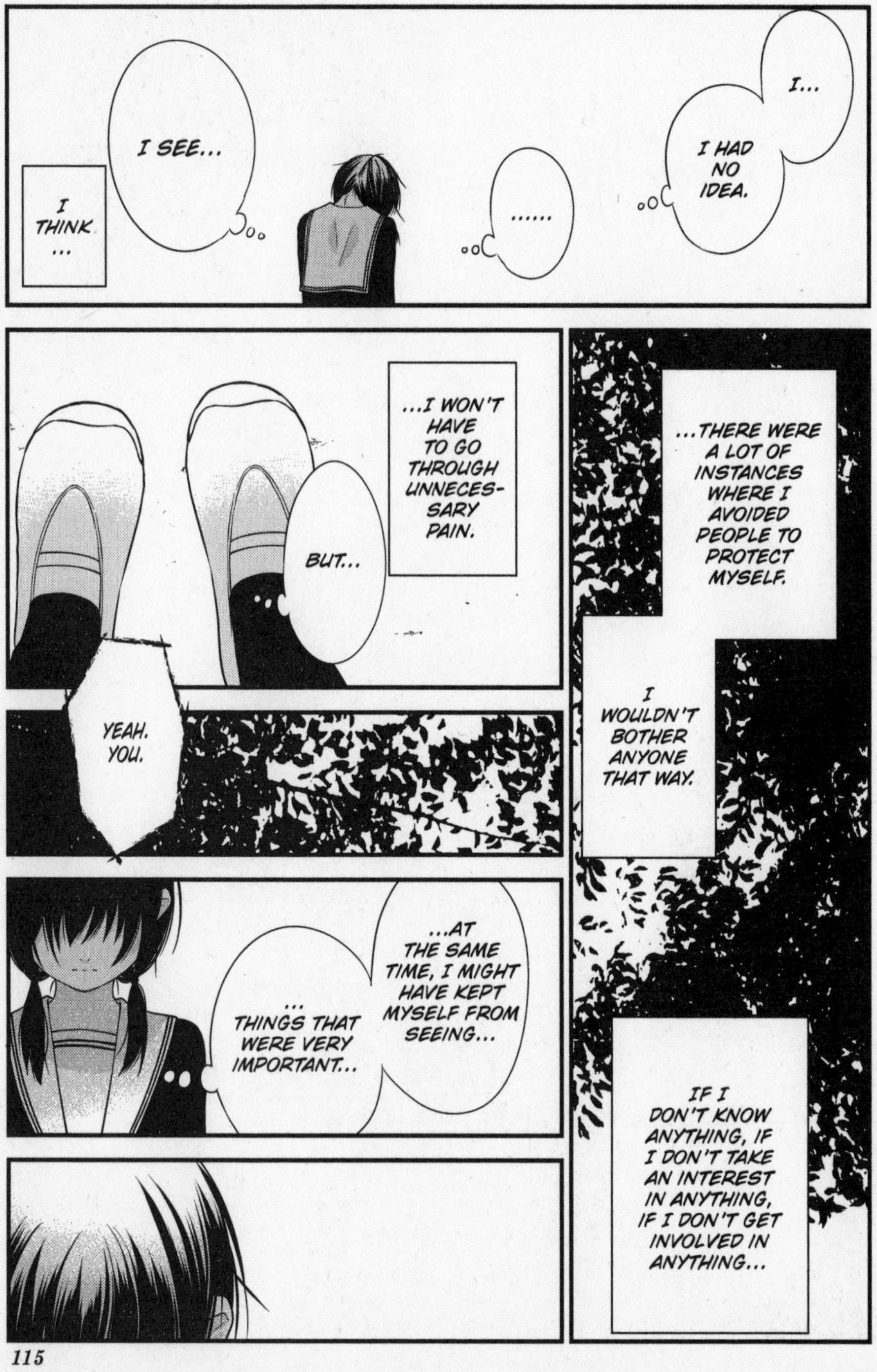
I...
I HAD NO IDEA.
......
I SEE...
I THINK...
...THERE WERE A LOT OF INSTANCES WHERE I AVOIDED PEOPLE TO PROTECT MYSELF.
I WOULDN'T BOTHER ANYONE THAT WAY.
IF I DON'T KNOW ANYTHING, IF I DON'T TAKE AN INTEREST IN ANYTHING, IF I DON'T GET INVOLVED IN ANYTHING...
...I WON'T HAVE TO GO THROUGH UNNECESSARY PAIN.
BUT...
YEAH. YOU.
...AT THE SAME TIME, I MIGHT HAVE KEPT MYSELF FROM SEEING...
...THINGS THAT WERE VERY IMPORTANT...

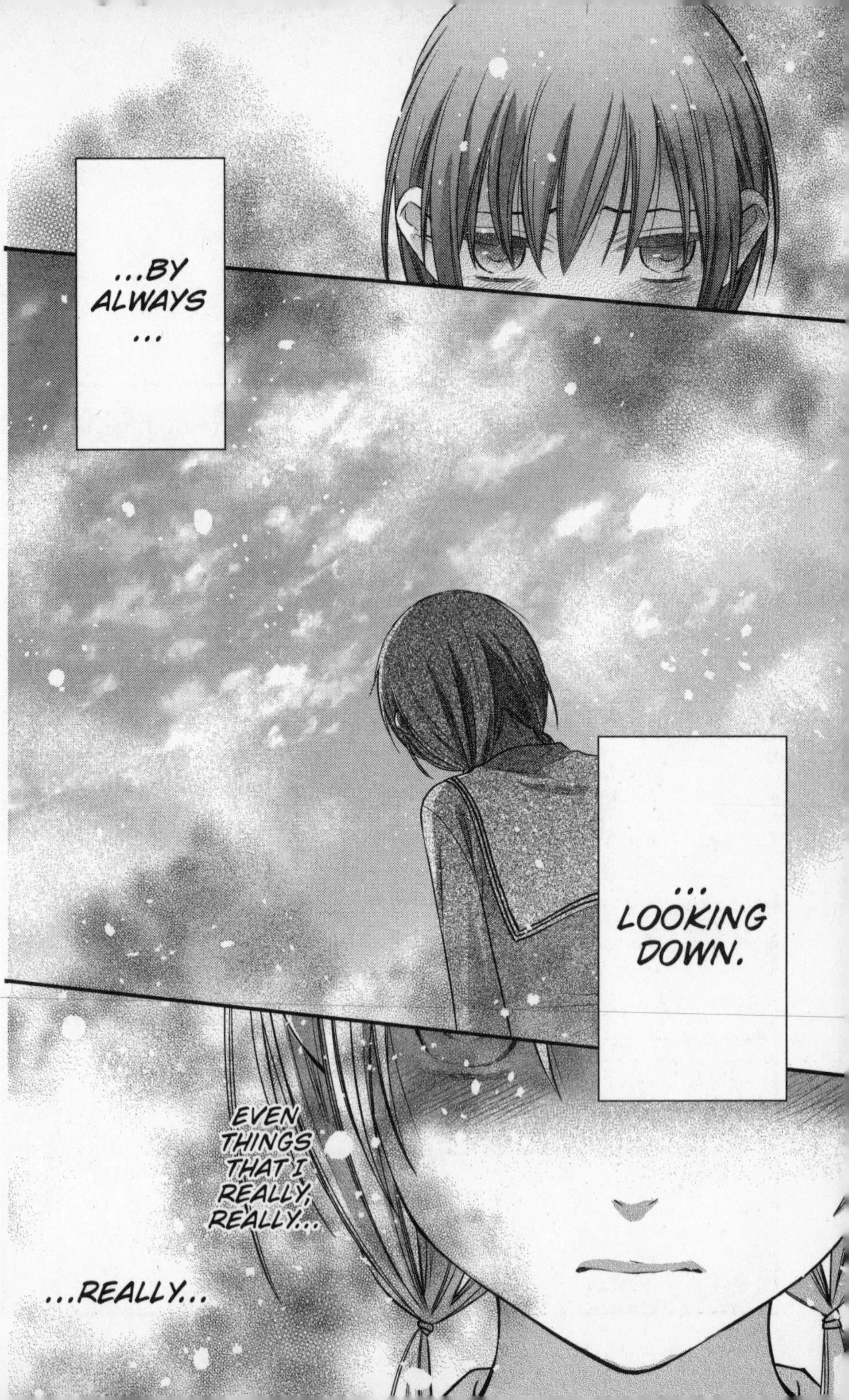
...BY ALWAYS ...
... LOOKING DOWN.
EVEN THINGS THAT I REALLY, REALLY...
...REALLY...

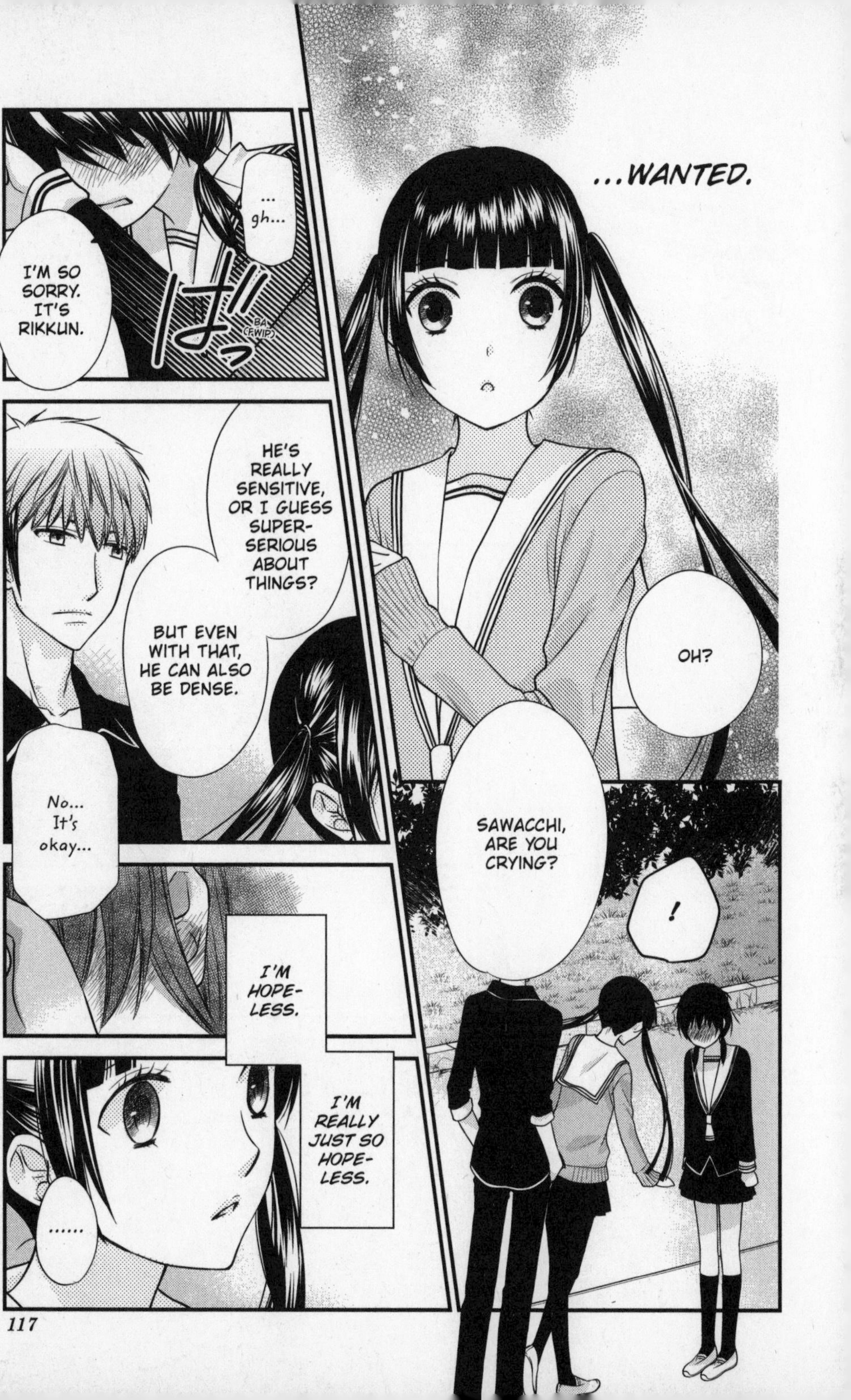
...WANTED.
OH?
SAWACCHI, ARE YOU CRYING?
!
... gh...
BA (FWIP)
I'M SO SORRY. IT'S RIKKUN.
HE'S REALLY SENSITIVE, OR I GUESS SUPER-SERIOUS ABOUT THINGS?
BUT EVEN WITH THAT, HE CAN ALSO BE DENSE.
No... It's okay...
I'M HOPE-LESS.
I'M REALLY JUST SO HOPE-LESS.
......

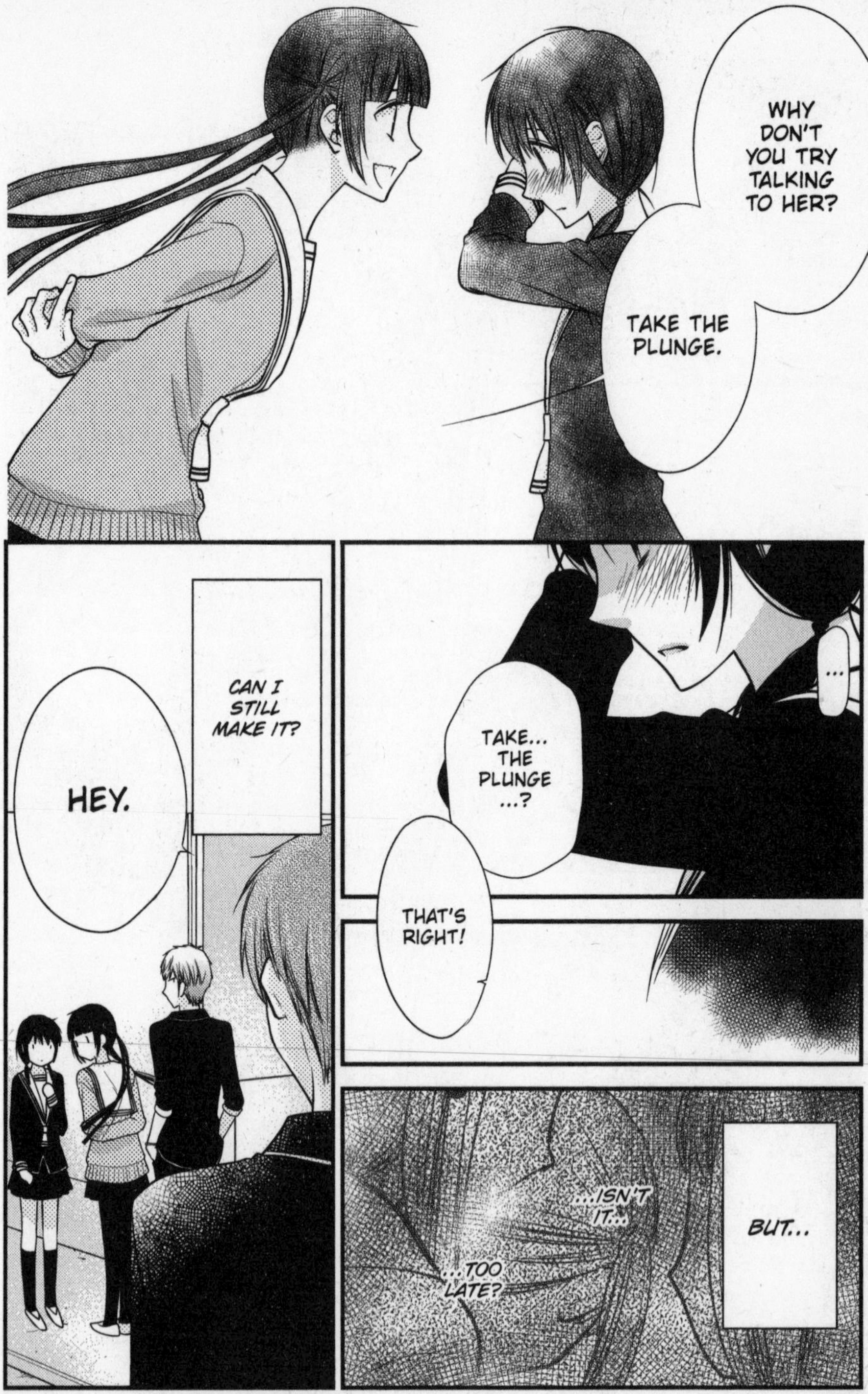
WHY DON'T YOU TRY TALKING TO HER?
TAKE THE PLUNGE.
...
TAKE... THE PLUNGE ...?
THAT'S RIGHT!
BUT...
...ISN'T IT...
...TOO LATE?
CAN I STILL MAKE IT?
HEY.

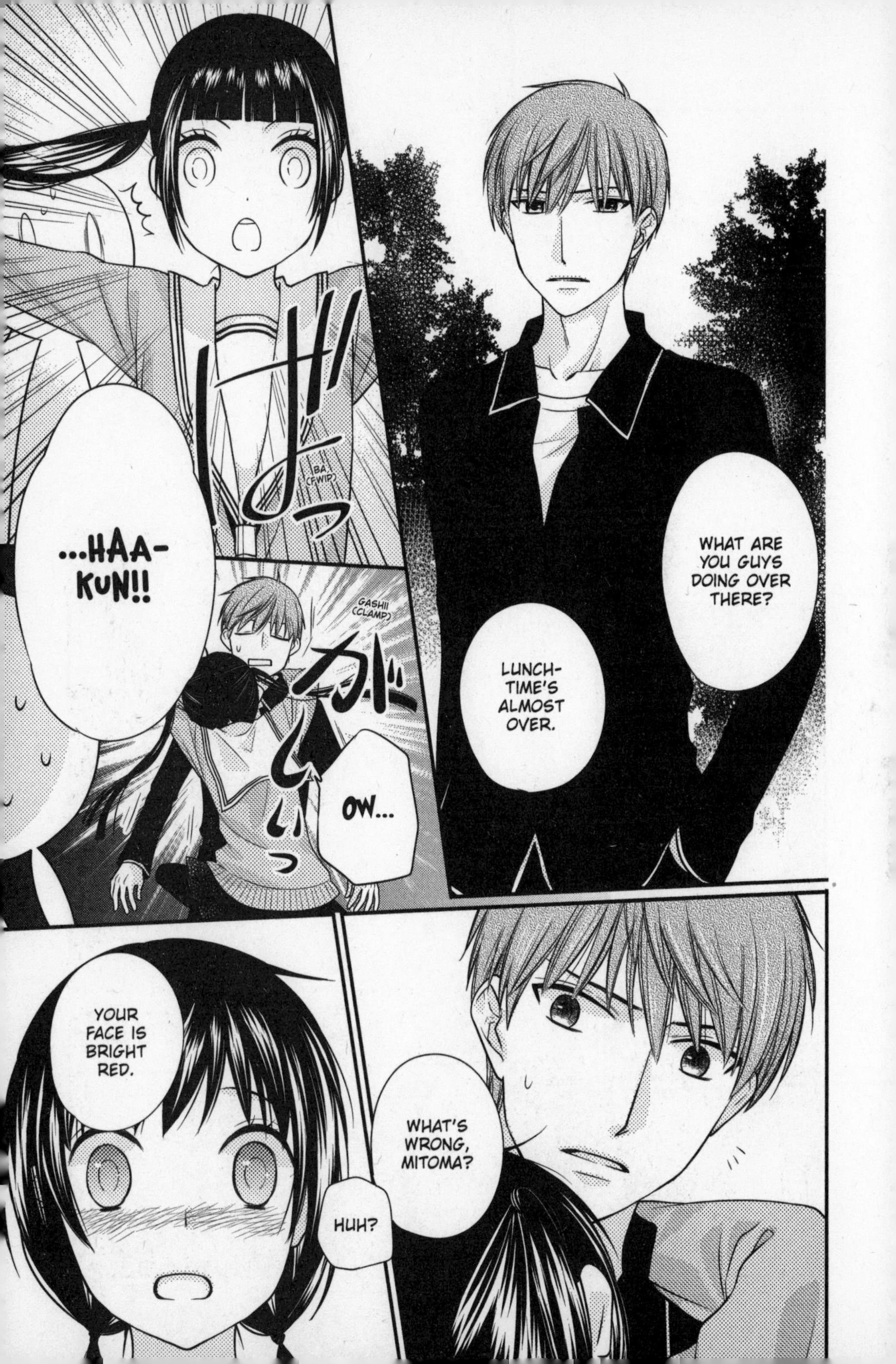
WHAT ARE YOU GUYS DOING OVER THERE?
LUNCH-TIME'S ALMOST OVER.
BA (FWIP)
...HAA-KUN!!
GASHII (CLAMP)
OW...
WHAT'S WRONG, MITOMA?
YOUR FACE IS BRIGHT RED.
HUH?

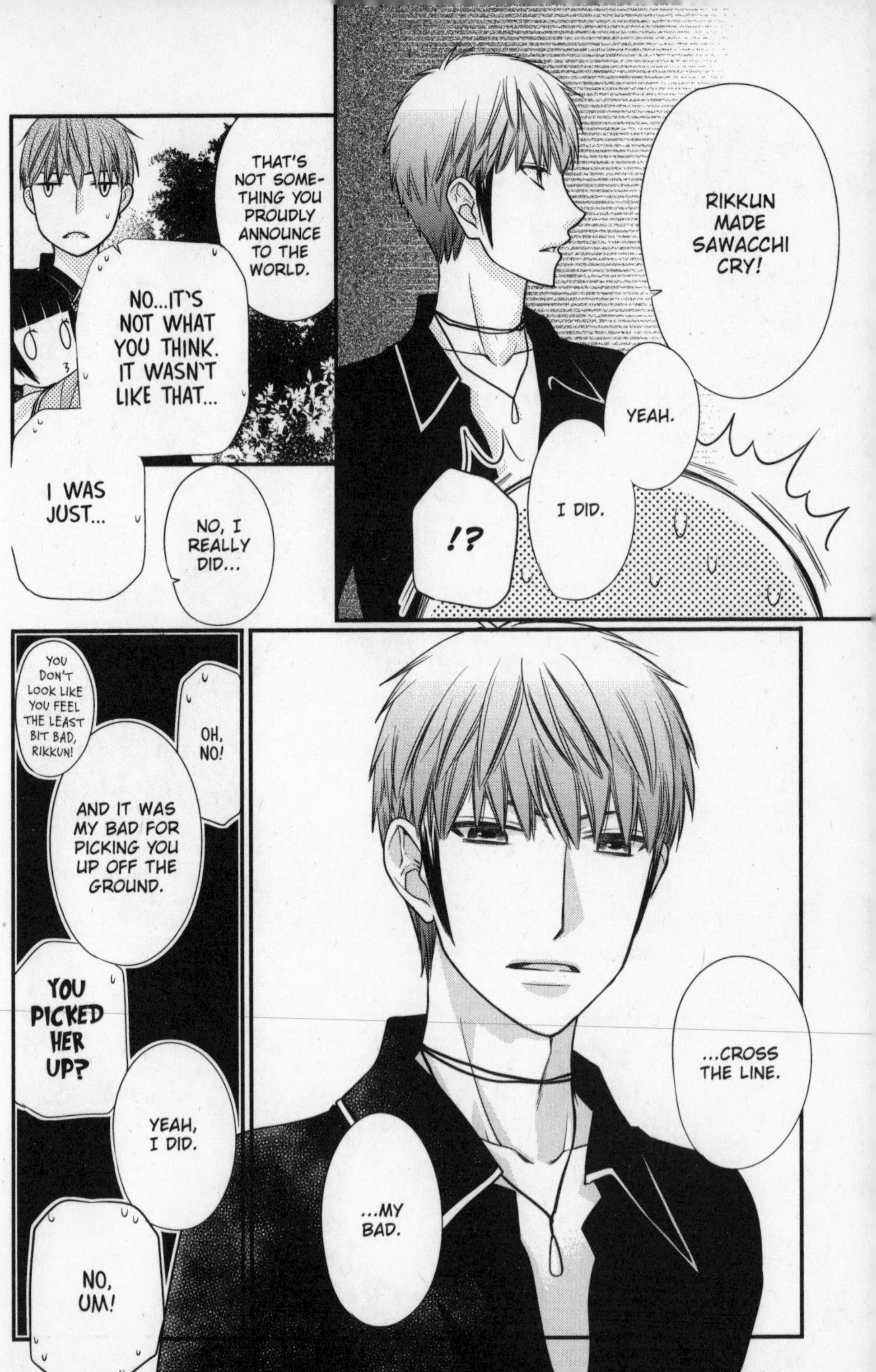
RIKKUN MADE SAWACCHI CRY!
YEAH.
I DID.
!?
THAT'S NOT SOME-THING YOU PROUDLY ANNOUNCE TO THE WORLD.
NO...IT'S NOT WHAT YOU THINK. IT WASN'T LIKE THAT...
NO, I REALLY DID...
I WAS JUST...
...CROSS THE LINE.
...MY BAD.
OH, NO!
YOU DON'T LOOK LIKE YOU FEEL THE LEAST BIT BAD, RIKKUN!
AND IT WAS MY BAD FOR PICKING YOU UP OFF THE GROUND.
YOU PICKED HER UP?
YEAH, I DID.
NO, UM!

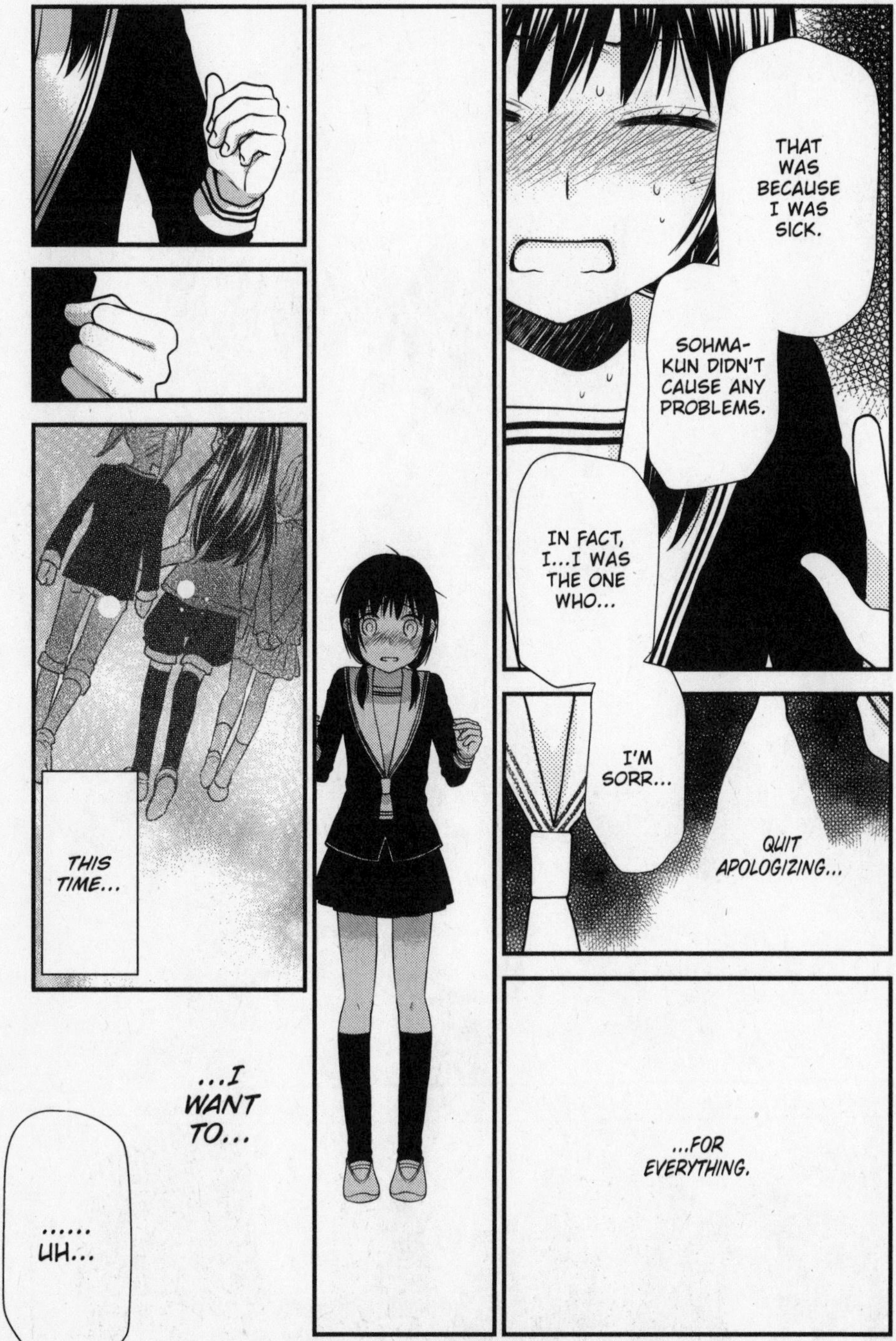
THAT WAS BECAUSE I WAS SICK.
SOHMA-KUN DIDN'T CAUSE ANY PROBLEMS.
IN FACT, I...I WAS THE ONE WHO...
I'M SORR...
QUIT APOLOGIZING...
...FOR EVERYTHING.
THIS TIME...
...I WANT TO...
...... UH...

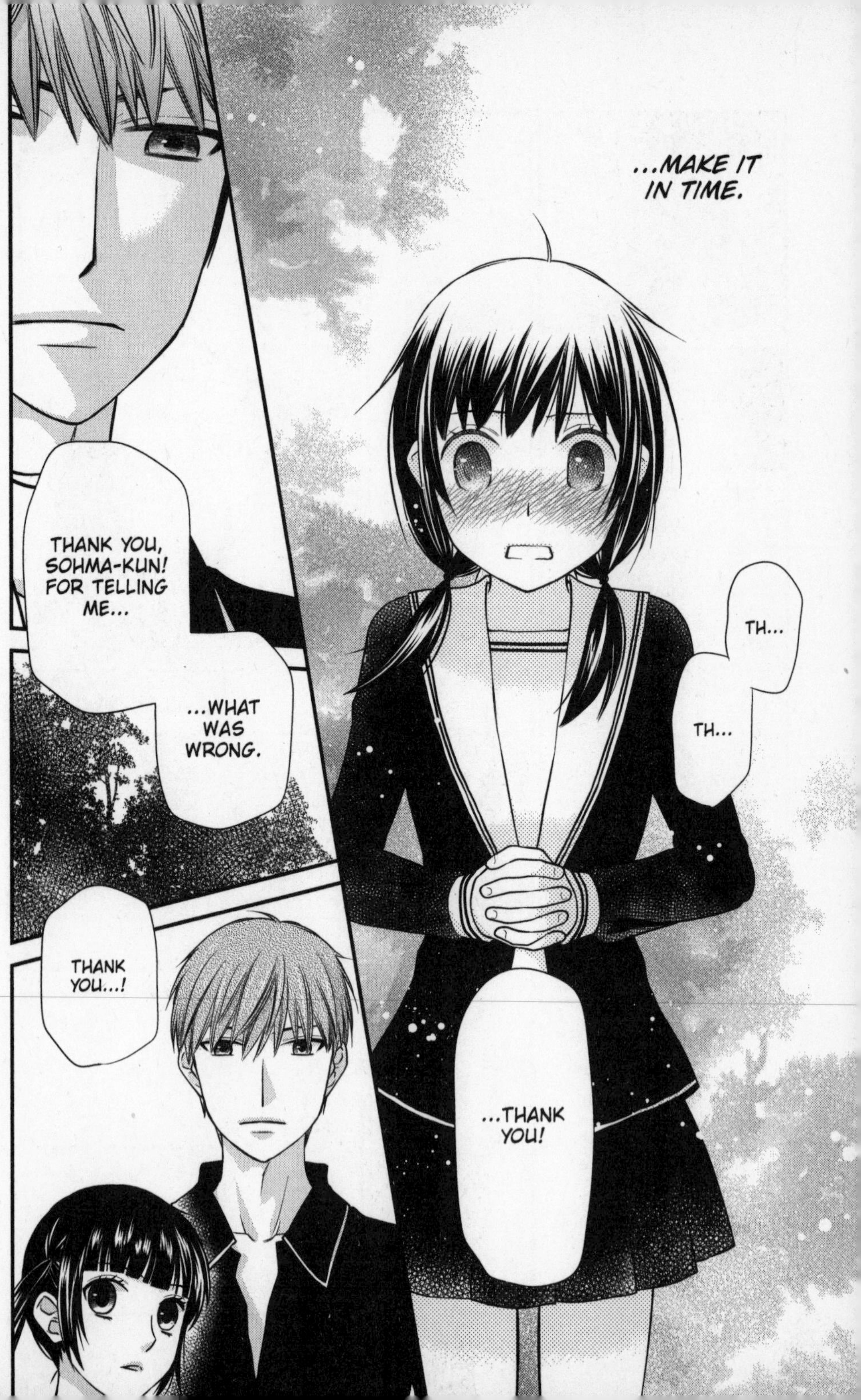
...MAKE IT IN TIME.
TH...
TH...
...THANK YOU!
THANK YOU, SOHMA-KUN! FOR TELLING ME...
...WHAT WAS WRONG.
THANK YOU...!

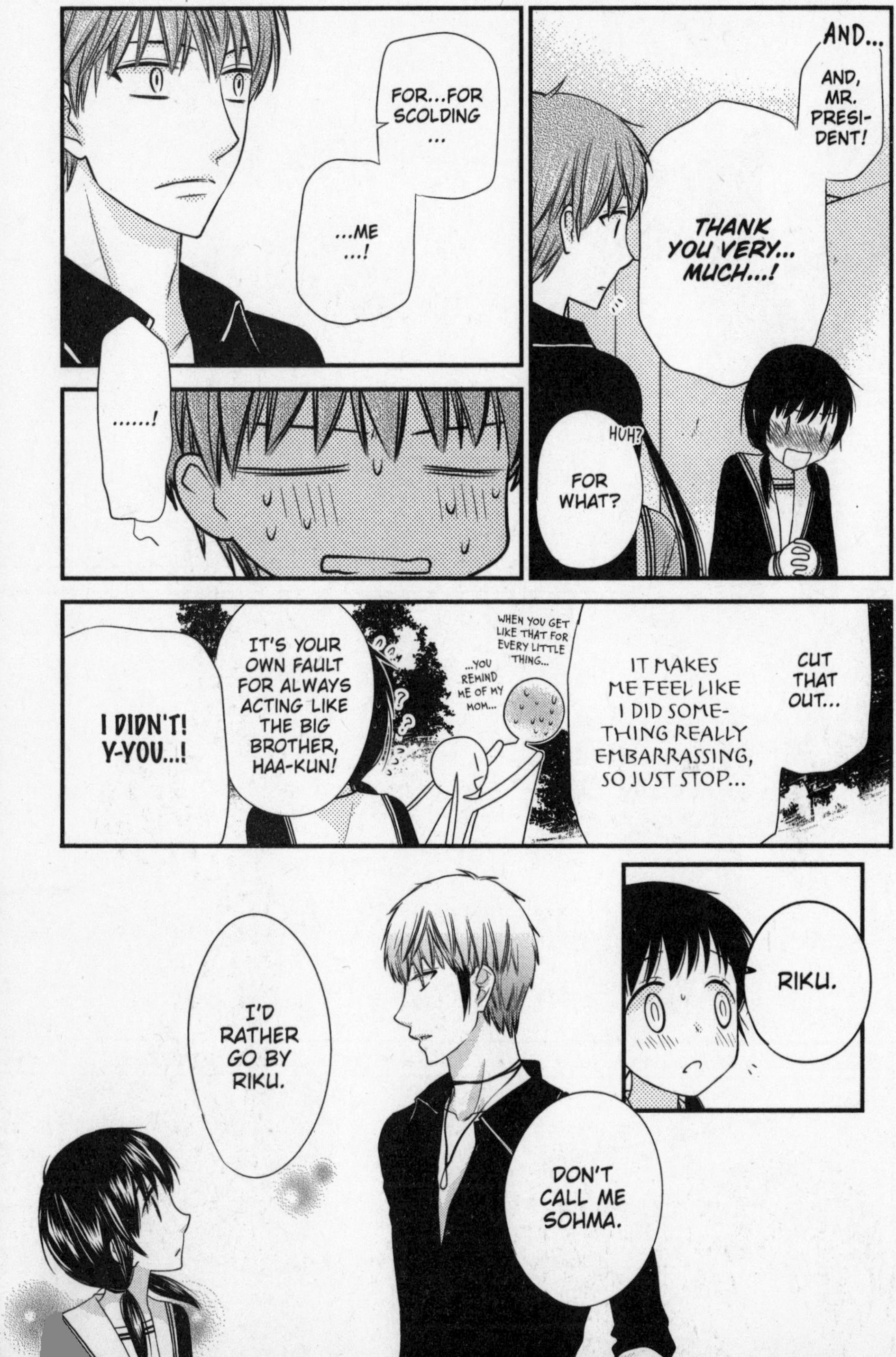
AND...
AND, MR. PRESIDENT!
THANK YOU VERY... MUCH...!
HUH?
FOR WHAT?
FOR...FOR SCOLDING ...
...ME ...!
......!
CUT THAT OUT...
IT MAKES ME FEEL LIKE I DID SOME-THING REALLY EMBARRASSING, SO JUST STOP...
WHEN YOU GET LIKE THAT FOR EVERY LITTLE THING...
...YOU REMIND ME OF MY MOM...
IT'S YOUR OWN FAULT FOR ALWAYS ACTING LIKE THE BIG BROTHER, HAA-KUN!
I DIDN'T! Y-YOU...!
RIKU.
DON'T CALL ME SOHMA.
I'D RATHER GO BY RIKU.

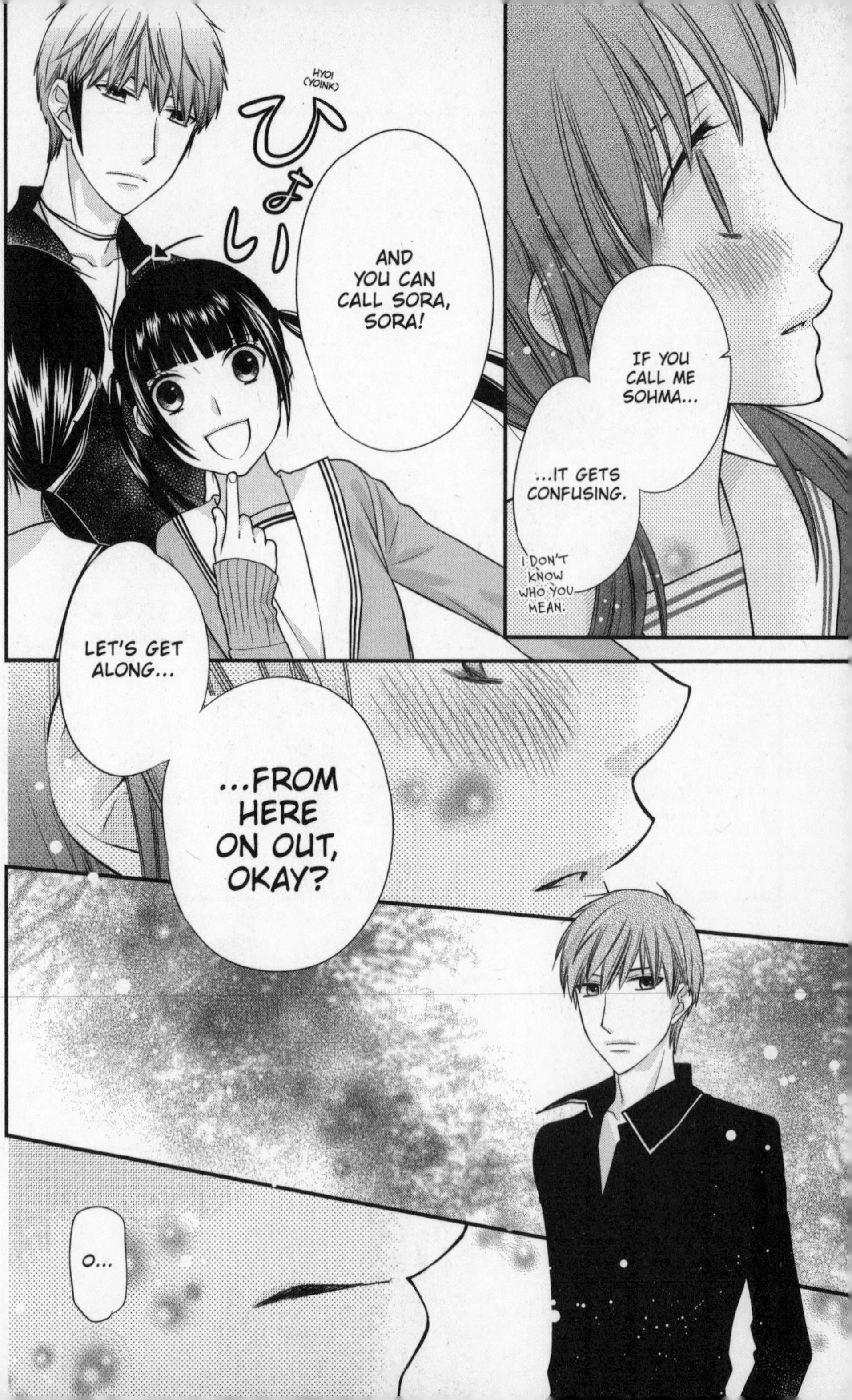
IF YOU CALL ME SOHMA...
...IT GETS CONFUSING.
I DON'T KNOW WHO YOU MEAN.
ひょい
HYOI (YOINK)
AND YOU CAN CALL SORA, SORA!
LET'S GET ALONG...
...FROM HERE ON OUT, OKAY?
O...

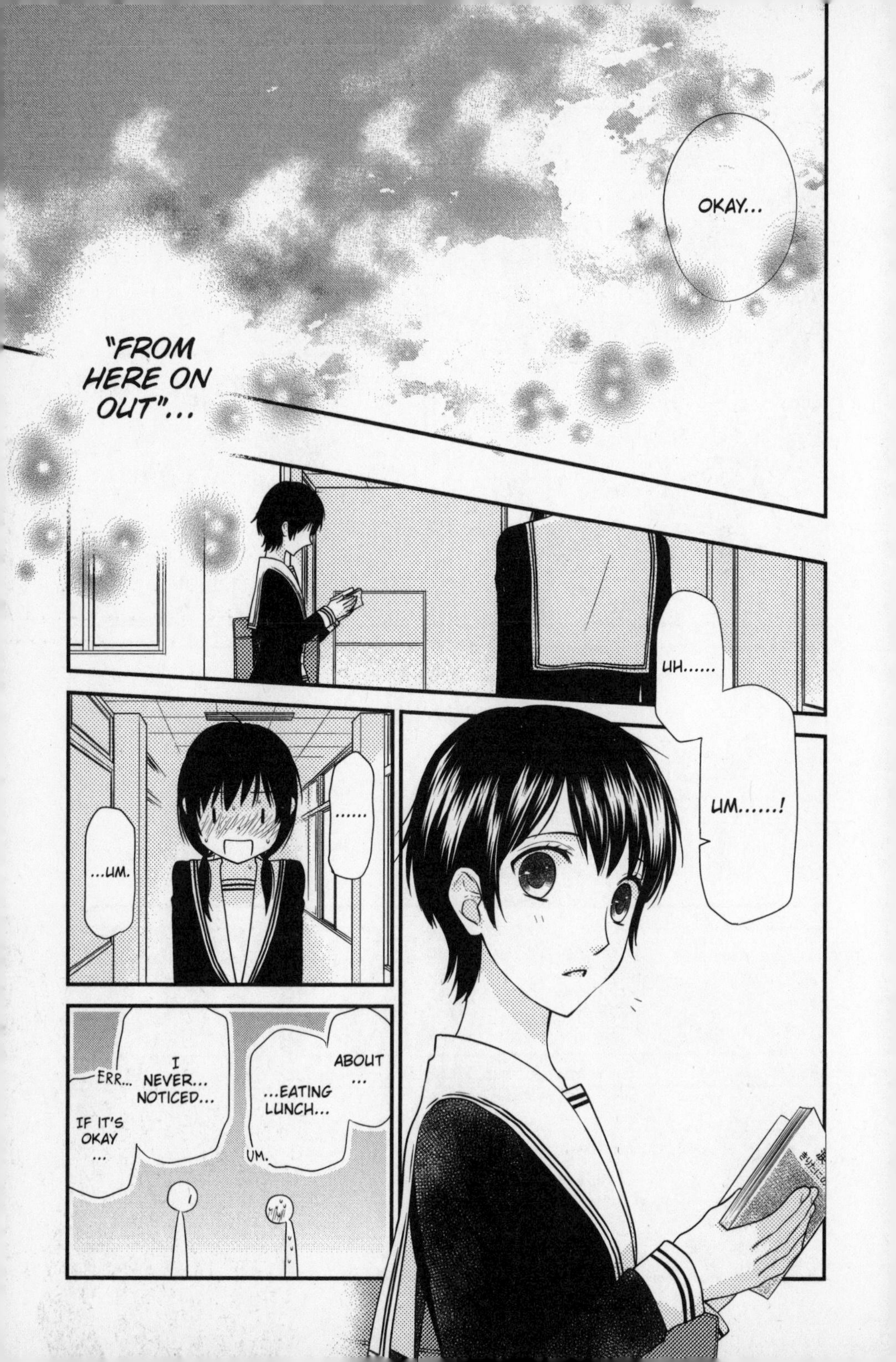
OKAY...
"FROM HERE ON OUT"...
UH......
UM......!
......
...UM.
ABOUT...
...EATING LUNCH...
UM.
I NEVER... NOTICED...
ERR...
IF IT'S OKAY...

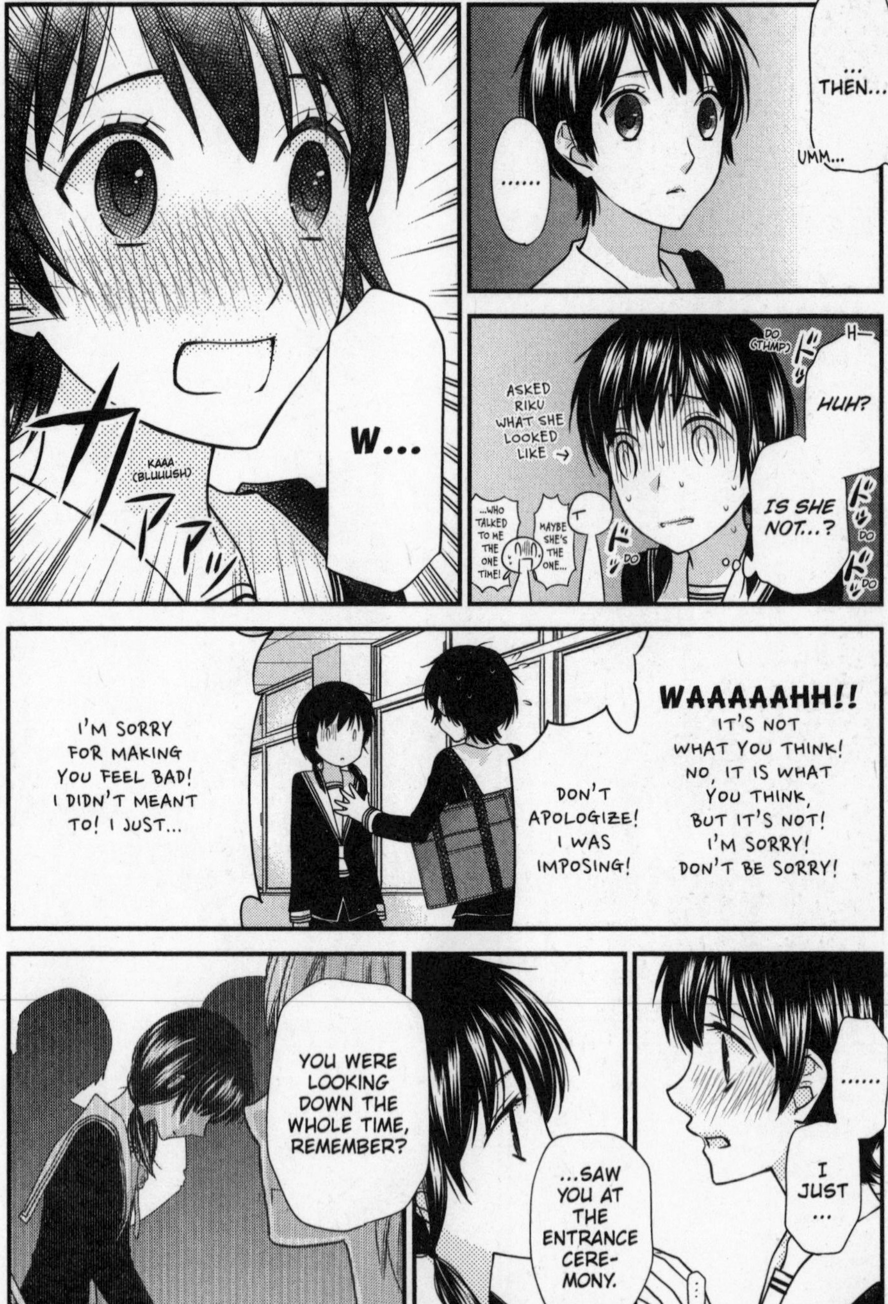
... THEN...
UMM...
......
H—
HUH?
DO (THMP)
IS SHE NOT...?
DO
DO
ASKED RIKU WHAT SHE LOOKED LIKE →
MAYBE SHE'S THE ONE...
...WHO TALKED TO ME THE ONE TIME!
DO
W...
KAAA (BLUUUSH)
WAAAAAHH!! IT'S NOT WHAT YOU THINK! NO, IT IS WHAT YOU THINK, BUT IT'S NOT! I'M SORRY! DON'T BE SORRY!
DON'T APOLOGIZE! I WAS IMPOSING!
I'M SORRY FOR MAKING YOU FEEL BAD! I DIDN'T MEANT TO! I JUST...
......
I JUST ...
...SAW YOU AT THE ENTRANCE CEREMONY.
YOU WERE LOOKING DOWN THE WHOLE TIME, REMEMBER?

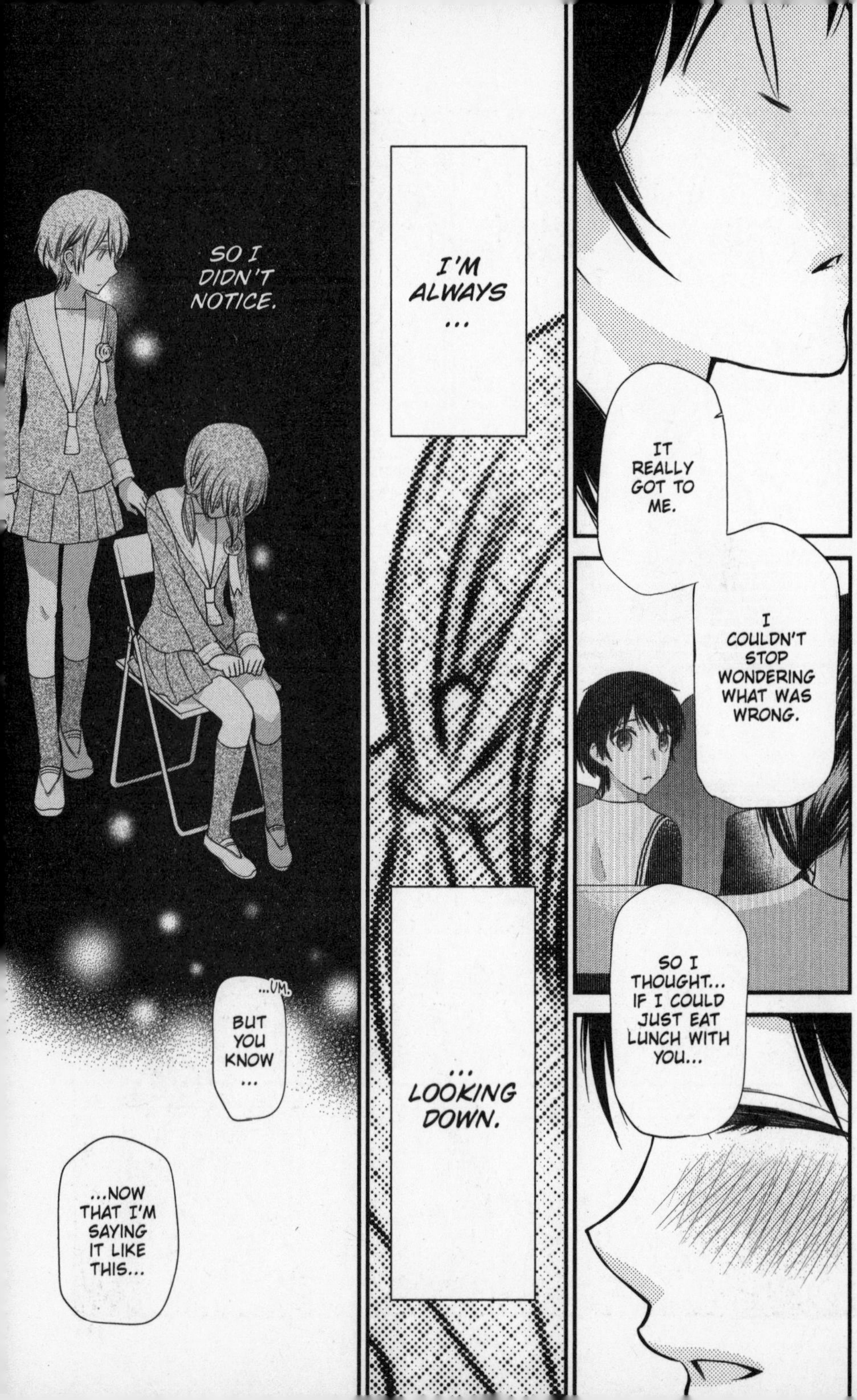
IT REALLY GOT TO ME.
I COULDN'T STOP WONDERING WHAT WAS WRONG.
SO I THOUGHT... IF I COULD JUST EAT LUNCH WITH YOU...
I'M ALWAYS ...
... LOOKING DOWN.
SO I DIDN'T NOTICE.
...UM.
BUT YOU KNOW ...
...NOW THAT I'M SAYING IT LIKE THIS...

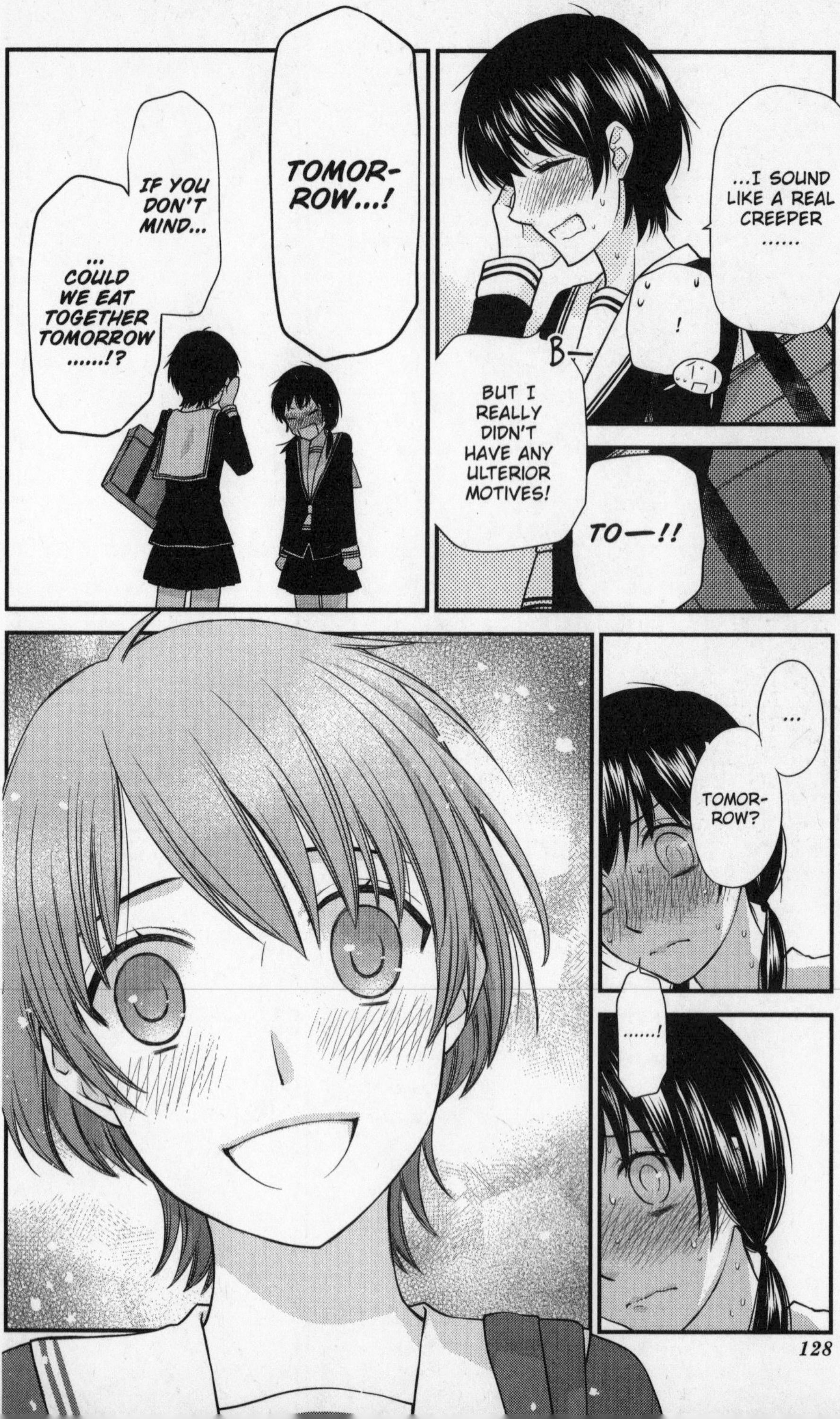

...I SOUND LIKE A REAL CREEPER ......
!
B—
BUT I REALLY DIDN'T HAVE ANY ULTERIOR MOTIVES!
TO—!!
TOMOR-ROW...!
IF YOU DON'T MIND...
...COULD WE EAT TOGETHER TOMORROW ......!?
...
TOMOR-ROW?
......!

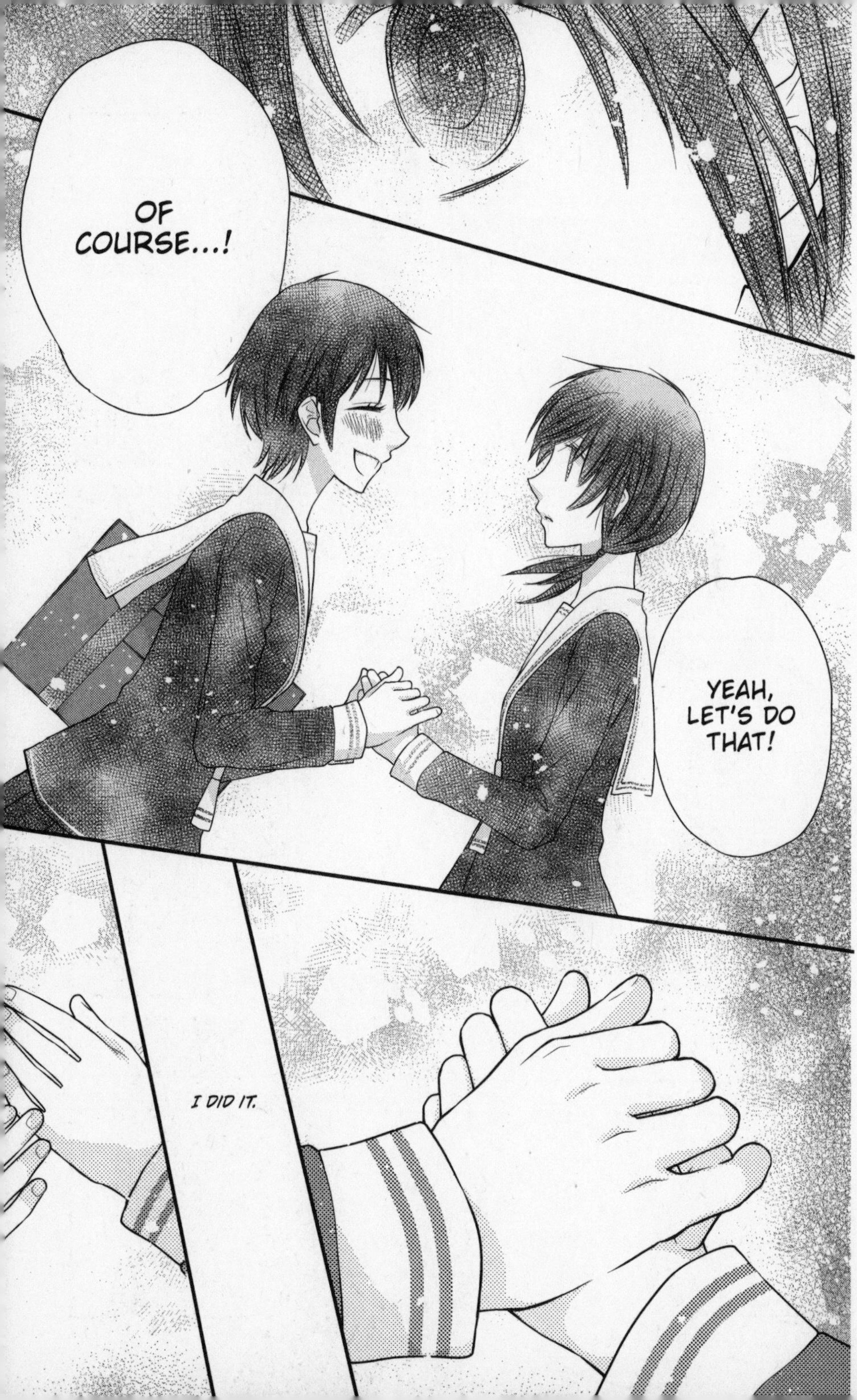
YEAH, LET'S DO THAT!
OF COURSE...!
I DID IT.

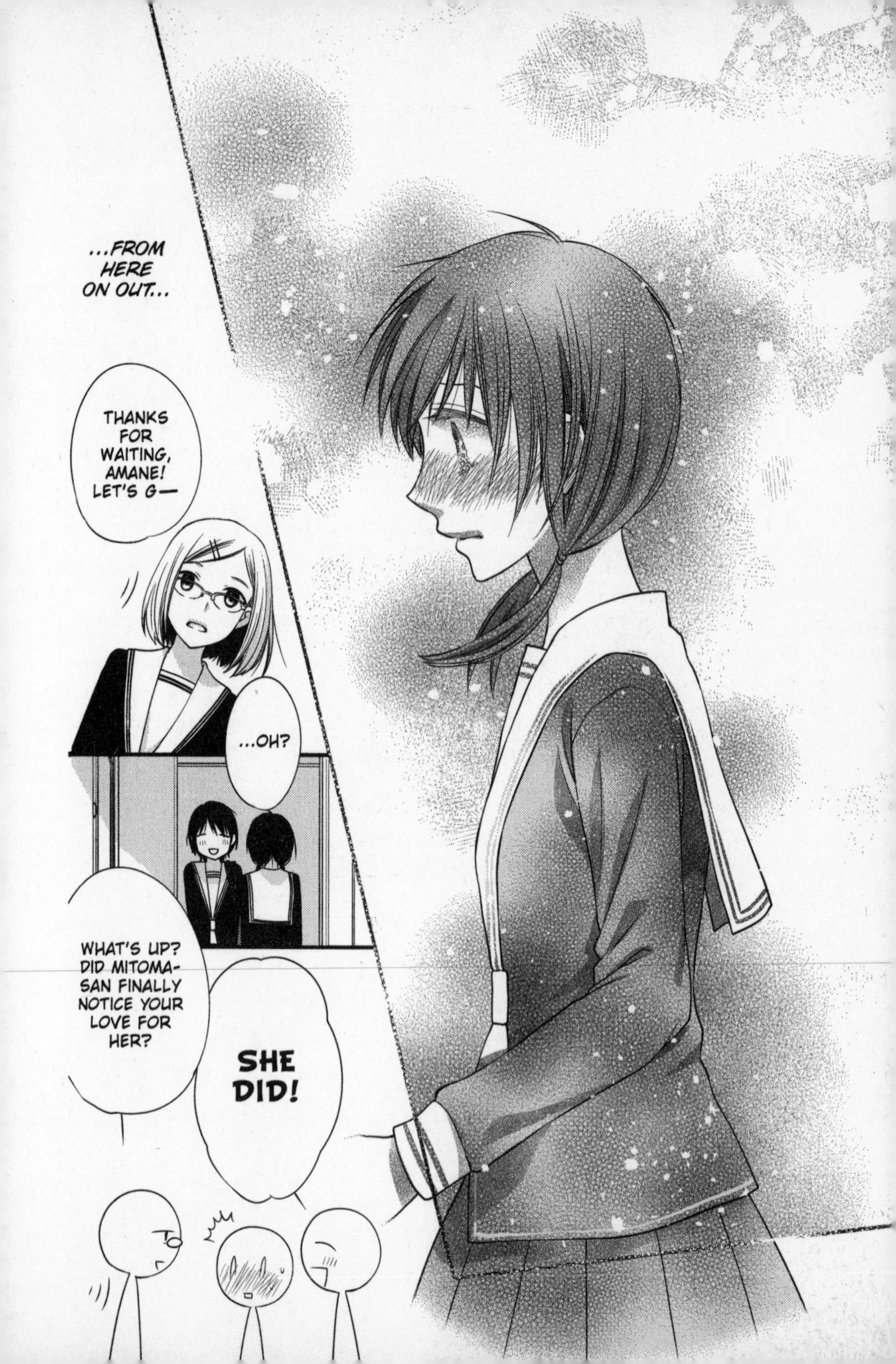
...FROM HERE ON OUT...
THANKS FOR WAITING, AMANE! LET'S G—
...OH?
WHAT'S UP? DID MITOMA-SAN FINALLY NOTICE YOUR LOVE FOR HER?
SHE DID!

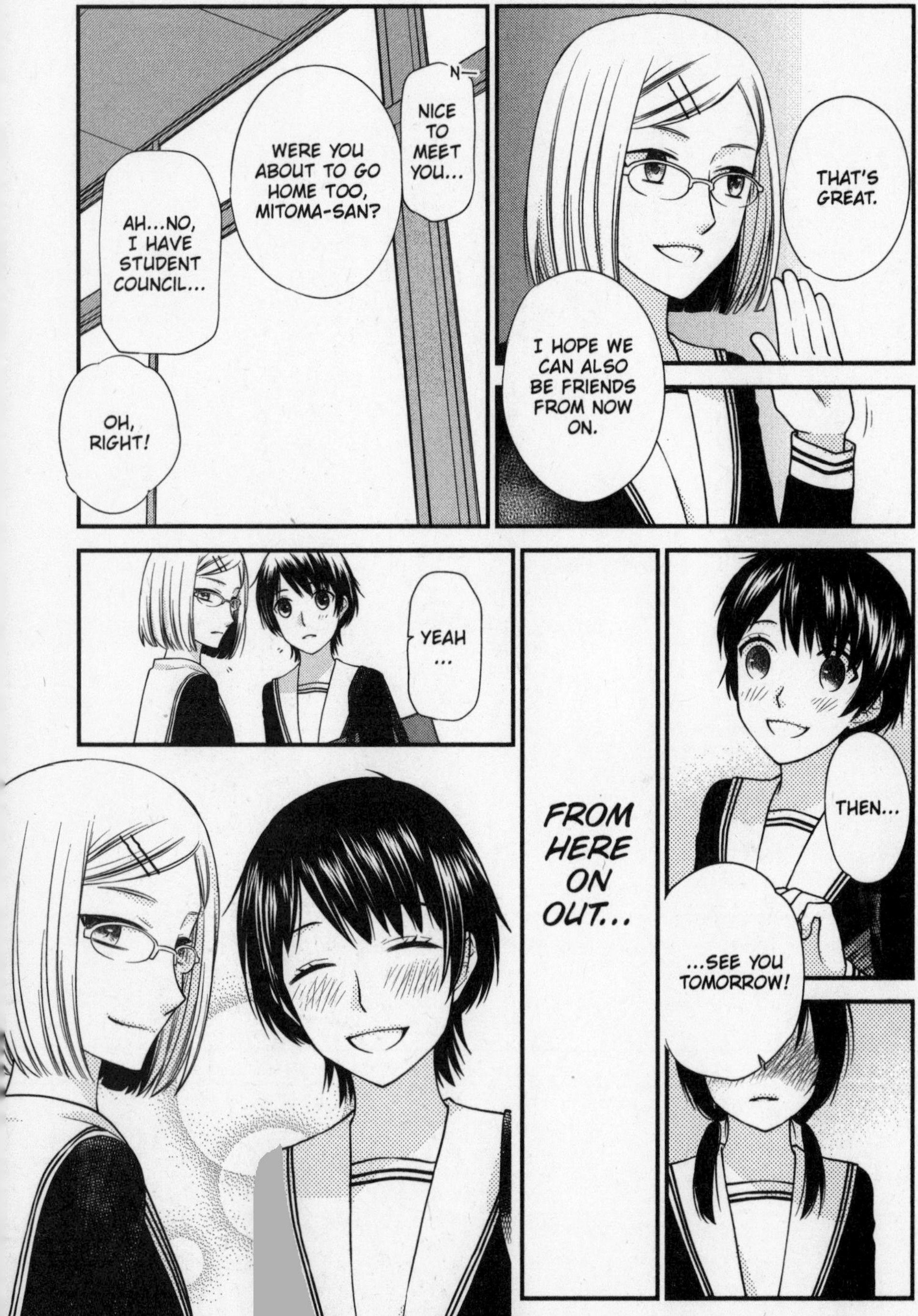

THAT'S GREAT.
I HOPE WE CAN ALSO BE FRIENDS FROM NOW ON.
N—
NICE TO MEET YOU...
WERE YOU ABOUT TO GO HOME TOO, MITOMA-SAN?
AH...NO, I HAVE STUDENT COUNCIL...
OH, RIGHT!
THEN...
...SEE YOU TOMORROW!
FROM HERE ON OUT...
YEAH...

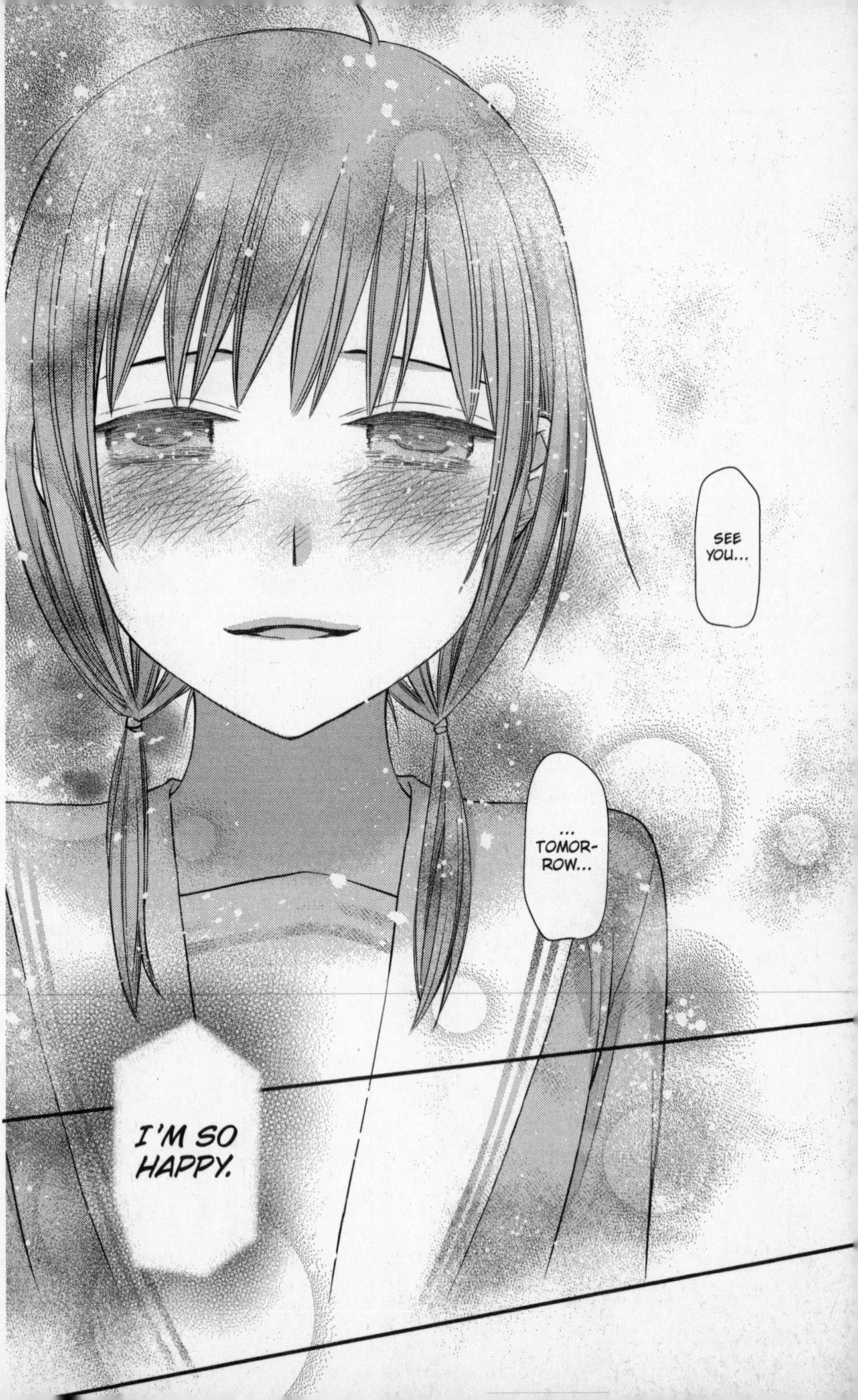
SEE YOU...
... TOMOR-ROW...
I'M SO HAPPY.

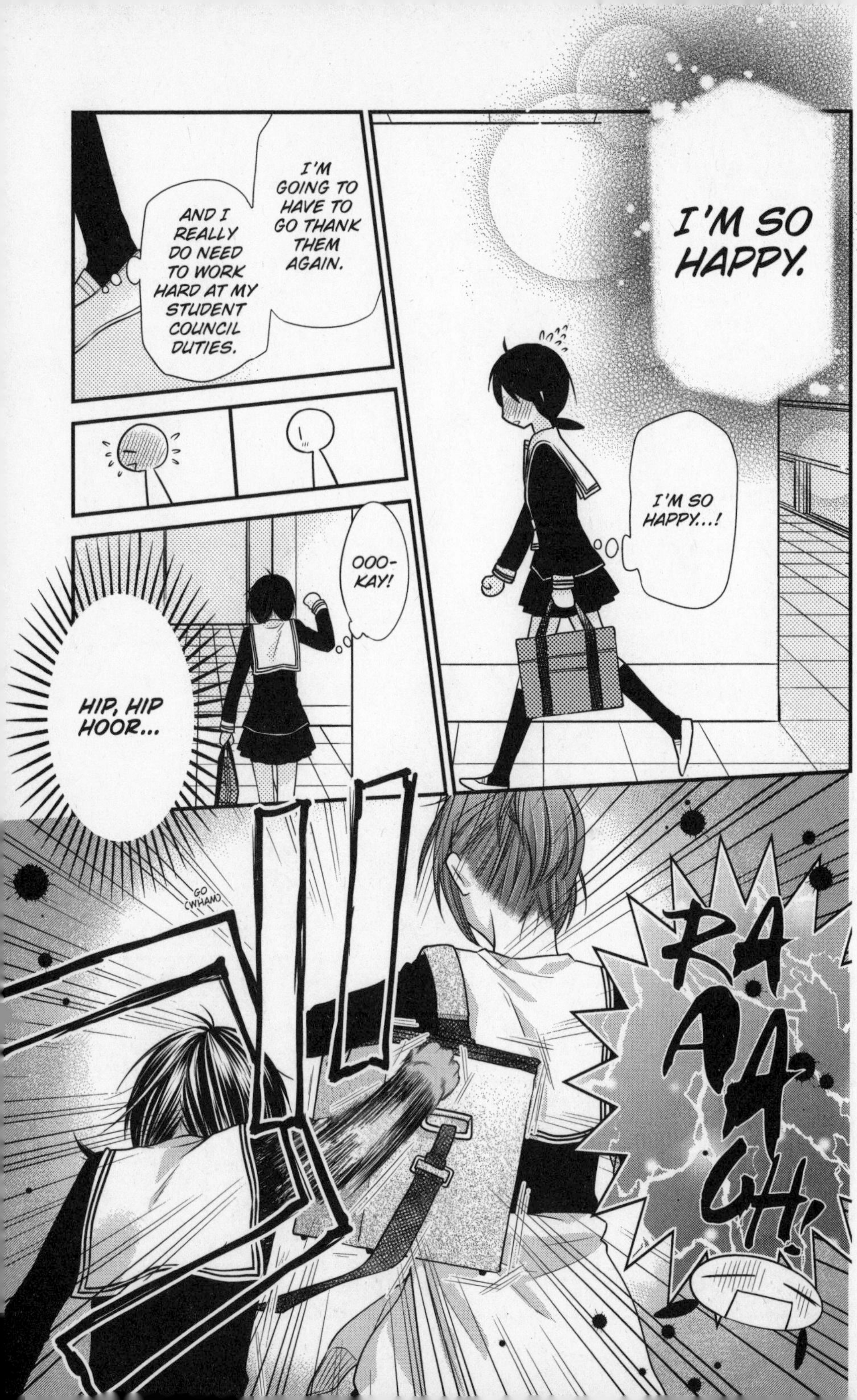
I'M SO HAPPY.
I'M SO HAPPY...!
I'M GOING TO HAVE TO GO THANK THEM AGAIN.
AND I REALLY DO NEED TO WORK HARD AT MY STUDENT COUNCIL DUTIES.
OOO-KAY!
HIP, HIP HOOR...
GO (WHAM)
RAAAGH!

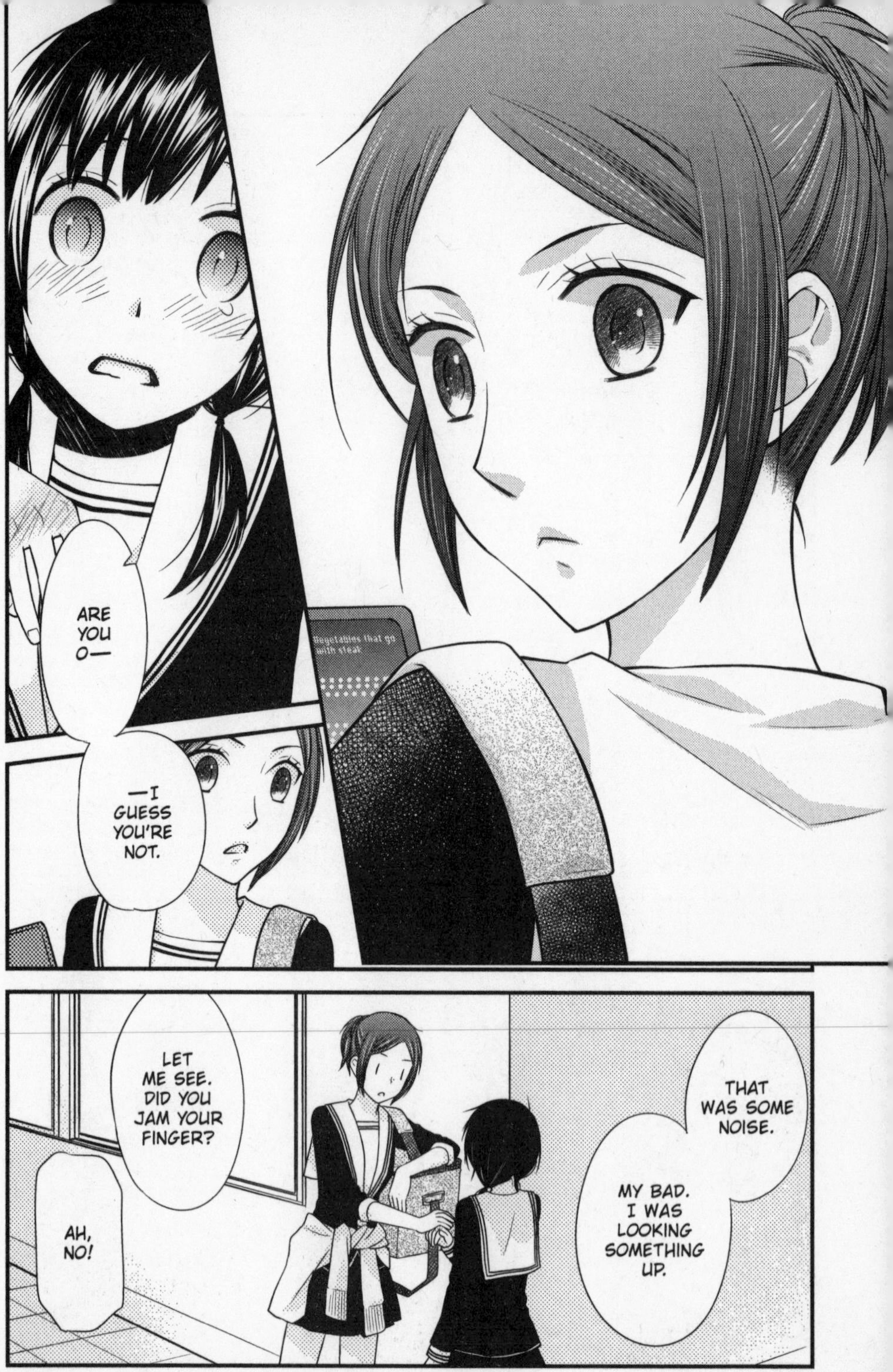
Vegetables that go with steak
ARE YOU O—
—I GUESS YOU'RE NOT.
THAT WAS SOME NOISE.
MY BAD. I WAS LOOKING SOMETHING UP.
LET ME SEE. DID YOU JAM YOUR FINGER?
AH, NO!

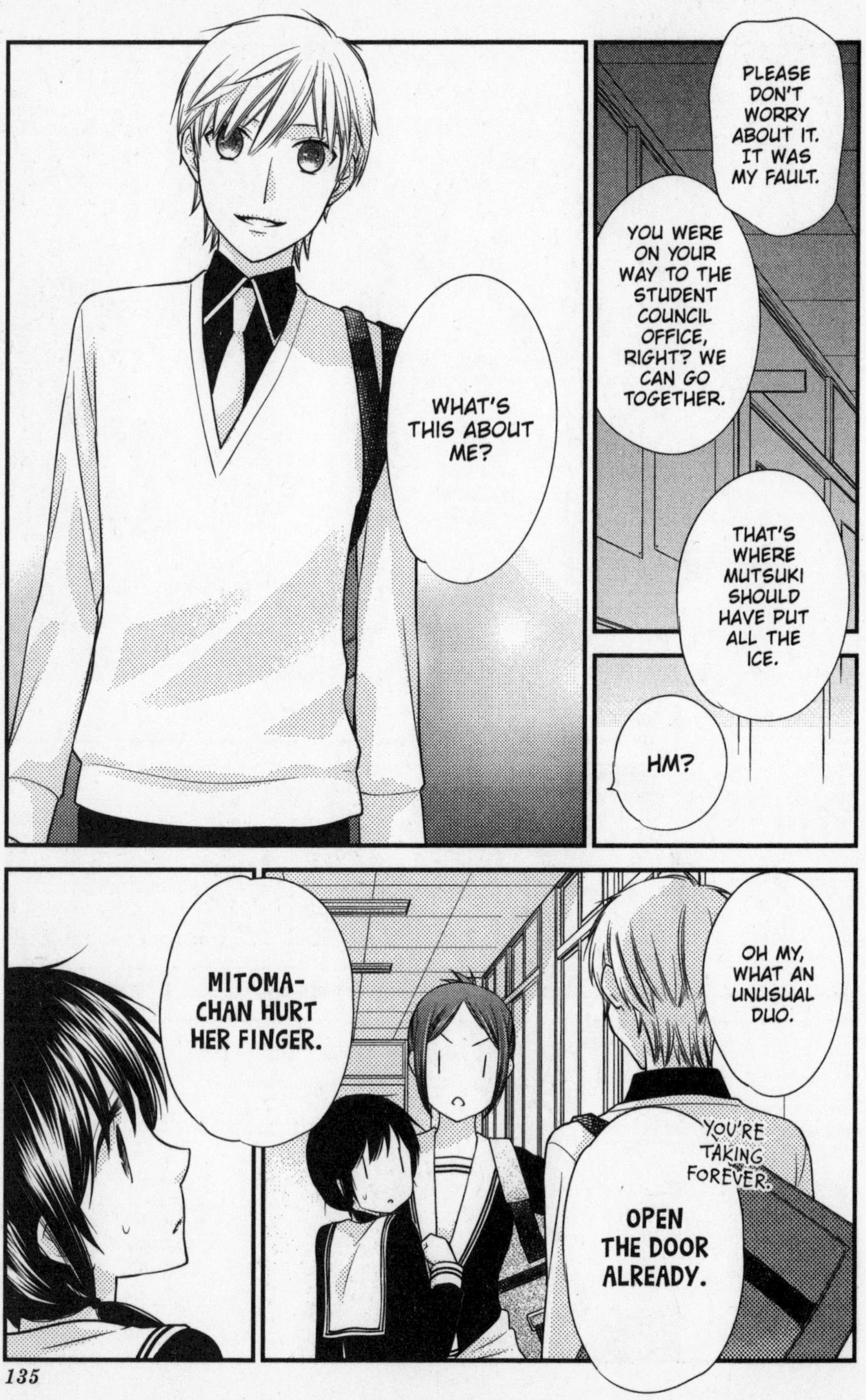
PLEASE DON'T WORRY ABOUT IT. IT WAS MY FAULT.
YOU WERE ON YOUR WAY TO THE STUDENT COUNCIL OFFICE, RIGHT? WE CAN GO TOGETHER.
THAT'S WHERE MUTSUKI SHOULD HAVE PUT ALL THE ICE.
HM?
WHAT'S THIS ABOUT ME?
OH MY, WHAT AN UNUSUAL DUO.
YOU'RE TAKING FOREVER.
OPEN THE DOOR ALREADY.
MITOMA-CHAN HURT HER FINGER.

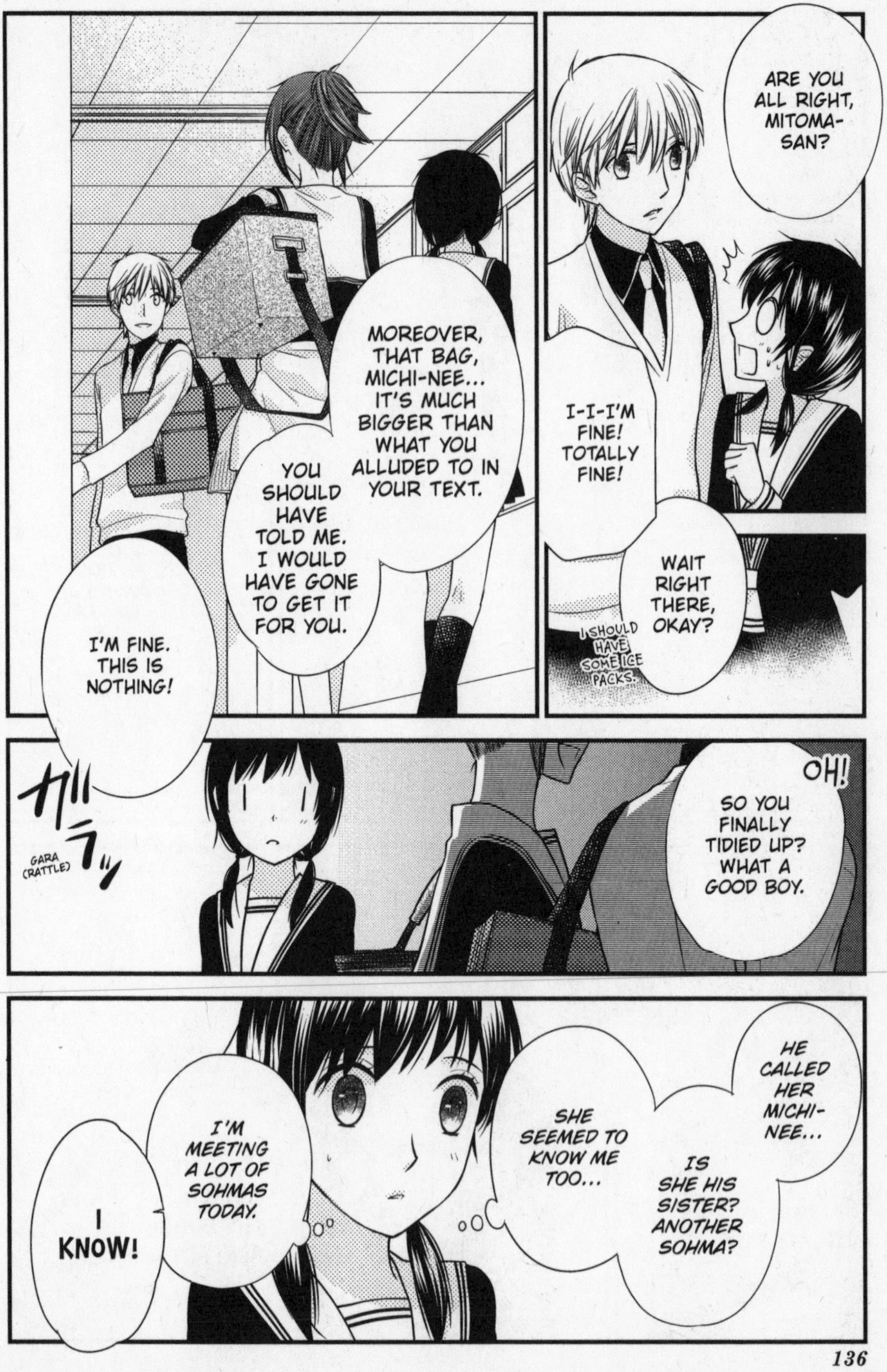
ARE YOU ALL RIGHT, MITOMA-SAN?
I-I-I'M FINE! TOTALLY FINE!
WAIT RIGHT THERE, OKAY?
I SHOULD HAVE SOME ICE PACKS.
MOREOVER, THAT BAG, MICHI-NEE... IT'S MUCH BIGGER THAN WHAT YOU ALLUDED TO IN YOUR TEXT.
YOU SHOULD HAVE TOLD ME. I WOULD HAVE GONE TO GET IT FOR YOU.
I'M FINE. THIS IS NOTHING!
OH!
SO YOU FINALLY TIDIED UP? WHAT A GOOD BOY.
ガラッ
GARA (RATTLE)
HE CALLED HER MICHI-NEE...
IS SHE HIS SISTER? ANOTHER SOHMA?
SHE SEEMED TO KNOW ME TOO...
I'M MEETING A LOT OF SOHMAS TODAY.
I KNOW!

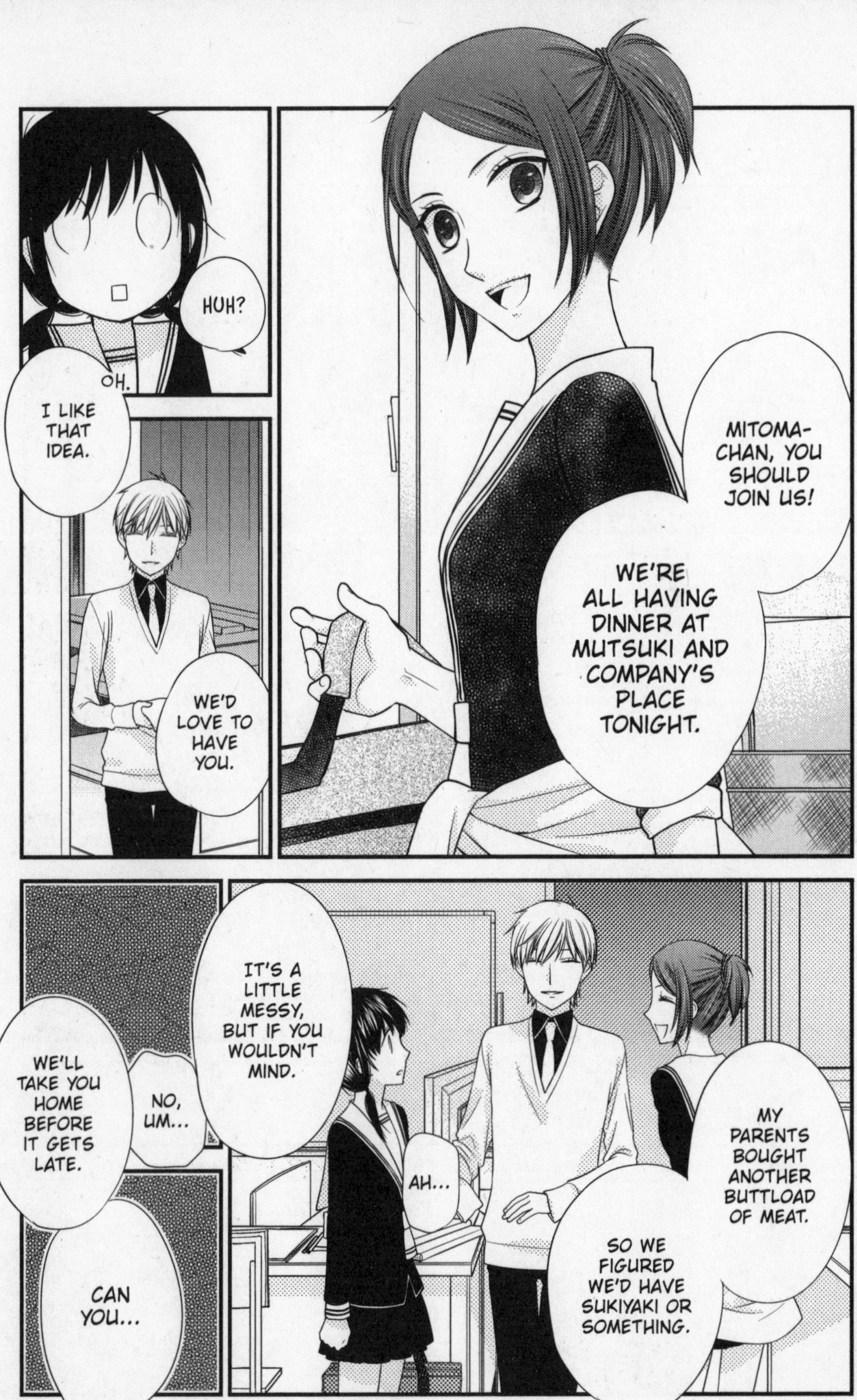
MITOMA-CHAN, YOU SHOULD JOIN US!
WE'RE ALL HAVING DINNER AT MUTSUKI AND COMPANY'S PLACE TONIGHT.
HUH?
OH.
I LIKE THAT IDEA.
WE'D LOVE TO HAVE YOU.
MY PARENTS BOUGHT ANOTHER BUTTLOAD OF MEAT.
SO WE FIGURED WE'D HAVE SUKIYAKI OR SOMETHING.
AH...
IT'S A LITTLE MESSY, BUT IF YOU WOULDN'T MIND.
NO, UM...
WE'LL TAKE YOU HOME BEFORE IT GETS LATE.
CAN YOU...

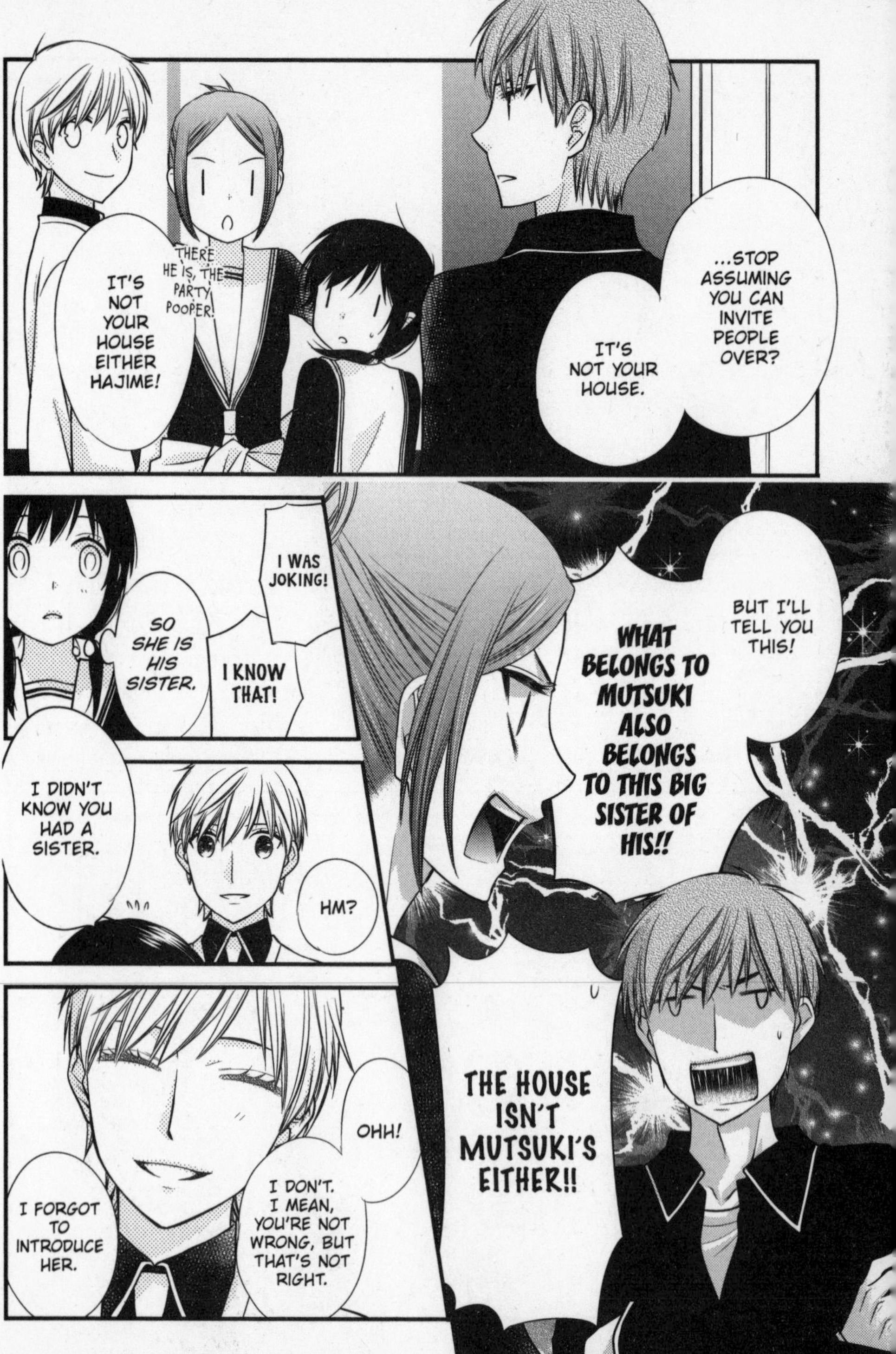
...STOP ASSUMING YOU CAN INVITE PEOPLE OVER?
IT'S NOT YOUR HOUSE.
THERE HE IS, THE PARTY POOPER!
IT'S NOT YOUR HOUSE EITHER HAJIME!
BUT I'LL TELL YOU THIS!
WHAT BELONGS TO MUTSUKI ALSO BELONGS TO THIS BIG SISTER OF HIS!!
THE HOUSE ISN'T MUTSUKI'S EITHER!!
I WAS JOKING!
I KNOW THAT!
SO SHE IS HIS SISTER.
HM?
I DIDN'T KNOW YOU HAD A SISTER.
OHH!
I DON'T. I MEAN, YOU'RE NOT WRONG, BUT THAT'S NOT RIGHT.
I FORGOT TO INTRODUCE HER.

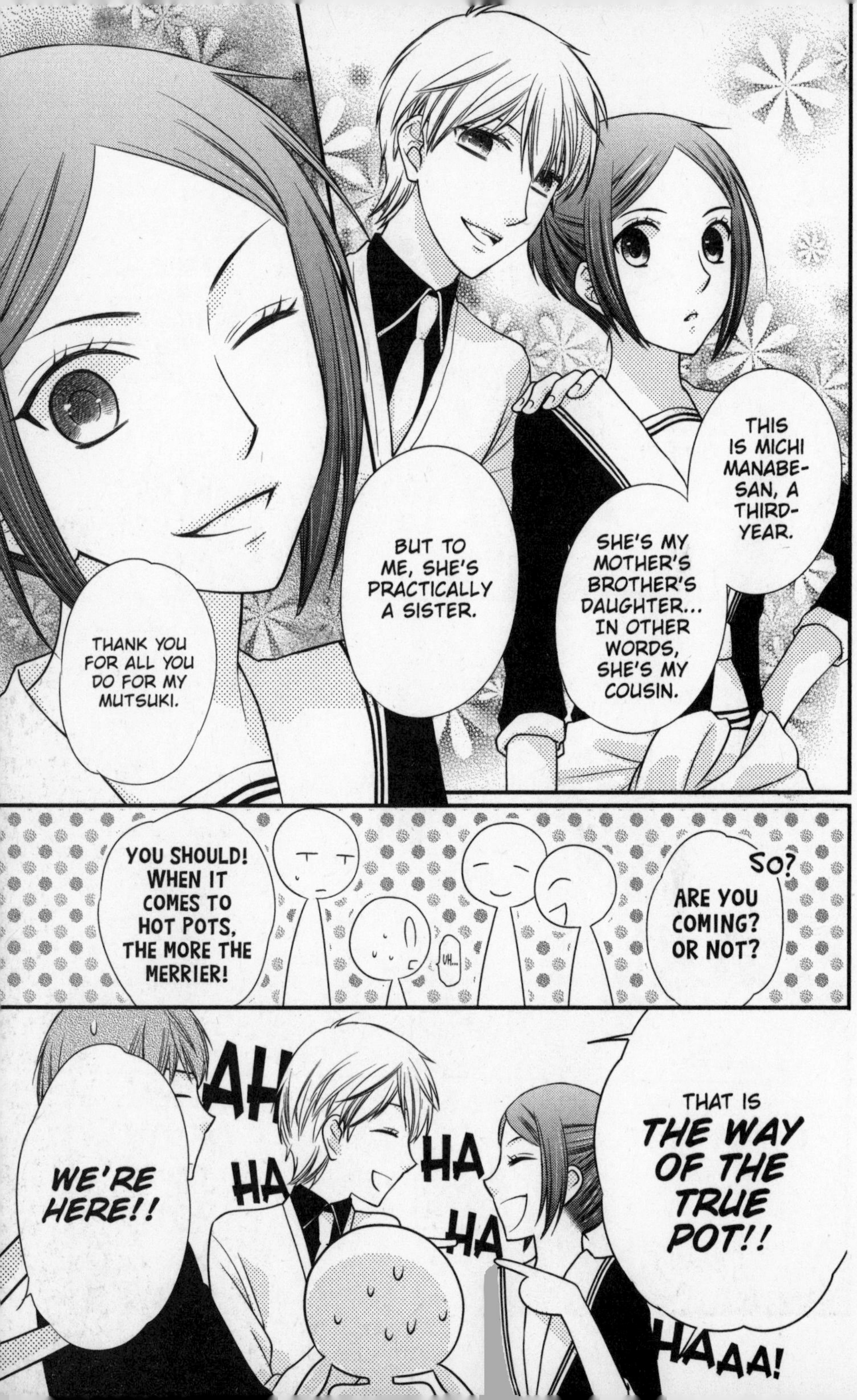
THIS IS MICHI MANABE-SAN, A THIRD-YEAR.
SHE'S MY MOTHER'S BROTHER'S DAUGHTER... IN OTHER WORDS, SHE'S MY COUSIN.
BUT TO ME, SHE'S PRACTICALLY A SISTER.
THANK YOU FOR ALL YOU DO FOR MY MUTSUKI.
SO?
ARE YOU COMING? OR NOT?
UH...
YOU SHOULD! WHEN IT COMES TO HOT POTS, THE MORE THE MERRIER!
THAT IS *THE WAY OF THE TRUE POT!!*
AH HA HA HA HA HAAA!
WE'RE HERE!!

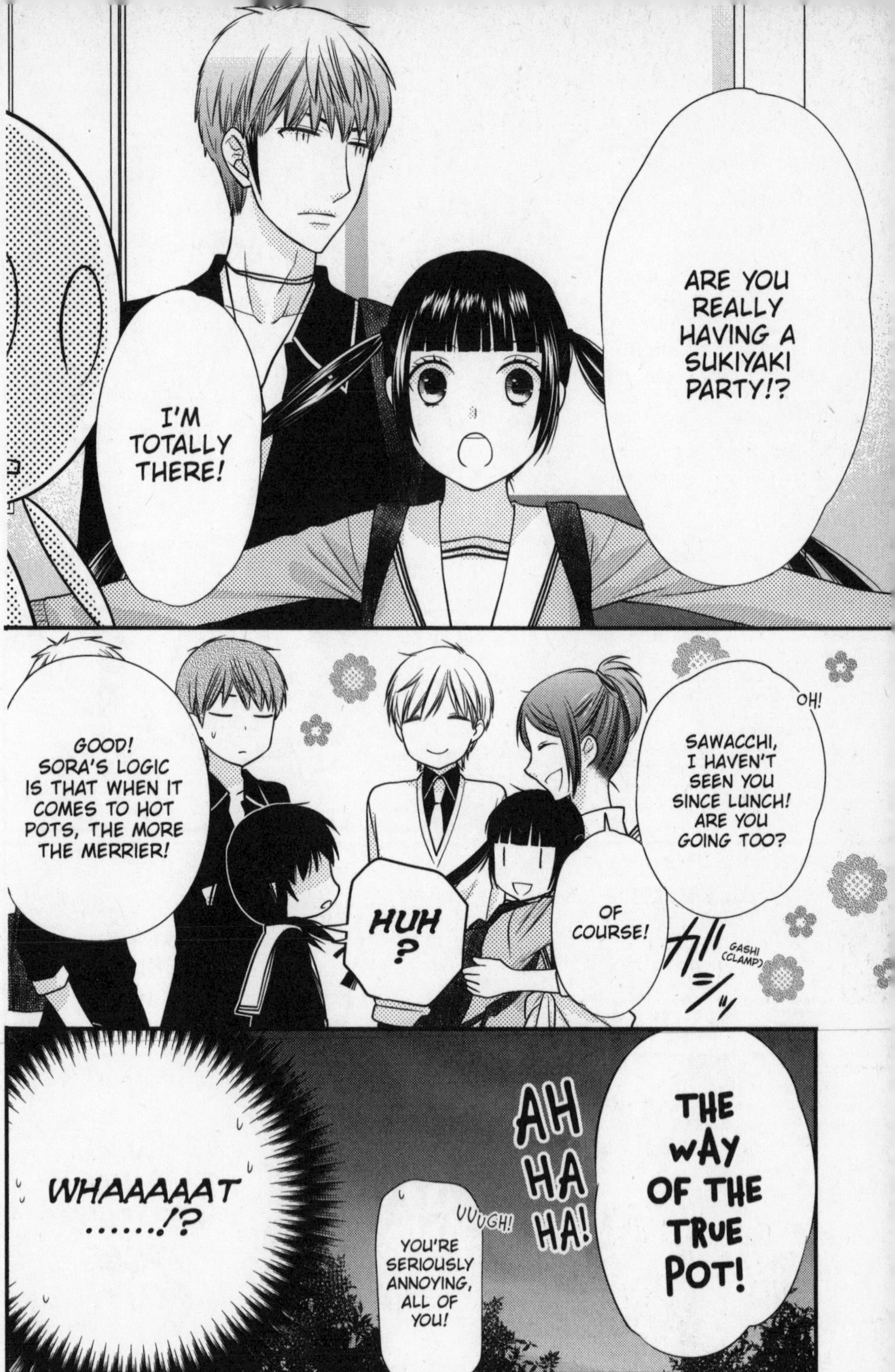
ARE YOU REALLY HAVING A SUKIYAKI PARTY!?
I'M TOTALLY THERE!
OH!
SAWACCHI, I HAVEN'T SEEN YOU SINCE LUNCH! ARE YOU GOING TOO?
GASHI (CLAMP)
OF COURSE!
HUH?
GOOD! SORA'S LOGIC IS THAT WHEN IT COMES TO HOT POTS, THE MORE THE MERRIER!
THE WAY OF THE TRUE POT!
AH HA HA!
UUUGH!
YOU'RE SERIOUSLY ANNOYING, ALL OF YOU!
WHAAAAAT ......!?

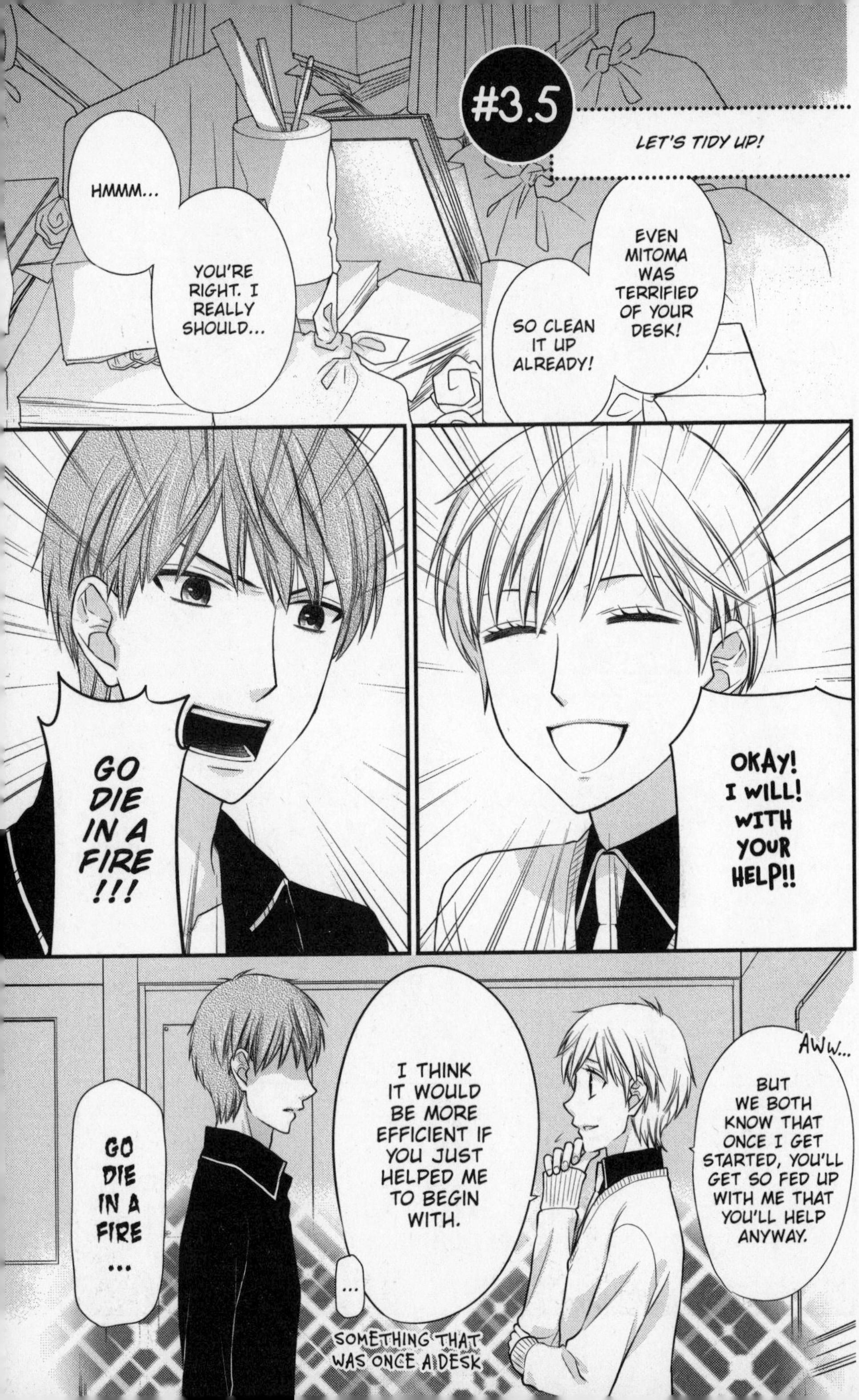
#3.5
LET'S TIDY UP!
EVEN MITOMA WAS TERRIFIED OF YOUR DESK!
SO CLEAN IT UP ALREADY!
HMMM...
YOU'RE RIGHT. I REALLY SHOULD...
OKAY! I WILL! WITH YOUR HELP!!
GO DIE IN A FIRE!!!
AWW...
BUT WE BOTH KNOW THAT ONCE I GET STARTED, YOU'LL GET SO FED UP WITH ME THAT YOU'LL HELP ANYWAY.
I THINK IT WOULD BE MORE EFFICIENT IF YOU JUST HELPED ME TO BEGIN WITH.
...
GO DIE IN A FIRE ...
SOMETHING THAT WAS ONCE A DESK

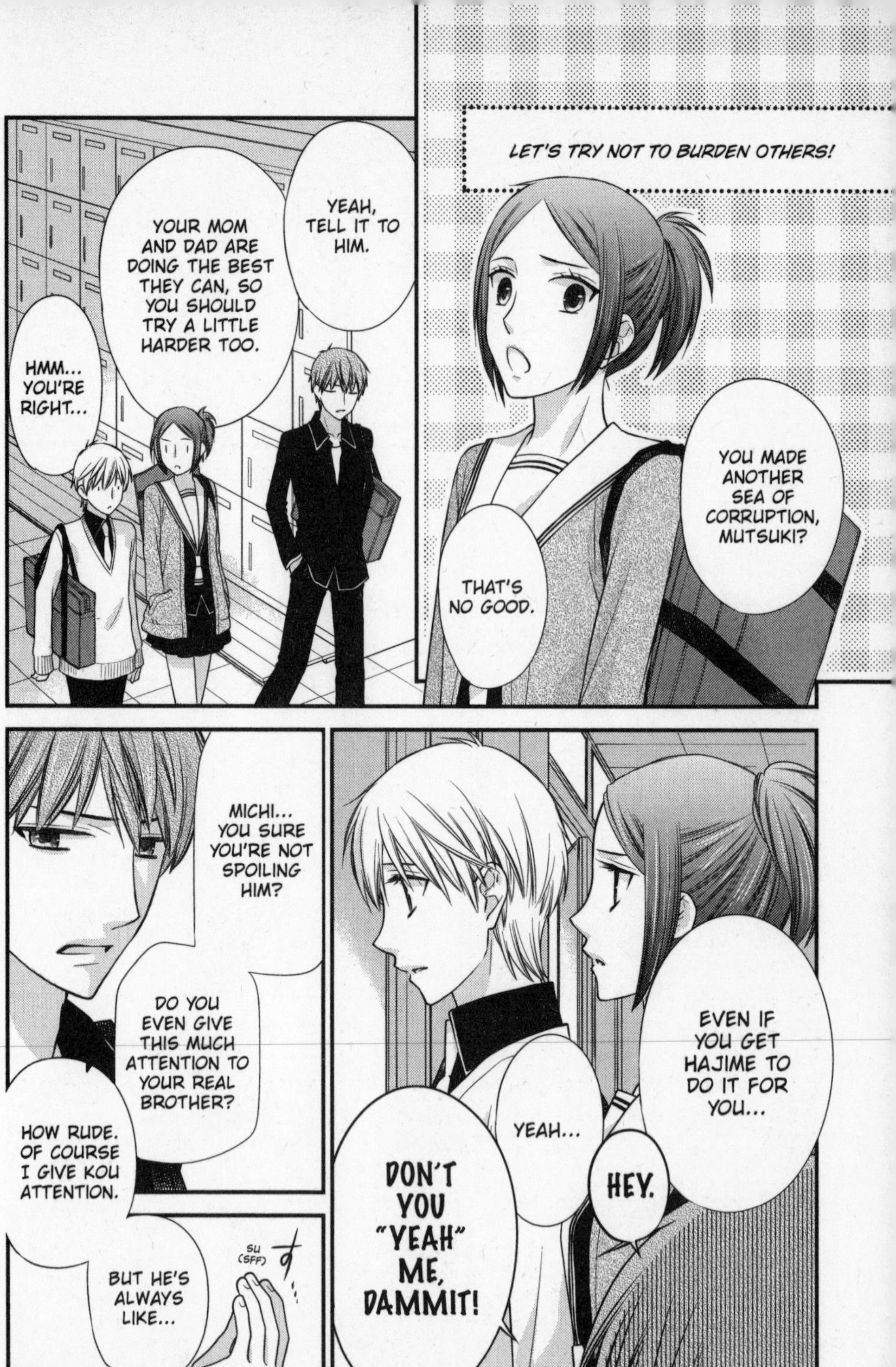
LET'S TRY NOT TO BURDEN OTHERS!
YOU MADE ANOTHER SEA OF CORRUPTION, MUTSUKI?
THAT'S NO GOOD.
YEAH, TELL IT TO HIM.
YOUR MOM AND DAD ARE DOING THE BEST THEY CAN, SO YOU SHOULD TRY A LITTLE HARDER TOO.
HMM... YOU'RE RIGHT...
EVEN IF YOU GET HAJIME TO DO IT FOR YOU...
HEY.
YEAH...
DON'T YOU "YEAH" ME, DAMMIT!
MICHI... YOU SURE YOU'RE NOT SPOILING HIM?
DO YOU EVEN GIVE THIS MUCH ATTENTION TO YOUR REAL BROTHER?
HOW RUDE. OF COURSE I GIVE KOU ATTENTION.
SU (SFF)
BUT HE'S ALWAYS LIKE...

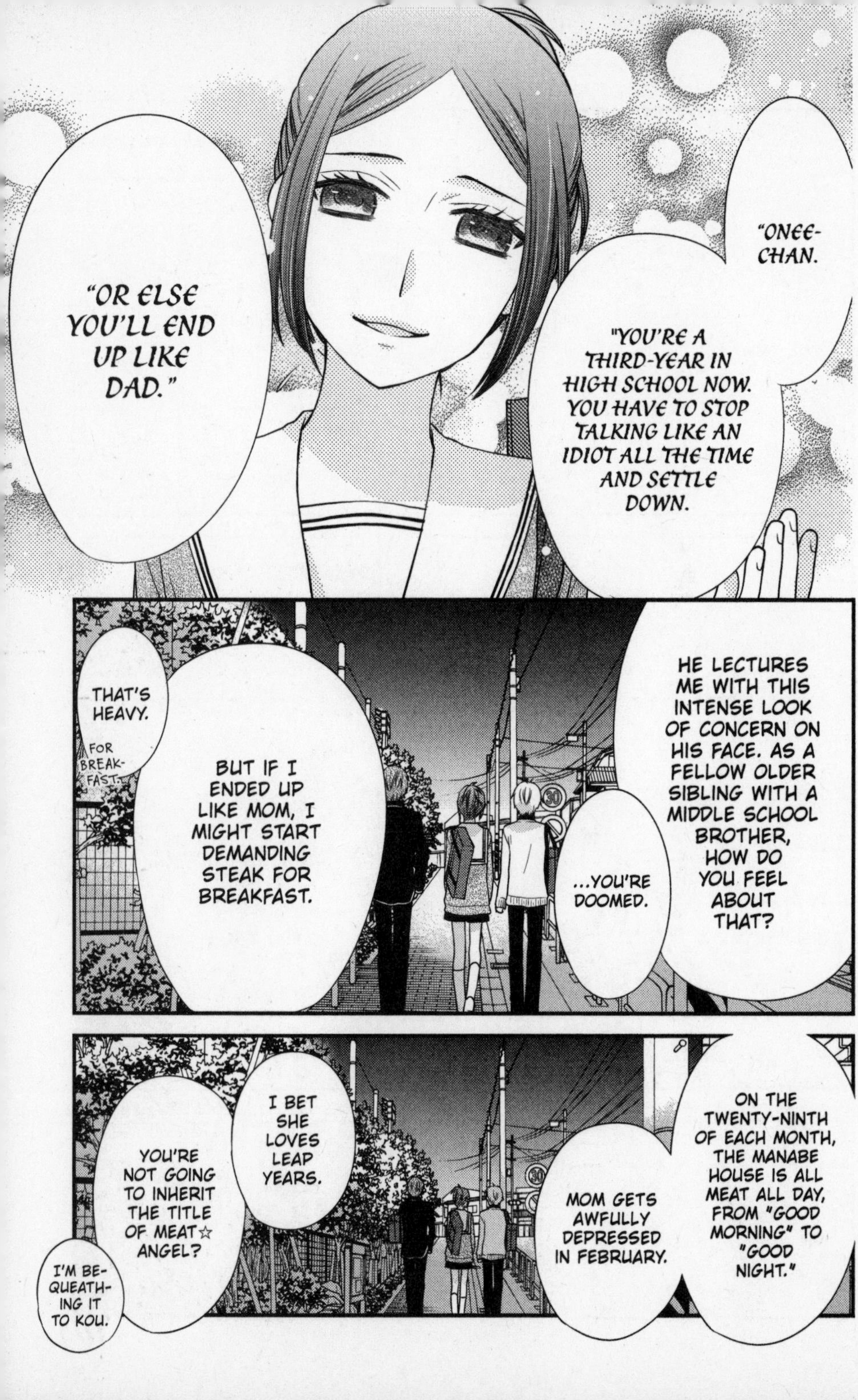
"ONEE-CHAN.
"YOU'RE A THIRD-YEAR IN HIGH SCHOOL NOW. YOU HAVE TO STOP TALKING LIKE AN IDIOT ALL THE TIME AND SETTLE DOWN.
"OR ELSE YOU'LL END UP LIKE DAD."
HE LECTURES ME WITH THIS INTENSE LOOK OF CONCERN ON HIS FACE. AS A FELLOW OLDER SIBLING WITH A MIDDLE SCHOOL BROTHER, HOW DO YOU FEEL ABOUT THAT?
...YOU'RE DOOMED.
BUT IF I ENDED UP LIKE MOM, I MIGHT START DEMANDING STEAK FOR BREAKFAST.
THAT'S HEAVY.
FOR BREAK-FAST.
ON THE TWENTY-NINTH OF EACH MONTH, THE MANABE HOUSE IS ALL MEAT ALL DAY, FROM "GOOD MORNING" TO "GOOD NIGHT."
MOM GETS AWFULLY DEPRESSED IN FEBRUARY.
I BET SHE LOVES LEAP YEARS.
YOU'RE NOT GOING TO INHERIT THE TITLE OF MEAT☆ANGEL?
I'M BE-QUEATH-ING IT TO KOU.

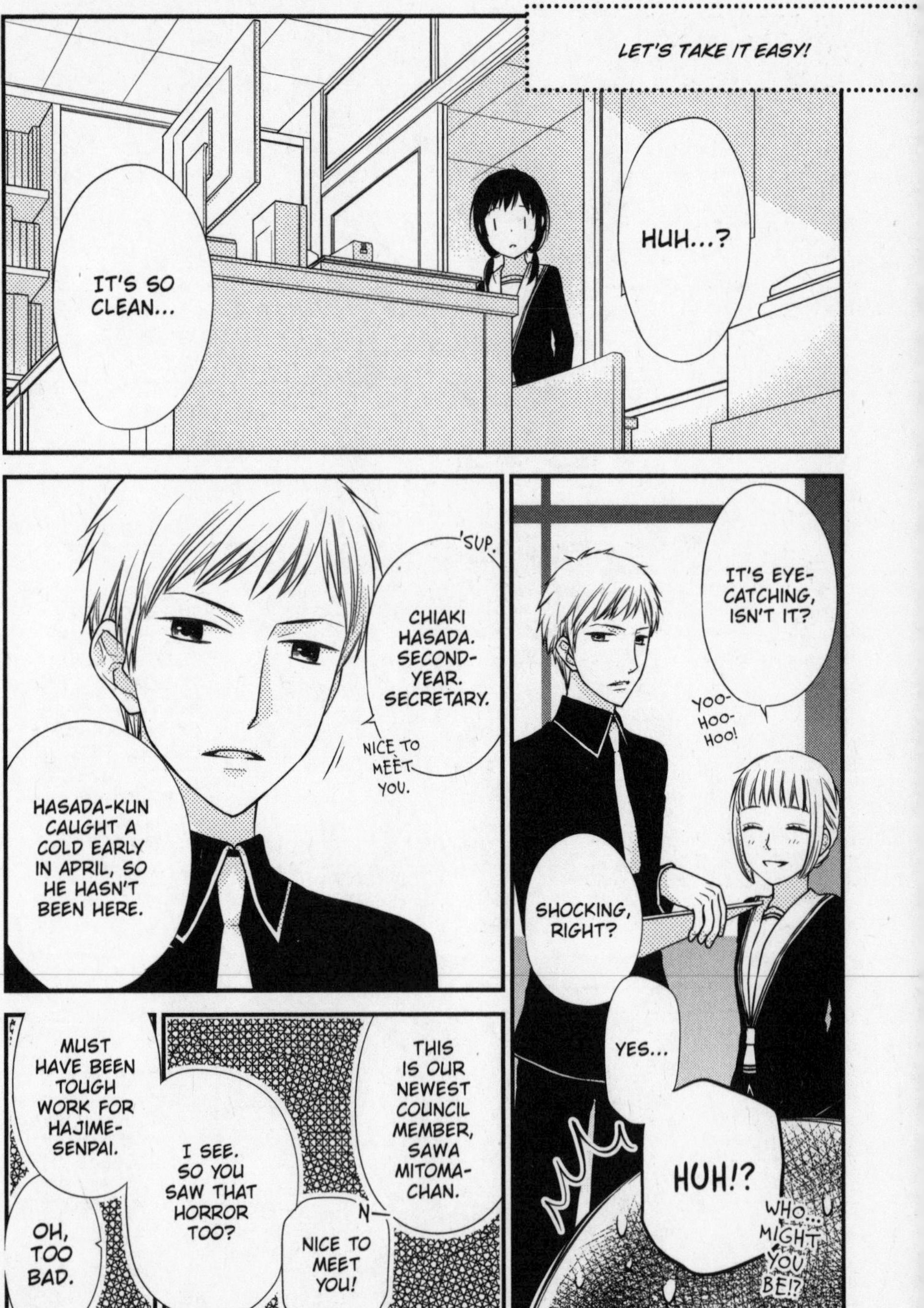
LET'S TAKE IT EASY!
HUH...?
IT'S SO CLEAN...
IT'S EYE-CATCHING, ISN'T IT?
YOO-HOO-HOO!
SHOCKING, RIGHT?
YES...
HUH!?
WHO... MIGHT YOU BE!?
'SUP.
CHIAKI HASADA. SECOND-YEAR. SECRETARY.
NICE TO MEET YOU.
HASADA-KUN CAUGHT A COLD EARLY IN APRIL, SO HE HASN'T BEEN HERE.
THIS IS OUR NEWEST COUNCIL MEMBER, SAWA MITOMA-CHAN.
N—
NICE TO MEET YOU!
I SEE. SO YOU SAW THAT HORROR TOO?
MUST HAVE BEEN TOUGH WORK FOR HAJIME-SENPAI.
OH, TOO BAD.

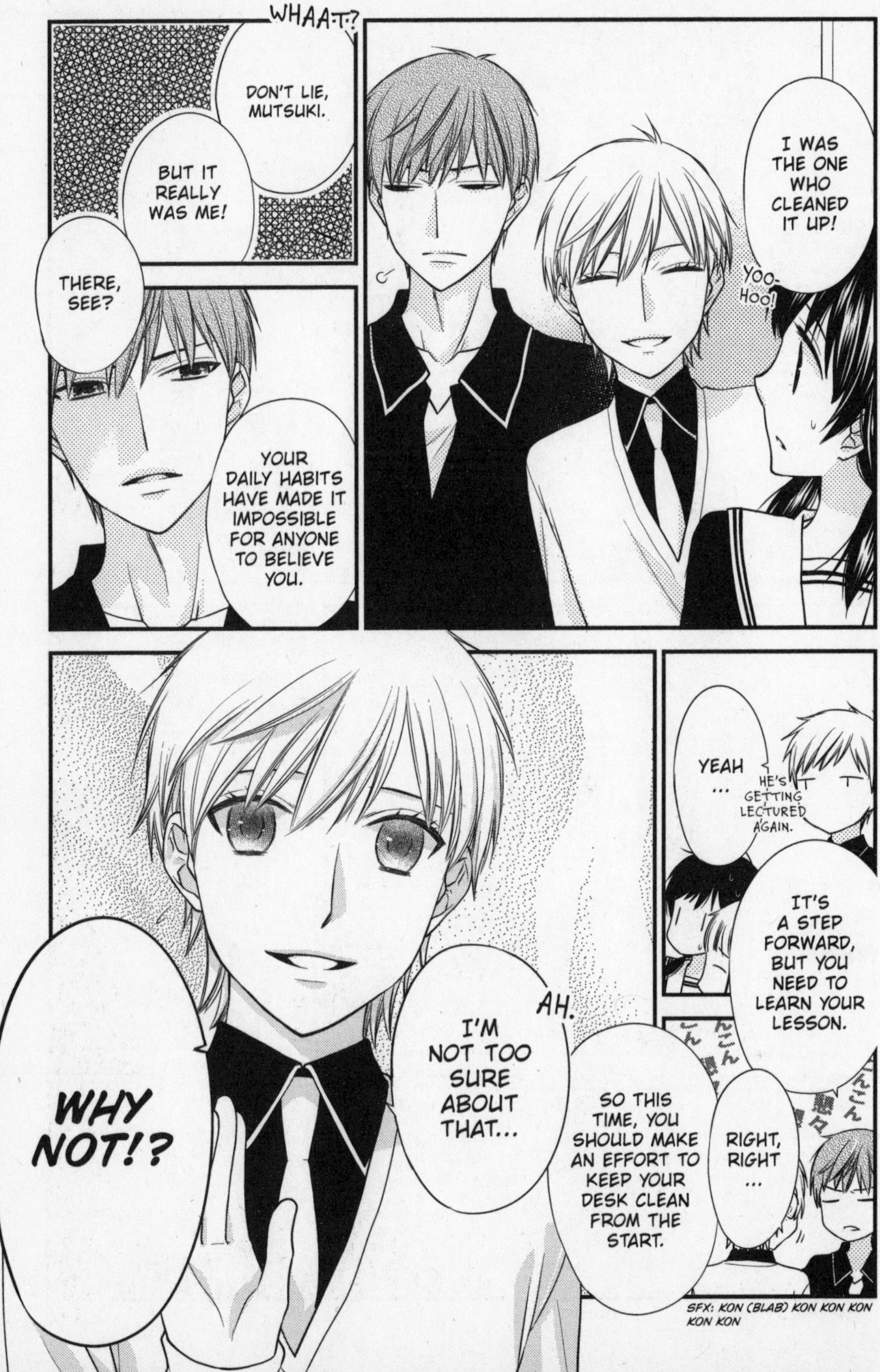
I WAS THE ONE WHO CLEANED IT UP!
YOO-HOO!
WHAA-T?
DON'T LIE, MUTSUKI.
BUT IT REALLY WAS ME!
THERE, SEE?
YOUR DAILY HABITS HAVE MADE IT IMPOSSIBLE FOR ANYONE TO BELIEVE YOU.
YEAH ...
HE'S GETTING LECTURED AGAIN.
IT'S A STEP FORWARD, BUT YOU NEED TO LEARN YOUR LESSON.
SO THIS TIME, YOU SHOULD MAKE AN EFFORT TO KEEP YOUR DESK CLEAN FROM THE START.
RIGHT, RIGHT ...
AH.
I'M NOT TOO SURE ABOUT THAT...
WHY NOT!?

SFX: KON (BLAB) KON KON KON KON KON

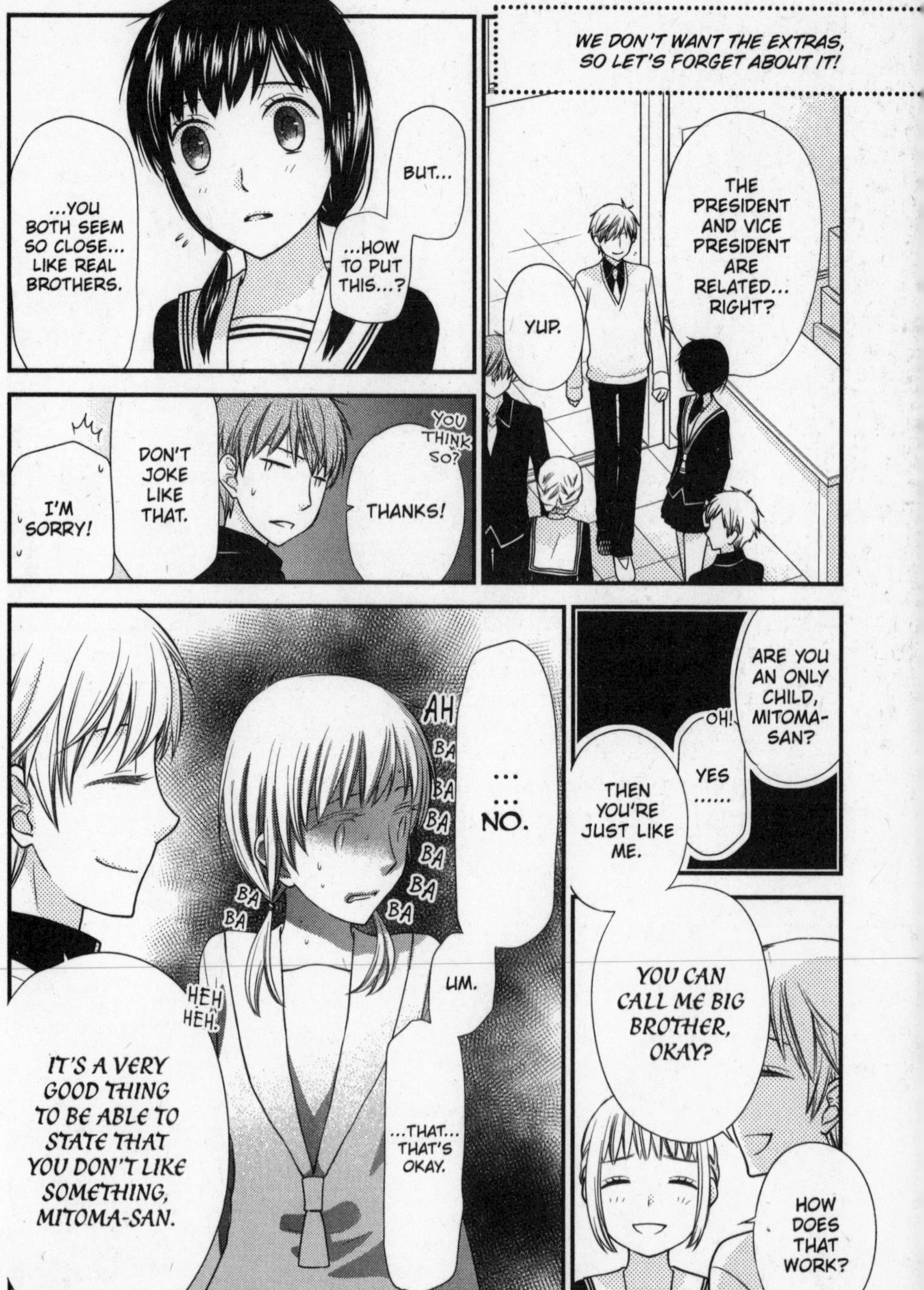

WE DON'T WANT THE EXTRAS, SO LET'S FORGET ABOUT IT!
THE PRESIDENT AND VICE PRESIDENT ARE RELATED... RIGHT?
YUP.
BUT...
...HOW TO PUT THIS...?
...YOU BOTH SEEM SO CLOSE... LIKE REAL BROTHERS.
YOU THINK SO?
THANKS!
DON'T JOKE LIKE THAT.
I'M SORRY!
ARE YOU AN ONLY CHILD, MITOMA-SAN?
OH!
YES ......
THEN YOU'RE JUST LIKE ME.
YOU CAN CALL ME BIG BROTHER, OKAY?
HOW DOES THAT WORK?
AH BA BA BA BA BA BA BA BA BA
... ... NO.
UM.
HEH HEH.
...THAT... THAT'S OKAY.
IT'S A VERY GOOD THING TO BE ABLE TO STATE THAT YOU DON'T LIKE SOMETHING, MITOMA-SAN.

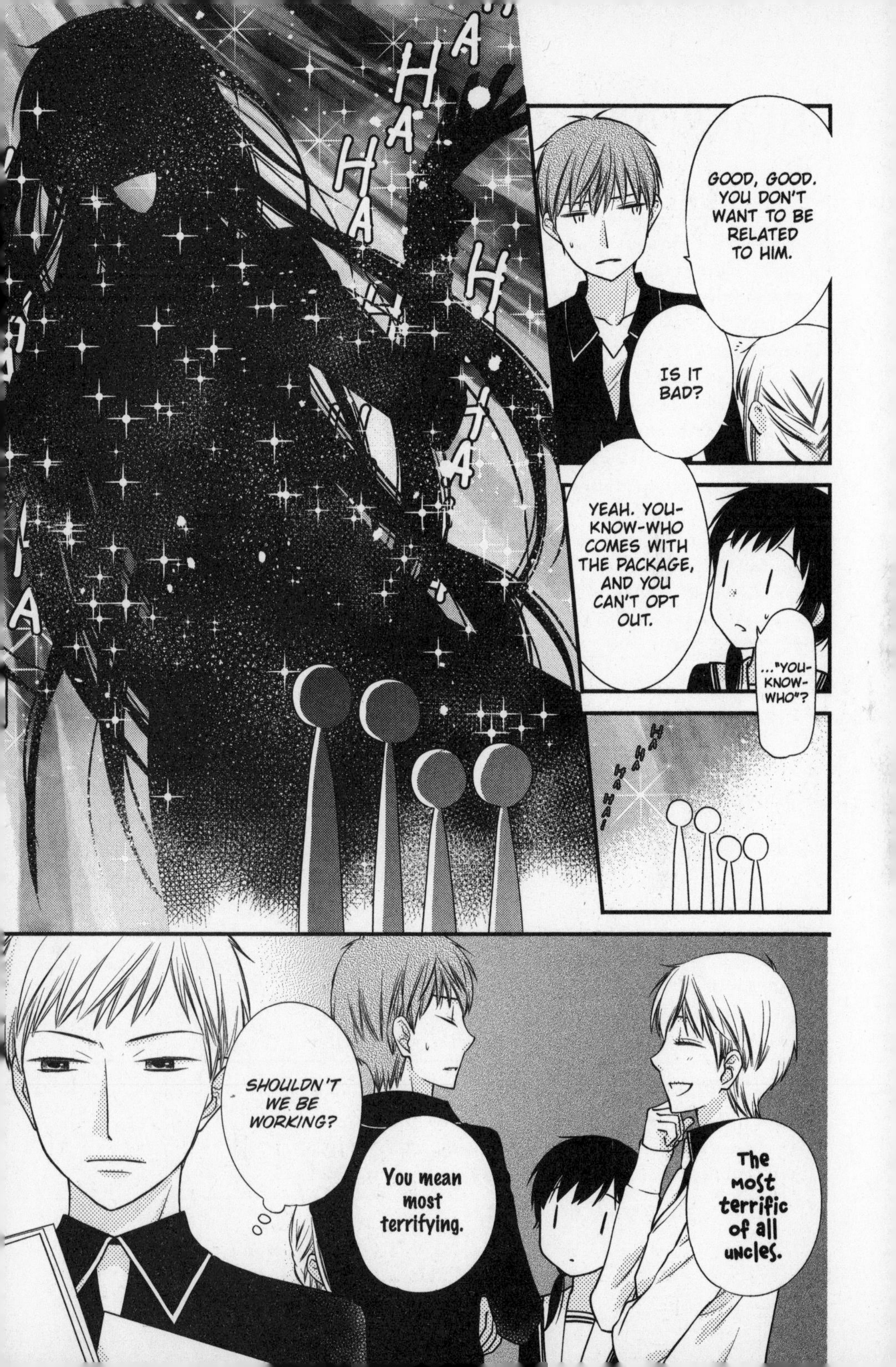
GOOD, GOOD. YOU DON'T WANT TO BE RELATED TO HIM.
IS IT BAD?
YEAH. YOU-KNOW-WHO COMES WITH THE PACKAGE, AND YOU CAN'T OPT OUT.
..."YOU-KNOW-WHO"?
HA HA HA HA
HA HA HA HA HA HA
The most terrific of all uncles.
You mean most terrifying.
SHOULDN'T WE BE WORKING?

TRANSLATION NOTES

COMMON HONORIFICS

no honorific: Indicates familiarity or closeness; if used without permission or reason, addressing someone in this manner would constitute an insult.

-san: The Japanese equivalent of Mr./Mrs./Miss. If a situation calls for politeness, this is the fail-safe honorific.

-sama: Conveys great respect; may also indicate that the social status of the speaker is lower than that of the addressee.

-kun: Used most often when referring to boys, this indicates affection or familiarity. Occasionally used by older men among their peers, but it may also be used by anyone referring to a person of lower standing.

-chan: An affectionate honorific indicating familiarity used mostly in reference to girls; also used in reference to cute persons or animals of either gender.

-senpai: A suffix used to address upperclassmen or more experienced coworkers.

-kouhai: A suffix used to address underclassmen or less experienced coworkers.

-sensei: A respectful term for teachers, artists, or high-level professionals.

Page 139
The Way of the True Pot: Longtime readers of *Fruits Basket* will recognize "the true pot" as Kakeru's translation of his last name. Michi's name means "way," in the sense of "the way things are," so her full name means "the way of the true pot." Ergo, her word is law when it comes to hot pot dishes, of which Japan has many.

Page 143
Meat all the time on the twenty-ninth: Everyone in Japan will know instantly that the twenty-ninth of the month is "meat day," because twenty-nine can be pronounced *niku*, which means "meat."

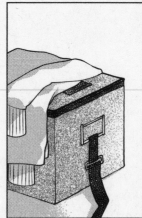

Page 144
A cold in April: In Japan, the school year starts in April, so if you catch a cold in early April, you're likely to miss your first day or so of school.

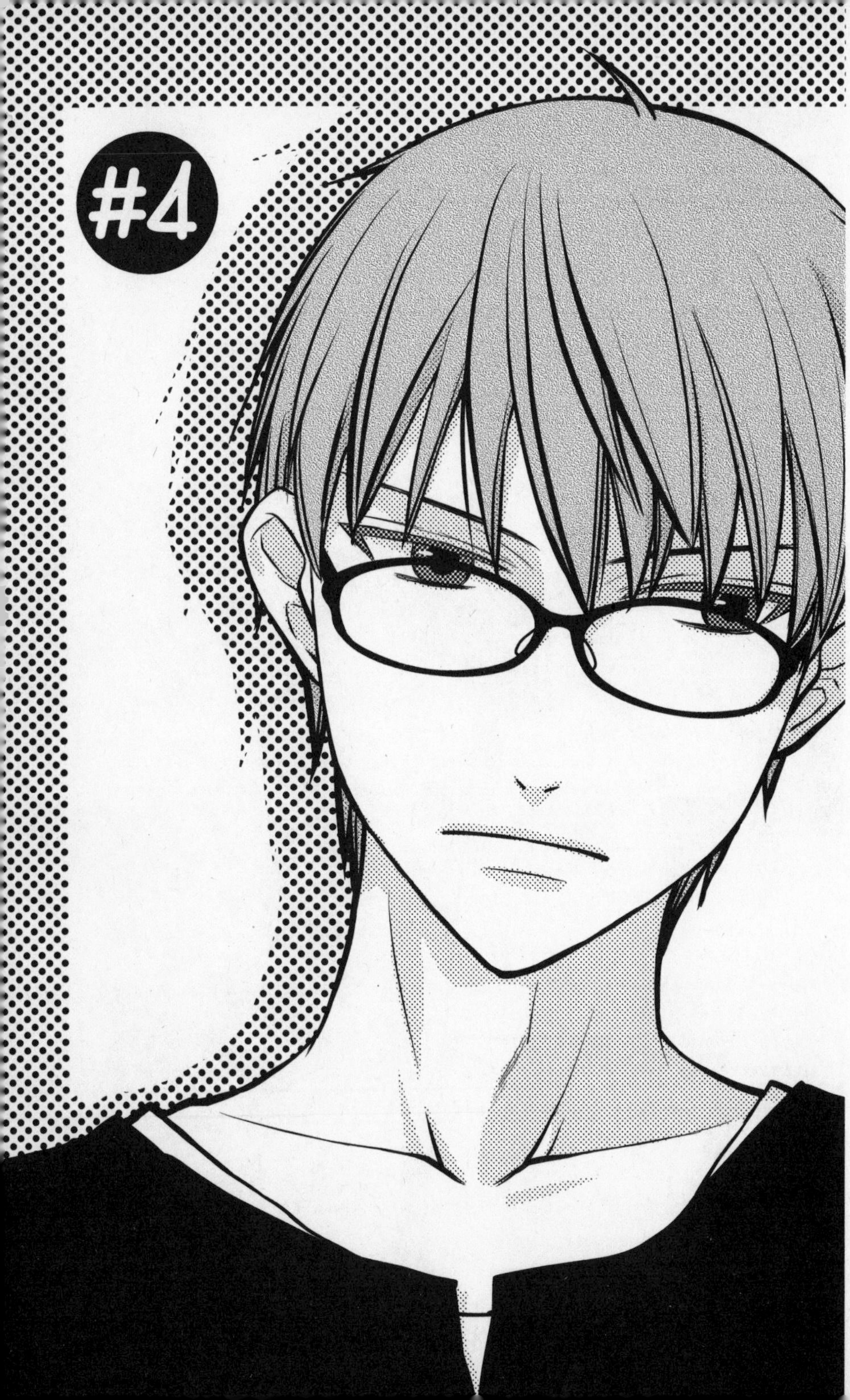
#4

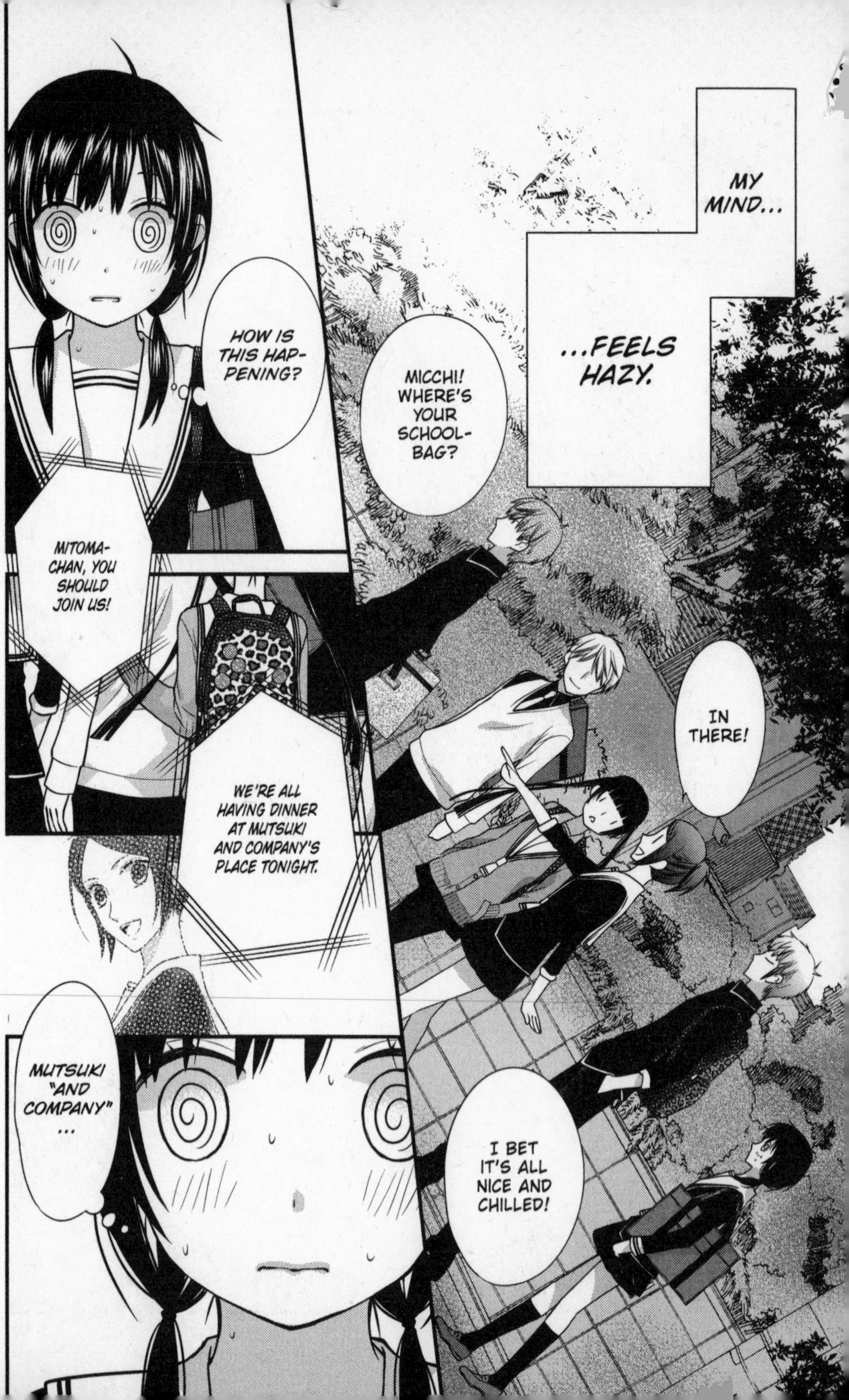
MY MIND...
...FEELS HAZY.
MICCHI! WHERE'S YOUR SCHOOL-BAG?
IN THERE!
I BET IT'S ALL NICE AND CHILLED!
HOW IS THIS HAP-PENING?
MITOMA-CHAN, YOU SHOULD JOIN US!
WE'RE ALL HAVING DINNER AT MUTSUKI AND COMPANY'S PLACE TONIGHT.
MUTSUKI "AND COMPANY"...

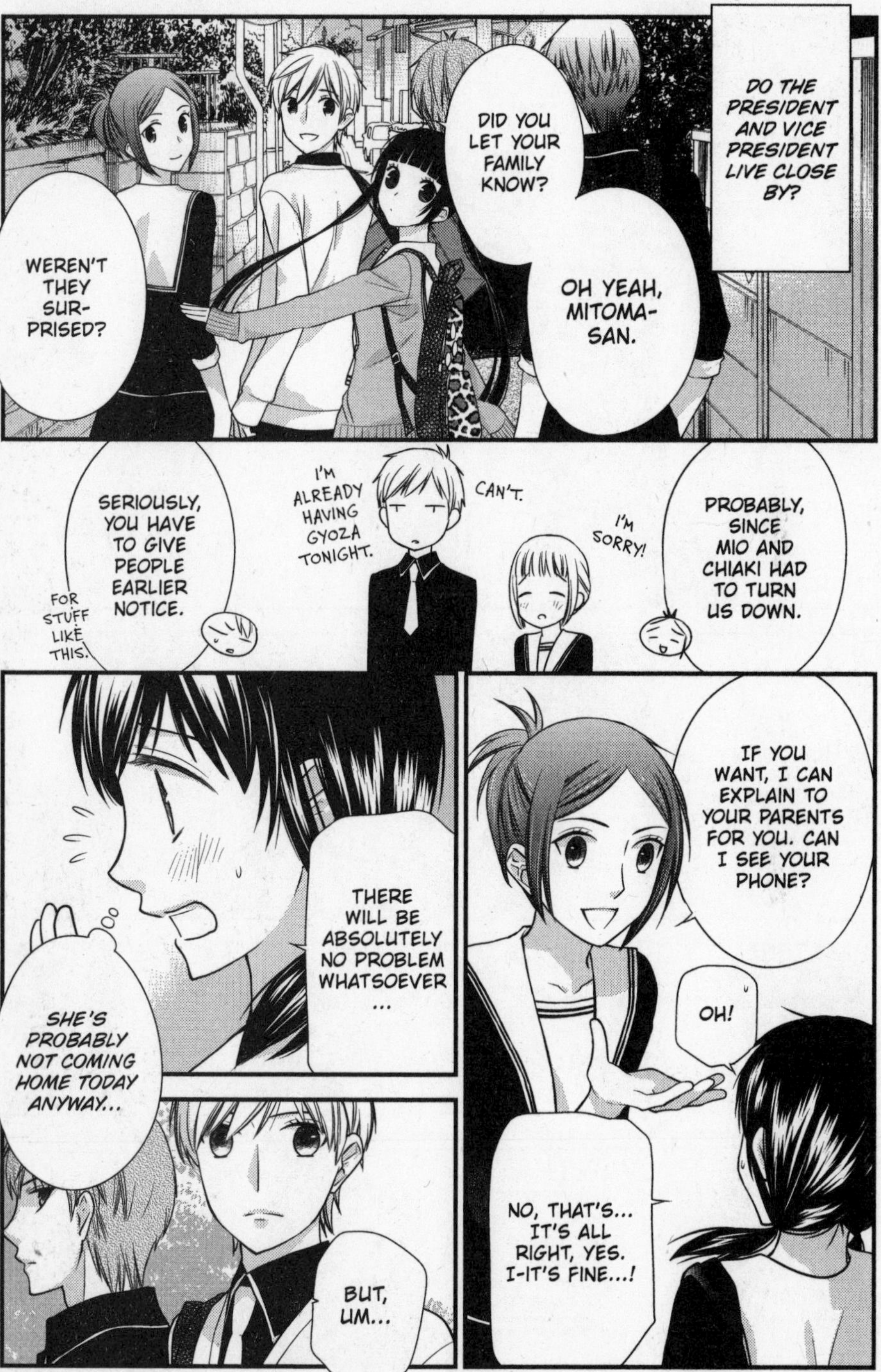
DO THE PRESIDENT AND VICE PRESIDENT LIVE CLOSE BY?
OH YEAH, MITOMA-SAN.
DID YOU LET YOUR FAMILY KNOW?
WEREN'T THEY SURPRISED?
PROBABLY, SINCE MIO AND CHIAKI HAD TO TURN US DOWN.
I'M SORRY!
CAN'T.
I'M ALREADY HAVING GYOZA TONIGHT.
SERIOUSLY, YOU HAVE TO GIVE PEOPLE EARLIER NOTICE.
FOR STUFF LIKE THIS.
IF YOU WANT, I CAN EXPLAIN TO YOUR PARENTS FOR YOU. CAN I SEE YOUR PHONE?
OH!
NO, THAT'S... IT'S ALL RIGHT, YES. I-IT'S FINE...!
THERE WILL BE ABSOLUTELY NO PROBLEM WHATSOEVER ...
SHE'S PROBABLY NOT COMING HOME TODAY ANYWAY...
BUT, UM...

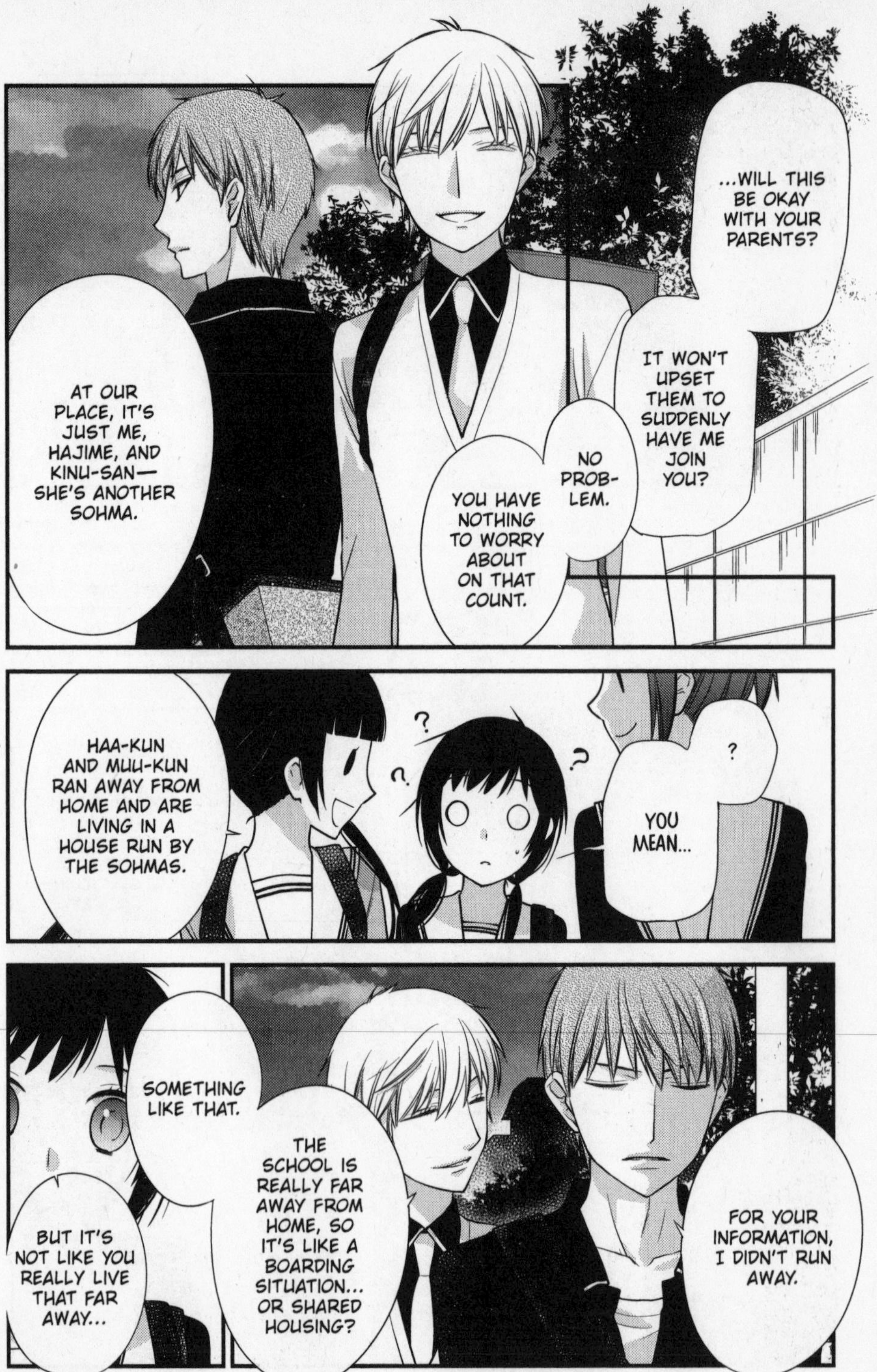
...WILL THIS BE OKAY WITH YOUR PARENTS?
IT WON'T UPSET THEM TO SUDDENLY HAVE ME JOIN YOU?
NO PROB-LEM.
YOU HAVE NOTHING TO WORRY ABOUT ON THAT COUNT.
AT OUR PLACE, IT'S JUST ME, HAJIME, AND KINU-SAN—SHE'S ANOTHER SOHMA.
?
YOU MEAN...
?
?
?
HAA-KUN AND MUU-KUN RAN AWAY FROM HOME AND ARE LIVING IN A HOUSE RUN BY THE SOHMAS.
FOR YOUR INFORMATION, I DIDN'T RUN AWAY.
THE SCHOOL IS REALLY FAR AWAY FROM HOME, SO IT'S LIKE A BOARDING SITUATION... OR SHARED HOUSING?
SOMETHING LIKE THAT.
BUT IT'S NOT LIKE YOU REALLY LIVE THAT FAR AWAY...

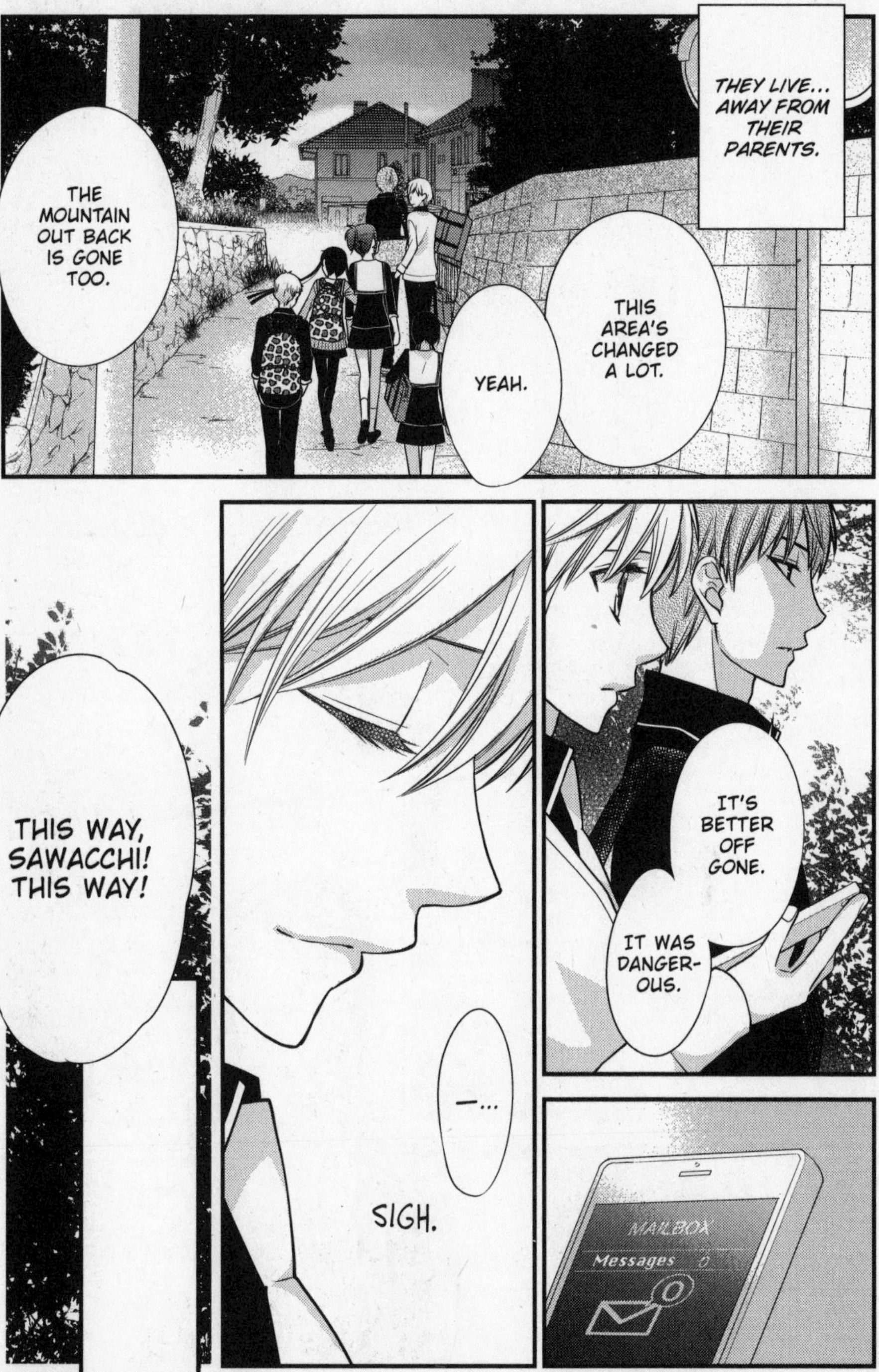
THEY LIVE... AWAY FROM THEIR PARENTS.
THIS AREA'S CHANGED A LOT.
YEAH.
THE MOUNTAIN OUT BACK IS GONE TOO.
IT'S BETTER OFF GONE.
IT WAS DANGER-OUS.
MAILBOX
Messages 0
—...
SIGH.
THIS WAY, SAWACCHI! THIS WAY!

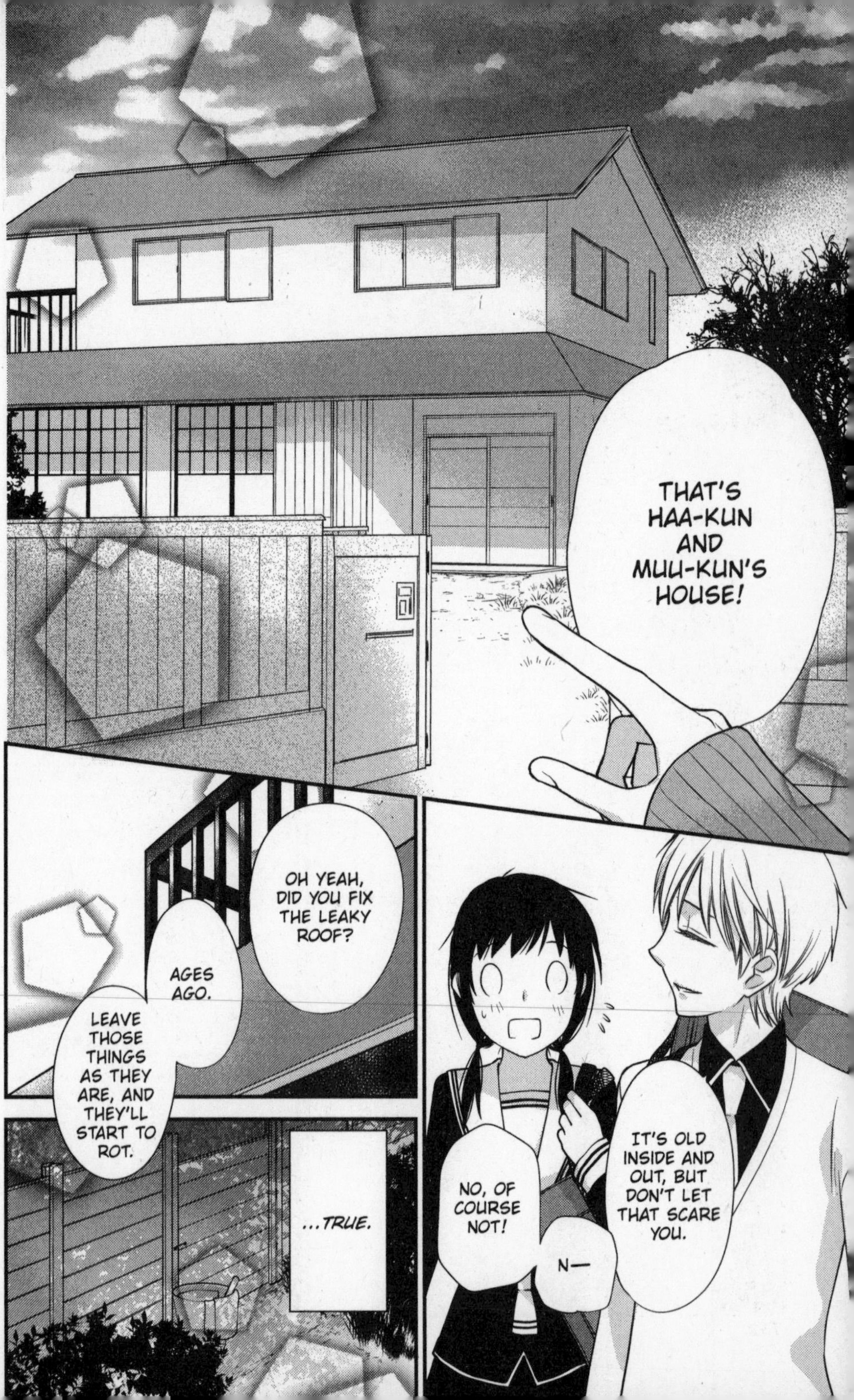
THAT'S HAA-KUN AND MUU-KUN'S HOUSE!
IT'S OLD INSIDE AND OUT, BUT DON'T LET THAT SCARE YOU.
N—
NO, OF COURSE NOT!
OH YEAH, DID YOU FIX THE LEAKY ROOF?
AGES AGO.
LEAVE THOSE THINGS AS THEY ARE, AND THEY'LL START TO ROT.
...TRUE.

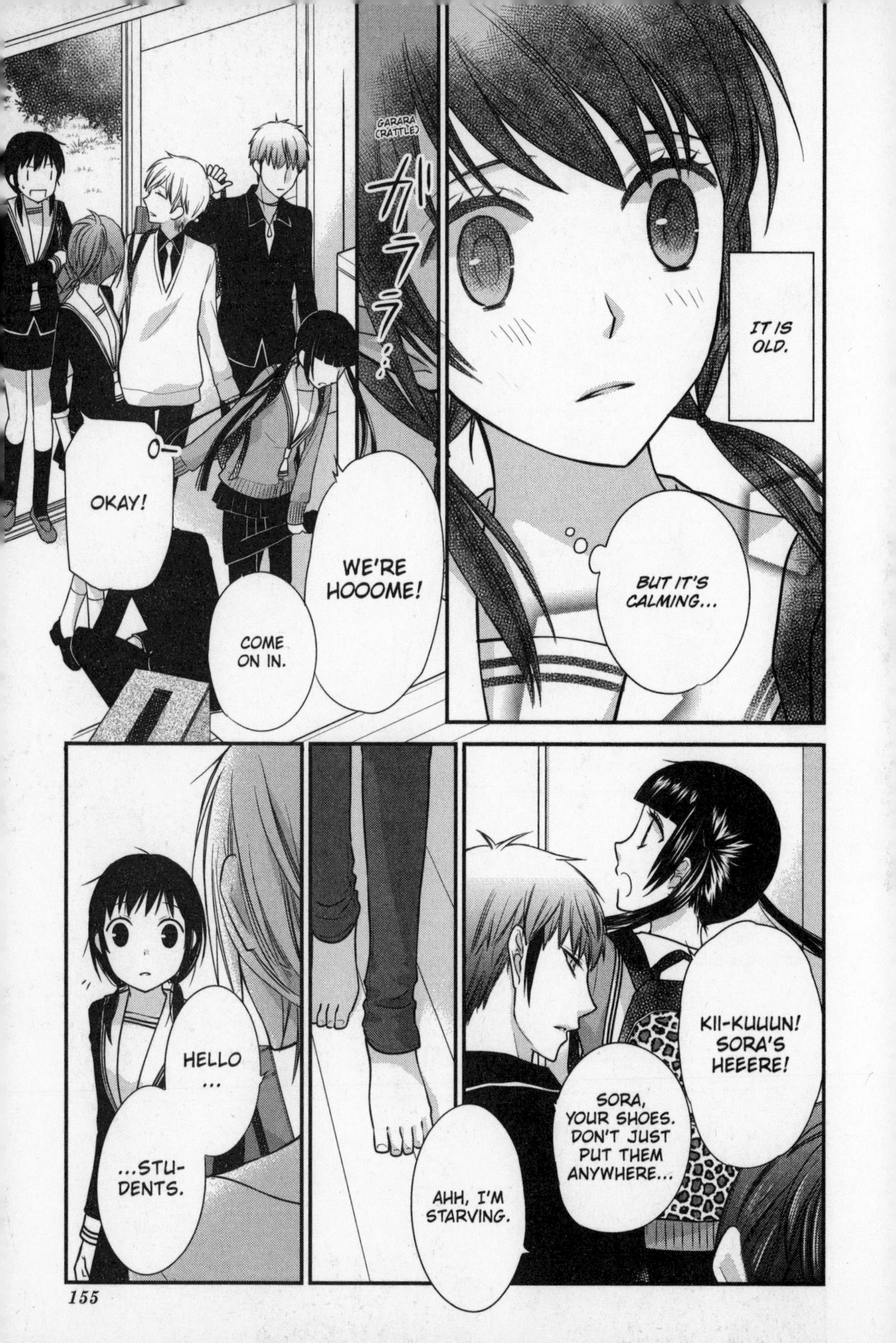
IT IS OLD.
BUT IT'S CALMING...
GARARA (RATTLE)
WE'RE HOOOME!
COME ON IN.
OKAY!
KII-KUUUN! SORA'S HEEERE!
SORA, YOUR SHOES. DON'T JUST PUT THEM ANYWHERE...
AHH, I'M STARVING.
HELLO...
...STU-DENTS.

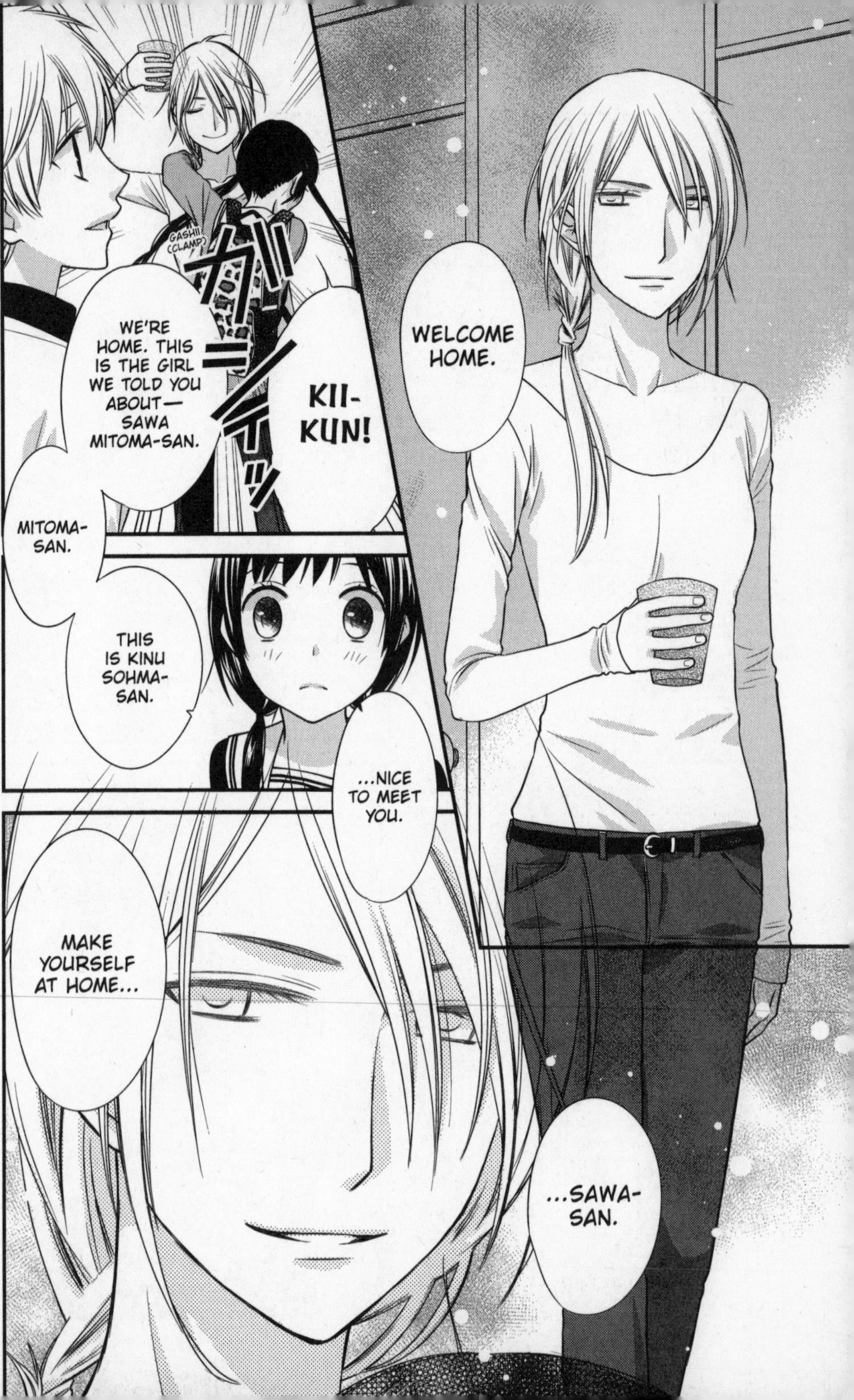
WELCOME HOME.
KII-KUN!
WE'RE HOME. THIS IS THE GIRL WE TOLD YOU ABOUT—SAWA MITOMA-SAN.
GASHII (CLAMP)
MITOMA-SAN.
THIS IS KINU SOHMA-SAN.
...NICE TO MEET YOU.
MAKE YOURSELF AT HOME...
...SAWA-SAN.

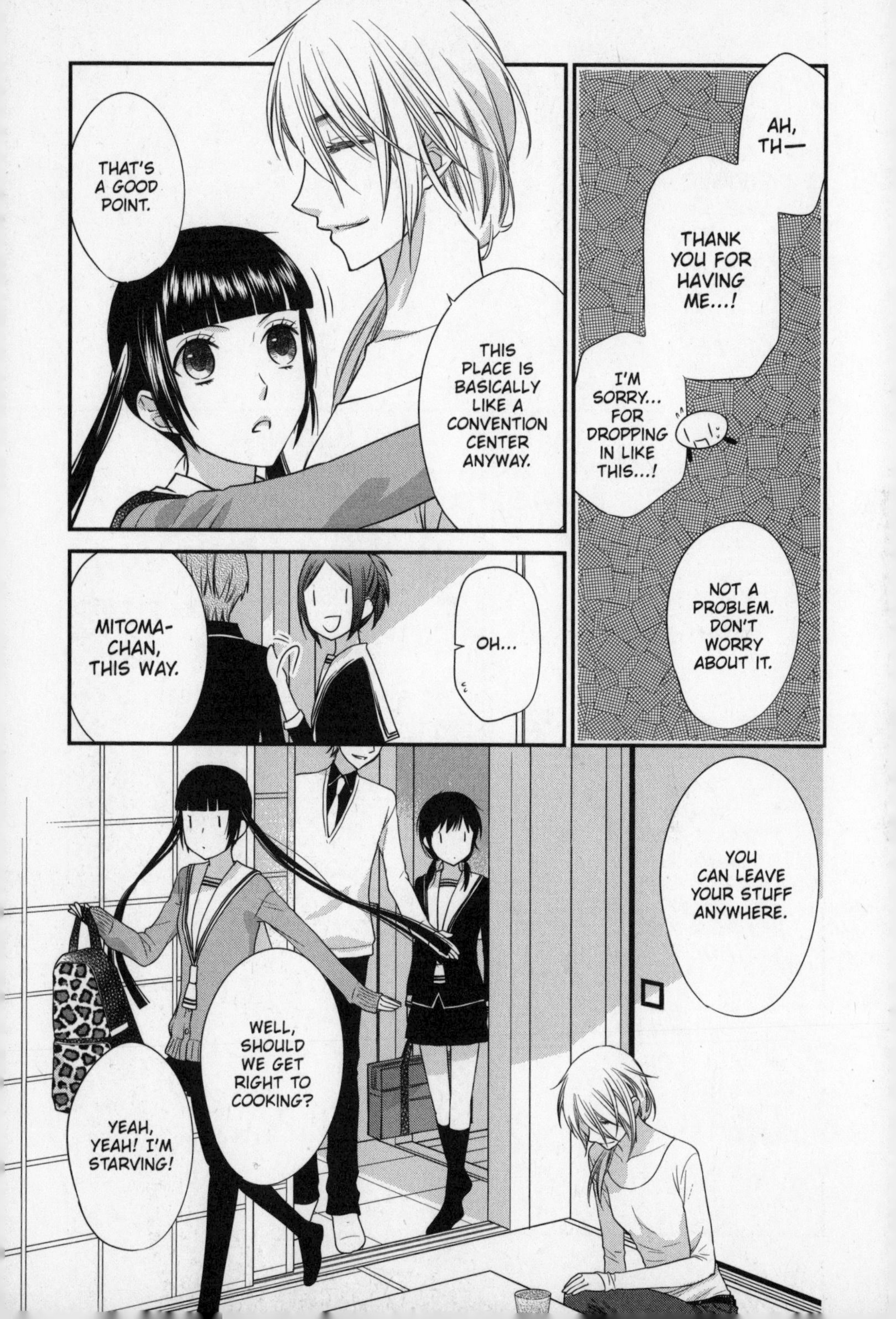
AH, TH—
THANK YOU FOR HAVING ME...!
I'M SORRY... FOR DROPPING IN LIKE THIS...!
NOT A PROBLEM. DON'T WORRY ABOUT IT.
THAT'S A GOOD POINT.
THIS PLACE IS BASICALLY LIKE A CONVENTION CENTER ANYWAY.
OH...
MITOMA-CHAN, THIS WAY.
YOU CAN LEAVE YOUR STUFF ANYWHERE.
WELL, SHOULD WE GET RIGHT TO COOKING?
YEAH, YEAH! I'M STARVING!

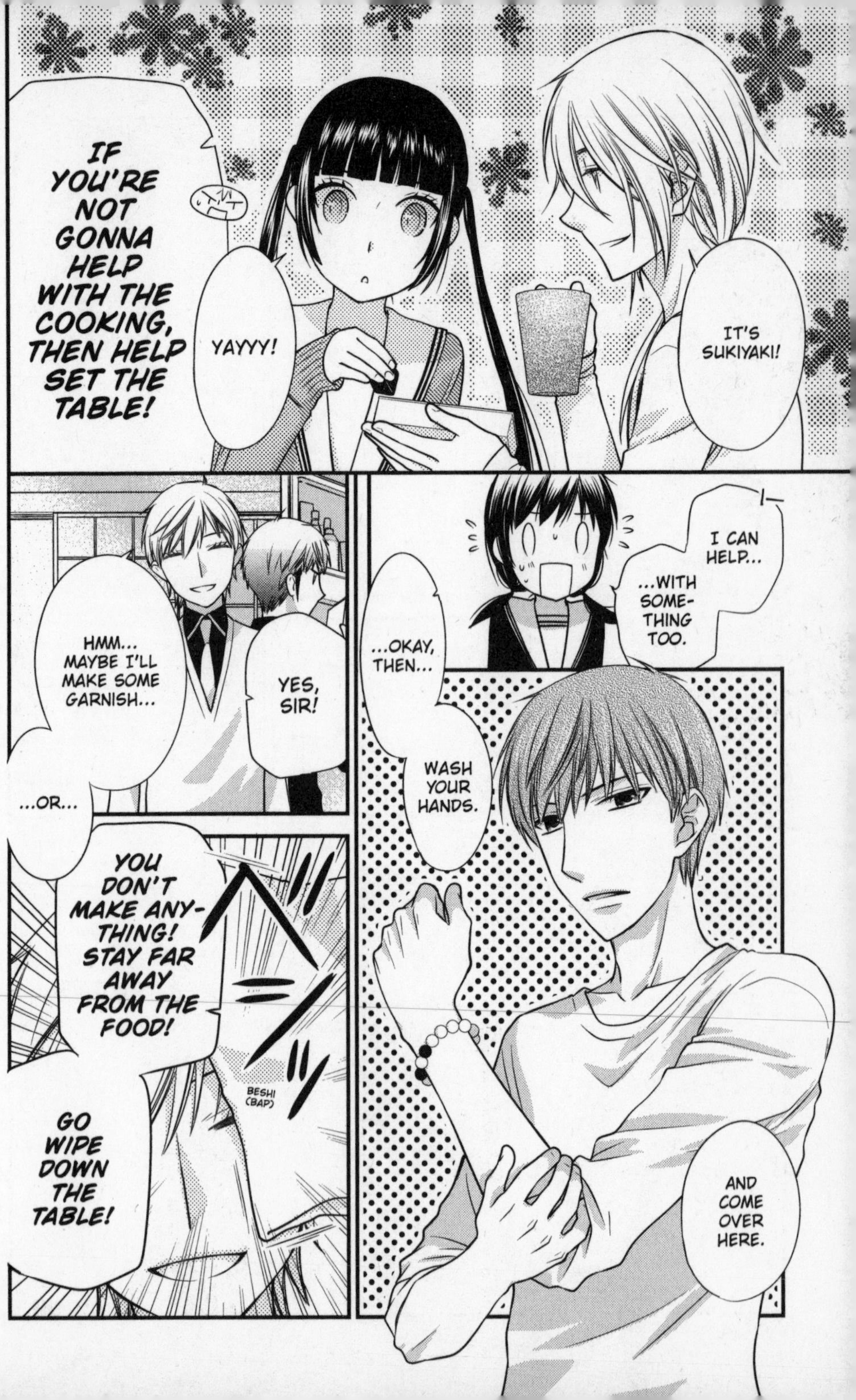
IT'S SUKIYAKI!
YAYYY!
IF YOU'RE NOT GONNA HELP WITH THE COOKING, THEN HELP SET THE TABLE!
I CAN HELP...
...WITH SOME-THING TOO.
...OKAY, THEN...
WASH YOUR HANDS.
AND COME OVER HERE.
HMM... MAYBE I'LL MAKE SOME GARNISH...
YES, SIR!
...OR...
YOU DON'T MAKE ANY-THING! STAY FAR AWAY FROM THE FOOD!
BESHI (BAP)
GO WIPE DOWN THE TABLE!

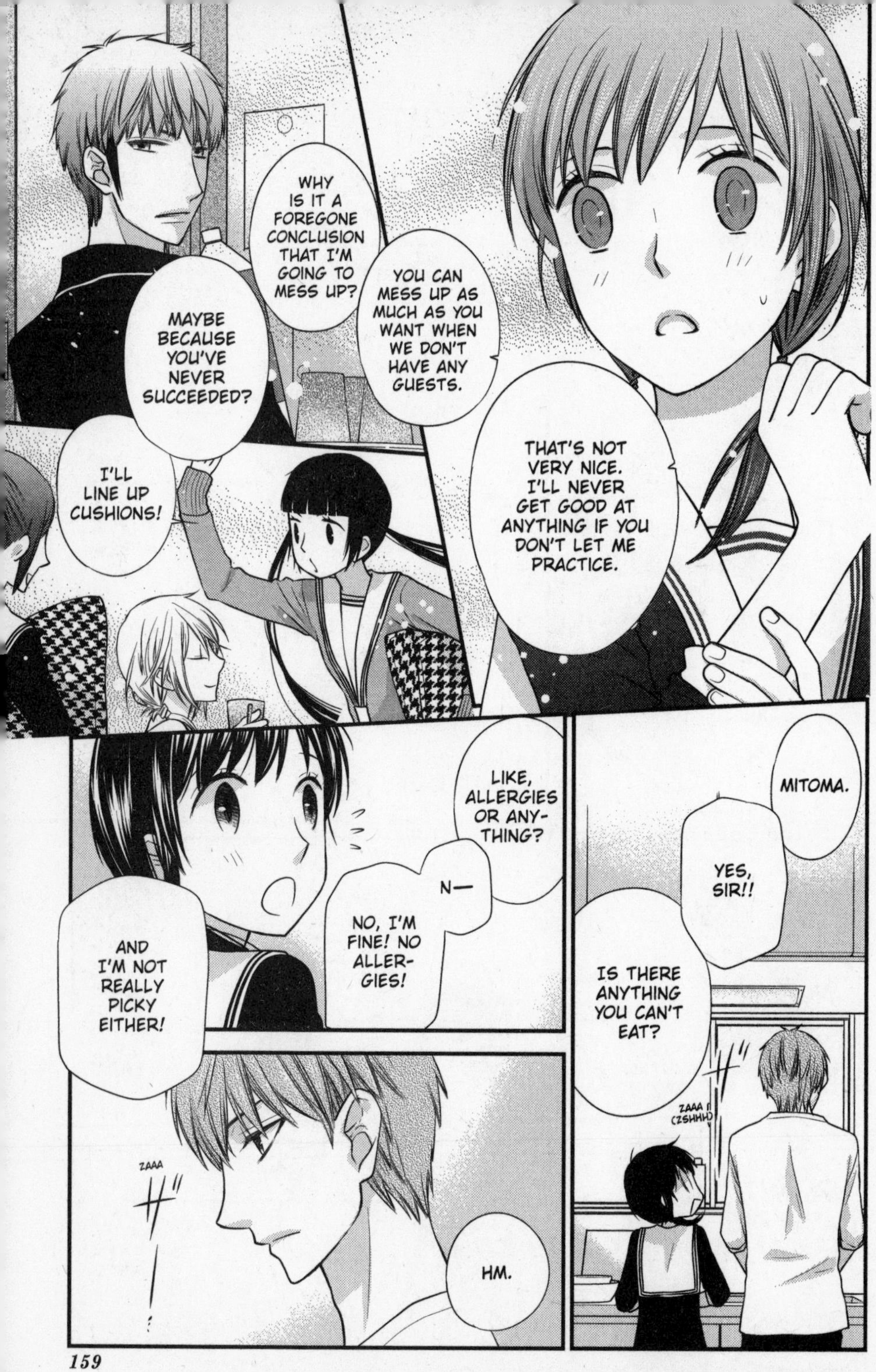

THAT'S NOT VERY NICE. I'LL NEVER GET GOOD AT ANYTHING IF YOU DON'T LET ME PRACTICE.
WHY IS IT A FOREGONE CONCLUSION THAT I'M GOING TO MESS UP?
YOU CAN MESS UP AS MUCH AS YOU WANT WHEN WE DON'T HAVE ANY GUESTS.
MAYBE BECAUSE YOU'VE NEVER SUCCEEDED?
I'LL LINE UP CUSHIONS!
MITOMA.
YES, SIR!!
IS THERE ANYTHING YOU CAN'T EAT?
ZAAA (ZSHHH)
LIKE, ALLERGIES OR ANY-THING?
N—
NO, I'M FINE! NO ALLER-GIES!
AND I'M NOT REALLY PICKY EITHER!
ZAAA
HM.

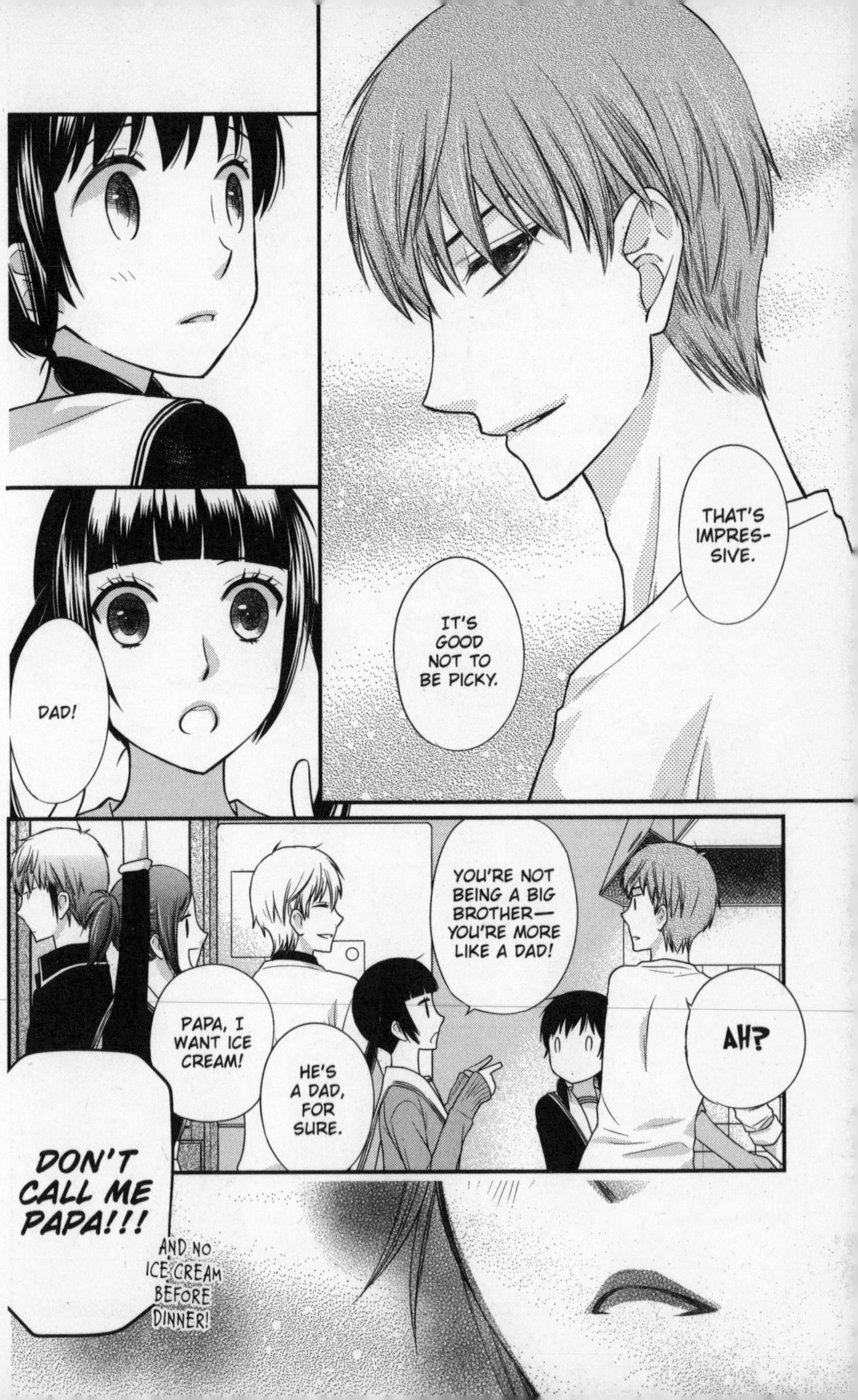
THAT'S IMPRES-SIVE.
IT'S GOOD NOT TO BE PICKY.
DAD!
AH?
YOU'RE NOT BEING A BIG BROTHER— YOU'RE MORE LIKE A DAD!
HE'S A DAD, FOR SURE.
PAPA, I WANT ICE CREAM!
DON'T CALL ME PAPA!!!
AND NO ICE CREAM BEFORE DINNER!

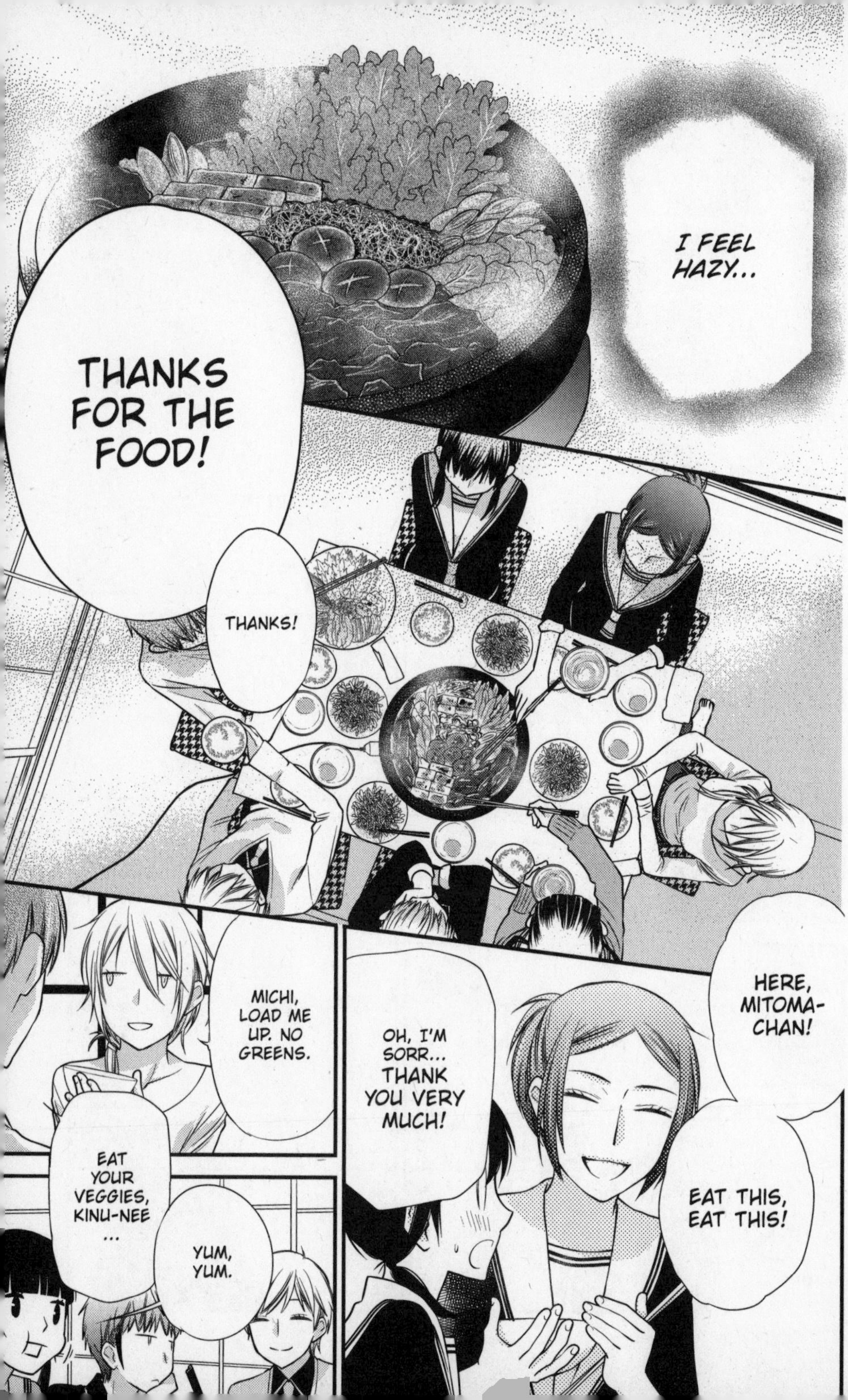
I FEEL HAZY...
THANKS FOR THE FOOD!
THANKS!
HERE, MITOMA-CHAN!
OH, I'M SORR... THANK YOU VERY MUCH!
EAT THIS, EAT THIS!
MICHI, LOAD ME UP. NO GREENS.
EAT YOUR VEGGIES, KINU-NEE ...
YUM, YUM.

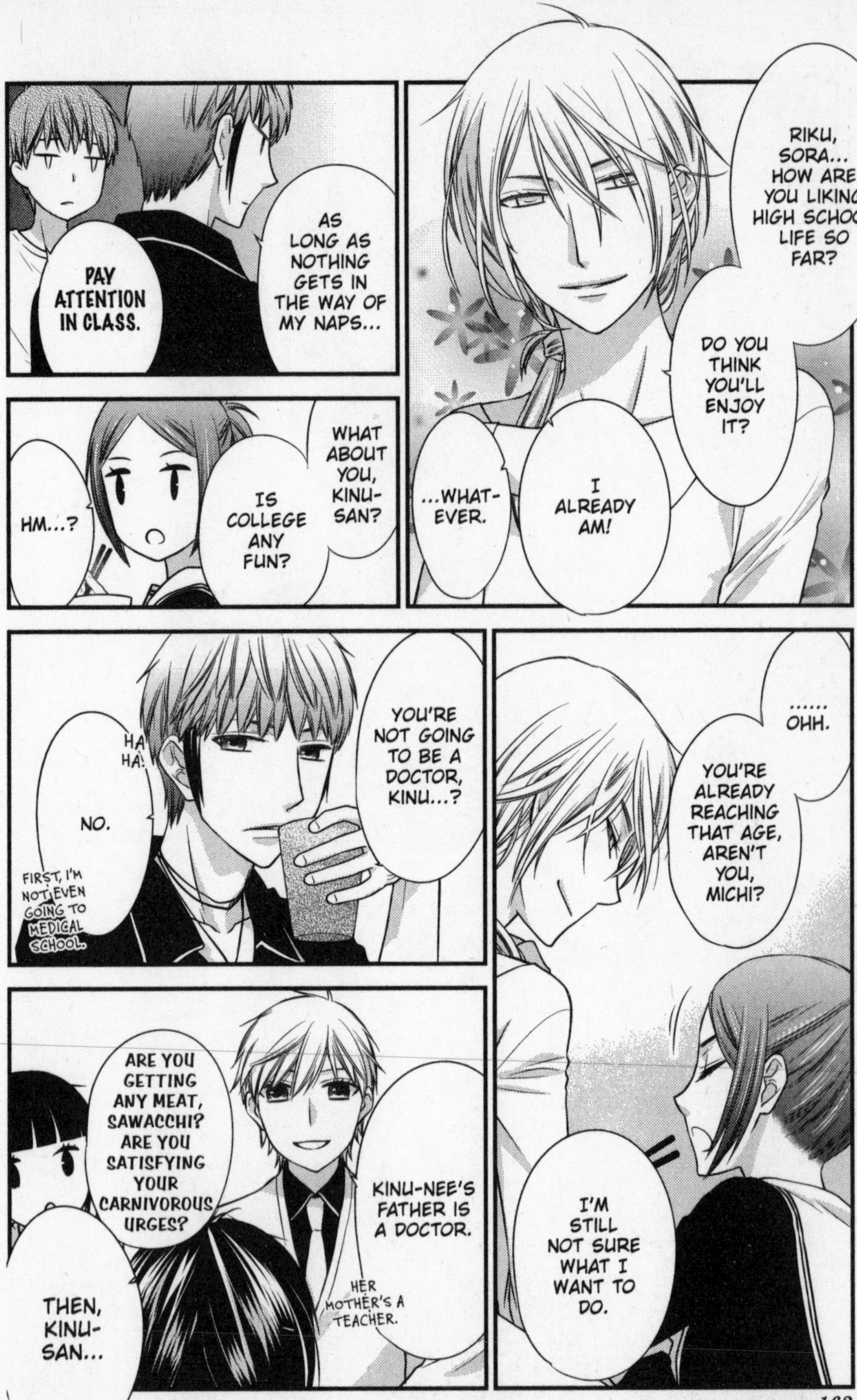
RIKU, SORA... HOW ARE YOU LIKING HIGH SCHOOL LIFE SO FAR?
DO YOU THINK YOU'LL ENJOY IT?
I ALREADY AM!
...WHAT-EVER.
AS LONG AS NOTHING GETS IN THE WAY OF MY NAPS...
PAY ATTENTION IN CLASS.
WHAT ABOUT YOU, KINU-SAN?
IS COLLEGE ANY FUN?
HM...?
......OHH.
YOU'RE ALREADY REACHING THAT AGE, AREN'T YOU, MICHI?
I'M STILL NOT SURE WHAT I WANT TO DO.
YOU'RE NOT GOING TO BE A DOCTOR, KINU...?
HA HA!
NO.
FIRST, I'M NOT EVEN GOING TO MEDICAL SCHOOL.
KINU-NEE'S FATHER IS A DOCTOR.
HER MOTHER'S A TEACHER.
ARE YOU GETTING ANY MEAT, SAWACCHI? ARE YOU SATISFYING YOUR CARNIVOROUS URGES?
THEN, KINU-SAN...

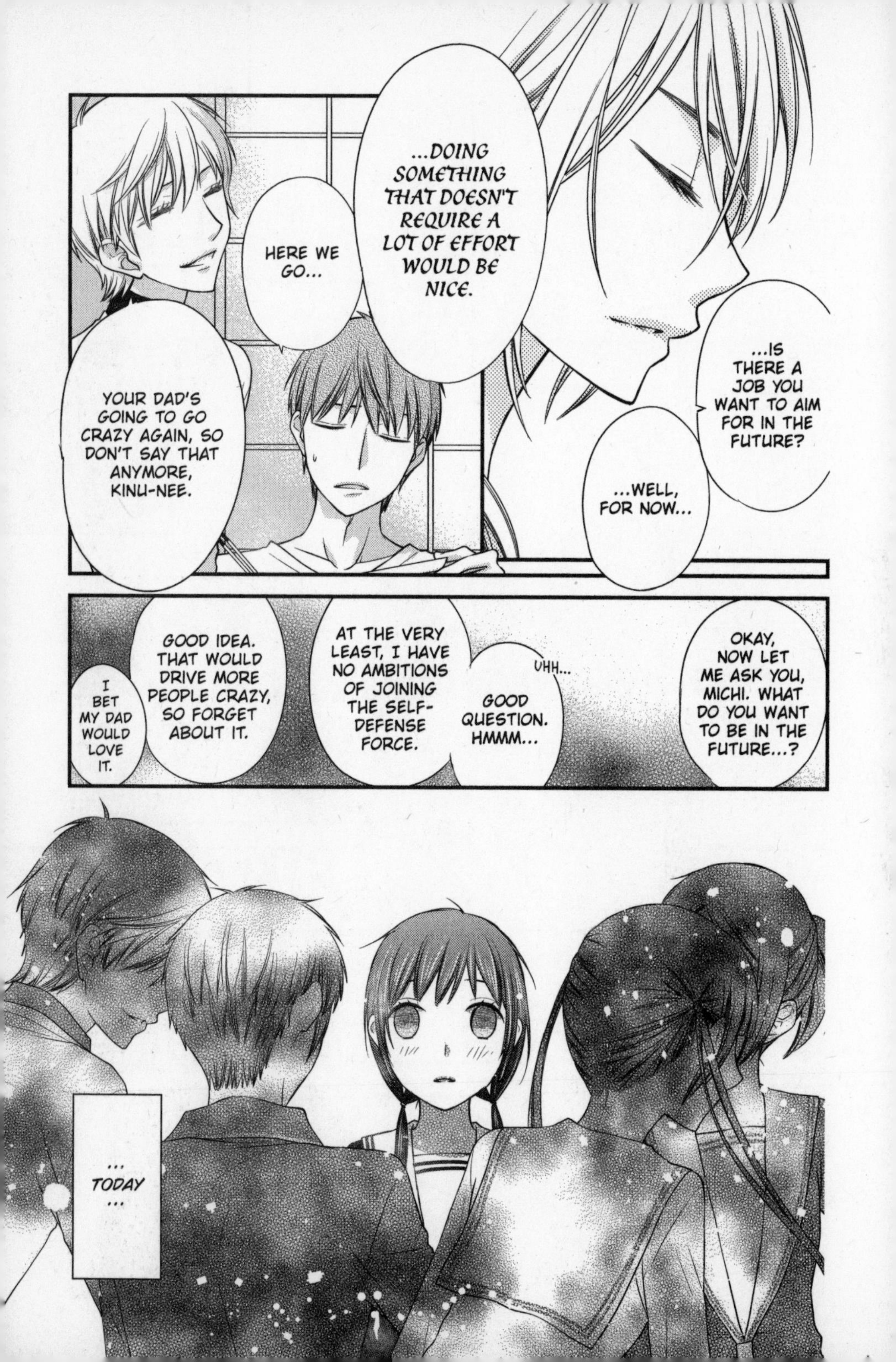

...IS THERE A JOB YOU WANT TO AIM FOR IN THE FUTURE?
...WELL, FOR NOW...
...DOING SOMETHING THAT DOESN'T REQUIRE A LOT OF EFFORT WOULD BE NICE.
HERE WE GO...
YOUR DAD'S GOING TO GO CRAZY AGAIN, SO DON'T SAY THAT ANYMORE, KINU-NEE.
OKAY, NOW LET ME ASK YOU, MICHI. WHAT DO YOU WANT TO BE IN THE FUTURE...?
UHH...
GOOD QUESTION. HMMM...
AT THE VERY LEAST, I HAVE NO AMBITIONS OF JOINING THE SELF-DEFENSE FORCE.
GOOD IDEA. THAT WOULD DRIVE MORE PEOPLE CRAZY, SO FORGET ABOUT IT.
I BET MY DAD WOULD LOVE IT.
...TODAY...

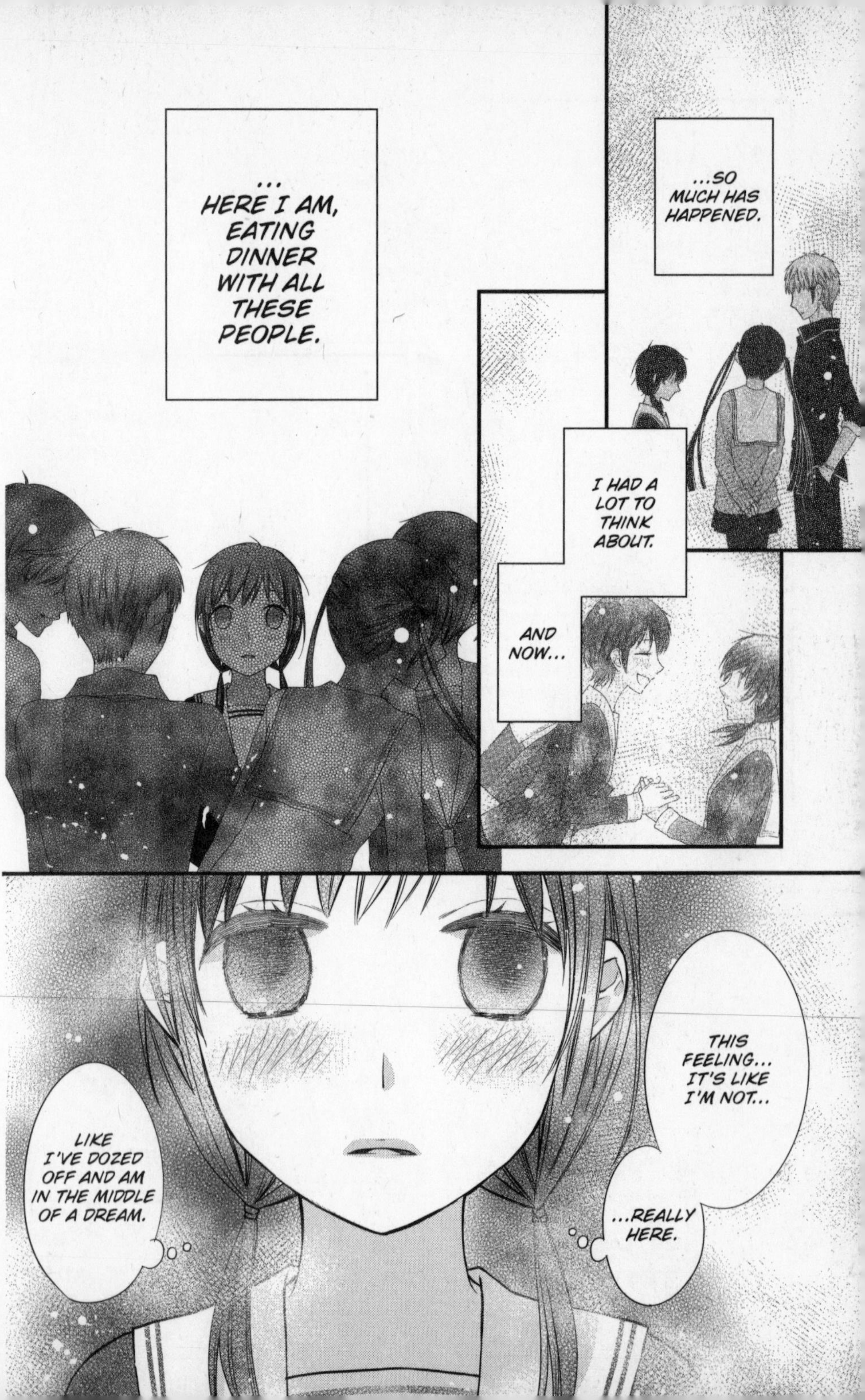

...SO MUCH HAS HAPPENED.
I HAD A LOT TO THINK ABOUT.
AND NOW...
... HERE I AM, EATING DINNER WITH ALL THESE PEOPLE.
THIS FEELING... IT'S LIKE I'M NOT...
...REALLY HERE.
LIKE I'VE DOZED OFF AND AM IN THE MIDDLE OF A DREAM.

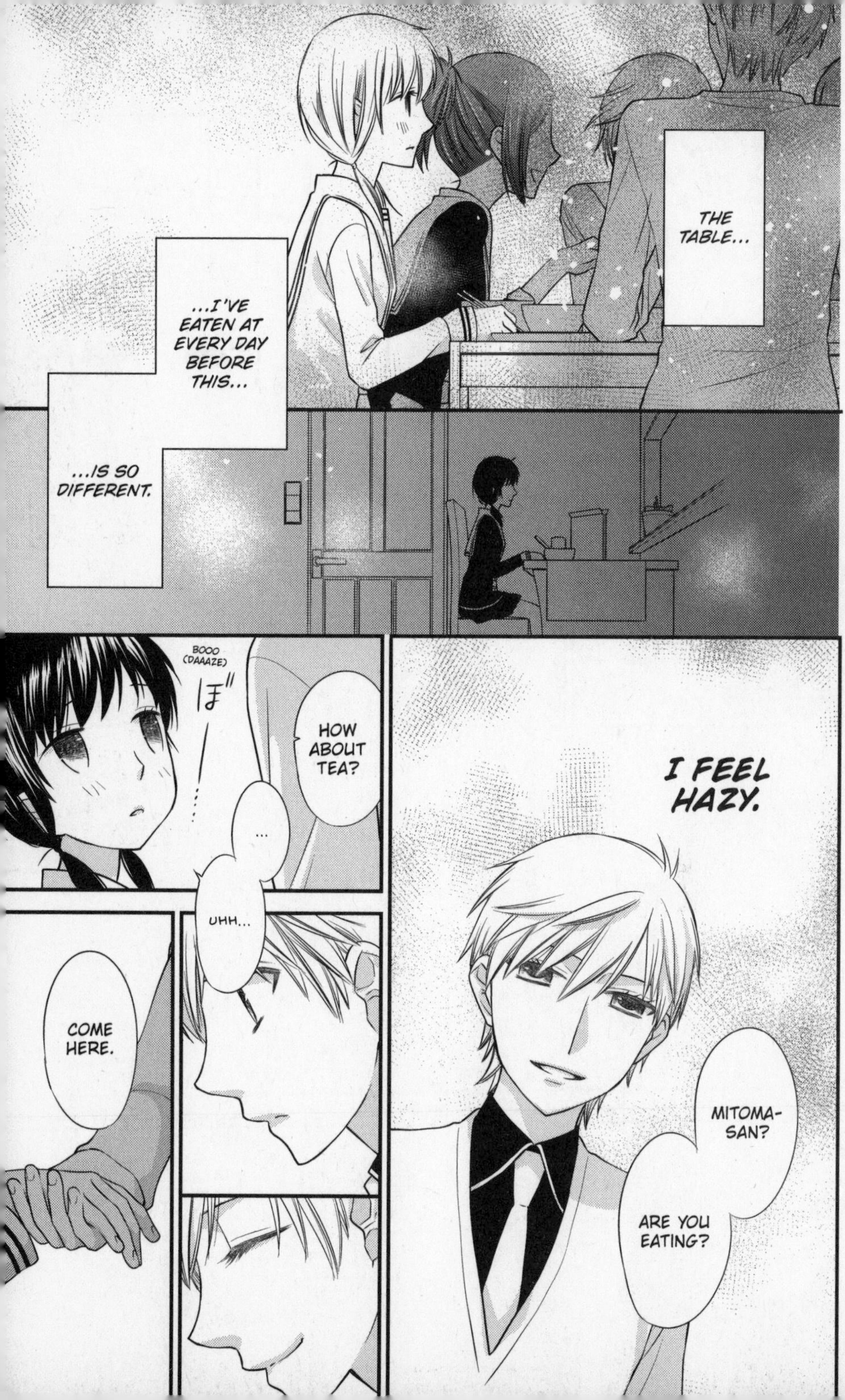
THE TABLE...
...I'VE EATEN AT EVERY DAY BEFORE THIS...
...IS SO DIFFERENT.
I FEEL HAZY.
MITOMA-SAN?
ARE YOU EATING?
HOW ABOUT TEA?
BOOO (DAAAZE)
ぼ゛
...
UHH...
COME HERE.

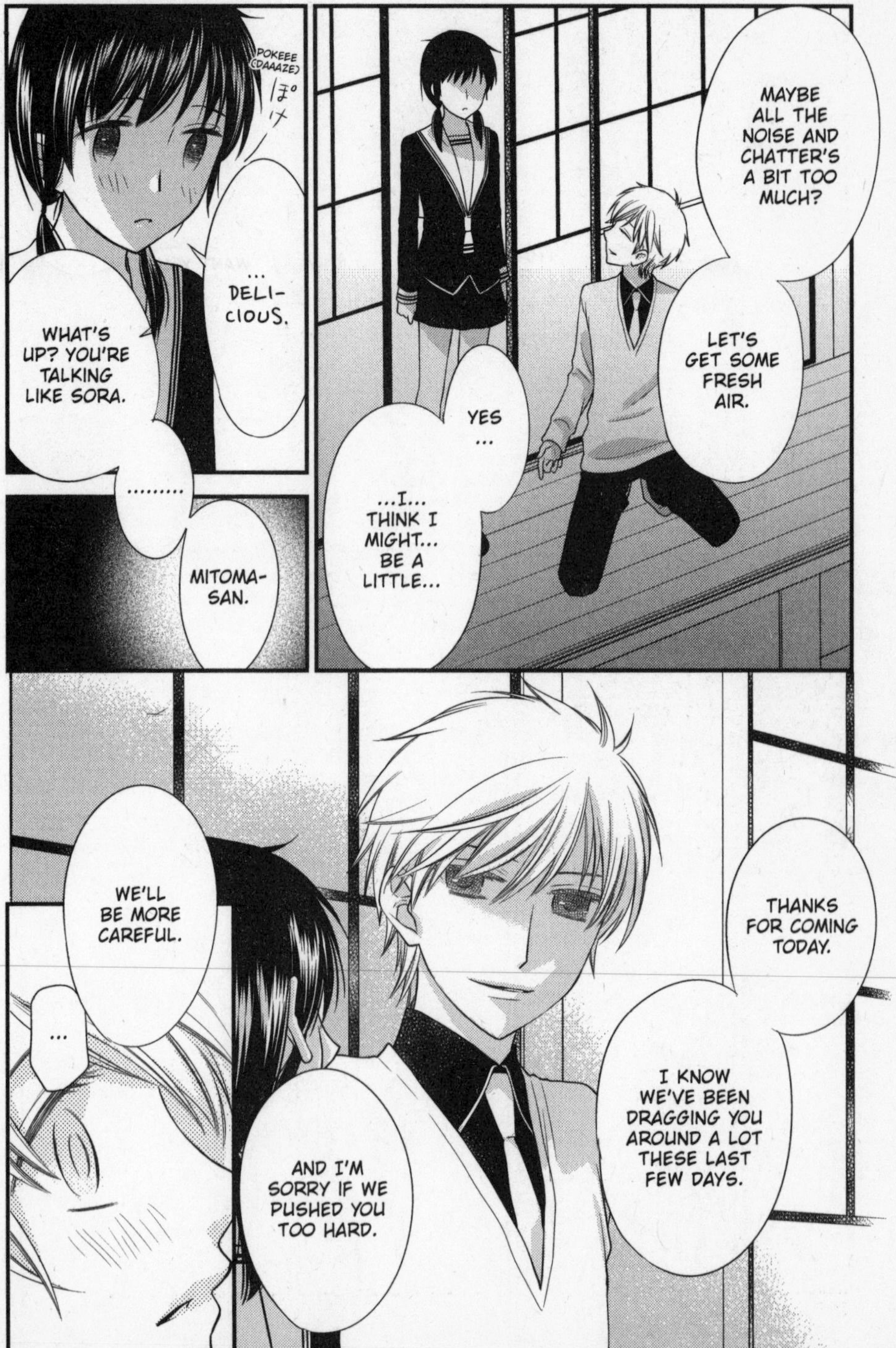
MAYBE ALL THE NOISE AND CHATTER'S A BIT TOO MUCH?
LET'S GET SOME FRESH AIR.
YES...
...I... THINK I MIGHT... BE A LITTLE...
POKEEE (DAAAZE)
ぽけ
...DELI-CIOUS.
WHAT'S UP? YOU'RE TALKING LIKE SORA.
....
MITOMA-SAN.
THANKS FOR COMING TODAY.
I KNOW WE'VE BEEN DRAGGING YOU AROUND A LOT THESE LAST FEW DAYS.
AND I'M SORRY IF WE PUSHED YOU TOO HARD.
WE'LL BE MORE CAREFUL.
...

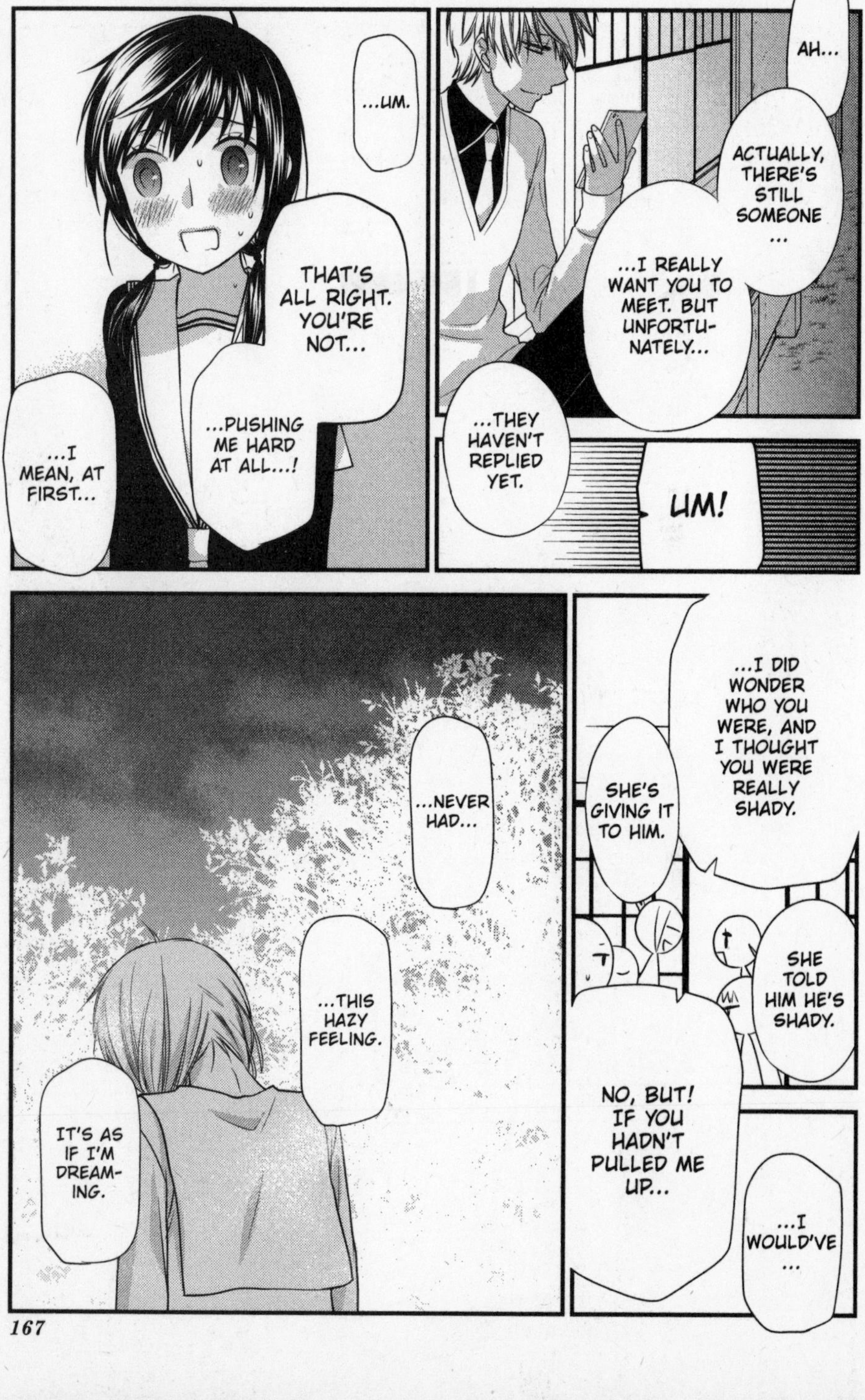
AH...
ACTUALLY, THERE'S STILL SOMEONE ...
...I REALLY WANT YOU TO MEET. BUT UNFORTU-NATELY...
...THEY HAVEN'T REPLIED YET.
UM!
...UM.
THAT'S ALL RIGHT. YOU'RE NOT...
...PUSHING ME HARD AT ALL...!
...I MEAN, AT FIRST...
...I DID WONDER WHO YOU WERE, AND I THOUGHT YOU WERE REALLY SHADY.
SHE'S GIVING IT TO HIM.
SHE TOLD HIM HE'S SHADY.
NO, BUT! IF YOU HADN'T PULLED ME UP...
...I WOULD'VE ...
...NEVER HAD...
...THIS HAZY FEELING.
IT'S AS IF I'M DREAMING.

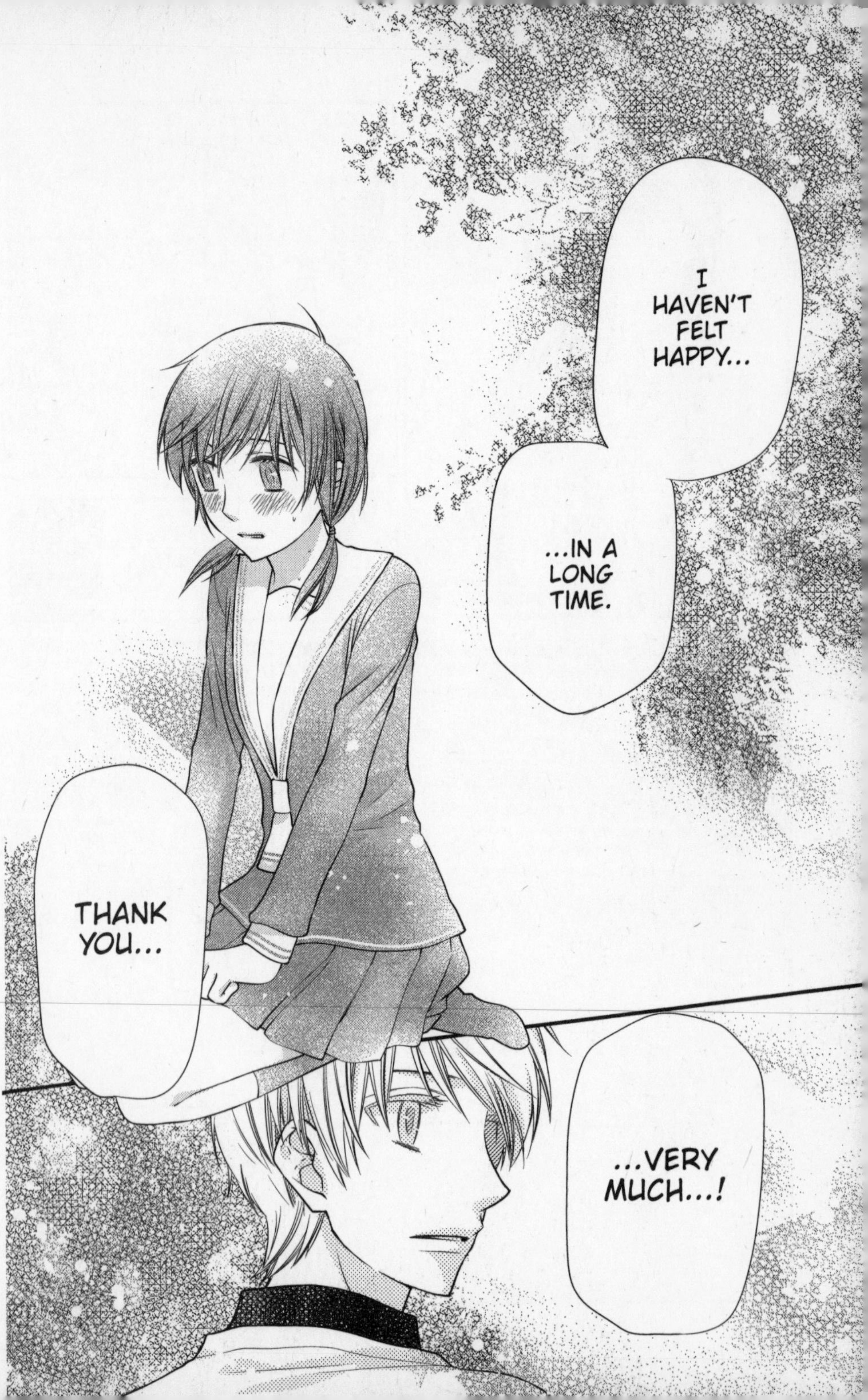
I HAVEN'T FELT HAPPY...
...IN A LONG TIME.
THANK YOU...
...VERY MUCH...!

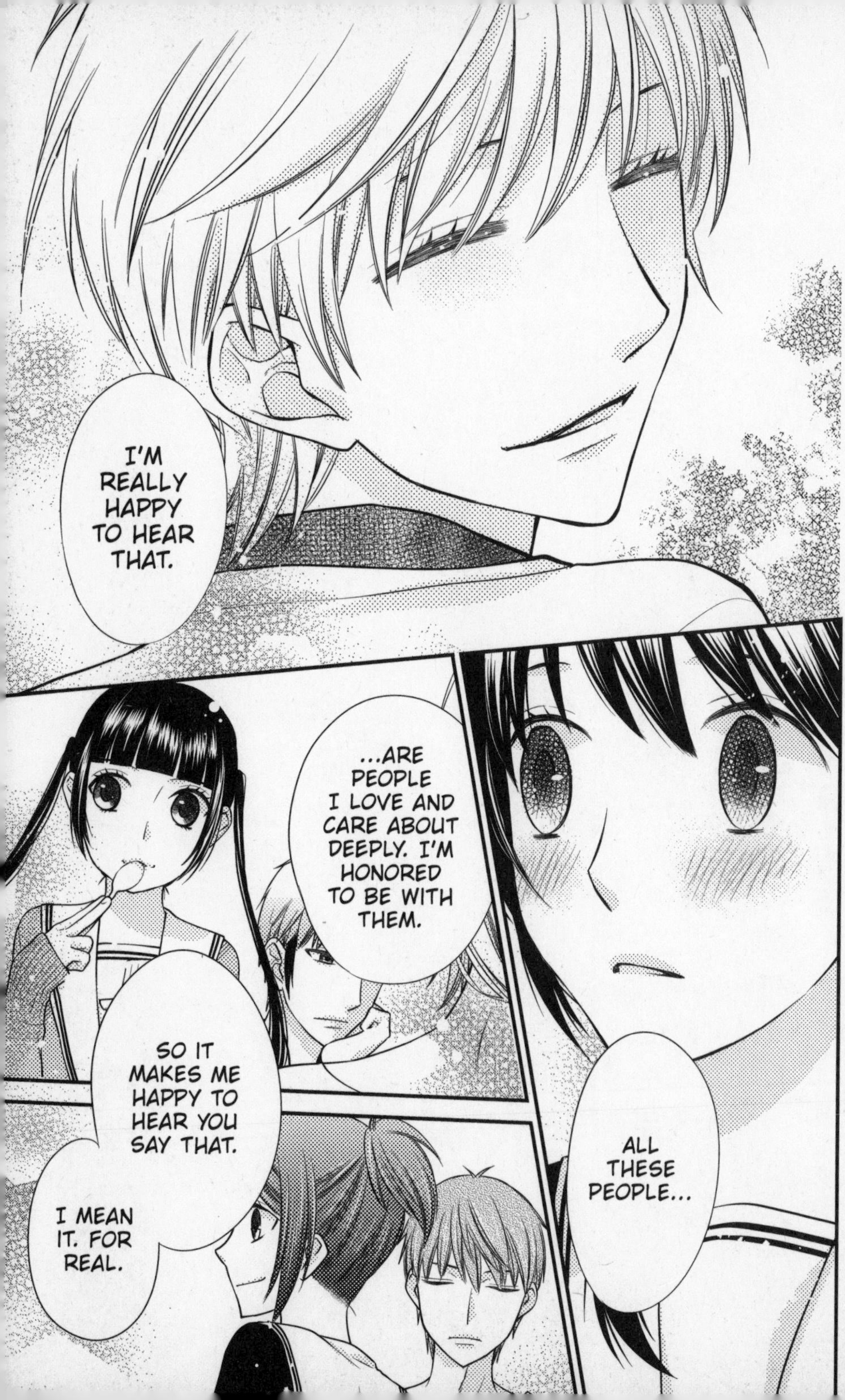
I'M REALLY HAPPY TO HEAR THAT.
ALL THESE PEOPLE...
...ARE PEOPLE I LOVE AND CARE ABOUT DEEPLY. I'M HONORED TO BE WITH THEM.
SO IT MAKES ME HAPPY TO HEAR YOU SAY THAT.
I MEAN IT. FOR REAL.

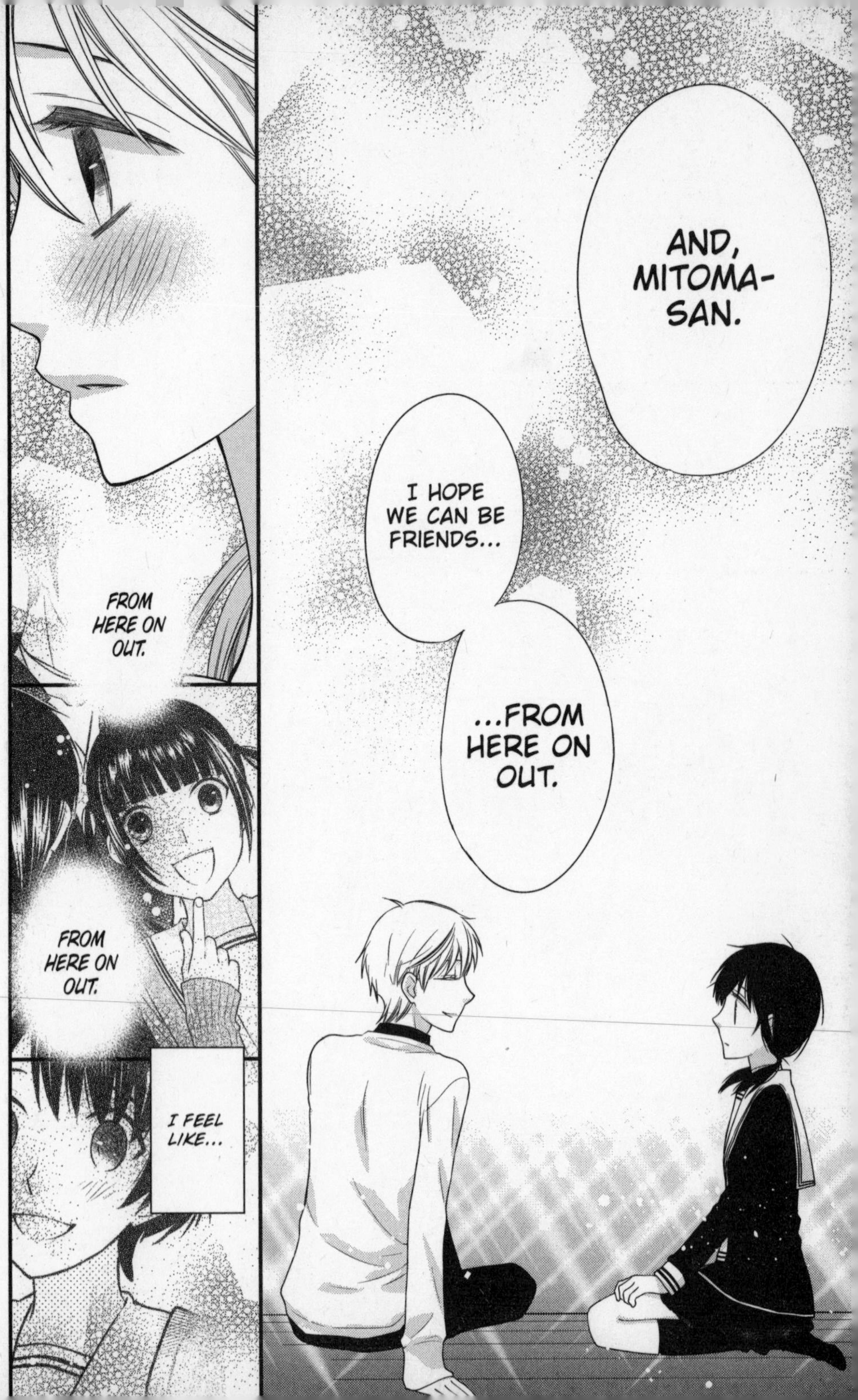
AND, MITOMA-SAN.
I HOPE WE CAN BE FRIENDS...
...FROM HERE ON OUT.
FROM HERE ON OUT.
FROM HERE ON OUT.
I FEEL LIKE...

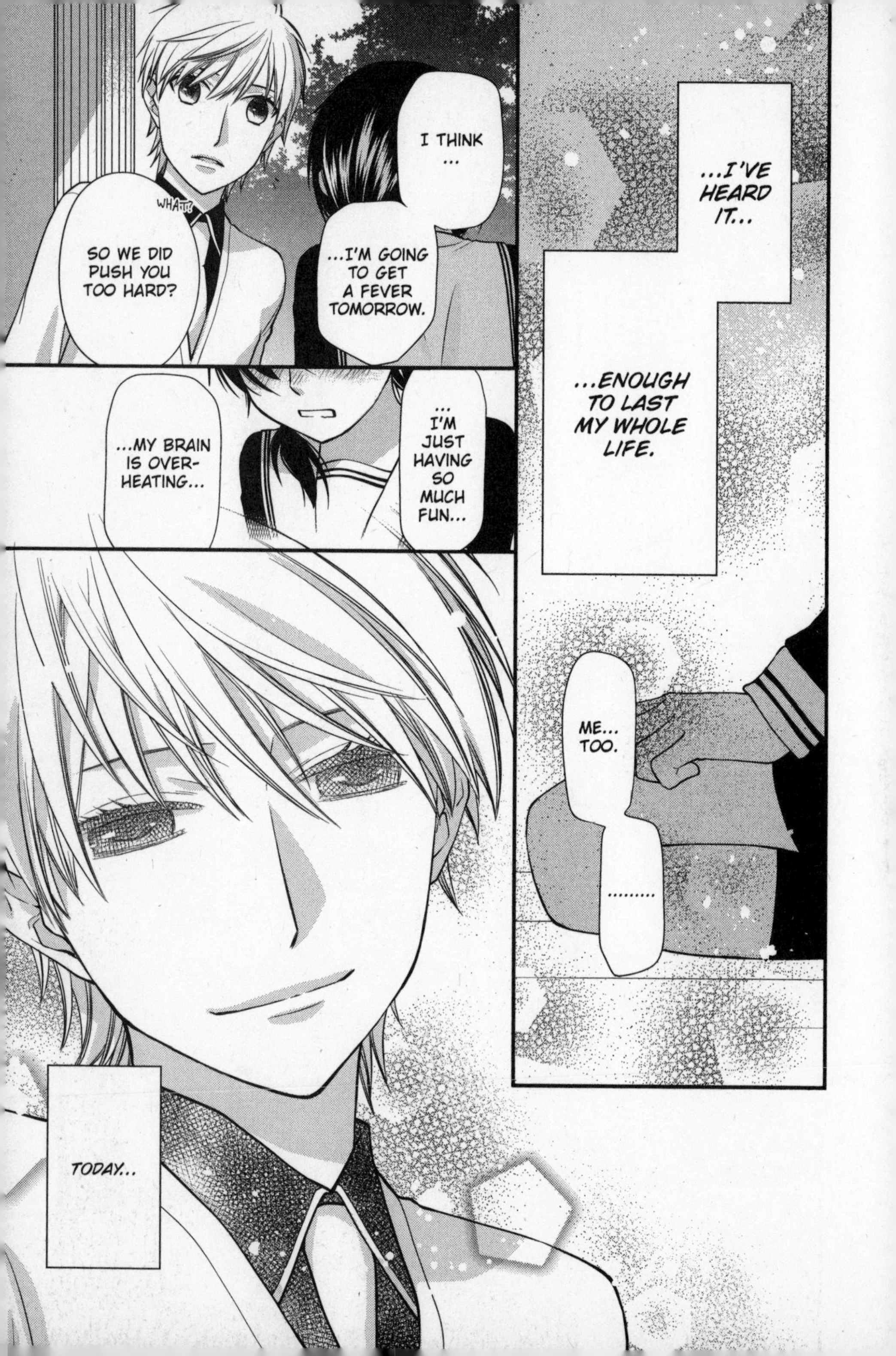
I THINK ...
...I'M GOING TO GET A FEVER TOMORROW.
WHAT!?
SO WE DID PUSH YOU TOO HARD?
... I'M JUST HAVING SO MUCH FUN...
...MY BRAIN IS OVER-HEATING...
TODAY...
...I'VE HEARD IT...
...ENOUGH TO LAST MY WHOLE LIFE.
ME... TOO.
....

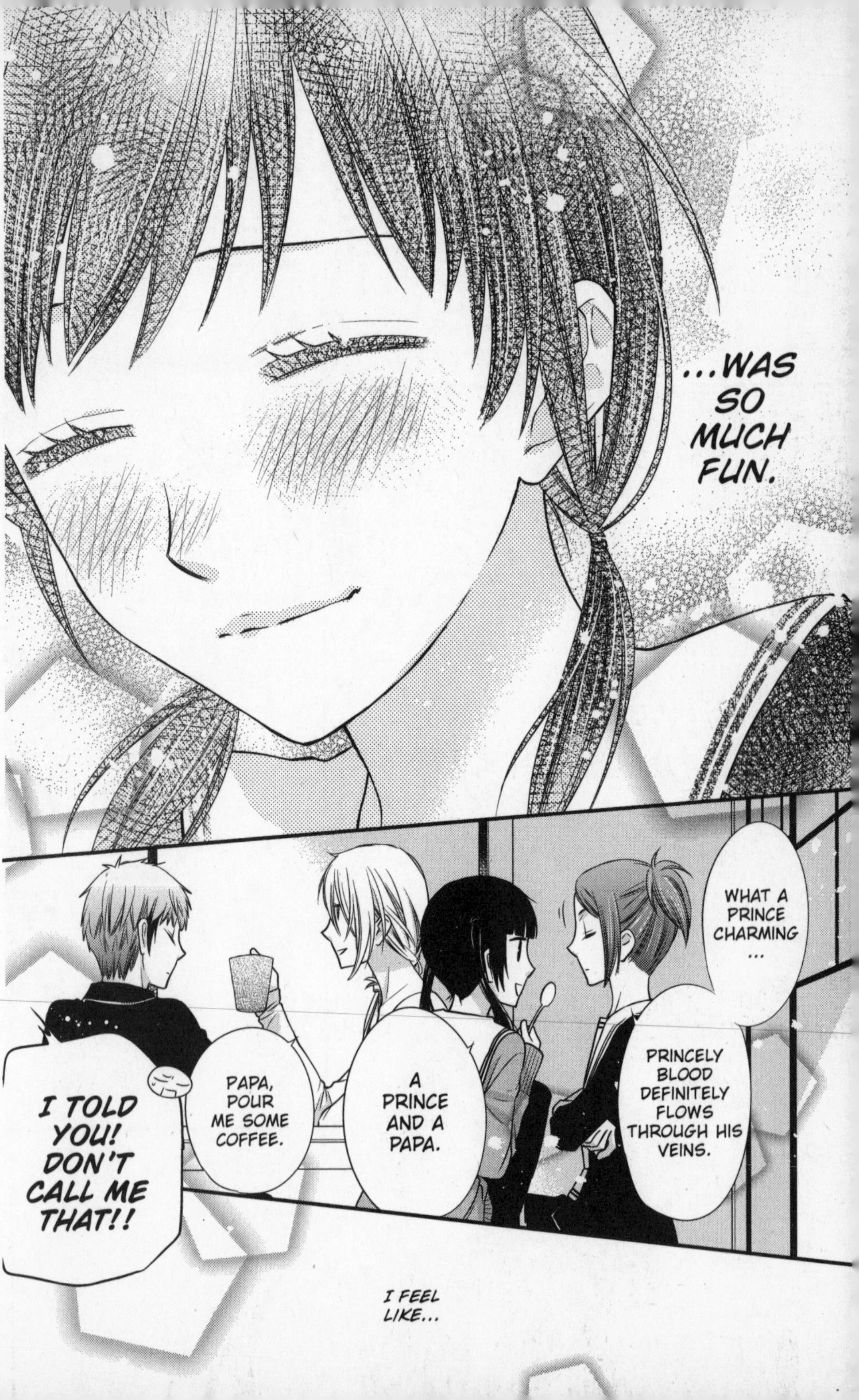
...WAS SO MUCH FUN.
WHAT A PRINCE CHARMING ...
PRINCELY BLOOD DEFINITELY FLOWS THROUGH HIS VEINS.
A PRINCE AND A PAPA.
PAPA, POUR ME SOME COFFEE.
I TOLD YOU! DON'T CALL ME THAT!!
I FEEL LIKE...

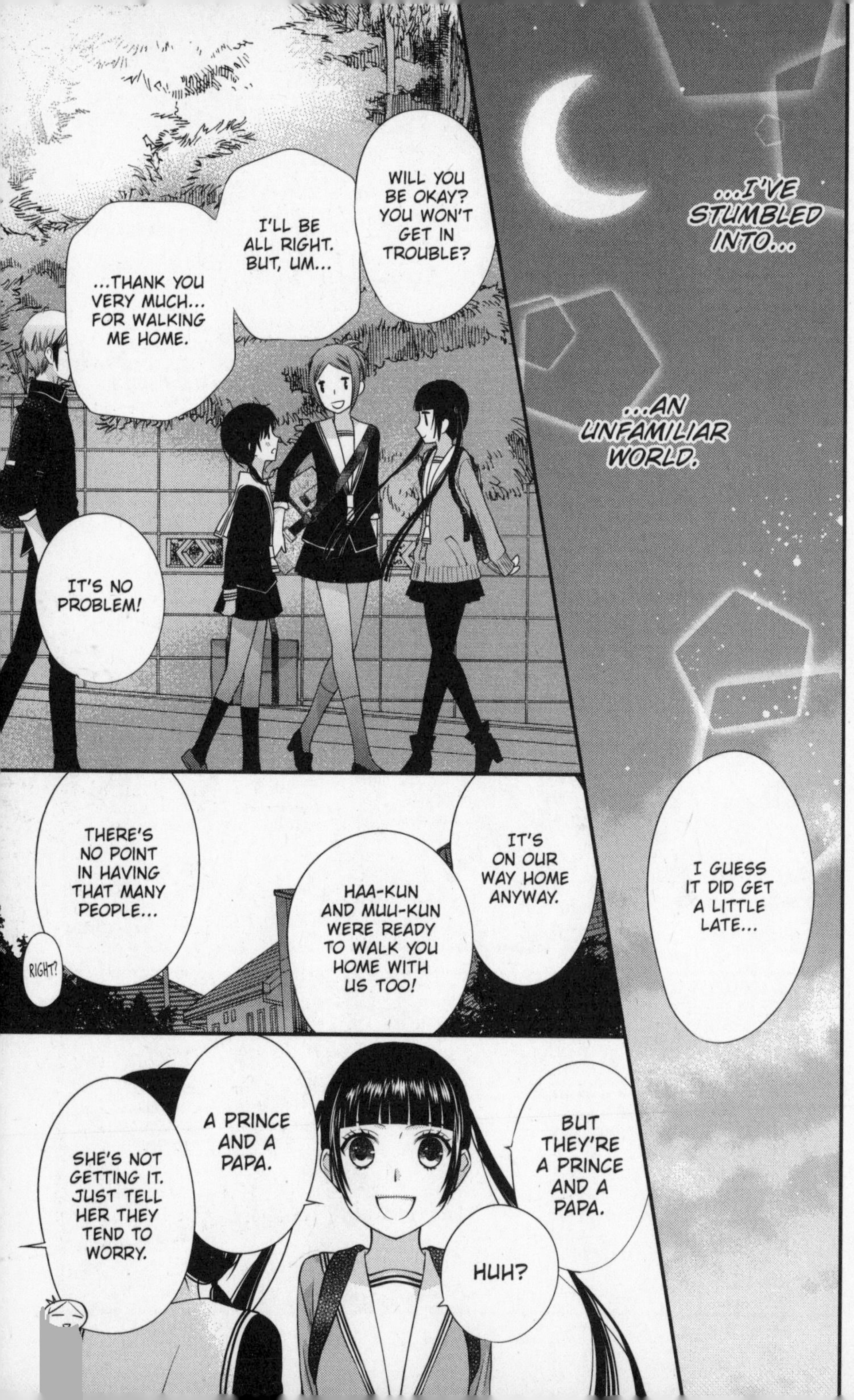
...I'VE STUMBLED INTO...
...AN UNFAMILIAR WORLD.
I GUESS IT DID GET A LITTLE LATE...
WILL YOU BE OKAY? YOU WON'T GET IN TROUBLE?
I'LL BE ALL RIGHT. BUT, UM...
...THANK YOU VERY MUCH... FOR WALKING ME HOME.
IT'S NO PROBLEM!
IT'S ON OUR WAY HOME ANYWAY.
HAA-KUN AND MUU-KUN WERE READY TO WALK YOU HOME WITH US TOO!
THERE'S NO POINT IN HAVING THAT MANY PEOPLE...
RIGHT?
BUT THEY'RE A PRINCE AND A PAPA.
HUH?
A PRINCE AND A PAPA.
SHE'S NOT GETTING IT. JUST TELL HER THEY TEND TO WORRY.

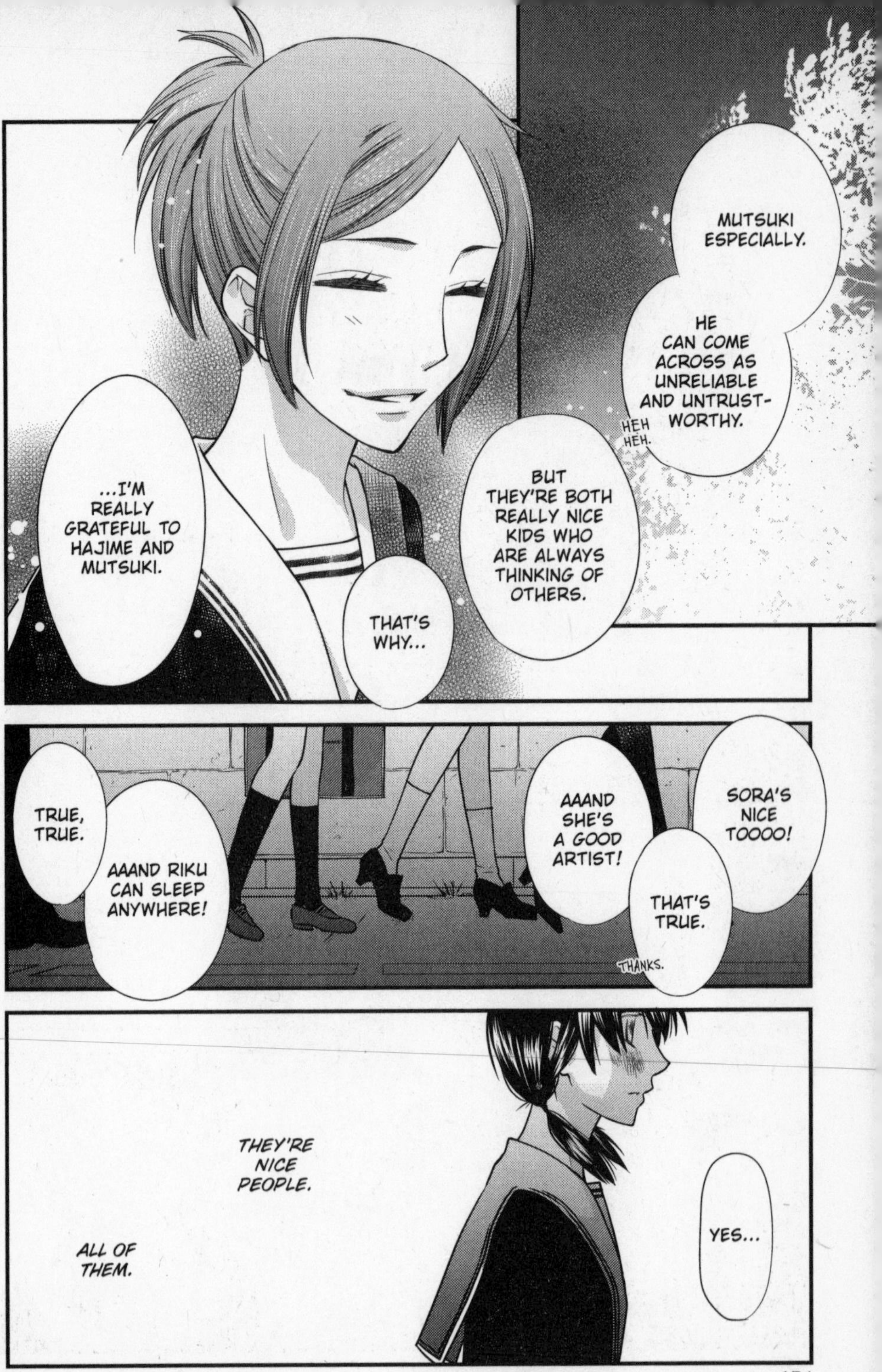
MUTSUKI ESPECIALLY.
HE CAN COME ACROSS AS UNRELIABLE AND UNTRUST-WORTHY.
HEH HEH.
BUT THEY'RE BOTH REALLY NICE KIDS WHO ARE ALWAYS THINKING OF OTHERS.
THAT'S WHY...
...I'M REALLY GRATEFUL TO HAJIME AND MUTSUKI.
SORA'S NICE TOOOO!
AAAND SHE'S A GOOD ARTIST!
THAT'S TRUE.
THANKS.
TRUE, TRUE.
AAAND RIKU CAN SLEEP ANYWHERE!
YES...
THEY'RE NICE PEOPLE.
ALL OF THEM.

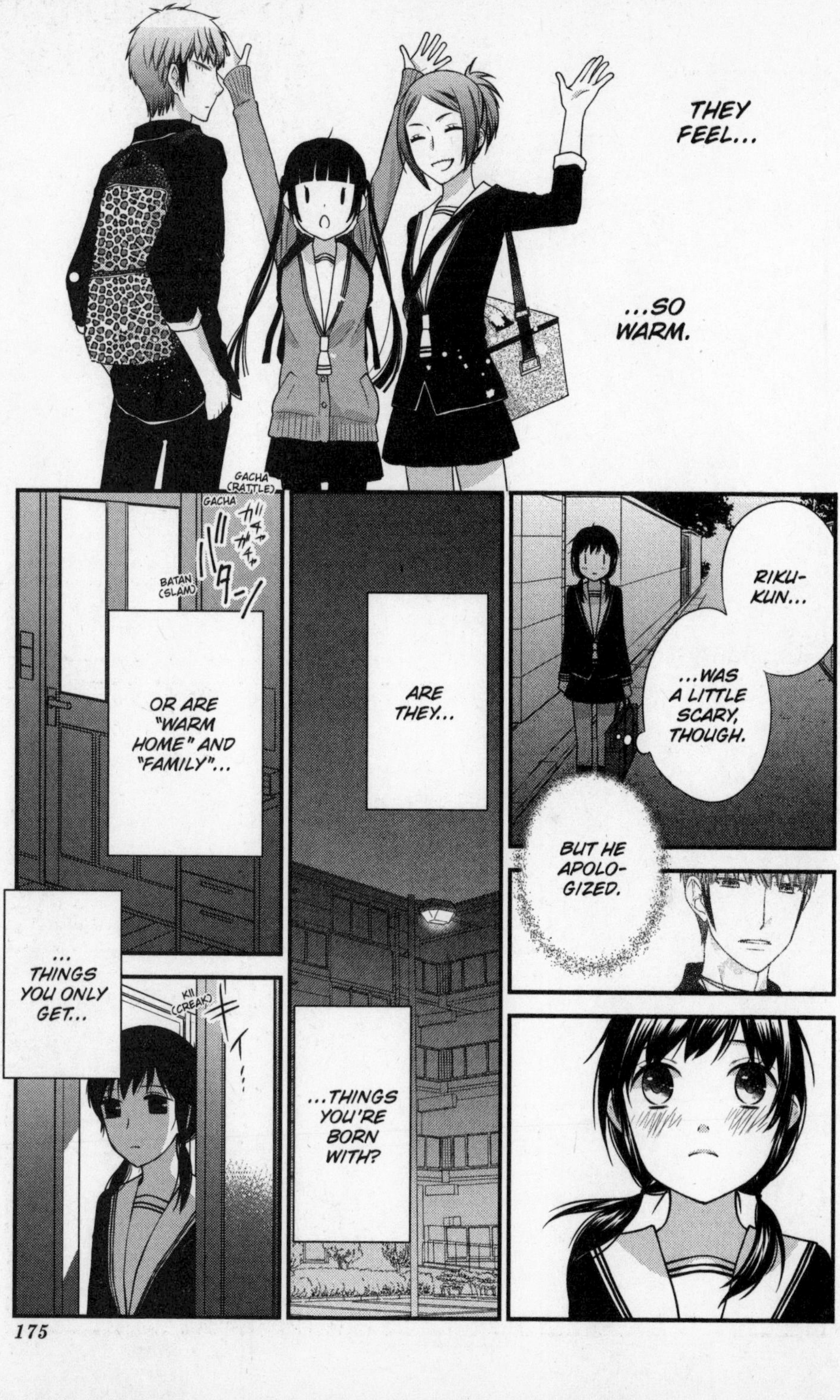
THEY FEEL...
...SO WARM.
RIKU-KUN...
...WAS A LITTLE SCARY, THOUGH.
BUT HE APOLOGIZED.
ARE THEY...
...THINGS YOU'RE BORN WITH?
GACHA (RATTLE)
GACHA
BATAN (SLAM)
OR ARE "WARM HOME" AND "FAMILY"...
...THINGS YOU ONLY GET...
KII (CREAK)

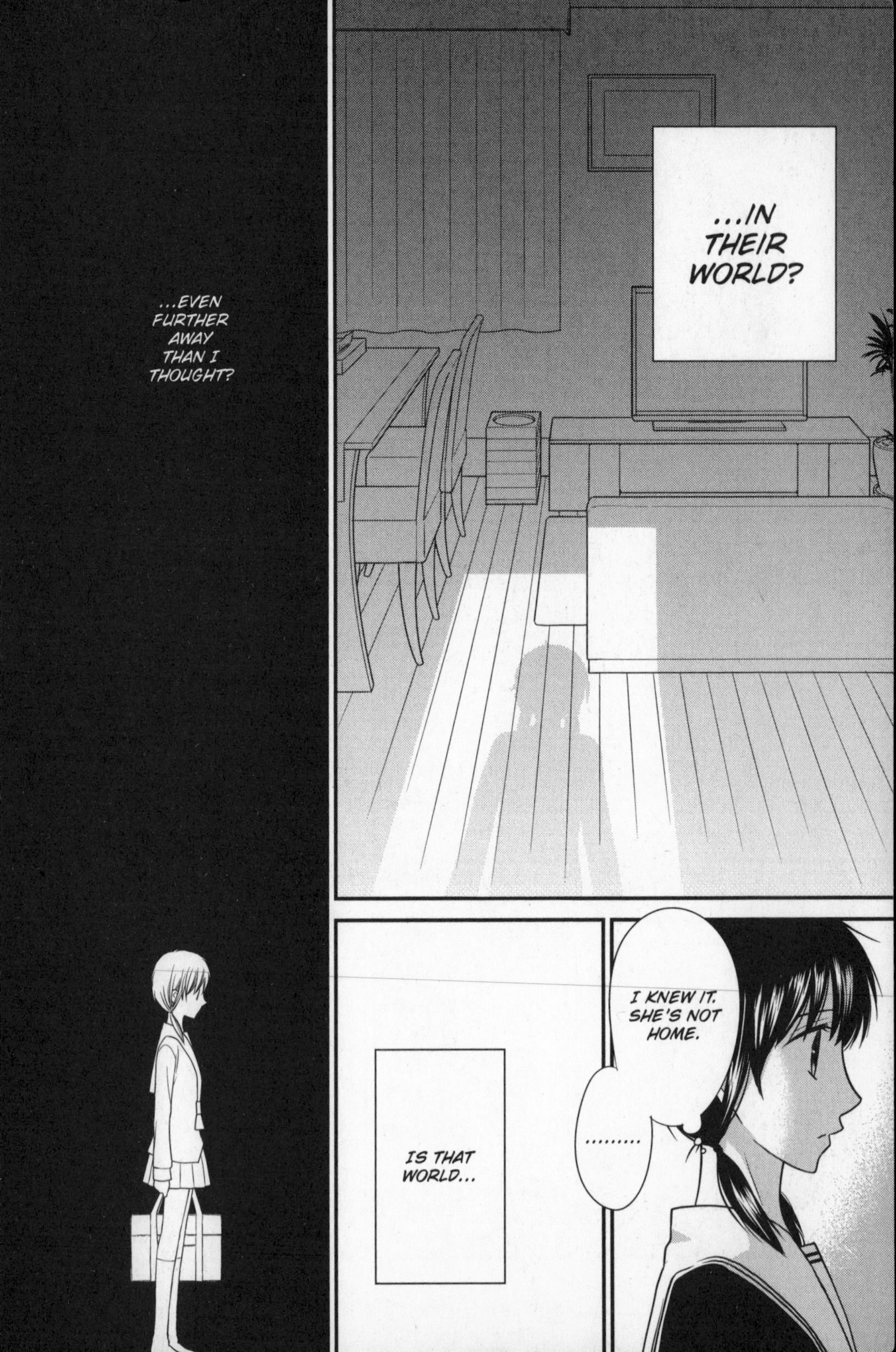
...IN THEIR WORLD?
I KNEW IT. SHE'S NOT HOME.
....
IS THAT WORLD...
...EVEN FURTHER AWAY THAN I THOUGHT?

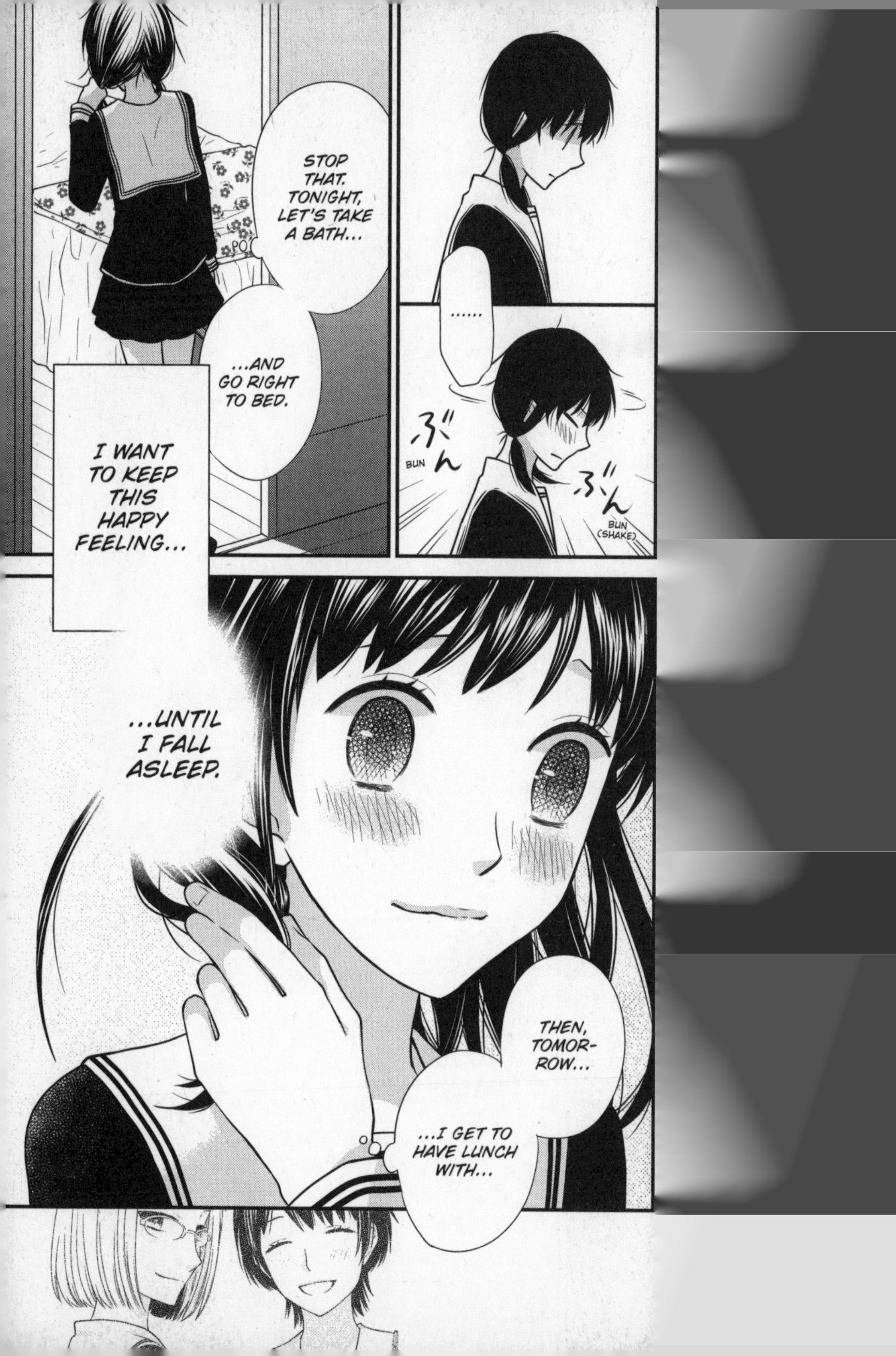
......
ぶん
BUN
ぶん
BUN (SHAKE)
STOP THAT. TONIGHT, LET'S TAKE A BATH...
...AND GO RIGHT TO BED.
PO
I WANT TO KEEP THIS HAPPY FEELING...
...UNTIL I FALL ASLEEP.
THEN, TOMORROW...
...I GET TO HAVE LUNCH WITH...

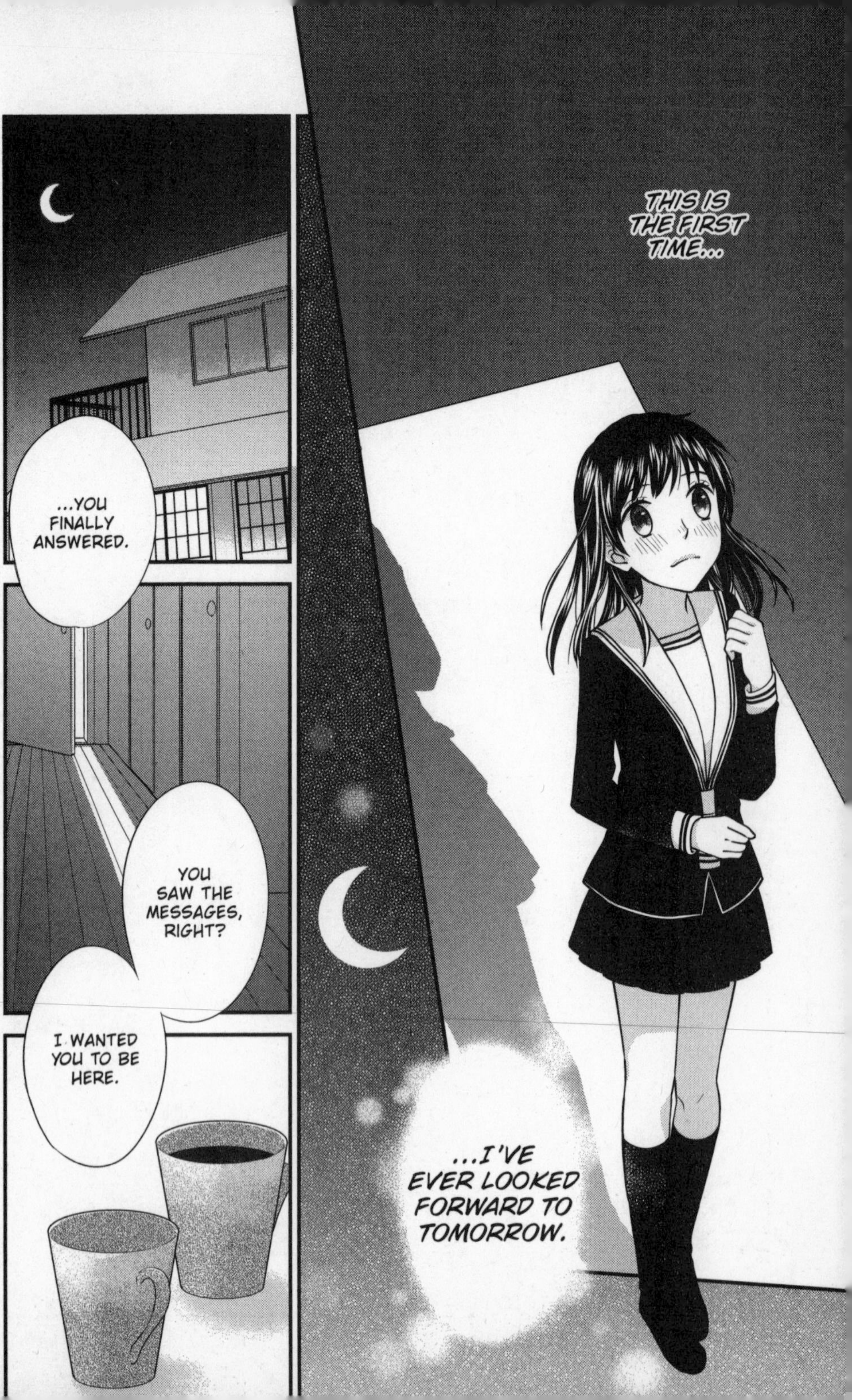
THIS IS THE FIRST TIME...
...I'VE EVER LOOKED FORWARD TO TOMORROW.
...YOU FINALLY ANSWERED.
YOU SAW THE MESSAGES, RIGHT?
I WANTED YOU TO BE HERE.

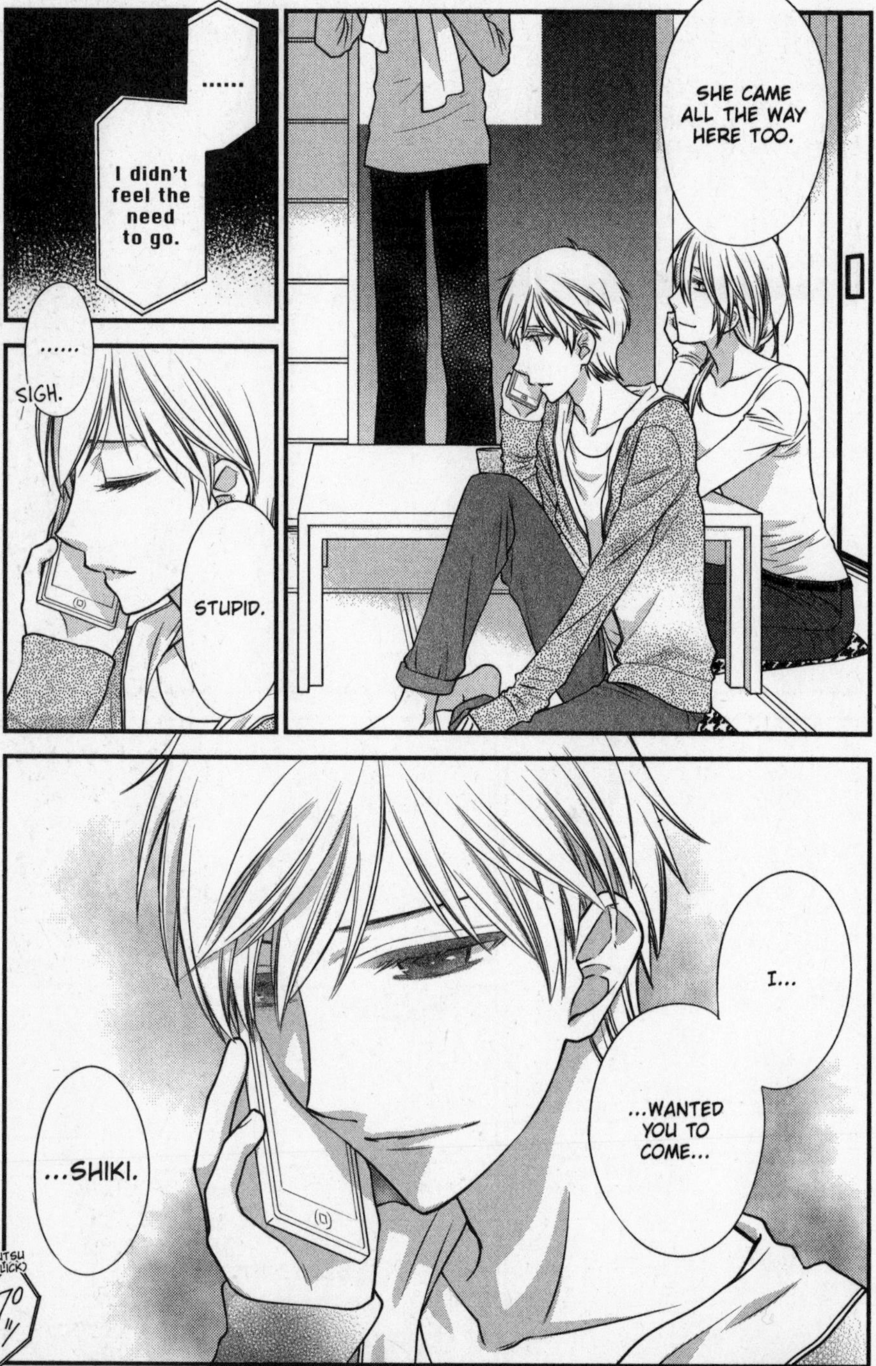
SHE CAME ALL THE WAY HERE TOO.
......
I didn't feel the need to go.
......
SIGH.
STUPID.
I...
...WANTED YOU TO COME...
...SHIKI.
PUTSU (CLICK)

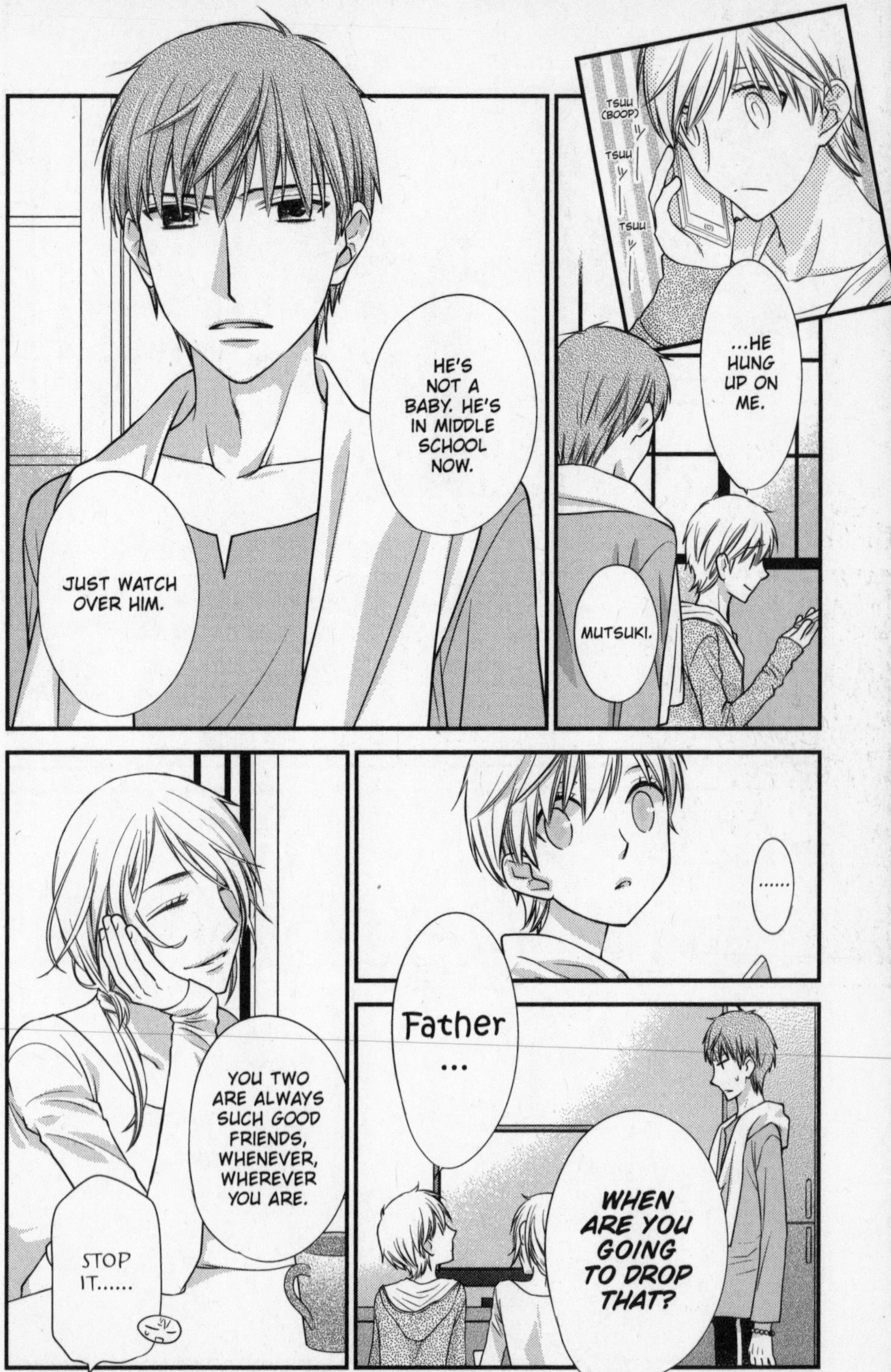
TSUU (BOOP)
ツ
TSUU
ツ
TSUU
ツ
...HE HUNG UP ON ME.
MUTSUKI.
HE'S NOT A BABY. HE'S IN MIDDLE SCHOOL NOW.
JUST WATCH OVER HIM.
......
Father...
WHEN ARE YOU GOING TO DROP THAT?
YOU TWO ARE ALWAYS SUCH GOOD FRIENDS, WHENEVER, WHEREVER YOU ARE.
STOP IT......

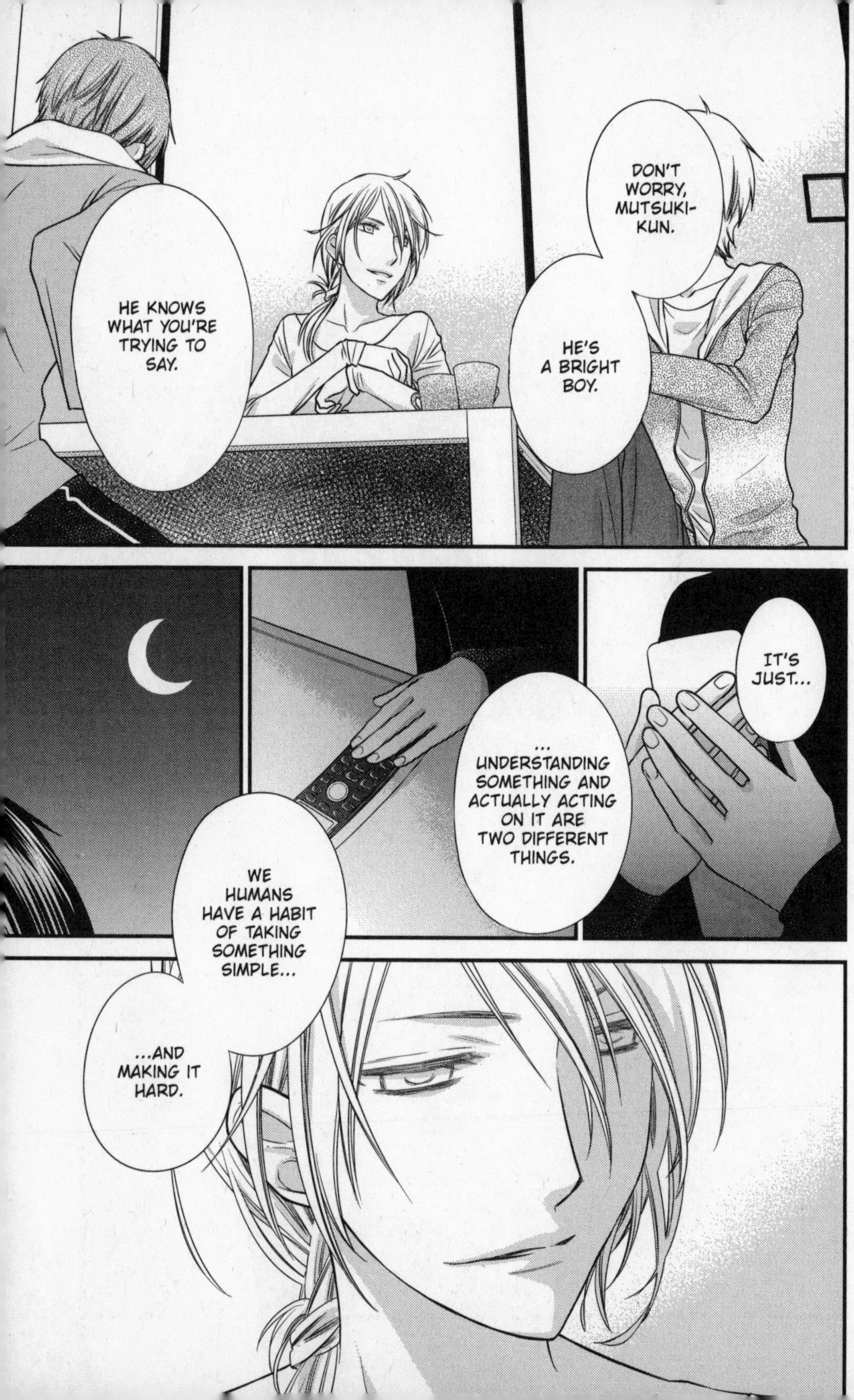
DON'T WORRY, MUTSUKI-KUN.
HE'S A BRIGHT BOY.
HE KNOWS WHAT YOU'RE TRYING TO SAY.
IT'S JUST...
...UNDERSTANDING SOMETHING AND ACTUALLY ACTING ON IT ARE TWO DIFFERENT THINGS.
WE HUMANS HAVE A HABIT OF TAKING SOMETHING SIMPLE...
...AND MAKING IT HARD.

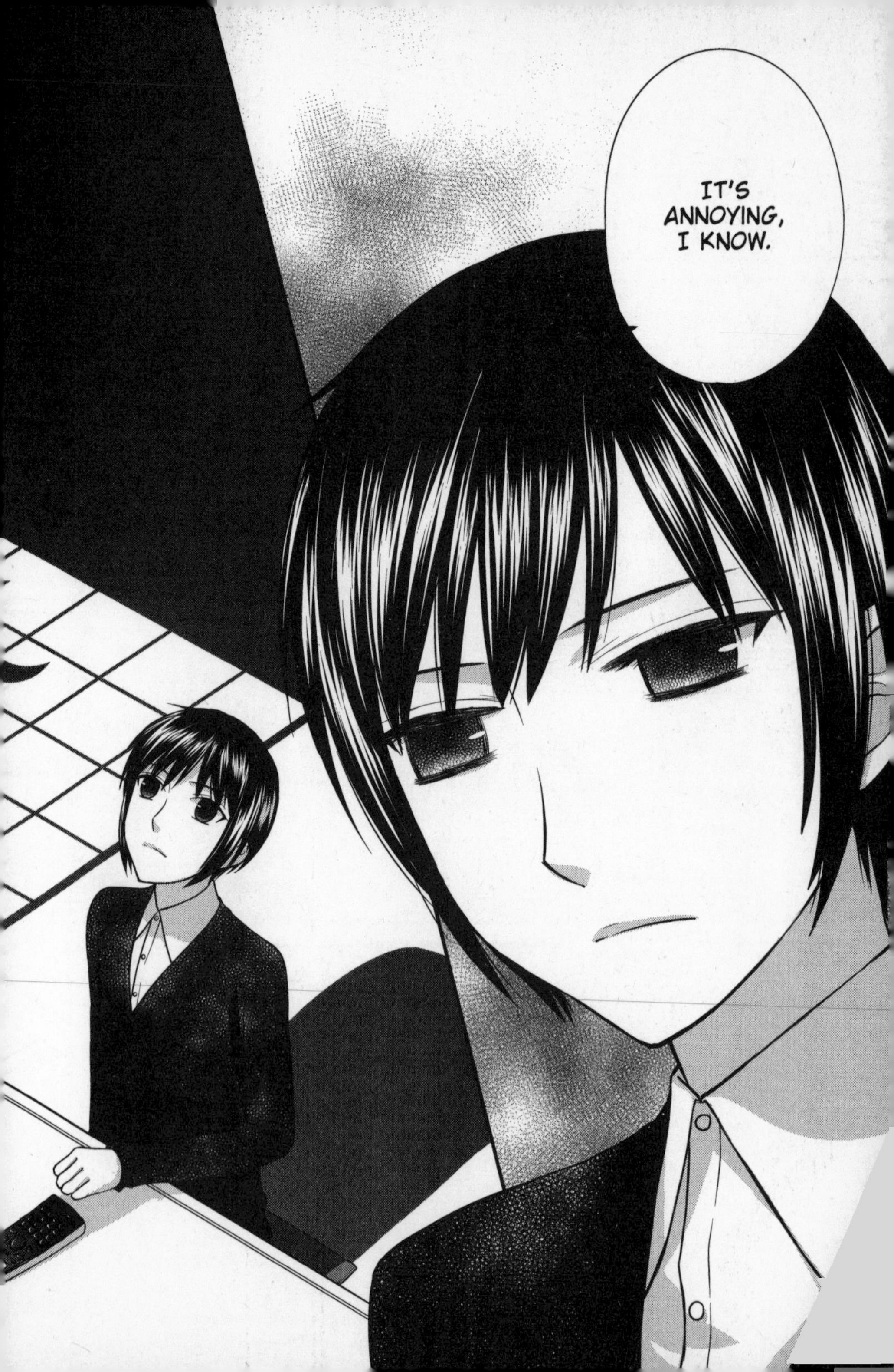
IT'S ANNOYING, I KNOW.

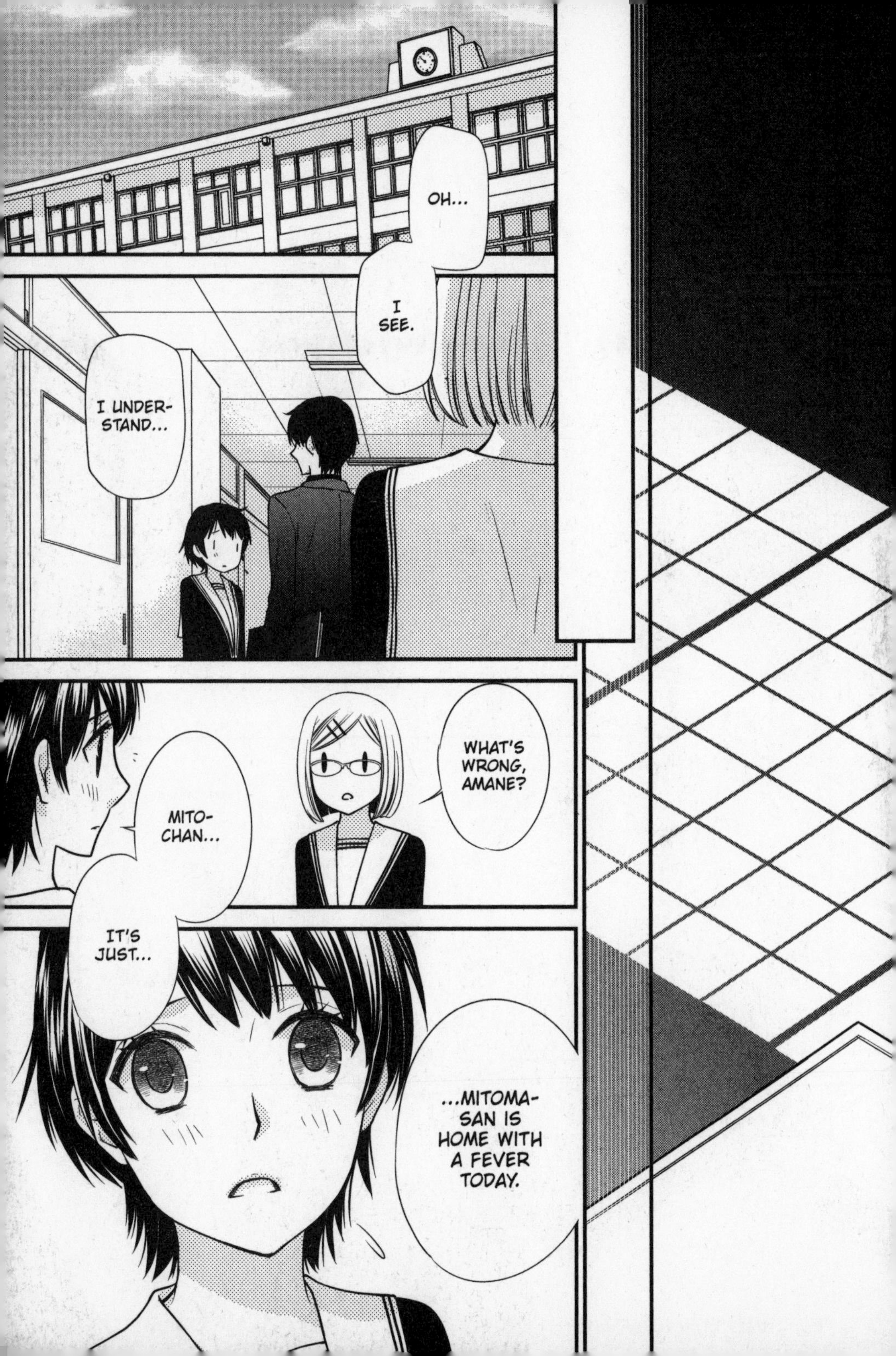
OH...
I SEE.
I UNDER-STAND...
WHAT'S WRONG, AMANE?
MITO-CHAN...
IT'S JUST...
...MITOMA-SAN IS HOME WITH A FEVER TODAY.

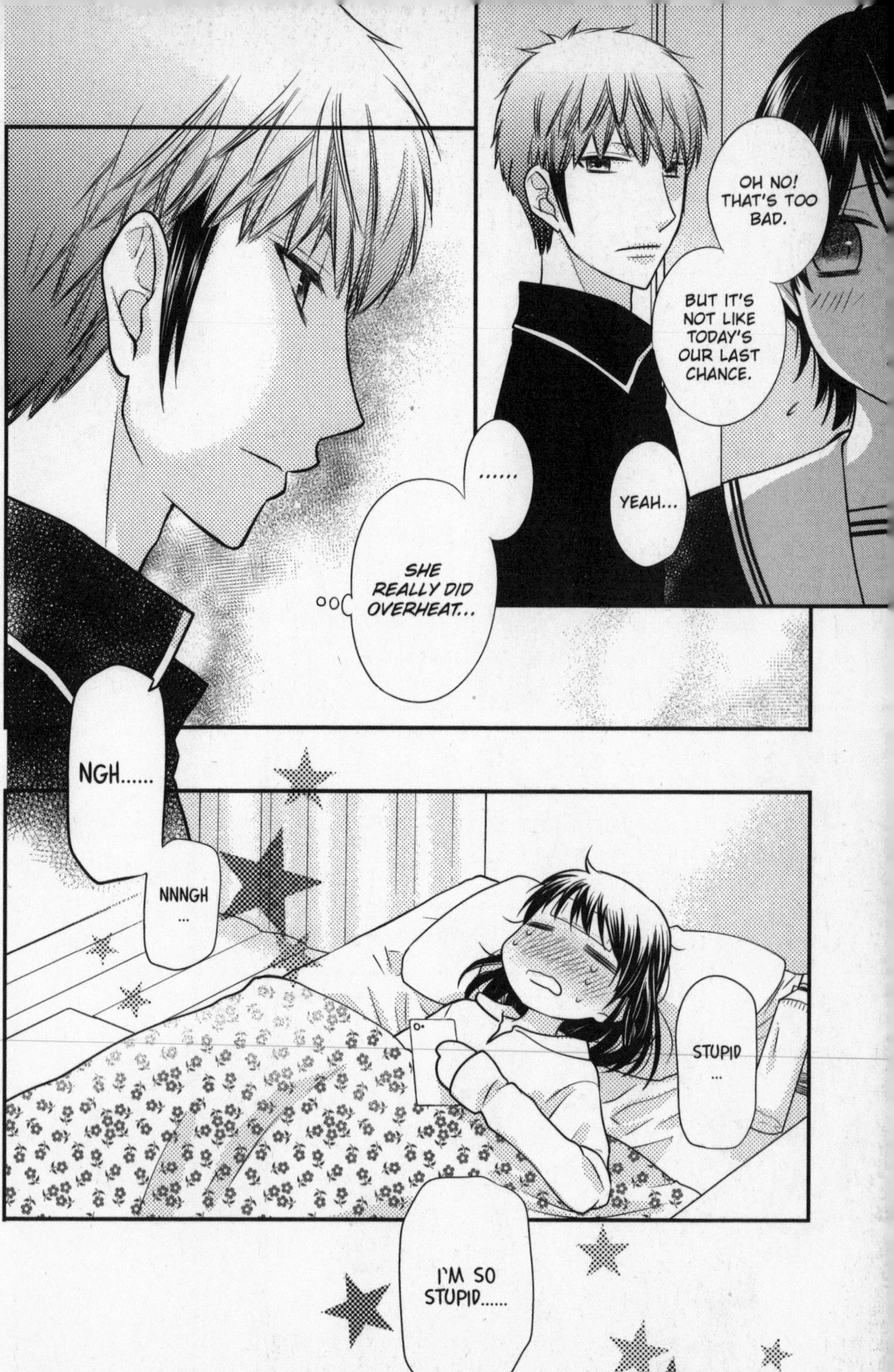
OH NO! THAT'S TOO BAD.
BUT IT'S NOT LIKE TODAY'S OUR LAST CHANCE.
YEAH...
......
SHE REALLY DID OVERHEAT...
NGH......
NNNGH ...
STUPID ...
I'M SO STUPID......

FRUITS BASKET ANOTHER 1 THE END

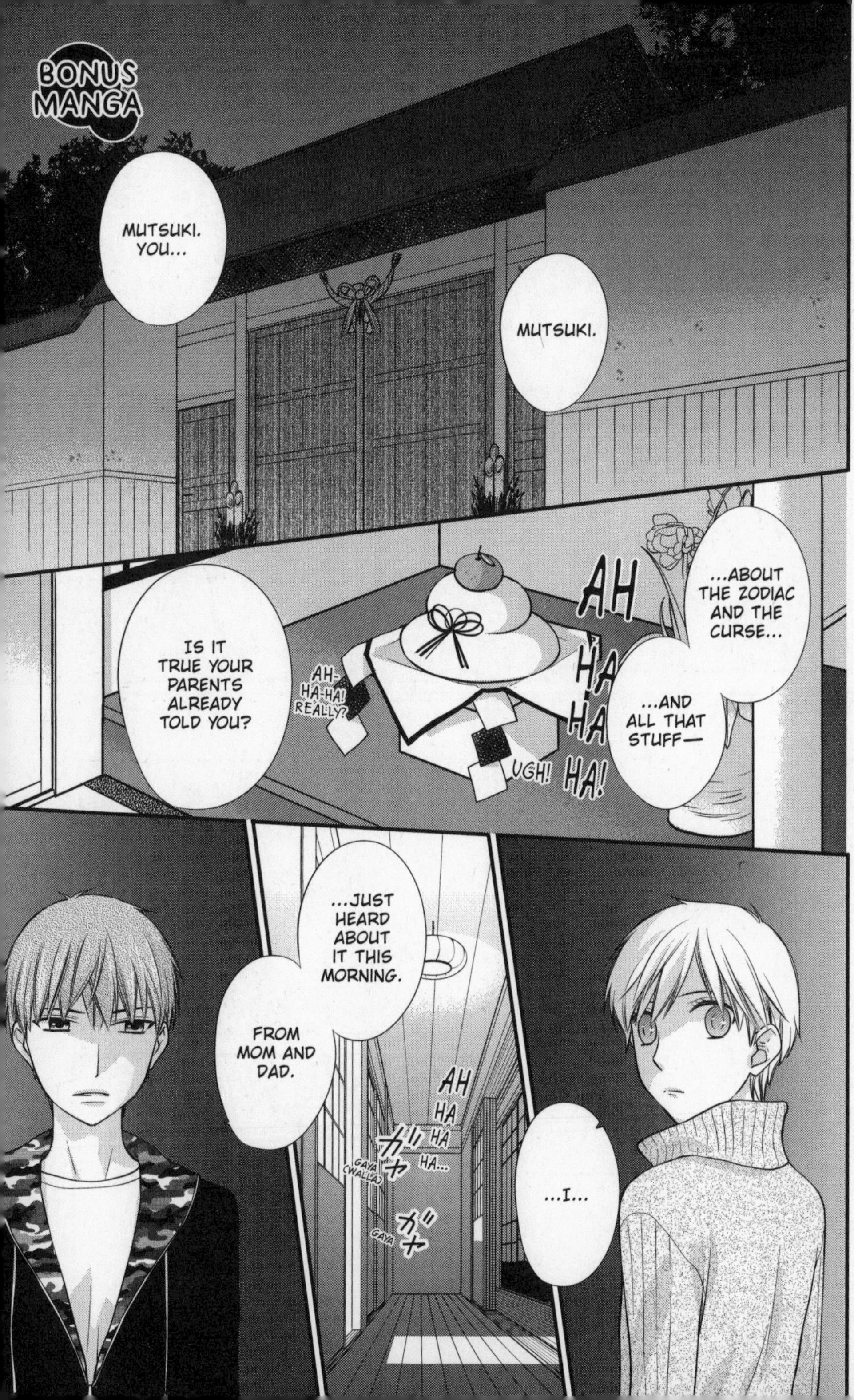
BONUS MANGA
MUTSUKI.
MUTSUKI. YOU...
...ABOUT THE ZODIAC AND THE CURSE...
...AND ALL THAT STUFF—
AH HA HA HA HA!
UGH!
AH-HA-HA! REALLY?
IS IT TRUE YOUR PARENTS ALREADY TOLD YOU?
...I...
...JUST HEARD ABOUT IT THIS MORNING.
FROM MOM AND DAD.
AH HA HA HA HA...
GAYA (WALLA)
GAYA

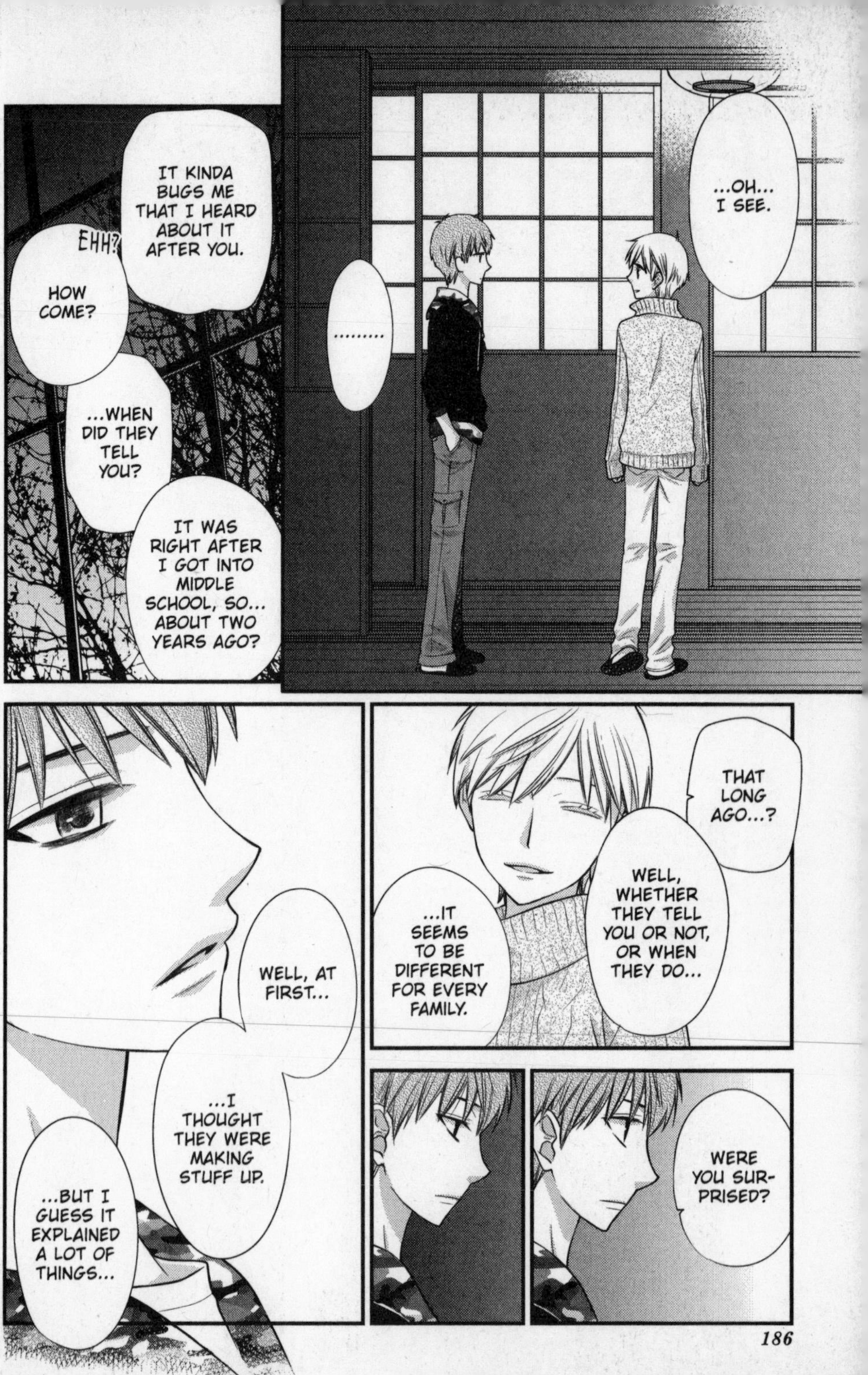
...OH... I SEE.
....
IT KINDA BUGS ME THAT I HEARD ABOUT IT AFTER YOU.
EHH?
HOW COME?
...WHEN DID THEY TELL YOU?
IT WAS RIGHT AFTER I GOT INTO MIDDLE SCHOOL, SO... ABOUT TWO YEARS AGO?
THAT LONG AGO...?
WELL, WHETHER THEY TELL YOU OR NOT, OR WHEN THEY DO...
...IT SEEMS TO BE DIFFERENT FOR EVERY FAMILY.
WERE YOU SURPRISED?
WELL, AT FIRST...
...I THOUGHT THEY WERE MAKING STUFF UP.
...BUT I GUESS IT EXPLAINED A LOT OF THINGS...

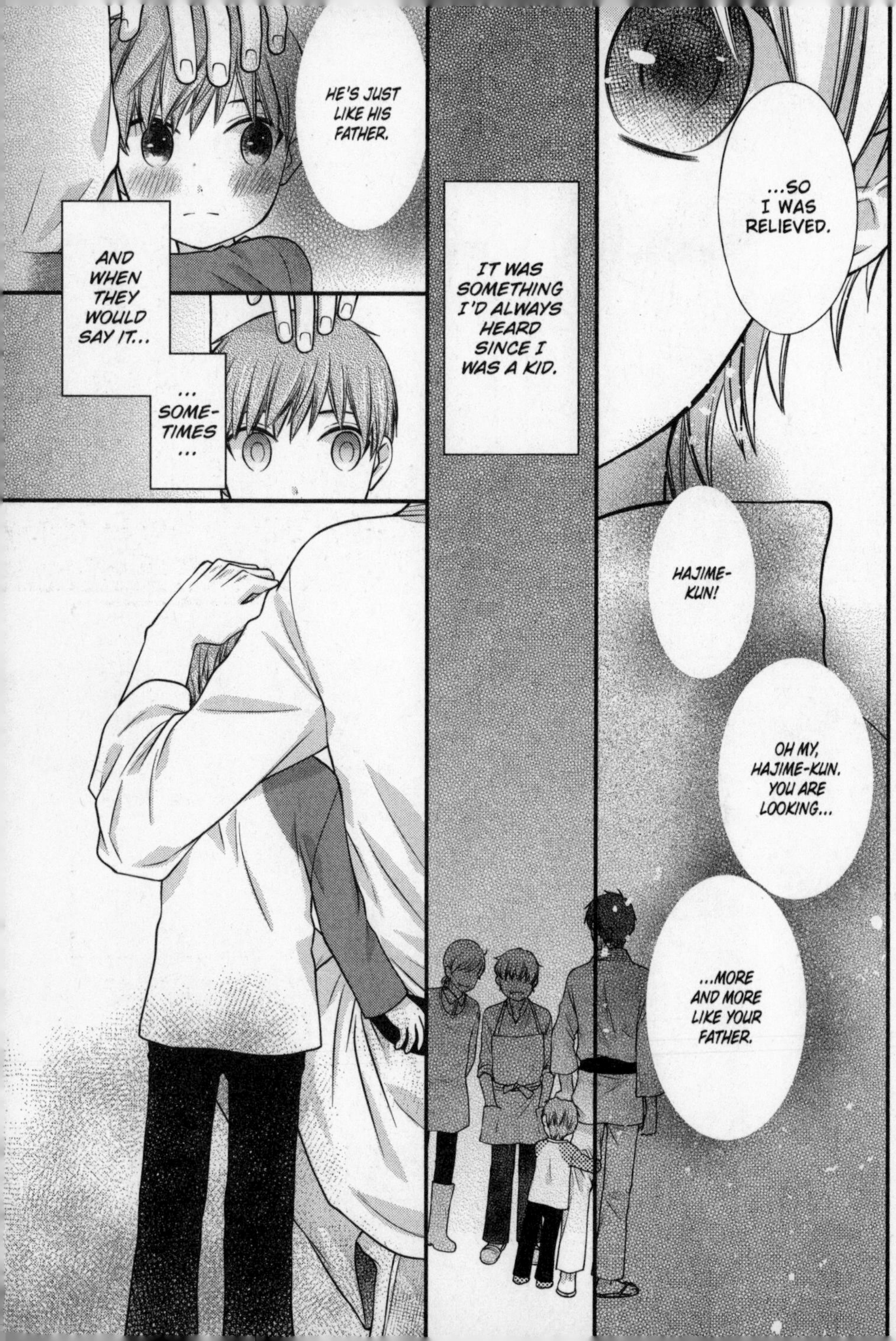
...SO I WAS RELIEVED.
HAJIME-KUN!
OH MY, HAJIME-KUN. YOU ARE LOOKING...
...MORE AND MORE LIKE YOUR FATHER.
IT WAS SOMETHING I'D ALWAYS HEARD SINCE I WAS A KID.
HE'S JUST LIKE HIS FATHER.
AND WHEN THEY WOULD SAY IT...
...SOMETIMES...

...I'D NOTICE MY DAD'S NERVOUS SMILE...

HEE HEE.

EVERY ONE OF THEM, ACTING AS IF THEY'RE LIKE EVERYBODY ELSE. IT'S HILARIOUS.

HEE HEE.

I HOPE YOU DON'T TURN INTO A MONSTER.

THE INTEN-TIONS...

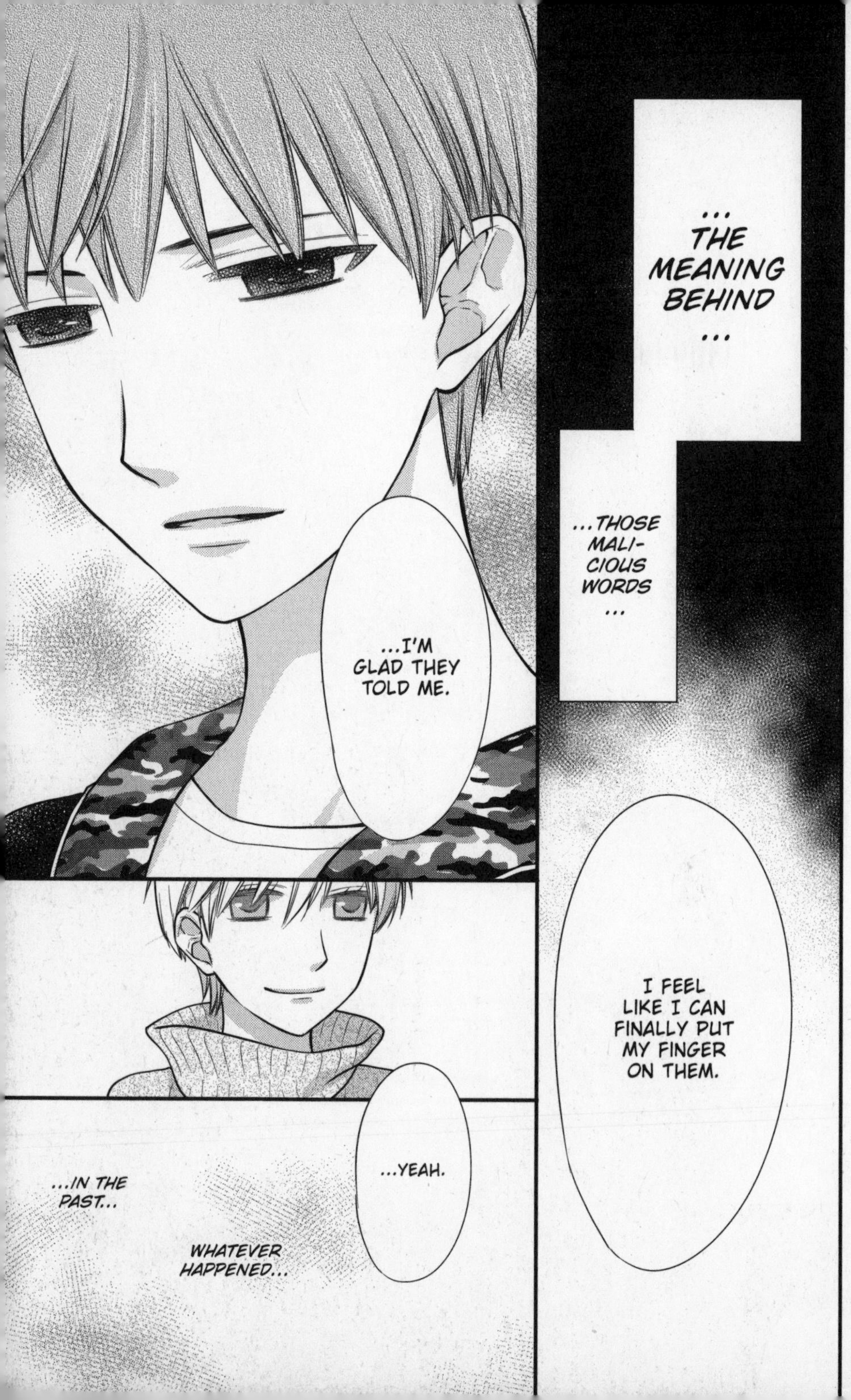
...THE MEANING BEHIND...
...THOSE MALICIOUS WORDS...
I FEEL LIKE I CAN FINALLY PUT MY FINGER ON THEM.
...I'M GLAD THEY TOLD ME.
...YEAH.
...IN THE PAST...
WHATEVER HAPPENED...

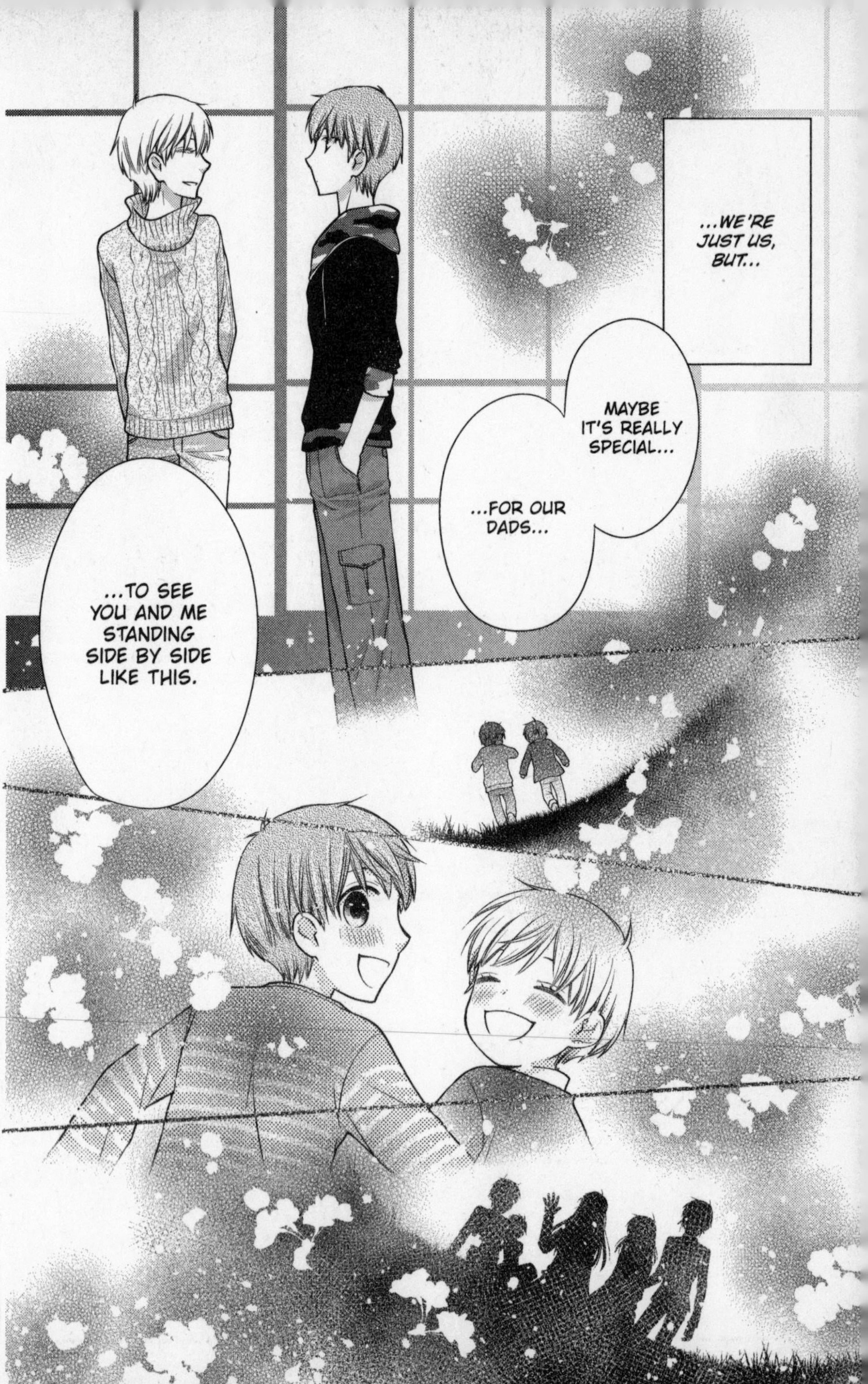
...WE'RE JUST US, BUT...
MAYBE IT'S REALLY SPECIAL...
...FOR OUR DADS...
...TO SEE YOU AND ME STANDING SIDE BY SIDE LIKE THIS.

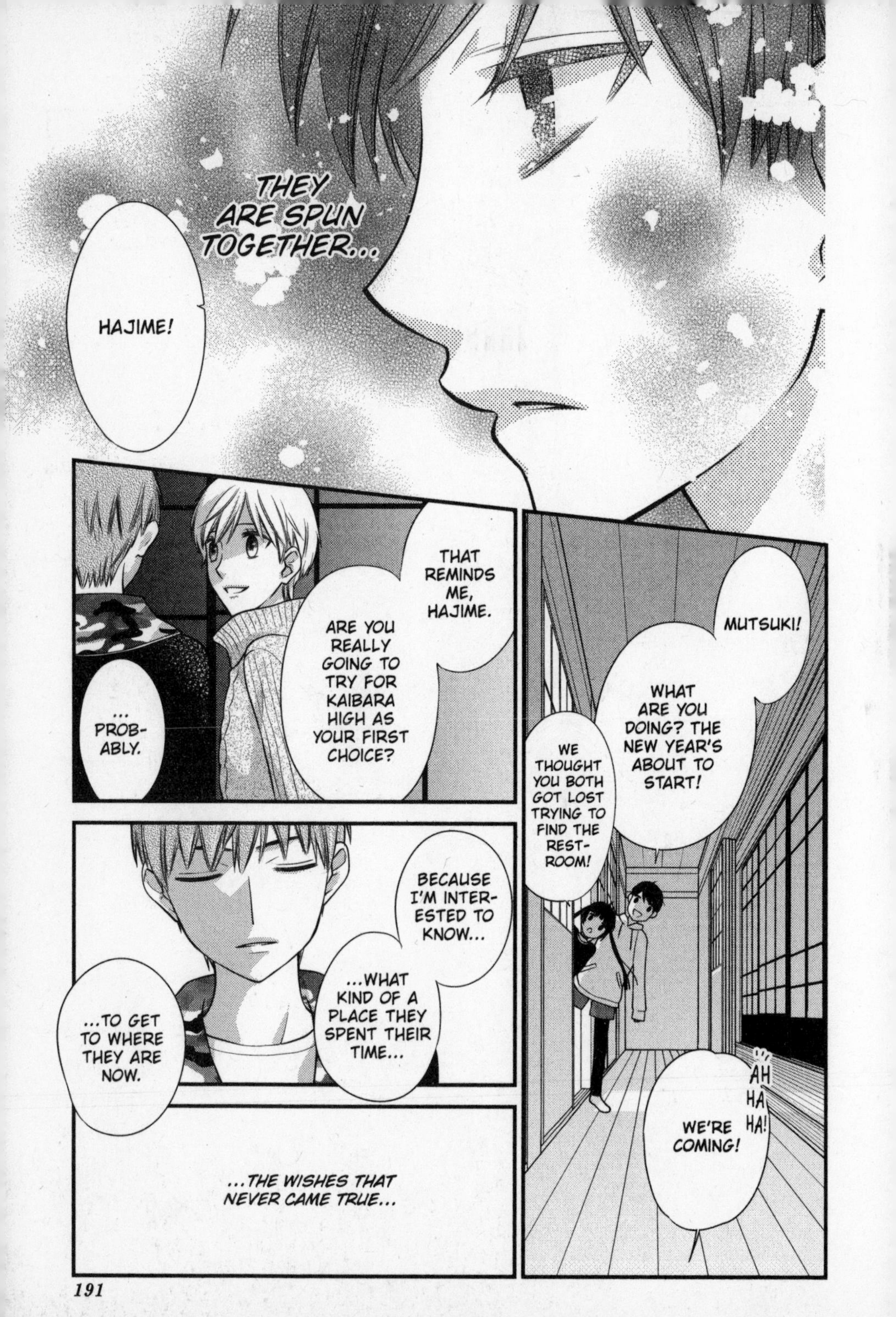
THEY ARE SPUN TOGETHER...
HAJIME!
MUTSUKI!
WHAT ARE YOU DOING? THE NEW YEAR'S ABOUT TO START!
WE THOUGHT YOU BOTH GOT LOST TRYING TO FIND THE REST-ROOM!
AH HA HA!
WE'RE COMING!
THAT REMINDS ME, HAJIME.
ARE YOU REALLY GOING TO TRY FOR KAIBARA HIGH AS YOUR FIRST CHOICE?
...PROBABLY.
BECAUSE I'M INTER-ESTED TO KNOW...
...WHAT KIND OF A PLACE THEY SPENT THEIR TIME...
...TO GET TO WHERE THEY ARE NOW.
...THE WISHES THAT NEVER CAME TRUE...

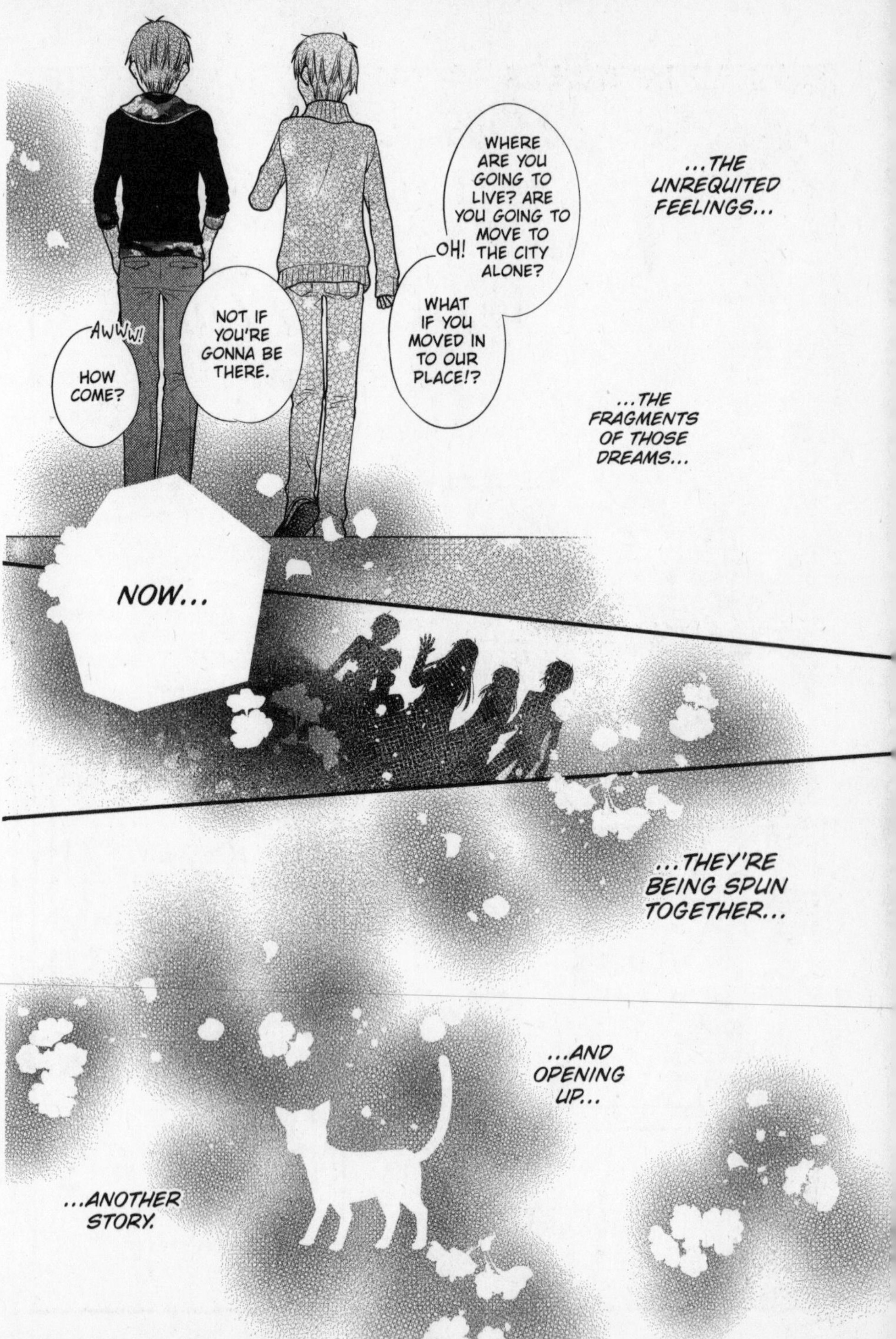
...THE UNREQUITED FEELINGS...
OH!
WHERE ARE YOU GOING TO LIVE? ARE YOU GOING TO MOVE TO THE CITY ALONE?
WHAT IF YOU MOVED IN TO OUR PLACE!?
NOT IF YOU'RE GONNA BE THERE.
AWWW!
HOW COME?
...THE FRAGMENTS OF THOSE DREAMS...
NOW...
...THEY'RE BEING SPUN TOGETHER...
...AND OPENING UP...
...ANOTHER STORY.

END OF BONUS MANGA